# AN INTRODUCTION TO
# EIGHTEENTH CENTURY FRANCE

# An Introduction to Eighteenth Century France

by

## JOHN LOUGH, M.A., Ph.D.

Professor of French in the University of Durham

LONGMAN

LONGMAN GROUP LIMITED

LONDON

*Associated companies, branches and representatives
throughout the world*

*First published* 1960

*Fifth Impression* 1970

SBN 582 31396 1 *cased edition*

SBN 582 31373 2 *paper edition*

Printed in Great Britain
by T. and A. CONSTABLE LTD., Hopetoun Street
Printers to the University of Edinburgh

# PREFACE

THIS book follows, broadly speaking, the same plan as *An Introduction to Seventeenth Century France*. It attempts to bring together in a narrow compass a sketch of the economic and social history of France in the eighteenth century; an account of the disintegration of Absolutism between the death of Louis XIV in 1715 and the meeting of the *États Généraux* in 1789; and a study of the relations between the writer and his public and the influence which these exercised on the literature and thought of the age. For the century of Voltaire and Montesquieu, Rousseau and Diderot in which literature and ideas are so inextricably mingled, a consideration of the background to the thought of the period seemed more essential than in the earlier volume. Yet the aim of the book is the same: to give the reader an introduction to the economic, social and political history of the age, and to show the connection of each with the world of literature.

Once again the different chapters have been illustrated by quotations drawn from all manner of contemporary sources; most of these have been left in their original French, but advantage has been taken of some of the fascinating travel books produced by English visitors, especially Arthur Young. Once again my publishers have been most co-operative in allowing me to include a number of plates reproducing a variety of paintings and engravings of the period, and photographs of some of its most attractive buildings. It is hoped that, with the aid of these, the book will succeed in its aim of bringing to life for the reader a civilization which, with all its defects and injustices, exerted an influence far beyond its frontiers in space and time.

J. L.

Durham

v

# A NOTE ON FRENCH MONEY IN THE EIGHTEENTH CENTURY

After various manipulations of the coinage during the latter part of the reign of Louis XIV and the Regency, especially during Law's *Système*, its value was finally fixed by a decree of 1726 and, apart from a minor technical change in 1785, remained unaltered until the Revolution.

The basic unit of money was the *livre tournois* or *franc*.

3 *livres* = 1 *écu*. 24 *livres* = 1 *louis*. The *livre* was divided into *sous* and *deniers*: 1 *livre* = 20 *sous*. 1 *sou* = 12 *deniers* (or 4 *liards*).

From 1726 onwards the pound sterling was worth approximately 24 *livres*. Reckoning the *livre* as being worth 10½d., Arthur Young, at the end of the Ancien Régime, gave a table of conversion from which the following figures are taken:

| *Livres* | £ | s. | d. |
|---:|---:|---:|---:|
| 5 | | 4 | 4½ |
| 10 | | 8 | 9 |
| 50 | 2 | 3 | 9 |
| 100 | 4 | 7 | 6 |
| 500 | 21 | 17 | 6 |
| 1,000 | 43 | 15 | 0 |
| 5,000 | 218 | 15 | 0 |
| 10,000 | 437 | 10 | 0 |

# CONTENTS

vii

# PLATES

ix

# NOTE

Photographs of No. 3 are by Alinari; Nos. 7, 8, 12, 21, 34, 38, 40 and 46 by Bulloz; Nos. 15, 22, 26, 30, 32, 33, 35 and 37 by Bulloz, © S.P.A.D.E.M. Paris; No. 19 by Commissiariat Général au Tourisme; No. 16 by Conservatoire National des Arts et Métiers; Nos. 6 and 13 by Giraudon; Nos. 4, 16 and 45 by W. F. Mansell; No. 14 by Éditions 'Tito', Bordeaux and No. 36 by J. C. D. Smith; No. 17 by Conservatoire National des Arts et Métiers.

## MAPS AND DIAGRAMS

# ACKNOWLEDGMENTS

We are indebted to the following for permission to quote copyright material:

MM. Calmann-Lévy, Paris, for extracts from *Mémoires de Talleyrand*, ed. by Duc de Broglie; Librairie Honoré Champion, Paris, for extracts from Besnard, *Souvenirs d'un Nonagénaire*, ed. by Célestin Port; Imprimerie Firmin-Didot et Cie, Paris, for extracts from Marie Antoinette, *Correspondance Secrète entre Marie-Thérèse et le Comte de Mercy-Argenteau avec les Lettres de Marie-Thérèse et de Marie-Antoinette*, ed. by A. d'Arneth and A. Geffroy; Éditions Garnier Frères, Paris, for extracts from Grimm (ed.), *Correspondance Littéraire, philosophique et critique*, ed. by M. Tourneux; Imprimerie Nationale, Paris, for extracts from *Remontrances du Parlement de Paris au XVIIIe siècle*, ed. by J. Flammermont; Éditions A. & J. Picard et Cie, Paris, for extracts from Hardy, *Mes Loisirs*, ed. by M. Tourneux and M. Vitrac; Presses Universitaires de France, Paris, for extracts from Turgot, *Oeuvres*, ed. by G. Schelle; Librairie Jules Tallandier, Paris, for extracts from Abbé de Véri, *Journal*, ed. by J. de Witte; and the Institut et Musée Voltaire, Geneva, for extracts from Voltaire, *Correspondence*, ed. by T. Besterman.

# INTRODUCTION

DURING the reign of Louis XV and Louis XVI France's position in Europe was markedly different from that which she occupies in the middle of the twentieth century. Though in the 1760s both Lorraine and Corsica had become part of France, she still lacked in 1789 Savoy, Nice and the territory around the Papal city of Avignon. Yet with this smaller territory she continued to dominate the Continent, thanks to her large and growing population, her rich natural resources and the fact that, while Germany and Italy were still divided into a mass of small states, she had long been unified.

Her population naturally fell far short of the 50 millions of the France of our day. Wars and, above all, economic distress at the end of the reign of Louis XIV had probably reduced the population to some 18 or 19 millions; but the prosperity which France enjoyed for a considerable part of the eighteenth century, together with the fall in the death rate which took place there as in other European countries, raised the population by 1789 to some 25 or 26 millions. Despite her 50 million inhabitants, France today has fallen behind not only the Soviet Union, but Germany, Britain and even Italy. In our period only the Austrian Empire with its motley collection of territories and peoples could rival France in population, and continued throughout the eighteenth century to show a comparable growth in numbers. At the beginning of the period the other European countries were very sparsely populated. The population of Russia, which appears to have caught up with that of France by 1789, is estimated at some 14 millions, that of Spain at 5, and that of Prussia at only 2. In contrast to the 18 or 19 million inhabitants of France at the beginning of the century, the population of England was only some 5 millions. When at last the censuses of 1801 provide more or less reliable figures, we find that the total population of England and Wales came to less than 9 millions, compared with 28 millions in France.

### France at the end of the Ancien Régime

Redrawn by permission from a map by Mary Potter in *France, Government and Society*, ed. Wallace-Hadrill and McManners, Methuen

The changes which have since taken place in the relative populations of the different European countries tend to make us forget the dominant position which, thanks to her population, France continued to occupy in Europe down to the time of Napoleon and even beyond.

Then, as now, France enjoyed all the advantages of a fertile soil and a varied climate. Backward as they might appear in many respects when judged by modern standards or even by those of a contemporary English traveller like Arthur Young, her agriculture, her trade and even her slowly expanding industry gave at any rate a considerable proportion of her people a standard of living higher than that of less favoured countries of the Continent. A writer of the end of our period, Joseph de Maistre, an impartial judge since he hailed from outside France, offers a vivid picture of the position of power and wealth which she occupied in eighteenth century Europe:

> Cherchons dans l'univers un État dont les différentes parties aient une liaison aussi intime et forment un ensemble plus imposant. La France a tout à la fois la masse et le volume; il n'existe point en Europe de corps politique plus nombreux, plus *compact*, plus difficile à entamer et dont le choc soit plus terrible. Sa population est immense, ses productions infiniment nombreuses et non moins diversifiées. Ses richesses ne tiennent ni à la mode ni à l'opinion; ses vins, ses huiles, ses bois, ses sels, ses chanvres, etc., la rendent indépendante des autres peuples qui cependant sont obligés de lui payer tribut. Et comme si ce n'était pas assez des richesses naturelles, elle a reçu encore le sceptre de la mode, afin que, régnant également sur les besoins et sur les fantaisies, il ne manque rien à son empire. (*Œuvres complètes*, I, 188-9)

In spite of the strength which her population and natural resources gave her, in the reigns of Louis XV and Louis XVI France experienced many military setbacks when she came into conflict with the other powers of Europe. If in these years she had brilliant victories to set beside humiliating defeats, her role in the affairs of Europe was far from being as striking as one might have expected. Between 1715 and 1789 her position in Europe was weakened. In the East two new figures on the European scene, Prussia and Russia, greatly strengthened their position, while in the West England inflicted a decisive defeat on France in their bitter struggle for commercial and colonial supremacy. True, France was once again to reassert her power in the Revolutionary and Napoleonic wars which lasted with only short breaks from 1792 to 1815. At its height, French power in these years extended over most of Europe; French armies fought all over the Continent from Spain to Russia; but the vast empire built up by Napoleon finally collapsed at Waterloo.

In contrast to the ups and downs of her diplomatic relations with the rest of Europe, France's cultural position remained throughout this age one of almost unchallenged supremacy. This position she owed not only to her population and resources, but also to the development of Absolutism and the concentration in Paris and Versailles of a brilliant social life which produced a refined taste in the arts and in all manner of luxury trades. There was too the happy accident of a long succession of outstanding writers—poets, playwrights, novelists and thinkers—whose works had a universal appeal.

In the eighteenth century, French superseded Latin as the international language. 'Les ouvrages français se répandirent si universellement,' declared Frederick the Great, 'que leur langue remplaça celle des Latins, et à présent quiconque sait le français peut voyager par toute l'Europe sans avoir besoin d'un interprète' (*Histoire de mon temps*, I, 97-8). When he arrived in Berlin in 1750, Voltaire wrote to his niece: 'La langue qu'on parle le moins à la cour, c'est l'allemand. Je n'en ai pas encore entendu prononcer un mot. Notre langue et nos belles-lettres ont fait plus de conquêtes que Charlemagne' (*Correspondence*, XVIII, 131). Although he became a German national hero, Frederick remained to the end entirely French both in language and culture.

Not only in Prussia, but all over Germany French was the language of the upper classes. 'The native language of the country', wrote the Scottish traveller, John Moore, in the 1770s, is treated like a vulgar and provincial dialect, while the French is cultivated as the only proper language for people of fashion. . . . Children of the first families are instructed in French before they acquire their mother tongue, and pains are taken to keep them ignorant of this, that it may not hurt their pronunciation of the other' (*A View of Society*, I, 427). It was the Academy of Berlin (its publications, like those of the Academy of St. Petersburg, appeared in French) which in 1782 offered a prize for the best essay on the following subject:

> Qu'est-ce qui a fait de la langue française la langue universelle de l'Europe?
> Par où mérite-t-elle cette prérogative?
> Peut-on présumer qu'elle la conserve?

The prize was shared between a German professor and a Frenchman, Antoine de Rivarol, whose essay appeared in 1784 under the title, *De l'Universalité de la Langue française*.

Perhaps the most striking proof of the diffusion of the French language all over eighteenth century Europe is the number of people, besides Frederick the Great, who wrote in French: at the beginning of the century, the German philosopher, Leibniz, and later Catherine the Great as well as the English historian, Gibbon, whose first work, his *Essai sur l'étude de la littérature*, appeared in London in 1761. The works of French writers and thinkers were read all over Europe. If large numbers of French books were printed and published abroad—in Holland, Switzerland, Germany and England—it was partly because the rigid censorship in France drove French writers to seek foreign publishers; it was also because there was a market for French books all over Europe, and to publish French books, with or without the permission of the author, was generally a profitable undertaking. In his memoirs Marmontel gives a lively account of an encounter with a foreign publisher who was doing very nicely out of pirated editions of his works:

> A Liège, où nous avions couché, je vis entrer chez moi, le matin, un bourgeois d'assez bonne mine, et qui me dit: 'Monsieur, j'ai appris hier au soir que vous étiez ici; je vous ai de grandes obligations, et viens vous en remercier. Mon nom est Bassompierre; je suis imprimeur-libraire dans cette ville; j'imprime vos ouvrages dont j'ai un grand débit dans toute l'Allemagne. J'ai déjà fait quatre éditions copieuses de vos *Contes*; je suis à la

troisième édition de *Bélisaire.*—Quoi! Monsieur, lui dis-je, en l'interrompant, vous me volez le fruit de mon travail, et vous venez vous en vanter à moi!—Bon, reprit-il, vos privilèges[1] ne s'étendent point jusqu'ici: Liège est un pays de franchise. Nous avons droit d'imprimer tout ce qu'il y a de bon; c'est là notre commerce'. (*Mémoires*, II, 315)

The influence of French civilization in eighteenth century Europe was not confined to language, literature and ideas. Before the first fashion paper, *Le Cabinet des Modes*, appeared in 1784, dolls dressed in the latest fashions were regularly dispatched to all the capitals of Europe by the *couturières* of the Rue Saint-Honoré. There was a great demand for the luxury articles produced by French skill and taste: furniture, tapestries, gold and silver plate, jewellery, porcelain and especially clothes, fans, gloves and cosmetics. French cooks were much sought after all over Europe; and so were French painters and sculptors. However small his territory every German prince, dazzled by Versailles, took on a *premier architecte* and ruined himself—and his subjects—in constructing buildings and gardens on the same pattern. Versailles was imitated all over Europe, at Potsdam and even in Russia, but nowhere was the influence of French architecture stronger than in the German states of the Rhineland. In Mannheim, for instance, a vast palace on the model of Versailles was constructed in the 1720s from plans furnished by two French architects. At the nearby Schwetzingen, the summer residence of the Electors of the Palatinate, another French architect built in 1752 a small theatre at which in the following year, after leaving the court of Frederick the Great, Voltaire saw two of his plays performed.

In the nature of things the degree of influence exercised by French civilization varied from country to country; it was stronger in Eastern and Central Europe than in, say, England. Moreover, one must not forget the development of a national spirit in countries like Germany, or the growing prestige of English literature and thought in France itself as well as on the rest of the Continent. In France the fashion for all things

---

[1] A licence from the government to publish a book.

English gave rise about the middle of the century to the derisive term of *anglomanie*. Yet great as was the influence of English literature and thought in eighteenth century Europe, French civilization still possessed one advantage: the French language was much better known on the Continent. Indeed the diffusion of English literature and ideas in eighteenth century Europe was often assisted by French writers. Many German translations of English works were based not on the original, but on the French translation. Whether it was of Shakespeare or the English constitution, it was often French works of popularization which first spread knowledge over the Continent. Thus, despite the ravages of *anglomanie* in France, there is no question that her civilization dominated eighteenth century Europe.

In the France of our period, as in England, there were already signs of the Industrial Revolution which was to transform Western Europe. Not that France ever experienced an upheaval comparable to that which, between about 1750 and 1850, changed England from a preponderantly agricultural country into a preponderantly industrial one. Even today the proportion of French people engaged in agriculture is several times as great as in England. To the very end of our period agriculture continued to dominate the economic life of France. When it prospered, trade and industry flourished; when the prices of agricultural products declined steeply or when, in years of scarcity, they rose to heights which brought hardship and suffering to the masses both of town and country, there followed a slump in trade and industry which added to the general misery.

The preponderance of agriculture in the economic life of eighteenth century France is illustrated in the theories of the Physiocrats, the group of writers who founded the new science of economics about the middle of the century. Like Adam Smith slightly later, they denounced all government interference in economic matters in the name of the principles of economic Liberalism (it is to them that we owe the famous formula: *'laissez faire, laissez passer'*), but in a country still dominated by agriculture they maintained that the land was the ultimate source of all wealth, and relegated to a secondary

position trade and industry which, they argued, merely transformed the produce of the soil.

The importance of agriculture in eighteenth century France
has been brilliantly demonstrated by the economic historian
Ernest Labrousse, in the last twenty years.[1] Thanks to the
material collected for the central government by its agents in
the provinces, it is possible to work out in detail for a great part

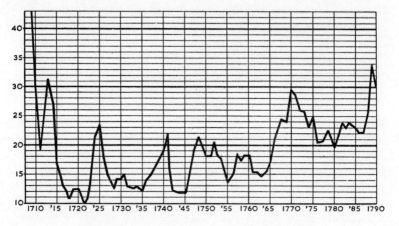

The Price of Wheat in France, 1709-1790

(Yearly averages; prices in *livres* per *setier*)

Reproduced by permission from E. Labrousse, *Esquisse du mouvement des prix
et des revenus au XVIIIe siècle*, Librairie Dalloz.

of the century the price movements of various commodities,
especially grain. The assembling and interpretation of this mass
of material enable us today to form a clearer picture both of the
lot of the various sections of the community in our period and
of the development of the economic life of the country. We can
now reconcile two conflicting views of the state of France before
1789 which have divided French historians for the last century.
For one school the French Revolution was the direct result of

[1] Particularly in two books, *Esquisse du mouvement des prix et des revenus au XVIIIe
siècle*, Paris, 1932, 2 vols., and *La Crise de l'économie française à la fin de l'Ancien Régime
et au début de la Révolution*, Vol. I, Paris, 1943.

the misery and impoverishment of the masses; for Michelet, writing almost a century ago, the upheaval was a last desperate revolt against poverty and suffering. In contrast to his picture of misery and despair which makes even La Bruyère's portrait of the seventeenth century peasant seem relatively mild, more recent historians, headed by the great French socialist, Jean Jaurès, have stressed the notion that, for all its black spots, eighteenth century France enjoyed a period of growing prosperity which saw in particular the expansion of the economic power of the middle classes. Not for them the notion that the Revolution of 1789 was the product merely of desperate poverty and suffering. The eighteenth century, in their eyes, was an age of economic as well as intellectual progress, an age in which, through the development of trade and industry, the middle classes came to play an ever more important part in the life of the nation and thus to seek a degree of political power commensurate with their importance in the economic life of the country. On this view the Ancien Régime came to an end in France, less because of the sufferings which it inflicted on the poorer sections of the community than because in an age of economic progress it barred the way to further advances.

These two contrasted views are, broadly speaking, reconciled by the work of economic historians like Labrousse. From the study of price movements, particularly those of agricultural products, there emerges a more precise picture of the economic state of the country, especially in the period from about 1730, when statistical material begins to be available in large quantities, down to the Revolution. In contrast to the period from about 1660 to 1730, an age of low agricultural prices (except in periods of great scarcity), the long-term trend in the years between about 1730 and the opening years of the Restoration, was towards high prices. This rise in agricultural prices was slow until about 1760, but extremely rapid for the next decade. In considering the long-term trends in prices, one has however to take into account shorter movements which could be very different—cyclical movements of prices over periods of twelve or fifteen years and seasonal movements which in years of bad harvests could be enormous, especially for cereals.

Characteristically, in an economy in which agriculture was still immensely more important than industry, this long-term rise in prices affected agricultural products, particularly cereals and meat, much more strongly than manufactured goods; but all sections of the economy benefited from the steady rise in prices which set in about 1730. Landowners and the better-off peasants prospered, and the flourishing state of a considerable sector of agriculture benefited the towns in their turn. Wealthy landowners mainly resided there and created a demand for luxury goods and above all for new and more comfortable houses. Moreover, many big landowners interested themselves in new industrial developments; great noblemen would often put their money into new forges and mines. The prosperity of the towns also helped to expand the market for such industrial products as textiles.

No doubt the prosperity produced by this long-term rise in agricultural prices was very unevenly spread. The majority of peasants did not benefit from it, as they did not produce for the market, and even had to buy such products as cereals at the higher prices, while both in town and country the rise in wages lagged far behind the rise in prices. Yet the half-century from about 1730 to 1778 was on balance a period of rapid economic advance and justifies the glowing picture of the progress achieved in eighteenth century France given by historians like Jaurès or Mathiez.

For the last dozen years or so of the Ancien Régime the situation was very different. After 1790 agriculture was gradually to recover from the depression of the period which began about 1778, but the closing years of the Ancien Régime undoubtedly brought hard times for many sections of the community. In a few years wine prices fell by half, with serious effects on the large number of small producers. The fall in the prices of cereals was less pronounced, but it came at a time when rents were being steadily raised to keep up belatedly with the general rise in prices. The agricultural depression had disagreeable consequences in the towns, where production both for the home market and for export fell rapidly. Unemployment was widespread both in town and country.

The economic depression which set in about 1778 was made worse, at a critical period in the history of France, by the bad harvest of 1788 and the moderate harvest of 1789. Scarcity had produced even higher prices earlier in the century, but the crisis which followed was worse because it occurred at a time when the economy as a whole was in a bad way. The mass of peasants were hard hit by the bad harvest of 1788; having little or no produce to sell, they could derive little benefit from high prices. Worse off still were the landless or nearly landless labourers, who suffered greatly from unemployment at the very moment when bread prices rocketed. The depression in agriculture had in turn marked repercussions on the state of industry. Cloth production, for instance, fell by half between 1787 and 1789. Thus in the towns in 1788 and 1789 unemployment coincided with a catastrophic rise in the price of bread.

The Revolution was not, of course, entirely due to the bad harvest of 1788 and the soaring prices of 1789. Its roots lay much deeper in the past. But it was undoubtedly precipitated by the economic depression of the last dozen years or so of the Ancien Régime; in that sense it can be described as 'une révolution de la misère'. Yet that was not the whole story. Historians like Jaurès or Mathiez were not wholly wrong in stressing the other side of the medal—that, viewed as a whole, the eighteenth century was a period of considerable prosperity. In the period which began about 1730 certain sections of the community profited from the prosperity of agriculture and from that of trade and industry. On a long-term view the Revolution of 1789 was indeed 'une révolution de la prospérité'.

Another complex problem in the history of eighteenth century France is the relative position of middle classes and aristocracy before 1789. It is possible to consider that history as the story of the continued rise of the middle classes and the gradual decline of the aristocracy, and to see in the Revolution with its destruction of absolutism and the aristocratic society of the Ancien Régime the translation of the economic power of the middle classes into political power. The truth is more complex. As a counterweight to the growing prosperity of the

middle classes in our period, recent historians have stressed the
efforts of the aristocracy to hold on to its position and even to
strengthen it. The privileged orders—the clergy and nobility—
profited from the long-term rise in agricultural prices; both their
rents and feudal dues were swollen by the upward surge of the
economy. A minority among the nobles played their part in the
development of new industries. As the century wore on, the
aristocracy tended more and more to deny to men of bourgeois
stock the opportunities to rise in society which they had enjoyed
in the France of Louis XIV; high posts in the army, the administration, the law courts and the Church became more and
more a monopoly of the aristocracy. Moreover, its members
became increasingly dissatisfied with the state of political
impotence to which absolutism had reduced them. Underlying
the fierce struggle between the Crown and the highest law
courts, the Parlements, which began as soon as Louis XIV had
breathed his last breath, was the determination of the French
aristocracy to regain a share of influence in the affairs of the
country. Neither on his estates nor in the government at the
centre did the French nobleman enjoy any influence or power;
he looked with envy on the part played in the political life of
England by the aristocracy and squires in Parliament and in
provincial life. As the power of French absolutism waned, the
privileged orders demanded more and more loudly a share in
political power until in the critical years 1787 and 1788 they
shook to its very foundations the authority of the Crown; by
their insistence on the summoning of the *États généraux* they
ended by destroying both Absolutism and their own privileges.

The revolt against Absolutism and indeed the whole society
of the Ancien Régime which marked the eighteenth century in
France stemmed thus from very different sources—from the
aristocracy as well as the Third Estate. The gradual disintegration of the power of the Crown and the increasing dissatisfaction with existing society produced a tremendous ferment of
political and social ideas. These ideas were of extraordinary
richness and complexity, ranging as they do from some of the
earliest manifestations of Socialist thought to a die-hard defence
of the *status quo*. Many of the reformers looked for the fulfilment

of their ideals to an enlightened despot; others again—Montesquieu is the most notable example—sought to limit the powers
of the monarchy by restoring and increasing the power of the
aristocracy. Few writers of the time foresaw what sort of France
was to emerge, after 1789, from the destruction of Absolutism
and of the privileges of the aristocracy. Dissatisfaction with the
*status quo* is more prominent in the political and social writings
of the age than agreement about the future; and yet this
ferment of ideas, despite the universal form it often took on,
was rooted in the complex realities of life in France before 1789.

CHAPTER I

# THE PEASANTRY

FOR all the gaps in our knowledge, we know considerably more about French agriculture and the peasants in the eighteenth century than in the age of Louis XIV; yet it still remains a difficult task to do justice to the extreme complexity of rural life in France before 1789. It is easy to paint a dark picture of the backwardness of French agriculture and the miserable lot of vast numbers of peasants and their families. On the other hand, if one chose one's documents carefully, it would be possible to produce a picture of prosperity and rapid technical progress on the land. For instance, it is possible (it has indeed been done) to quote Rétif de la Bretonne's description of the patriarchal scene when his father and mother, along with their numerous children and farm servants, male and female, sat down to their evening meal, as evidence of the prosperity of French peasants in the 'good old days' before the Revolution:

> Les soirs, à souper, qui était le seul repas où toute la famille pouvait être réunie, il se voyait comme un patriarche vénérable, à la tête d'une maison nombreuse: car on était ordinairement vingt-deux à table, y compris les garçons de charrue et les vignerons, qui, en hiver, étaient batteurs,[1] le bouvier, le berger, et deux servantes, dont l'une suivait les vignerons, et l'autre avait le gouvernement des vaches et de la laiterie. Tout cela était assis à la même table: le père de famille au bout, du côté du feu; sa femme à côté de lui, à portée des plats à servir (car c'était elle seule qui se mêlait de la cuisine; les servantes qui avaient travaillé tout le jour, étaient assises, et mangeaient tranquillement); ensuite les enfants de la maison, suivant leur âge, qui seul réglait leur rang; puis le plus ancien des garçons de charrue et ses camarades; ensuite les vignerons; après lequel venaient le bouvier et le berger; ensuite les deux servantes formaient la clôture. . . . (*Vie de mon père*, p. 208)

[1] Threshers.

If Arthur Young's account of French agriculture in the years
1787-9 offers on the whole a gloomy picture of poverty and
technical backwardness, on the other hand the Norwich doctor,
Edward Rigby, himself a practical farmer and agricultural
reformer, could write of what he saw in the year 1789 on a
journey from Calais to Lille in almost lyrical terms:

> The most striking character of the country through which we
> passed yesterday is its astonishing fertility. We went through an
> extent of seventy miles, and I will venture to say that there is not
> a single acre but what was in a state of the highest cultivation.
> The crops are great beyond any conception I could have had
> of them—thousands and ten thousands of acres of wheat superior
> to any that can be produced in England; oats extraordinarily
> large. (*Letters from France in 1789*, p. 10)

This favourable impression persisted not only during his
journey through the north-eastern corner of France which
was one of the most fertile and technically advanced regions,
but as far south as Burgundy. After travelling through Paris
to Dijon, he wrote with the same enthusiasm:

> My astonishment at the magnitude of this empire, its wonderful
> population, the industry of the inhabitants, and the excellence
> of the climate only increases the further we penetrate into the
> country. We have now travelled between four and five hundred
> miles in France, and have hardly seen an acre uncultivated,
> except two forests and parks . . ., and these were covered with
> woods. In every other place almost every inch had been ploughed
> or dug, and at this time appears to be pressed with the weight
> of the incumbent crop. On the roads, to the very edge where the
> travellers' wheels pass, and on the hills, to the very summit,
> may be seen the effects of human industry. Since we left Paris we
> have come through a country where the vine is cultivated. This
> grows on the sides and even the tops of the highest hills. It will
> also flourish where the soil is too poor to bear corn, and on the
> sides of precipices where no animal could draw the plough.
> (ibid. pp. 96-7)

From passages like these one could construct a remarkable
picture of agricultural prosperity.

The difficulty is that there is not and never has been such a person as a typical French peasant; then, as now, the lot of the individual peasant depended on the kind and the amount of land which he had at his disposal, and the region in which he happened to live.

Today the French rural landscape varies enormously from region to region, from the pastures of Normandy to the great corn-producing plateau of the Beauce west of Paris and the vast vineyards of Languedoc along the Mediterranean coast. Before the Revolution there was much less of such specialization. In an age oppressed by the fear of bad grain harvests, every district felt compelled to grow so far as possible its own cereals, since a primitive transport system made it difficult to draw supplies from regions which had been less affected by the disaster. Cereals, known then collectively as 'le blé', a term which included not only wheat, but rye, oats, barley and other grains,[1] were the staple crop of all regions before the Revolution. Yet even then the beginnings of specialization were visible. Nowhere was this more obvious than in winegrowing, even though it was carried on, at least in small pockets, almost everywhere, despite unfavourable geographical conditions which have driven it out in the last hundred years or so. By the eighteenth century the production of wine in France made it next in importance to cereals in the internal trade of the country and the leading article of export. Moreover, the regions in which the vine was grown were heavily populated, as it requires a large labour-force and the small peasant could obtain a large production from quite a small area of land.

Not only did the lot of the peasant differ according to the varying types of farming which were more and more clearly emerging in eighteenth century France; it inevitably depended also both on the amount of land which he owned or rented and on the fertility of the region in which he happened to live. Then, as now, there was an enormous difference between seeking to earn a living in, say, the fertile regions of Northern France,

[1] 'Blé, s.m. Plante qui produit le grain dont on fait le pain. . . . On appelle *Grands blés*, les blés froment et les blés seigle. *Blés méteil*, le blé moitié froment, moitié seigle. *Petits blés*, l'orge et l'avoine. Et *Blé noir*, ou *Blé sarrasin*, une autre plante qui porte par petites grappes un grain noir, et qui a des angles aigus' [='buckwheat']. (*Dictionnaire de l'Académie Française*, 1762)

1  Agriculture: Labourage (*Encyclopédie*)

2   Agriculture: Batteurs en grange (*Encyclopédie*)

such as Picardy, Flanders, Beauce or Normandy, and trying to do so in the poorer, often mountainous or semi-mountainous regions of Central and Southern France. Moreover, vast regions of Western and Central France, which modern farming methods have improved out of all recognition in the last hundred years or so, were then poor and unproductive.

Then, as now, there were all manner of differences between the peasants not only from region to region, but within each community. In one respect, it is true, the peasant before 1789 was in a very different position from the peasant of today; he still lived under what remained of the manorial system (the *régime seigneurial*). In France serfdom had lost much ground since the height of the Middle Ages. The lot of the great majority of French peasants in our period was vastly different from that of their brethren in many parts of Central and Eastern Europe where serfdom was to continue to survive, and in a much more severe form than anywhere in eighteenth century France, long after 1789. As Saint-Lambert put it, in a sentimental style typical of the period, in the notes to his poem, *Les Saisons*:

> La manière dont les cultivateurs sont traités dans la plus grande partie de l'Europe, en Espagne, en Portugal, en Pologne, dans une partie de l'Allemagne, etc. doit intéresser au sort de ces malheureux les hommes de toutes les nations. En France on a souvent déploré le sort de nos agriculteurs; il s'en faut de beaucoup qu'ils soient aussi à plaindre que ceux des pays que je viens de nommer. (*Œuvres*, I, 173)

Yet though by the eighteenth century the overwhelming majority of French peasants were free men, serfdom lingered on right down to the Revolution, though in a much mitigated form, particularly in such provinces as Burgundy and Franche-Comté. In his last years Voltaire campaigned vigorously against its survival, especially on certain estates of the Church. In 1779 Louis XVI was induced to abolish serfdom on the Crown lands and to express the hope that this example would be followed by noble and clerical landowners. It was left, however, to the National Assembly in 1789 to abolish the remnants of serfdom without compensation in one of the famous decrees of 'la nuit du 4 août'.

Yet long before our period the vast majority of French peasants had ceased to be serfs and enjoyed a freedom denied to many other peasants on the Continent. They continued, however, almost without exception, to be under the authority of a *seigneur* (lord of the manor), whether lay or ecclesiastical, for the clergy still owned a considerable amount of land and levied feudal dues on an even greater area. Whatever their status, the peasants continued to pay to their lord feudal dues on such land as they held on his estates. These dues were quite distinct from the rent of land; the peasant had to continue to pay them, even though by the eighteenth century such land as he held had become for all practical purposes his own property, in the sense that, unless he was a serf, he could sell, exchange or bequeath it as he wished. Moreover, feudal dues had long since lost their original justification: the help and protection which in an unsettled age the lord of the manor had given. The maintenance of law and order had long ceased to be the concern of the nobles; the task had been taken over by the central government to the upkeep of which the peasant had to contribute heavy taxes. Yet he still had to pay feudal dues to his lord in return for absolutely nothing.

The peasant's obligations towards his lord varied from region to region and even from manor to manor; but, despite all sorts of differences in terminology as well as practice, certain broad generalizations can be made. The *aveu* (sometimes known as *dénombrement*)—the obligation for all the peasants on an estate to produce a document giving an exact description of their holdings and the dues with which they were encumbered—was both an expensive and vexatious duty in our period, whenever the time (thirty years, or twenty or even less) came round, since the lord tended to take advantage of it to increase his exactions.

On the other hand, other obligations had become less onerous since the Middle Ages. The *corvée*—the obligation to work for a specified number of days a year on the lord's domain—had long ceased to have the importance in the peasant's life which it had had in earlier centuries when this could involve several days' work a week; by the eighteenth century it had long been reduced to no more than a few days a year, and had often been commuted for a small money payment. Again, the *cens*—a money payment due annually from the peasant according to the amount of land which he held—had ceased to be a heavy burden, as the decline in the value of money had reduced the sum to such an insignificant amount that it was only worth collecting because payment of the *cens* involved more important obligations.

Chief of these in the eighteenth century were payments in kind (*redevances en nature*). One of the most common was the *champart*, which closely resembled the tithe and was levied particularly on grain-crops; its amount varied from one manor to another, but a rough average might be something like 12 per cent. The burden of such dues had obviously been in no way mitigated by the fall in the value of money since mediaeval times. Indeed, in our period, in years of scarcity and high agricultual prices, they could make still more desperate the lot of the peasant, who, although driven to buy grain to feed himself and his family, was compelled to hand over to his lord this fixed proportion of his total crop, at the very moment when it was worth a very high price. Despite the poor harvest, rocketing prices might well make the lord's income from such dues rise higher than usual, but the peasant would be trampled further into the mire.

Feudal dues levied on the value of property when it changed hands could also be a considerable burden to the peasant and a valuable source of income to his lord. The most important of such dues was the *droit de lods et ventes*, which was levied on any piece of land which changed hands by sale or its equivalent, and amounted to some 8 or 10 per cent. of the purchase price.

The peasant's relations with his lord were not confined to the payment, in money or in kind, of a variety of feudal dues. In most places he was compelled to take his grain to his lord's mill to be ground (*banalité du moulin*), and in addition he was often obliged to take his bread to be baked in his lord's oven (*banalité du four*) or his grapes to be pressed in his lord's wine-press (*banalité du pressoir*). All these obligations which gave rise to inconvenience and even fraud were extremely unpopular.

In addition, the lord of the manor possessed the hated *droit de chasse*, the sole right to kill game on his estates. A royal edict of 1669 expressly forbade all *roturiers*, whatever their social class, to take any part whatsoever in hunting, a pastime reserved exclusively for the nobility. Moreover, the game laws were framed with complete disregard for the interests of the peasants; they were not allowed, for instance, to cut their hay before midsummer or even to enclose a piece of land with a stone wall without permission. Their land thus suffered severely from the ravages of game. These seem to have been worst of all in the regions around Paris reserved for the favourite sport of both Louis XV and Louis XVI, but over the country as a whole the lord's monopoly of hunting had most serious consequences for the peasants. The *droit de chasse* was the most detested of all the privileges of the aristocracy.

Finally there remained the manorial courts (*la justice seigneuriale*), several of which might function in the same village since it could lie in the estates of several noblemen. Theoretically there were various grades of courts; a nobleman might possess rights of *haute, moyenne et basse justice* or only more limited powers. In practice, since mediaeval times the Crown had succeeded in reducing the judicial powers of the nobility. A great many cases had been transferred to the royal courts, but what remained could often prove vexatious to the peasants. In general, the lord of the manor had little interest in trying criminal offences as these could involve him in considerable expense; by the eighteenth century the manorial courts were mainly occupied with civil cases. It is true that the lord of the manor could not himself try cases, but as he appointed (and dismissed) the judge, the peasant could expect but scant justice in disputes with his lord over such matters as feudal dues.

In this context we must not forget a process which had long been going on in France, but which seems to have received fresh impetus in the eighteenth century: the so-called *réaction seigneuriale*. The members of the older aristocracy, often living

in dire financial straits, or even if they led a luxurious life in
Paris or at court, still constantly in debt and anxious to increase
their income, strove to wring the last farthing in feudal dues
out of their peasants. Moreover, the aristocracy was constantly
being renewed by the admission of the wealthier members of
the middle classes to its ranks. These newcomers, who were often
judges and high officials with a legal training, were determined
to obtain the highest possible return from the capital invested
in their land. Much better business men than the members of
the often profligate *noblesse d'épée*, they too were determined to
have their pound of flesh. In the decades before the Revolution
the members of the French aristocracy employed either their
own time or that of paid experts delving into their archives to
discover old rights which had fallen into disuse or inventing
new ones, which they imposed on their peasants at each new
*dénombrement* on their estates, often claiming up to twenty-nine
years' arrears. As the burden of feudal dues was automatically
made heavier in years of bad harvests, to increase these further
by more or less dubious devices was scarcely calculated to win
the hearts of the peasants; it helps to explain the alacrity with
which in 1789 the archives of so many of the châteaux of France
(and sometimes the châteaux themselves) were given over to
the flames.

Some ten years before the Revolution a tax official, on a tour
of inspection in the South of France, wrote of this exploitation
of the peasants (in this case by an abbey):

> Comment se défendre contre les parchemins qu'on ne sait pas lire
> et qu'on ne peut pas se faire expliquer, faute d'argent? Les
> archives des seigneurs sont remplies de titres inconnus et qu'on
> tire successivement de la poussière, sauf à les y faire rentrer si
> l'abus du pouvoir ou si la chicane ne peuvent parvenir à leur
> donner de la valeur. (Richeprey, *Journal de voyage*, I, 70)

The same writer gives us some idea of the effects of the *réaction
seigneuriale* on a nearby estate, owned by a judge of the Toulouse
Parlement:

> Il n'y a pas d'exemple d'aussi rigoureuses recherches des droits
> seigneuriaux que celles exercées dans cette terre. On y a rétabli

beaucoup de droits et de censives[1] inconnues ou oubliées. On y a
fait exercer la plus rigoureuse corvée lors de la réparation du
château. Je croyais que le droit de taille, *dans les quatre cas*,[2]
n'avait plus lieu, qu'il était oublié avec tous les usages des temps
gothiques. Mais le seigneur de St-Bauzely l'exige encore. Quand
il achète des terres, et cela lui arrive malheureusement souvent,
ses vassaux lui payent une taille extraordinaire. Il a exigé celle
de 2,000 l. quand il a acheté la terre d'Espalion. (I, 118)

Linked with this movement were the frequent inroads into
the common lands (*communaux*) made in our period by aristocratic and other wealthy landowners. Common lands still
played an important part in the economic life of the village,
since they provided a place for the peasants to graze their sheep
and cattle and, if they were partly forest, also furnished wood.
For centuries the common lands had given rise to disputes
between the lord and his peasants, but now the struggle was
intensified as the urge to increase agricultural production grew.
Sometimes the lord—or even a wealthy peasant—would simply
go ahead and enclose part of the *communaux* and add them to
his fields. More often the lord would make use of the legal
machinery for the division of the common lands and demand
the third share which the law, under the name of *droit de triage*,
conferred upon him; or sometimes village communities, heavily
in debt, would sell the whole or part of their common lands.
In France, however, the enclosure movement did not take on
the same proportions as in eighteenth century England. The
law courts (Parlements) whose members were almost invariably
big landowners, gave the movement their full support, but the
government, partly because the peasants were so important as
taxpayers, was inclined to come to their aid. However, in the
closing decades of the Ancien Régime when the agricultural
revolution was beginning to make itself felt, it gave fresh
impetus to the enclosure movement, which benefited not only
the feudal landowners, but also the wealthier peasants.

[1] 'Redevance en argent ou en denrées, que certains biens doivent annuellement
au seigneur du fief dont ils relèvent' (*Dictionnaire de l'Académie Française*, 1762).
[2] 'Une taille seigneuriale que dans certains lieux les seigneurs ont droit de lever
sur leurs hommes taillables' (*Encyclopédie*). Its payment had generally fallen into
disuse.

Important as the manorial system remained in France until the Revolution, one must penetrate beyond it if one is to form some reasonably precise notion of the lot of the peasants before 1789. One must first consider which social classes owned the land in our period. Today the land of France is in the hands not only of a very large number of small peasants, but also of a much smaller number of medium and large landowners; that was exactly the situation in the century before 1789. Then, of course, the medium and large landowners included not only rich bourgeois from the towns or well-to-do peasants, but also members of the two privileged orders, the nobility and the clergy, who, in addition, exacted feudal dues from the peasants on their estates.

The amount of land owned by the nobility, the clergy, the middle classes and the peasants varied enormously from province to province. In general the landed property of the Church was not nearly as great as has often been imagined; in reality its wealth was probably derived less from the ownership of agricultural land than from tithes, feudal dues and from its valuable urban property. Its holdings rarely exceeded 20 per cent. of the total land in any region, and in some were less than 1 per cent.; 6 per cent. as an average over the country as a whole is generally accepted by historians, and it is also agreed that they decreased in importance as one moved further south. The holdings of the nobility, while much more considerable, also appear to have varied sharply, from 9 per cent. to 44 per cent. In general, they were greatest in the west of France, but they were also large near some of the bigger towns, where the wealthy bourgeois had bought land and risen up into the aristocracy. The share of the middle classes was equally varied, ranging from 12 per cent. to 45 per cent.; it too was obviously greater near the towns.

A considerable proportion of the total land of France—some historians argue that the amount actually increased in the decades before the Revolution—was in the hands of the peasants, subject, of course, in almost all cases to the payment of feudal dues. Once again, the amount varied enormously from region to region, from 22 per cent. to 70 per cent. Moreover, as the peasants were by far the largest single group of land-owners, their individual holdings were mostly extremely small. Inevitably the amount of land in peasant hands varied considerably from village to village, as well as from region to region; and inside each village community there were all sorts of grades of landed wealth, ranging from the wealthy *coq de paroisse*, with his large holding, down to the completely landless labourer, with peasants owning medium and especially tiny holdings in between. Landless labourers were numerous in certain regions of France before 1789, even though ownership of the land was spread over an extraordinarily large number of peasants. The growth in population brought about in the eighteenth century both by the progress of medicine and by the disappearance of the worst type of famine, undoubtedly led to over-population of the countryside and to the growth of the class of landless or nearly landless labourers.

It is not, however, sufficient to confine our attention merely to the ownership of land, if we are to form some relatively precise notion of life in the French countryside before 1789. The very considerable amount of land in the hands of the nobility, clergy and middle classes was mostly let out, under different forms of tenancy, to the peasants. In addition to farming his own land, a peasant who possessed the necessary capital, might become a tenant-farmer (*fermier*) and take on the lease of quite an extensive farm. The importance of these large-scale tenant-farmers who were particularly numerous in the more fertile regions of the northern half of France, was stressed by Turgot when he wrote:

Ce qui distingue véritablement les pays de grande culture de ceux de petite culture, c'est que, dans les premiers, les propriétaires trouvent des *fermiers* qui leur donnent un revenu constant de leur terre et qui achètent d'eux le droit de la cultiver pendant un certain nombre d'années. Ces fermiers se chargent de toutes les dépenses de la culture, des labours, des semences, de meubler la ferme de bestiaux de toute espèce, des animaux et des instruments de labour. Ces fermiers sont de véritables *entrepreneurs de culture*, qui ont à eux, comme les entrepreneurs dans tout autre genre de commerce, des fonds considérables et qui les font valoir par la culture des terres. Lorsque leur bail est fini, si le propriétaire ne veut plus le continuer, ils cherchent une autre ferme où ils puissent transporter leurs richesses et les faire valoir de la même manière.

Such peasants, he adds,

ont, non pas seulement des bras, mais des richesses, à consacrer à l'agriculture. [Ils] n'ont d'autre état que de labourer, non pas à gagner leur vie à la sueur de leur front comme des ouvriers, mais pour employer d'une manière lucrative leurs capitaux, comme les armateurs de Nantes et de Bordeaux emploient les leurs dans le commerce maritime. (*Œuvres*, II, 448-9).

Large farms of this type, rented by well-to-do peasants generally from big landowners from among the privileged orders, seem to have tended to increase in the closing decades of the Ancien Régime, to the indignation of the less prosperous peasants who found it increasingly difficult to find land to rent.

Such large-scale farmers, equipped with considerable capital, were naturally a small, if economically important minority amongst the peasants. A much more numerous class, especially in the west, centre and south of France, were the so-called *métayers*—peasants without capital who rented a small piece of land, and received from their landlord the necessary stock, seed and implements, in return for which they handed over to him a share of the produce, generally a half. Sometimes part of their rent was paid in money. *Métayage* (or 'culture à moitié fruits') was denounced by Arthur Young as 'a miserable system, that perpetuates poverty' (*Travels in France*, I, 12). Its disadvantages are brought out by the following observations of Turgot:

Les pays de *petite culture*, c'est-à-dire au moins les quatre septièmes de l'étendue du royaume, sont ceux où il n'existe point d'entrepreneurs de culture, où un propriétaire qui veut faire valoir sa terre ne trouve pour la cultiver que des malheureux paysans qui n'ont que leurs bras, où il est obligé de faire à ses frais toutes les avances de la culture, bestiaux, instruments, semences, d'avancer même à son *métayer* de quoi se nourrir jusqu'à leur première récolte, où, par conséquent, un propriétaire qui n'aurait d'autre bien que sa terre, serait obligé de la laisser en friche. . . .

Après avoir prélevé la semence et les rentes[1] dont le bien est chargé, le propriétaire partage avec le métayer ce qui reste des fruits, suivant la convention qu'ils ont faite entre eux. Le propriétaire, qui fait les avances, court tous les risques des accidents des récoltes, des pertes de bestiaux; il est le seul véritable entrepreneur de la culture. Le métayer n'est qu'un simple manœuvre, un valet auquel il abandonne une part des fruits pour lui tenir lieu de gages. Mais le propriétaire n'a pas dans son entreprise les mêmes avantages que le fermier, qui la conduit lui-même avec attention et avec intelligence: le propriétaire est forcé de confier toutes ses avances à un homme qui peut être négligent ou fripon, et qui n'a rien pour en répondre.

Ce métayer, accoutumé à la vie la plus misérable, et qui n'a l'espérance ni même le désir de se procurer un état meilleur, cultive mal, néglige d'employer les terres à des productions commerçables et d'une grande valeur; il s'occupe par préférence à faire venir celles dont la culture est moins pénible et qui lui procurent une nourriture plus abondante, comme le sarrasin et surtout la châtaigne, qui ne donne d'autre peine que de la ramasser. Il est même assez peu inquiet sur sa subsistance: il sait que, si la récolte manque, son maître sera obligé de le nourrir pour ne pas voir abandonner son domaine. (*Œuvres*, II, 449-50)

These were the two extremes amongst the tenant-farmers of France before the Revolution: the well-to-do peasant with sufficient capital to run a large farm and to produce for the market, and the miserably poor *métayer*, living from hand to mouth and concerned primarily with subsistence agriculture, with producing enough food for himself and his family. There were, of course, all kinds of intermediate types of tenant-farmers enjoying different degrees of prosperity.

The variety of social classes covered by the term 'peasant' was thus considerable. At the top came a relatively small, but economically powerful class of men who owned or were able to rent a considerable amount of land and who possessed sufficient capital to run their farms efficiently and to make a comfortable living. They formed a kind of rural bourgeoisie raised far above the great mass of the peasantry. Beneath them came other

---

[1] Feudal dues.

peasants who owned or rented enough land to make a reasonable living in times of prosperity, but who could be hard hit
when grain and other prices were low, and especially when
their crops failed and prices rocketed. Over a great part of the
country there came next, in descending order of prosperity, the
mass of *métayers*, landless or nearly landless peasants who could
offer their landlord merely a share in the crops, and who needed
to be provided with seed, stock and implements. Finally there
came the army of landless or nearly landless labourers who
depended for a living on being able to find agricultural work
and who, in the neighbourhood of the towns, managed to eke
out a subsistence by working with their families in domestic
industry.[1] These were the sections of the community which
suffered most in years of bad harvests and high grain prices,
for at best they lived just about at the subsistence level.

In the villages and hamlets of France there were also other
social groups, the members of which might own or rent land,
but found their main living, not in agriculture, but in some
other occupation. There were artisans and innkeepers, cattle
dealers and corn merchants, of varying degress of prosperity
or poverty. There were men too who collected the feudal dues
of one or more *seigneurs*, lay or ecclesiastical, or who rented all
the available land on an estate and let it out to tenant-farmers
or *métayers*; such men were often well-to-do.

Rural society before 1789 was thus extremely complex. The
prosperous *laboureur* who owned enough land to make a comfortable living and the tenant-farmer with sufficient capital to
rent a large farm had little in common with the agricultural
labourer at their gate, or even with the mass of poverty-stricken
*métayers*. Yet all bore the label 'peasant'. All of them, it is true,
found their way of living largely conditioned by the fluctuations
in the prices of agricultural products, but even here they were
affected differently according to their economic status.

To grasp the importance of grain prices in eighteenth century
France, one has to consider their effect both on the producer
and on the masses who were large consumers of bread, the main
item in their diet. 'Le pain est en France', wrote a contem-

[1] See pp. 78-80

porary, 'le principal aliment du pauvre dans les grandes villes, et il compose à la campagne presque sa seule nourriture. Or qui dit le pauvre, dit la moitié de la nation' (Mercier, *Tableau de Paris*, VIII, 92). After calculating the total consumption of grain in the whole kingdom, the great chemist, Lavoisier, goes on: 'Si l'on prend en masse la valeur de toutes les autres consommations, le blé en forme plus de la moitié, et il entre même pour les deux tiers dans la dépense des ménages très pauvres' (*Œuvres*, VI, 409-10). Large sections of the peasantry—not only agricultural labourers, but the winegrower and the many peasants who did not farm enough land to supply all their needs in grain—had to buy part or even all their requirements. Wheat was seldom made use of; rye was much more important in the diet of the masses, and such cheaper grains as maize and buckwheat in the regions where they could be grown. Bread was the basis of the various kinds of soup, varying from region to region, which the peasant consumed at his three main meals; vegetables were added, of course, and occasionally bacon, butter or salt meat, but the essential ingredient was bread. If sharp variations in the price of bread had little importance for the wealthier classes, with their much more varied diet and longer purse, to the millions of families who lived on a bare subsistence level, not only the long-term trends in grain prices, but the startling seasonal rises which frequently took place, were a matter of vital interest, since, in the words of Arthur Young, 'a very small deficiency of the crop will make an enormous difference in the price' (*Travels in France*, I, 489).

No doubt a considerable proportion of the peasant community profited from the half-century or so of agricultural prosperity which France enjoyed between about 1730 and 1778. The rise in the price of wheat, taking the years 1726-41 as 100, is revealed in the following figures:

| | |
|---|---|
| 1726-41 . . . . | 100 |
| 1742-57 . . . . | 109 |
| 1758-70 . . . . | 129 |
| 1771-89 . . . . | 156 |

(Labrousse, *Esquisse du mouvement des prix*, p. 147)

If in the period from 1778 onwards various factors were unfavourable to those peasants producing wheat and even more
to the winegrowers, the general picture of a steady upward
surge in wheat prices from about 1730 onwards stands out
clearly. Naturally these averages for the whole country fail to
bring out the extraordinary range of prices in the different parts
of the country at any given moment, and especially the
tremendous seasonal variations which took place in districts
where there was a grain shortage, for then, particularly in the
spring and summer months before the harvest was brought in
(what the French call *la soudure*), prices might rocket very high,
a long way above the average for the particular year and the
country as a whole.

No doubt all classes on the land profited in some degree from
the prosperity of agriculture in this half-century or so. Though
the growth in population led to a larger number of agricultural
labourers competing for such work as was available, the demand
for labour no doubt grew in these years of expansion. On the
other hand, wages—on the land as in the towns—failed to keep
pace with the rise in the cost of living, so that while money
wages did not remain unchanged, real wages fell. Again, years
of shortage and high prices not only reduced the demand for
labour, but they did so at the very time when the landless
labourer, never in a position to save, was entirely at the mercy
of the high bread prices which followed on poor harvests.
Moreover, it was precisely the cheaper grains such as rye and
buckwheat which furnished the bread of the poorer sections
of the community that increased most in price when there was
a bad harvest. Thus we find Turgot, writing of the effects of
the bad harvest of 1769 in his *généralité*:

Dans les endroits où le prix des grains a été le plus bas, le froment
a valu environ 45 l. le setier de Paris, et le seigle de 33 à 36 l.
Dans une grande partie de la province ce grain a même valu
jusqu'à 42 l. C'est à ce prix qu'a constamment payé sa subsistance
un peuple accoutumé à ne payer cette même mesure de seigle
qu'à 9 l. et souvent moins, et qui, même à ce prix, trouve le
seigle trop cher, et se contente de vivre une grande partie de
l'année avec des châtaignes ou de la bouillie de blé noir. Le

peuple n'a pu subsister qu'en épuisant toutes ses ressources, en vendant à vil prix ses meubles et jusqu'à ses vêtements; une partie des habitants ont été obligés de se disperser dans d'autres provinces pour chercher du travail ou des aumônes, abandonnant leurs femmes et leurs enfants à la charité des paroisses. (*Œuvres*, III, 358)

It was not only the landless labourer who suffered from rocketing prices in years of scarcity and, more generally, from the steady rise in food prices in the two middle quarters of the century. Many of the smaller peasants, whether they cultivated their own small plots or rented land as *métayers*, were not in a position to profit from the steep rise in grain prices. By the time the *métayer* had delivered to his landlord his share of the crop, by the time the small peasant landowner had laid aside the seed for the next year's harvest (often, given the backward state of much of French agriculture, a very high proportion of his grain) and had handed over the share of it demanded by his lord and the Church, there was not enough left to feed him and his family throughout the year. If the *métayer* and the small peasant landowner had to buy in grain for bread, they often had to do so at the time of the year when prices were highest; and in years of bad harvest they might have no grain to speak of from their own land, at the very moment when prices were reaching extraordinary levels. Moreover, at the best of times many small peasants did not have enough land to cultivate for them to make a real living from it and were thus compelled to eke out a precarious existence by devoting part of their time to working as agricultural labourers on the land of their more prosperous neighbours. They too were affected by the failure of wages to keep pace with prices in the middle part of the century, and they were also hard hit when bad harvests and high prices brought increased competition for the smaller number of jobs available on the land.

It was true, at least on paper, that the poorer sections of the community in town and country, the agricultural labourer and the artisan, the *métayer* and the small peasant landowner, could profit from those periods when grain prices were low. At such times some of them no doubt put by some money against the hard times of fantastically high bread prices and possible unemployment, but for people living on a meagre income this was no easy task.

A picture of the sufferings inflicted on the poorer sections of the community in the regions affected by bad harvests and the accompanying high price of bread is provided by a great number of contemporary documents. In July 1725 Mathieu Marais relates in his journal how the high price of bread led to a riot in the Faubourg Saint-Antoine in Paris, in the course of which the troops fired on the mob, two of whom were hanged. He mentions similar riots in Rouen and Caen. In the following month the price, which in times of plenty was normally about 2 sous a pound, rose to 5, then 6, then 7 sous; the shortage, according to Marais, was now confined to the Paris region, for he adds:

Le pain n'a pas manqué d'être à sept sols la livre au marché du samedi 25 août, et on a vu avec effroi que, pendant qu'à quinze ou vingt lieues de Paris et presque par toute la France, il y a abondance, et que le pain est à 2 ou 3 sols, on en manque dans Paris, et le peuple est désespéré. (III, 210-15)

In a letter written on 10 September he gives a still blacker picture of the situation:

La misère publique est toujours très grande; le pain est à huit sols la livre, et n'est pas bon à manger. Les marchés sont toujours garnis de gens de guerre, de crainte des séditions. (III, 360)

These observations give one some idea of the extraordinary variations in bread prices between different parts of the country at exactly the same time, and show how high prices could soar. However, this particular crisis does not appear to have been as prolonged or widespread as the one which began in the summer of 1738 and became particularly violent in the spring of the following year.

In May 1739 the Marquis d'Argenson noted in his journal:

La misère depuis un an avance donc au dedans du royaume à un degré inoui; les hommes meurent drus comme mouches, de pauvreté et en broutant l'herbe, surtout dans les provinces de la

Touraine, du Maine, de l'Angoumois, du Haut-Poitou, du Périgord, de l'Orléanais et du Berry, et cela approche déjà des environs de Versailles. (II, 149)

Later in the same month he wrote:

La disette vient d'occasionner trois soulèvements dans les provinces; à Ruffec en Angoumois, à Caen et à Chinon. On a assassiné sur les chemins des femmes qui portaient des pains. Cette simple nourriture y est plus enviée aujourd'hui qu'une bourse d'or en d'autres temps, et, en effet, la faim pressante et l'envie de conserver ses jours excuse plus le crime que l'avarice d'avoir des moyens accumulés pour les besoins à venir . . . M. le duc d'Orléans[1] porta l'autre jour au Conseil un morceau de pain de fougère; à l'ouverture de la séance il le mit devant la table du roi et dit: Sire, voilà de quel pain se nourrissent aujourd'hui vos sujets! (II, 159)

D'Argenson is suspect to many historians, not without reason, as a man of thwarted ministerial ambitions who painted everything around him in the darkest of colours. One therefore reads with some scepticism the following entry in his journal for the same month:

On parle donc de misère à Versailles plus que jamais; ce n'est plus seulement la Touraine qui en est le siège, c'est toutes les provinces qui approchent de Paris. L'évêque de Chartres a tenu sur cela des discours singulièrement hardis au lever du roi et au dîner de la reine; tout le monde le poussa à les redoubler. Le roi l'interrogeant sur l'état de ses peuples, il a répondu que la famine et la mortalité y étaient; que les hommes mangeaient l'herbe comme des moutons et crevaient comme mouches, et que bientôt on allait y voir la peste, ce qui était pour tout le monde (et il y comprenait Sa Majesté). (II, 165)

Yet this very same incident is related in the memoirs of the Duc de Luynes, a more reliable if less interesting witness.

By July 1739 it was clear that in many parts of France the coming harvest was also going to be a poor one, a serious matter in an age when as d'Argenson put it, 'la récolte, bonne ou mauvaise, décide de la misère générale' (II, 197). Throughout

---

[1] The son of the Regent, Philippe d'Orléans.

3  *Oudry*, La Ferme

4 *Greuze,* L'Accordée de village

the late summer and autumn and the following winter his
journal is full of allusions to the sufferings caused over a wide
area of the country by the high price of bread. As usual, it
reached its climax in the months which preceded the new
harvest. In June 1740 he noted that bread was 7 sous a pound
at Calais and 5 sous in Flanders, and that the high price had
led to riots in the Paris markets. According to the journal of
the Paris lawyer, Barbier, the situation was particularly serious
between September and December 1740, when, despite the
efforts of the authorities, bread remained at 4½ sous a pound.
In December he relates the following anecdote:

> On dit que M. le contrôleur général a eu l'impudence de dire
> au roi que dans Paris le pain ne valait que dix-huit deniers pour
> les pauvres et deux sols six deniers pour les riches, et que le
> marquis de Souvré, qui était présent, s'écria: 'Ah! mon Dieu,
> je suis volé!' Le roi lui demanda ce qu'il voulait dire, il répondit:
> 'Sire, mes gens me comptent depuis longtemps le pain à cinq
> sols.' (III, 246)

D'Argenson contributes his usual gloomy observations on the
situation in the closing months of this year. In September he
writes:

> Le pain augmente ici d'un sol chaque jour; il est présentement
> à six sols; aucun marchand n'ose ni ne veut apporter ici son blé.
> Mercredi, la halle était presque révoltée, le pain y manqua dès
> sept heures du matin. Les commissaires allaient haranguant le
> peuple et disaient que M. le contrôleur général était venu exprès
> à Paris pour travailler avec M. de Marville,[1] et sur cela le peuple
> criait: 'Eh! les bons chiens! Il n'y aurait qu'à mettre le feu à
> l'hôtel de ce Orry,[2] le brûler, lui et sa maison, et nous aurions
> du pain. C'est ce vieux chien de cardinal qui empêche les
> laboureurs de travailler, et qui fait que nous manquions de pain.'
> (III, 171)

The King himself was not allowed to remain unaware of
popular discontent, for on the same day d'Argenson records:

> Le roi passa dimanche par Issy pour voir le cardinal, il allai
> de là à Choisy; il passa par le faubourg Saint-Victor; on le savai

---

[1] The *Lieutenant de police* of Paris.    [2] *Contrôleur général* from 1730 to 1745.

le peuple s'amassa et criait, non Vive le roi! mais Misère! Du pain! Du pain! Le roi en fut fort mortifié.

A few days later it was the turn of his chief minister, Cardinal Fleury:

Le cardinal, traversant hier Paris, a été entouré de deux cents femmes qui se tenaient à la bride de ses chevaux, ne voulaient pas le laisser passer, ouvraient la portière et criaient avec fureur: Du pain! Du pain! nous mourons de faim! Il mourait de peur, il a jeté quelques écus, ce qui a amusé ces pauvres, et il s'est échappé. (III, 171-2)

After the grain shortage which lasted from the summer of 1738 to the spring of 1741, the next serious crisis came in 1751, after another bad harvest, with the usual inflated prices and the inevitable distress for the poorer classes in both town and country. When the Dauphin and Dauphine visited Paris in November of that year, d'Argenson records that 'passant au pont de la Tournelle, il y avait plus de deux mille femmes assemblées dans ce quartier-là qui leur crièrent: "Donnez-nous du pain, nous mourons de faim!" ' (VII, 29). When in the following month he went to his country-house outside Paris, he notes:

Dans les bourgs où je me suis arrêté sur la route et dans le village voisin de ma maison, on crie avec raison sur la cherté du pain qui est excessive; les pauvres gens n'en peuvent manger pour leur nourriture. Mon curé m'a dit que huit familles qui vivaient de leur travail avant mon départ mendiaient aujourd'hui leur pain. On ne trouve point à travailler, les gens riches se retranchant à proportion comme les pauvres. (VII, 55)

By January 1752 news was coming in of revolts in the provinces affected by the famine, first at Arles, then at Rennes, Bordeaux and Rouen. D'Argenson quotes one of the *curés* on his estates in Touraine as declaring that he had never seen greater suffering, even in 1709, the catastrophic famine year towards the end of the reign of Louis XIV.

The good harvest of 1752 was far from bringing immediate relief. When at the end of August, the King, Queen and

Dauphine went from Versailles to Notre-Dame to a thanks-
giving service for the convalescence of the Dauphin, d'Argenson notes in his journal:

> On avait fait baisser le pain au marché de samedi, pour faire
> mieux recevoir Leurs Majestés. Cependant un pauvre homme
> s'attacha au carrosse de la reine, dès l'endroit du chemin qu'on
> nomme le Point du jour, pour crier en montrant du pain noir:
> 'Voilà, Madame, ce qu'on nous fait payer 3 sous la livre!' La
> reine le renvoyait au roi, et enfin ordonna à ses gardes de prendre
> son nom pour qu'il vînt la trouver et pour qu'elle l'assistât.

A few days later he adds further details:

> A l'entrée du roi, dimanche dernier, pour le *Te Deum* à Notre-
> Dame, il y eut un grand silence sur les bénédictions que le peuple
> donne ordinairement au roi. Il n'y avait que quelques voix
> solitaires: d'autres les faisaient taire, et criaient: 'Vive M. le
> Dauphin! Donnez-nous du pain!' (VII, 289-90)

All through the autumn and winter he continues to speak of
the effects of high bread prices. In October, for instance:

> J'apprends qu'au dernier marché le pain est encore augmenté
> d'un liard, de sorte que le gros pain est présentement à 3 s. 6 d., ce
> qui est exorbitant, vu l'abondance de cette année qui est le triple
> de l'année dernière. (VII, 321-2)

The continued high prices he attributes to the government's
intervention in the grain market which only causes alarm:
'Chacun veut faire sa provision pour deux années, et personne
ne veut apporter au marché, comme ci-devant.' Later in the
month he writes: 'Chaque jour de marché les grains aug-
mentent de prix dans les provinces. Hier, au marché voisin de
ma campagne, le blé était à 26 et l'avoine à 16 l. le setier, ce
qu'on n'a jamais vu dans une année belle et abondante' (VII,
327-8). In his journal notes on high bread prices continue all
through the winter and spring, and it is not until September
1753 that at last we find a completely different tune:

> Le blé froment diminue de prix; on en porte en abondance dans
> les marchés. Ce qui se vendait 27 livres le setier l'an passé, en

pareil temps, ne s'est vendu que 18 l. au dernier marché de Montlhéry.[1] (VIII, 129)

The next bread crisis arose in the last part of the 1760s, after government decrees of 1763 and 1764 had removed a great many of the restrictions on the free movement of grain inside France and on its export. These restrictions which aimed at avoiding bread shortages had been severely criticised by the Physiocrats, the new school of economists, who held that only complete freedom for the grain trade could both secure a fair price to the farmer and prevent periods of famine. When shortages and high prices followed the poor harvest of 1767 the Physiocrats were bitterly attacked for their policy, until, as shortages continued over a great part of the country, in 1770 the government re-imposed restrictions on the grain trade inside France and stopped all exports.

Unquestionably the 1760s saw a considerable rise in the average price of cereals, which benefited many peasants and especially the big landlords. On the other hand, the shortages which began in 1767 brought suffering to the poorer sections of the community in country and town. The Paris bookseller, Hardy, noted in his journal in December 1767:

> Le pain, qui depuis le mois d'août précédent qu'on le payait 2 sols 6 deniers la livre, avait toujours été en augmentant, fut vendu au marché sur le pied de 3 sols 3 deniers, quoique la récolte n'eût pas été mauvaise cette année, ce qu'on attribua à la trop grande exportation des blés hors du royaume. (*Mes Loisirs*, I, 81)

This was only the beginning of the rise in prices, nor was it confined to Paris. In March, 1768, Hardy wrote:

> On apprend qu'il y avait eu à Rouen le mardi précédent et le jeudi 24, par continuation, une révolte assez considérable, occasionnée par la cherté du pain qui s'y vendait 4 sols la livre, que la plupart des manufactures étaient fermées et les ouvriers ne travaillant pas et manquant de pain et d'argent pour s'en procurer, s'etaient livrés à différents excès. (I, 89)

So great was discontent that in September 1768 the inhabitants

---

[1] Near Corbeil (Seine-et-Oise).

of places near Versailles determined to bring their plight to the attention of the King himself:

> Le roi chassant dans la plaine de Boulogne avec le prince de Soubise et plusieurs autres seigneurs, les habitants de Saint-Cloud et de Boulogne qui avaient préparé des mémoires en forme de placets sur la cherté du pain dans l'intention de les présenter au roi en se jetant à ses pieds, ne purent les remettre qu'aux principaux officiers de la maréchaussée ou des chasses qui les passèrent au duc de Villeroy, capitaine des gardes du quartier, au moment que le roi montait en carrosse au bout du pont de Sèvres, vers 5 heures du soir; 12 femmes de Meudon s'étaient aussi mises à genoux, la veille, sur le chemin de Bellevue et l'une d'elles avait fait voir au roi un morceau de pain noir comme de l'encre. (I, 108)

Hardy's journal records high prices for bread from December 1767 until the latter end of 1771. Although prices fell in the winter of 1769-70 and the following spring, he records two peaks when they rose to about 4 sous a pound. The first was in October and November 1768, when on a number of occasions seditious posters, such as that described below, were put up in Paris.

> Dans la matinée on trouva à la Halle un nouveau placard abominable et séditieux qu'on avait eu la précaution d'appliquer avec de la colle forte sur une planche qu'on avait ensuite collée à la muraille. Il était si affreux que le commissaire qui en fit la levée crut devoir le faire couvrir d'un linge pendant qu'on détachait la planche, pour qu'on ne pût pas le lire plus longtemps. Le pain n'augmenta pas au marché de ce jour, mais il demeura toujours au taux de 4 sols la livre. (I, 114)

The second was reached in October 1770.

> Le pain de 4 livres est porté dans les marches de 15 sols et demi à 16 sols; on continuait d'assurer qu'il irait jusqu'à 20 sols. (I, 221)

However, this pessimism was not justified, as a fairly rapid fall in bread prices began in the following month, even though they continued to remain relatively high for some time to come.

Meanwhile, in the far-away province of Limousin, the *Intendant*, the famous Liberal economist Turgot, who was passionately keen on maintaining the recently won freedom of the grain trade, was grappling with the problem of the shortage. His task was made all the more difficult by the backwardness and poverty of the region; even under normal conditions the peasants subsisted on a meagre diet, not rising as high even as rye bread. 'Vous savez, Monsieur,' he wrote to the *Contrôleur général* in December 1769, 'que la plus grande partie de cette généralité ne produit que du seigle au lieu de froment'. While in normal times some wheat and rye were imported from neighbouring provinces for the inhabitants of the towns,

> ceux de la campagne ne mangent que très peu de froment ou de seigle; ils subsistent la plus grande partie de l'année des productions d'une moindre valeur. En Angoumois et en bas Limousin les paysans vivent principalement de maïs, qu'ils appellent blé d'Espagne; ceux du Limousin vivent de gros navets appelés raves, de châtaignes, surtout de blé noir, connu sous le nom de sarrasin. Ces productions qui sont communément assez abondantes, suppléent au vide du froment et du seigle, et il en résulte que ces deux grains sont ordinairement à un prix bas parce qu'on en consomme peu. (*Œuvres*, III, 112)

Given their poverty, it was, he explains, a matter of indifference to the mass of the peasants in his *généralité* that the prices of wheat and rye should soar, so long as the things they normally ate remained abundant and cheap.

> A l'égard des habitants de la campagne, tant que les denrées dont ils font leur nourriture ordinaire sont abondantes, ce haussement dans le prix leur est indifférent puisque, même lorsque les seigles étaient au plus bas prix, ils étaient trop pauvres pour en consommer habituellement. En effet, les recherches les plus exactes que j'ai pu faire sur les ressources des paysans non propriétaires, m'ont convaincu que, l'un portant l'autre, ils ne dépensent ou ne consomment pas la valeur de 30 à 35 l. par an.

Now, Turgot explains, even the cheap forms of food to which they are accustomed have failed them, and at the very time when the dearer grains like wheat and rye, which are normally beyond their reach, have risen to prices utterly beyond them.

> Vous concevez, monsieur, dans quel excès de misère des malheureux, pour qui cette situation est un état d'abondance, doivent

être plongés, lorsque toutes les ressources de leur subsistance ordinaire leur sont enlevées et que les grains dont ils sont obligés de se passer, dans les années mêmes où ils sont à bas prix, sont montés à un prix excessif et double du prix moyen.
... Pour trouver une année aussi désastreuse que celle-ci, il faut remonter jusqu'en 1739. ... De tous côtés on me présente le tableau de la plus excessive misère; des familles entières sont prêtes à périr. Exactement, la plus grande partie des colons ou métayers ne subsistent que des avances que leur font leurs maîtres dont plusieurs ont l'inhumanité de les renvoyer, dans une saison où la terre n'exige que peu de travaux, pour en prendre d'autres au bout de quelques mois. ...
Je sais que les paysans voisins des villes viennent acheter, des boulangers, le son pour le mêler dans leur pain et tromper ainsi leur besoin par un aliment sans substance. (III, 113-14)

The harvest of the following year (1770) was also poor. Already by October, as Turgot explained to the *Contrôleur général*, grain prices had soared:

Les propriétaires des biens de campagne qui, l'année dernière, ont été obligés d'acheter des grains pour la nourriture de leur famille, de leurs colons et des pauvres gardent ce qu'ils ont recueilli, tandis que les décimateurs et ceux qui ont pu percevoir leur rente en nature[1] envisagent l'étendue du vide et le long intervalle qui reste à passer jusqu'à la récolte, comptent sur une augmentation excessive et ne veulent vendre à aucun prix. D'un autre côté, tout bourgeois aisé veut s'approvisionner pour ne pas être exposé à manquer; aussi la crainte produit l'excès de la demande d'un côté, et de l'autre le resserrement de la denrée. Mais cette crainte est fondée, et ce resserrement est l'effet d'un vide réel et constaté. (III, 142-3)

In a postscript Turgot gives further details about the grain shortage in his *généralité*:

Il n'y a de grain disponible qu'une partie de celui des décimateurs, et ce qui a pu rentrer des rentes en grains dues aux seigneurs ou à leurs fermiers,[2] mais c'est un très petit objet, parce que la modicité de la récolte est telle que peu de censitaires sont en état

[1] Those who drew tithes and feudal dues in kind.
[2] Many owners of feudal dues farmed out their collection to peasants or lawyers.

de payer, surtout dans la Montagne,[1] malgré les frais dont on les accable,[2] nouveau poids ajouté à leur misère; un grand nombre préfère de payer en argent à une évaluation exorbitante. Ce n'est point exagérer de dire qu'il me paraît inévitable qu'une partie des habitants de ce malheureux canton meure de faim. (III, 153)

The heavy burden which feudal dues paid in kind imposed on the peasants in years of bad harvests had caused concern to Turgot several months earlier; he had endeavoured to secure the promulgation of a law to prevent the peasant having to make heavy cash payments if he was unable to produce the necessary grain.

Dans les temps de disette [he wrote to the Chancellor] il est humain et même juste que la loi vienne au secours du censitaire accablé de tous côtés; le propriétaire de la rente, que la cherté enrichit,[3] ne pourrait, sans montrer une avidité odieuse, prétendre tirer de la cruelle circonstance où se trouve son tenancier un profit plus exorbitant. (III, 249)

Despite the troubles which grain shortages and excessively high bread prices involved him in, Turgot defended freedom in the grain trade in a series of letters to the *Contrôleur général*, but in vain, for at the end of 1770 the government, alarmed by the situation in the last two years, reimposed controls and virtually abolished free trade in grain, a policy which he was to reverse as soon as he himself became *Contrôleur général* four years later.[4]

There is thus no question that for the medium and poorer peasants—not only for the landless labourer, but for all the small landowners and *métayers* who, far from having a surplus for sale, were compelled to buy grain for their own consumption —the steady rise in prices in the two middle quarters of the eighteenth century, had many disadvantages; when prices rocketed in years of scarcity, many went hungry and were exposed to appalling hardships. Yet, as recent historians have pointed out, there was one vital difference between the famine years of the reigns of Louis XV and Louis XVI, and those of

---

[1] A district of his *généralité*.
[2] By sending in the bailiffs until the amount was paid.
[3] Because he had grain to sell when prices were at their very highest point.
[4] See pp. 205-6.

the reign of Louis XIV. In earlier days the violent upsurge of grain prices had had devastating effects on the poorer sections of the community, in the country and the towns, and had led to heavy mortality in the regions affected. The eighteenth century saw a striking change in this respect. Periods of shortage and high bread prices still recurred, but their effects were less catastrophic than in earlier reigns, even than in the recent disaster of 1709. One outstanding fact in the history of eighteenth century France is the increase in the population from about 18 millions in 1715 to some 26 millions in 1789. The masses at least survived these catastrophes, and although their very numbers kept wages far below the long-term rise in prices, their meagre share in the general prosperity which reached its high point in the years between the end of the Seven Years War in 1763 and 1770, made them better off than they had been earlier or were to be in the last decade or so before 1789.

Moreover, though well-to-do peasants, whether they themselves owned enough land to make a comfortable living or had enough capital to rent a large farm, were undoubtedly a small minority, they were an important section of the agricultural community. If they profited less from the long-term rise in agricultural prices than the landowners of the privileged orders who drew not only higher rents, but also increased feudal dues, they too prospered, since, unlike their poorer brethren, they had a surplus to dispose of and could generally afford to wait to sell their grain until prices reached their peak. The wealthier type of farmer also benefited from the fact that for most of the century rents lagged behind prices, so that during each lease he profited from the gap between the rise in grain prices and a rent which had not yet caught up with them. Again, the winegrowers, an important section of the agricultural community even though they mostly operated on a small scale, produced for the market and only incidentally for domestic consumption; they too profited from the agricultural prosperity of these fifty years.

Some notion of the agricultural prosperity of France during the last part of the reign of Louis XV is given in the memoirs of the son of a man who had farmed the land, feudal dues and tithes of a priory:

> Le blé, boisseau du poids de 30 livres, se vendait en moyenne de 1765 à 1771, 3 fr., les autres grains en proportion, et ce prix, comparé à celui des dix années précédents, qui s'élevait à peine à 1 f. 15 sols, augmenta sensiblement la rente des propriétaires et l'aisance des cultivateurs. Ma mère dut à cette circonstance d'avoir promptement acquitté les dettes contractées par mon père,[1] ainsi qu'elle nous l'a souvent répété. (Besnard, *Souvenirs d'un nonagénaire*, I, 82-3)

A broader picture of the general prosperity of France at this period of the century is offered in several passages of the journal of Abbé de Véri, a friend of Turgot, and an extremely well-informed man. Take, for instance, the following lines, written in 1774:

> La population française est fort augmentée depuis vingt ans. C'est ce que j'appris l'année dernière par les évêques, les curés et les subdélégués des intendants dans les trois quarts des provinces que je parcourus. J'y trouvai nombre de villages que je n'avais pas vus depuis quinze ans, rebâtis à neuf par moitié. J'y trouvai les maisons de paysan aisé plus commodes que les anciennes des bourgeois. J'y appris l'augmentation graduelle des denrées et des baux à prix d'argent. J'y vis un mobilier plus abondant. Mon voyage fut de Paris jusqu'en Provence, de là à Bordeaux par le Languedoc et de Bordeaux à Paris par Nantes. (I, 167-8)

Thus these years of high agricultural prices did help a considerable number of peasants to improve their position and to enjoy a higher standard of living.

These years of high prices and agricultural prosperity were to last, through the Revolution and the Napoleonic era, down to about the year 1817. Once the disorders of the Revolution had been overcome, there opened a new period of prosperity for the French peasant, years of high prices in which moreover he no longer had to bear the burden of feudal dues and tithes. Yet, between these two periods there intervened, from about 1778 to the opening phase of the Revolution, roughly the reign

---

[1] His father, who died in 1766, was a drunkard.

of Louis XVI, a period of agricultural depression, culminating in the two bad harvests of 1788 and 1789 and the familiar phenomenon of rocketing bread prices, which had their effect on the events of 1789 and 1790. 'The deficit', wrote Arthur Young the day after the fall of the Bastille, 'would not have produced the revolution but in concurrence with the price of bread.' (*Travels in France*, I, 151)

After the period of rising prices which reached its peak in 1770, there began about 1778 a gradual reversal of the trend in two highly important branches of agriculture. The decade which followed was one of low prices for wines, with serious consequences for the large numbers of small peasants engaged in this form of agriculture; then, on a much less violent scale, came a fall in the price of grain, which affected particularly the great cereal-producing regions of the northern half of the country, from Flanders and Lorraine to Normandy and the Beauce region. The tenant-farmers found themselves caught between falling prices and increased rents, which were now based on the profits of the earlier period of prosperity. The large numbers of landless or nearly landless labourers in these regions found it harder to obtain work, especially as the population continued to rise at the very time when economic depression grew worse.

It was on top of this period of recession that there came the violent crisis of the years 1788-90. The grain harvest of 1788 was particularly bad. From the second half of that year prices shot up to a level higher even than in the previous crisis of 1770. Even the fairly prosperous peasant who normally had something left over to sell after he had kept what he needed for his family and handed over the share of his crop taken for feudal dues and tithe, had now little left to take to market. The lot of the peasant who even in normal times had to buy some grain, was much worse, as he had to buy as grain prices rose steeply. The winegrower, it is true, had the consolation of a moderate harvest and good prices, but he too had to buy his grain on a market in which prices were soaring. The mass of landless or nearly landless labourers found once again that there was less work for them at the very time when bread prices rose to record

heights. Already on the 10th June 1789, over a month before
the fall of the Bastille, Arthur Young noted in his travel diary:

> Everything conspires to render the present period in France
> critical; the want of bread is terrible; accounts arrive every
> moment from the provinces of riots and disturbances, and calling
> in the military, to preserve the peace of the markets. The prices
> reported are the same as I found at Abbeville and Amiens; 5 s.
> (2½ d.) a pound for white bread, and 3½ s. to 4 s. for the common
> sort, eaten by the poor; these rates are beyond their faculties, and
> occasion great misery. (*Travels in France*, I, 118)

Later in the same month, after describing how Louis XVI had
finally been compelled to eat his words and to urge the nobility
and clergy to join the Third Estate in the National Assembly,
Arthur Young writes:

> It was represented to him that the want of bread was so great
> in every part of the kingdom that there was no extremity to which
> the people might not be driven; that they were nearly starving,
> and consequently ready to listen to any suggestions, and on the
> *qui vive* for all sorts of mischief; that Paris and Versailles would
> inevitably be burnt . . . (I, 137-8)

On 28 June Young left Paris and could now observe for himself
what was going on in the provinces. At Nangis, south-east of
the capital, he noted a conversation with his barber:

> He gave me a frightful account of the misery of the people; whole
> families in the utmost distress; those that work have a pay in-
> sufficient to feed them—and many that find it difficult to get
> work at all. I inquired of Mons. de Guerchy[1] concerning this,
> and found it true. By order of the magistrates no person is allowed
> to buy more than two bushels of wheat at a market, to prevent
> monopolizing. . . . Being here on a market-day, I attended, and
> saw the wheat sold out under this regulation, with a party of
> dragoons drawn up before the market-cross to prevent violence.
> The people quarrel with the bakers, asserting the prices they
> demand for bread are beyond the proportion of wheat, and pro-
> ceeding from words to scuffling, raise a riot, and then run away
> with bread and wheat for nothing. This has happened at Nangis,
> and many other markets; the consequence was that neither

---

[1] His host, the Marquis de Guerchy.

farmers nor bakers would supply them till they were in danger of starving, and prices under such circumstances must necessarily rise enormously, which aggravated the mischief, till troops became really necessary to give security to those who supplied the markets. (I, 142-3)

In his account of a visit to nearby Coulommiers he gives us another vivid glimpse of the consequences of the bad harvest of 1788 when prices reached their seasonal peak in the following summer:

> Conversation here, as in every other town of the country, seems more occupied on the dearness of wheat than on any other circumstance; yesterday was market-day, and a riot ensued of the populace, in spite of the troops that were drawn up as usual to protect the corn. It rises to 46 livres (£2.0.3) the septier, or half-quarter, and some is sold yet higher. (I, 144)

The better harvest which followed did something to bring down prices, but this fall was soon wiped out by a new upward surge, brought on partly by political disorders. In the summer of 1790 prices rose even higher than in 1789, and it was only the good harvest of that year which brought to an end—at least temporarily—the fierce crisis which coincided with great political events between the summer of 1788 and the summer of 1790.

The decade of economic depression and the final rocketing of prices in the years 1788-90 undoubtedly sharpened the tensions which already existed in the countryside between the peasantry and the great feudal landowners, particularly in the matter of feudal dues and tithes. Not only did the so-called *reaction seigneuriale* which increased the exactions of the lord of the manor weigh heavily upon the peasant in this period of economic depression; in addition, in these years of low prices tithe and payments in kind like the *champart*, both levied on the gross produce of the land, absorbed a high proportion of the net profit, indeed sometimes all of it. The violent hostility to the privileged orders, their property, their feudal dues and tithes, which boiled over in 1789 was no doubt heightened by the decade of economic depression which preceded the Revolution.

If on the whole the eighteenth century brought prosperity, at least for a considerable period, to the wealthier minority of the peasantry, those who owned enough land to make a comfortable living or had sufficient capital to rent a substantial farm, the much more numerous class of medium to small peasants, while no doubt sharing up to a point in the general prosperity, could suffer very severely during the years of crisis. Worse still was the lot of the *métayers* and the landless or nearly landless agricultural labourers; the economic trends of the period worked against them as prices rose and wages failed to keep pace with them, and in years of crisis their sufferings were severe. One serious flaw in the society of the Ancien Régime was its failure to solve the problem of 'la mendicité', of the hordes of beggars who, especially in years of bad harvests, were driven from their homes to eke out a living on charity or even crime.

No doubt the French peasant of our period was better off than peasants in most other parts of the Continent; but the standard of living of a great part of the agricultural population was still very low. This was partly due to the over-population of the countryside, but mainly to the relatively backward state of French agriculture, at least compared with that of England. At the end of our period, Arthur Young gave high marks to the agriculture of one or two regions of France. But he was appalled by the low yields obtained from arable land as a whole (he estimated them as only 5 to 1, as against 12 to 1 in England) and by the prevalence in the rich arable lands of Northern France of the open field system and the practice of leaving the land fallow one year in three. In this northern region of France he found the land still farmed in scattered strips, unenclosed by hedges and still subject to rights of pasture by the peasants of the village, and with large areas of waste subject to similar grazing rights. There had been a move in the direction of something approaching the English enclosures, but even by 1789 it had not gone very far. Relatively little was achieved in the redistribution and enclosure of holdings to form compact farms; consequently it was seldom possible to follow the English example of abolishing fallow, and introducing such

crops as turnips which made it possible to feed sheep, which in
their turn manured the arable land. All Arthur Young found
in this rich arable region of Northern France was a countryside
'lying under the unprofitable neglect of open fields and dis-
graced with the execrable system of fallowing' (*Travels in
France*, I, 322), although, in Flanders, for instance, he found
that 'the land is cropped every year'.

There were, however, in eighteenth century France other
agricultural systems besides the open field with the land left
fallow one year in three. Over a large area of Central and
Southern France the fields remained unenclosed, but instead
of consisting, as in the north, of long, parallel strips, they were
arranged quite haphazard in plots of all shapes and sizes;
moreover, although the land in these regions was unenclosed,
there was not the same compulsory rotation of crops as in the
north, nor were the communal grazing rights any longer
enforced for the most part. Over a considerable part of this
region, especially in the south, the land was left fallow as often
as one year in two. There remained a third section of the
country, chiefly in the west, from Brittany to the Basque
country, in which most of the arable land was enclosed by
hedges or walls, but where the meadows and waste land remained unenclosed and subject to communal grazing rights.
Although the arable land was protected by hedges or walls, the
peasants still remained attached to a rotation of crops which
left the land fallow one year in every two or three. Arthur
Young was naturally horrified by this state of affairs:

The marvellous folly is that in nine-tenths of all the enclosures of
France the system of management is precisely the same as in the
open fields; that is to say, fallows as regularly prevail, and
consequently the cattle and sheep of a farm are nothing in comparison of what they ought to be. . . . Sologne is enclosed, yet it
is the most miserable province in France, of the same rank with
Bretagne itself. The Bourbonnais and great part of the Nivernais
are enclosed; yet the course[1] pursued is 1. fallow, 2. rye, and 1.
fallow, 2. rye, 3. left to weeds and broom—and all these on soils,
as Bretagne, Sologne and the Bourbonnais, highly improveable

[1] Rotation of crops.

and capable of the best Norfolk husbandry. With such miserable systems of what use are enclosures?—Hence we may draw this conclusion, that when we find half of France enclosed, we are not to suppose that kingdom in the state of improvement and cultivation which this circumstance implies among us. On the contrary, it indicates no such thing; for some of the poorest and most unimproved provinces are precisely those which are enclosed. (I, 398)

Even in the eyes of such a critical traveller, accustomed to the achievements of the agricultural revolution on this side of the Channel, there were some regions of France in 1789 which deserved high praise:

Throwing these several rich districts together . . . we cannot but admit that France is in possession of a soil, and even of a husbandry, that is to be ranked very high amongst the best in Europe. Flanders, part of Artois, the rich plain of Alsace, the banks of the Garonne, and a considerable part of Quercy are cultivated more like gardens than farms. . . . The rapid succession of crops, the harvest of one being but the signal of sowing immediately for a second, can scarcely be carried to greater perfection; and this in a point perhaps of all others the most essential to good husbandry, when such crops are so justly distributed as we generally find them in these provinces, cleaning and ameliorating ones being the preparation for such as foul and exhaust. These are provinces which even an English farmer might visit with advantage. (I, 364)

But Young was horrified at the persistence of the open field system and of what he calls the 'detestable common rights':

When we see some of the finest, deepest and most fertile loams that are to be met with in the world, such as those between Berney and Elbeuf, and part of the Pays de Caux, in Normandy, and the neighbourhood of Meaux, in the Isle of France, destined to the common barbarous course of 1. fallow, 2. wheat, 3. spring corn, and the product of this spring corn beneath contempt, the whole exertion and produce being seen in a crop of wheat, we must be convinced that agriculture in such a kingdom is on the same footing as in the tenth century. If these lands were then tilled at all, they were in all probability as well tilled as at present. (I, 359)

5   Le Seigneur chez son fermier

6   Château de Combourg

7, 8 'A faut esperer q'eu se jeu la finira bentot' (popular engravings of 1789)

Modern historians agree that Arthur Young gives too black a picture of French agriculture in 1789, yet even so there is no question that it lagged far behind English agriculture at that date and even further behind French agriculture in our own day. Despite the propaganda of agricultural reformers, inspired in part by English theory and practice, despite some efforts by the government, despite the undoubted pressure towards new methods, towards enclosures and the ending of common rights on the land, a considerable part of French agriculture was still in a backward state in 1789.

It was with the produce of an often primitive agriculture that the French peasant had to bear the burden, not only of feudal dues and tithes, but also of the heavy direct and indirect taxes levied by the state. Inevitably that burden varied not only from one period of the century to another (in war time taxes rose steeply), but, given the incoherent administrative system, also from province to province. The principal direct tax, the *taille*, could be *personnelle*, i.e. levied on the estimated income of the taxpayer, or *réelle*, i.e. levied on the amount of land which he held; and there were also experiments with other systems. The other two direct taxes, first introduced towards the end of the reign of Louis XIV, the *capitation* and the *vingtième*—the latter being nominally a tax of 5 per cent. of income (there were often two *vingtièmes* levied, and occasionally even three)— varied enormously in their incidence. As far as the *vingtième* was concerned, those provinces with Estates (*pays d'états*) generally succeeded in getting off more lightly than the others, as they contracted to pay a lump sum which came to much less than if the tax had been levied directly by the government's agents, while the *capitation* was proportionately much more of a burden to the *roturier* than to the nobleman. Of the numerous indirect taxes the most hated was the *gabelle* or salt-tax; yet this fell very unevenly on the different provinces of France. In a considerable number salt was not taxed at all, while in the so-called *pays de grandes gabelles* the price was very high and each household was compelled to take a certain minimum quantity each year. In between these two extremes there were all manner of inter-mediate rates of tax; in the *pays de petites gabelles* the cost of salt was roughly half what it was in the last group of provinces, and so on. The *aides* (excise duties) were also levied differently from province to province.

The result was, as Necker showed in a book which appeared five years before the Revolution, that there were gross inequalities between the burden of taxation in the different provinces of France. Some of these anomalies were not altogether as crazy as they appeared, as exemption from one tax might lead to a heavier burden from another tax. Again some regions were more prosperous than others. If the inhabitants of Brittany paid on an average only about two-fifths of the taxes borne by their neighbours in Normandy, this could be explained up to a point; not only had Brittany provincial estates whereas Normandy had not, but in addition Normandy was a much more fertile and prosperous province. Yet there were shocking anomalies. The inhabitants of the *généralité* of Châlons which covered most of the province of Champagne paid more than half as much again a head in taxation as those of the Bordeaux region:

> La généralité de Châlons contient six cent mille âmes de moins que celle de Bordeaux; elle a plus de manufactures, mais bien moins de commerce; et cependant le produit de ces deux généralités se trouve à peu près le même. C'est que la Guyenne, rédîmée de l'impôt du sel,[1] est encore exempte des aides, tandis que la Champagne y est assujettie et fait de plus partie des grandes gabelles. Ces deux impôts forment une augmentation de charge pour la Champagne d'environ sept millions; et ce tribut particulier balance ce que la généralité de Bordeaux paie de plus en taille, vingtièmes, capitation, tabac, droits de traites,[2] de contrôle et autres impositions, du genre de celles qui sont proportionnées à l'étendue des richesses et de la population.

Again, the burden of taxation in Champagne was nearly twice what it was in the neighbouring province of Franche-Comté:

> La Champagne n'est que d'un cinquième plus considérable en population que la Franche-Comté, et cependant elle paie au moins six cinquièmes de plus. C'est que la Franche-Comté est

---

[1] Its inhabitants paid only a very light tax on salt.
[2] Customs duties (see below pp. 69-71).

exempte des aides et du privilège exclusif du tabac, et que le fisc y vend le sel au quart du prix fixé pour la Champagne. Ainsi pour ces deux seuls impôts il en coûte près de six millions et demi de plus à cette dernière province. Les trois vingtièmes en Champagne se montent à deux millions 900 mille livres; ceux de la Franche-Comté, à la faveur d'anciens abonnements, ne vont pas à 1,600 mille livres. Enfin la taille, la capitation et toutes les impositions générales sont encore plus fortes en Champagne qu'en Franche-Comté. (*De l'Administration des Finances*, I, 186-7)

No doubt some peasants profited from the lower level of taxes in their particular region, but others, in the more heavily taxed provinces, suffered a corresponding degree of hardship. And there is no question that, given the exemptions which the privileged orders and even the inhabitants of the towns had won for themselves, it was on the peasants that the main burden of taxation continued to fall.

Before and since the Revolution various writers have argued that the privileges of the nobility and clergy in the matter of taxation were largely illusory. According to Sénac de Meilhan, a former *Intendant*, writing after the fall of the Ancien Régime, the privileges of the aristocracy were relatively trivial, since most noblemen let out their land to tenant-farmers or *métayers*, and these, because of the burden of taxation, paid correspondingly less rent to their landlords who were thus in fact taxed indirectly:

Dans les derniers temps il ne leur était resté de leur antique splendeur et de leur indépendance que le privilège d'une exemption de taille pour l'exploitation de trois charrues[1]; mais il fallait que le noble qui voulait en jouir fît valoir par lui-même sa terre; le privilège cessait dès qu'elle était affermée. Si l'on considère combien peu de gentilshommes étaient à portée de profiter de cette exemption, elle paraîtra bien peu considérable. Les grands propriétaires et tous les nobles qui avaient des emplois à la cour et à l'armée; tous ceux qui vivaient dans la capitale ou exerçaient des charges dans les villes de province, affermaient leurs biens, et une partie de la plus pauvre noblesse jouissait seule de cet

[1] Noblemen were exempt from paying the *taille* on three (or in some provinces four) *charrues* (i.e. the amount of land which could be cultivated with that number of ploughs) provided they farmed it themselves.

avantage. Si l'on porte au cinquantième du produit de la taille, c'est-à-dire à deux millions environ, le montant de ce privilège de la noblesse, je crois que l'on sera plutôt au delà qu'en deçà de la vérité. (*Le Gouvernement, les Mœurs et les Conditions en France avant la Révolution,* pp. 110-11)

This view was not shared by Turgot. In a letter which he wrote while he was *Contrôleur général,* he showed how not only the *taille,* but also the more modern direct taxes such as the *capitation* and the *vingtième* which had been intended to apply to all sections of the community in proportion to their wealth, bore most heavily on the Third Estate. The nobleman's privilege of four *charrues,* he declared, meant an exemption of something near 2,000 francs in taxation in the Paris region. Moreover, this privilege affected only arable land, and the nobleman's woods, meadows, vineyards and parks paid no tax. 'Il y a des cantons très vastes dont la principale production est en prairies ou en vignes; alors le noble qui fait régir ses terres s'exempte de toute l'imposition, qui retombe à la charge du taillable.—*Second avantage,* qui est immense.' Again, the nobles paid only the *vingtième* on their feudal dues, but not the *taille.*

In addition to other forms of privilege as far as the *taille* was concerned, there were, Turgot adds, inequalities in the assessment of the *capitation*:

Les nobles sont imposés, à la vérité, à la capitation comme les taillables, mais ils ne le sont pas dans la même proportion. La capitation est une imposition arbitraire de sa nature. Il a été impossible de la répartir sur la totalité des citoyens autrement qu'à l'aveugle. On a trouvé plus commode de prendre pour base les rôles des tailles qu'on a trouvés tout faits. La capitation des taillables est devenue une imposition accessoire de la taille; on a fait un rôle particulier pour les nobles; mais comme les nobles se défendent et comme les taillables n'ont personne qui parle pour eux, il est arrivé que la capitation des nobles s'est réduite à peu près dans les provinces à un objet excessivement modique, tandis que la capitation des taillables est presque égale au principal de la taille. Il est encore arrivé de là que tous les privilèges dont les terres des nobles sont avantagées, entraînent un privilège proportionné sur la capitation, quoique suivant son institution, ce dernier impôt doive être réparti sur tous les sujets du roi à raison de leurs facultés.

It was no doubt true, Turgot concedes, that the numerous class of poorer peasants known as *métayers* were often so overwhelmed by taxes that the landowner was compelled to share part of the burden:

> Mais il est à observer que cette condescendance des propriétaires étant libre, et la loi étant toute contre le colon,[1] le propriétaire borne cette espèce de libéralité au point précis qui est nécessaire pour que sa terre ne reste point en friche, et qu'ainsi il laisse au cultivateur toute la charge que celui-ci peut absolument supporter sans tomber dans le désespoir et l'impuissance de travailler.

Moreover, if in a sense it was the landowner who paid the taxes of the tenant-farmer and *métayer*, it was on the peasants that all the abuses in the assessment and collection of the direct taxes fell:

> Ce sont eux, par conséquent, qui supportent tous les frais, toutes les suites des retards de payements, les saisies, les exécutions des huissiers, des collecteurs, enfin tout ce qu'entraîne de vexations et d'abus le payement d'un impôt très fort, souvent mal réparti, et levé sur la portion du peuple que son ignorance et sa pauvreté privent le plus de tous les moyens de se défendre contre toute espèce de vexations.

Finally, he adds, when the tenant-farmer signs his lease, he has no means of calculating exactly how much he will have to pay in taxes over the period concerned. If a war breaks out, his *taille* will have all manner of additions made to it, possibly with ruinous effects. (*Œuvres*, V, 170-3)

Moreover, the peasant's obligations were not limited to the payment of direct taxes in money. In the course of the eighteenth century there grew up the practice of imposing on the peasants—and on the peasants alone—the *corvée royale*, which meant so many days a year of forced labour on the making and repair of roads. The magnificent road system built up in the course of the century, the admiration of foreign travellers like

---

[1] 'Celui qui cultive une terre' (*Dictionnaire de l'Académie française*, 1762).

Arthur Young, was mostly founded on the *corvée royale*. Some of the abuses and hardships of the system are brought out (not without a certain sentimental exaggeration) in the following lines from Saint-Lambert's poem, *Les Saisons*:

J'ai vu le magistrat qui régit la province,[1]
L'esclave de la cour et l'ennemi du prince,
Commander la corvée à de tristes cantons,
Où Cérès et la faim commandaient les moissons.
On avait consumé les grains de l'autre année;[2]
Et je crois voir encor la veuve infortunée,
Le débile orphelin, le vieillard épuisé,
Se traîner, en pleurant, au travail imposé.
Si quelques malheureux, languissants, hors d'haleine,
Cherchent un gazon frais, le bord de la fontaine,
Un piqueur inhumain les ramène aux travaux;
On leur vend au prix d'or un moment de repos. . . .

(*L'Été*)

This institution was severely criticized by contemporaries, and when Turgot was *Intendant* of Limousin, he replaced it by a money tax. Among the edicts which led to his dismissal from the post of *Contrôleur général* in 1776 was one abolishing the *corvée* and raising the money needed for the building and upkeep of roads by a tax which would be paid by the privileged orders as well as the peasants.[3] Although the edict was withdrawn after his dismissal, in practice by 1789 the *corvée royale* had generally been replaced by some sort of a money payment.

Yet another imposition which fell heavily on the peasantry in our period was the *milice*. These were second-line troops, recruited by the drawing of lots mainly from the lower orders of town and country. There were inevitably all manner of exemptions for the sons of both the wealthier peasants and bourgeois, since anything approaching equality in such matters would have been rejected by public opinion. Although in peace time the service demanded was almost nil, and even in time of war was generally limited to guarding fortresses and communications, the institution was profoundly unpopular in the countryside.

[1] The *Intendan* .    [2] 'The previous year.'    [3] See pp. 206-8.

One must not forget the effect on the peasants of such indirect taxes as the *gabelle* and the *aides* (excise duties). The salt-tax produced a considerable slice of the King's revenues, and in the most heavily taxed provinces was an extremely heavy burden, bringing in more than the *taille*. Inevitably the variations in the price of salt from province to province made smuggling (*faux-saunage*) almost an industry in certain regions. In the words of Necker:

> Une pareille bigarrure, effet du temps et de plusieurs circonstances, a dû nécessairement faire naître le désir de se procurer un grand bénéfice, en portant du sel d'un lieu franc dans un pays de gabelle, tandis que pour arrêter ces spéculations destructives des revenus publics, il a fallu établir des employés, armer des brigades et opposer des peines graves à l'exercice de ce commerce illicite; ainsi s'est élevée de toutes parts dans le royaume une guerre intestine et funeste. Des milliers d'hommes, sans cesse attirés par l'appât d'un gain facile, se livrent à un commerce contraire aux lois. L'agriculture est abandonnée pour suivre une carrière qui promet de plus grands et de plus prompts avantages; les enfants se forment de bonne heure et sous les yeux de leurs parents à l'oubli de leurs devoirs, et il se prépare ainsi, par le seul effet d'une combinaison fiscale, une génération d'hommes dépravés. (*Compte rendu au roi*, pp. 82-3)

An army of officials, derisively known as *gabelous*, waged an endless struggle against the smugglers—men, women and children—and even at times fought pitched battles with gangs of brigands, composed frequently of ex-soldiers or even soldiers and their officers.

There were similar inequalities in the incidence of the *aides* in the different provinces of France. Although they covered a wide range of goods, these taxes were levied mainly on wines and spirits. No doubt many contemporary complaints about this tax were grossly exaggerated, but the various forms which it took could be very vexatious. Particular unpopularity fell upon the tax known as the *trop bu*, a duty levied on any wine used by the winegrower and his family beyond their normal consumption, the presumption being that the excess had been sold surreptitiously, without payment of the tax on sales of wine; armed men might descend upon persons suspected of this tax evasion, and heavy fines be levied—justly or otherwise. What added above all to the unpopularity of these taxes on wines and spirits was that, in the eyes of the winegrowers—a large and important class in eighteenth century France—they reduced the demand for their products, especially in those periods, such as the years immediately preceding the Revolution, when they could not sell their wine except at prices which left little or no room for profit. Here again, in addition to the inequalities between the different provinces, there were advantages for the privileged orders, as their members did not have to pay some of the taxes in question on wines from their estates.

Voltaire and Rousseau, the two greatest writers of the age, have both left behind a page in which they describe the inequalities of the arbitrary taxation system of their day and the fear which it inspired in the peasant that, unless he feigned abject poverty, he would have to pay more. In his *Lettres philosophiques* Voltaire sums up in a famous page the differences between the English and French taxation systems. Professing to write from England, he boldly declares:

> Un homme, parce qu'il est noble ou parce qu'il est prêtre, n'est point ici exempt de payer certaines taxes. . . . Chacun donne, non selon sa qualité (ce qui est absurde), mais selon son revenu; il n'y a point de taille ni de capitation arbitraire, mais une taxe réelle sur les terres: elles ont toutes été évaluées sous le fameux roi Guillaume III, et mises au-dessous de leur prix.
>
> La taxe subsiste toujours la même, quoique les revenus des terres aient augmenté; ainsi personne n'est foulé, et personne ne se plaint. Le paysan n'a point les pieds meurtris par des sabots; il mange du pain blanc; il est bien vêtu; il ne craint point d'augmenter le nombre de ses bestiaux ni de couvrir son toit de tuiles, de peur que l'on ne hausse ses impôts l'année d'après. (Lettre IX)

Here, as throughout the *Lettres philosophiques*, the reader is left to work out for himself the contrast with conditions in France which Voltaire is seeking to imply. He must think of the France Voltaire knew where there did exist the 'absurdity' that what people paid in taxes was largely determined, not by their wealth, but by their social rank; where in place of a uniform and moderate land-tax there were such arbitrary taxes as the *taille* and the *capitation*; where many peasants were poorly dressed and wore wooden shoes, when they did not go barefoot; and where even those who were moderately prosperous dared not add to their stock or make their houses more habitable for fear of attracting the attention of the tax-collector.

A page from Rousseau's *Confessions*, almost too well known to quote, relates how in his youth, in 1731, while walking from Paris to Lyons, he got lost and, tired and hungry, sought refreshment in a modest peasant's house:

> Je priai celui-ci de me donner à dîner en payant. Il m'offrit du lait écrémé et de gros pain d'orge, en me disant que c'était tout ce qu'il avait. Je buvais ce lait avec délices, et je mangeais ce pain, paille et tout; mais cela n'était pas fort restaurant pour un homme épuisé de fatigue. Ce paysan, qui m'examinait, jugea de la vérité de mon histoire par celle de mon appétit. Tout de suite, après m'avoir dit qu'il voyait bien que j'étais un bon jeune honnête homme qui n'était pas là pour le vendre, il ouvrit une petite trappe à côté de sa cuisine, descendit, et revint un moment après avec un bon pain bis de pur froment, un jambon très appétissant quoique entamé, et une bouteille de vin dont l'aspect me réjouit le cœur plus que tout le reste. On joignit à cela une omelette assez épaisse, et je fis un dîner tel qu'autre qu'un piéton n'en connut jamais. Quand ce vint à payer, voilà ses inquiétudes et ses craintes qui le reprennent; il ne voulait point de mon argent, il le repoussait avec un trouble extraordinaire; et ce qu'il y avait de plaisant était que je ne pouvais imaginer de quoi il avait peur. Enfin, il prononça en frémissant ces mots terribles de *commis* et de *rats de cave*.[1] Il me fit entendre qu'il cachait son vin à cause des aides, qu'il cachait son pain à cause de la taille, et qu'il serait un homme perdu si l'on pouvait se douter qu'il ne mourût pas de faim. Tout ce qu'il me dit à ce sujet, et dont je n'avais pas la moindre idée, me fit une impression qui ne s'effacera jamais. Ce fut là le germe de cette haine inextinguible qui se développa depuis dans mon cœur contre les vexations qu'éprouve le malheureux peuple, et contre ses oppresseurs. Cet homme, quoique aisé, n'osait manger le pain qu'il avait gagné à la sueur de son front,

---

[1] 'Parmi le peuple on appelle *Rats de cave* certains commis des aides qui visitent le vin dans les caves' (*Dictionnaire de l'Académie française*, 1762).

et ne pouvait éviter sa ruine qu'en montrant la même misère qui régnait autour de lui. Je sortis de sa maison aussi indigné qu'attendri, et déplorant le sort de ces belles contrées[1] à qui la nature n'a prodigué ses dons que pour en faire la proie des barbares publicains. (*Confessions*, Book IV)

Such were the results of an arbitrary system of taxation; even the reasonably well-to-do peasant was compelled to hide the outward signs of his modest prosperity in order to avoid being burdened with ruinous taxes.

Large numbers of the inhabitants of the countryside did not have to feign poverty; their miserable state, especially in periods of economic depression, was only too obvious. No doubt we must not take as gospel everything that a traveller like Arthur Young has to say; occasionally it may be that he gives too gloomy a view of French agriculture and the condition of the peasants. Yet some of the details which he gives about the clothes and housing of the French peasantry at the very end of our period, remain imprinted on one's memory. In his journal for 1787, as he approached the Pyrenees, he made such entries as these:

Pass Payrac, and meet many beggars, which we had not done before. All the country girls and women are without shoes or stockings; and the ploughmen at their work have neither sabots nor stockings to their feet. This is a poverty that strikes at the root of national prosperity; a large consumption among the poor being of more consequence than among the rich. . . . It reminded me of the misery of Ireland.

. . . Pass by several cottages, exceedingly well built, of stone and slate or tiles, yet without any glass to the windows; can a country be likely to thrive where the great object is to spare manufactures? Women picking weeds into their aprons for their cows, another sign of poverty I observed during the whole way from Calais. (*Travels in France*, I, 18.)

A year later when he visited Brittany, he passed by the ancestral home of Chateaubriand, who left behind a vivid account of his childhood there in his *Mémoires d'outre-tombe*:

---

[1] In France. Rousseau was a native of Geneva.

To Combourg, the country has a savage aspect; husbandry not much further advanced, at least in skill, than among the Hurons, which appears incredible amidst enclosures; the people almost as wild as their country, and their town of Combourg one of the most brutal filthy places that can be seen; mud houses, no windows, and a pavement so broken, as to impede all passengers, but ease none; yet here is a château, and inhabited. Who is this Mons. de Chateaubriand, the owner, that has nerves strung for a residence amidst such filth and poverty?[1] (I, 97)

Brittany, of course, confirmed his first impression that it was 'a miserable province'.

To Montauban. The poor people seem poor indeed; the children terribly ragged, if possible worse clad than if with no clothes at all; as to shoes and stockings they are luxuries. A beautiful girl of six or seven years playing with a stick, and smiling under such a bundle of rags as made my heart ache to see her. They did not beg, and when I gave them anything seemed more surprised than obliged. One third of what I have seen of this province seems uncultivated, and nearly all of it in misery. (I, 98)

A year later, two days before the fall of the Bastille, while visiting Lorraine on his third tour of France, Young records the following conversation:

Walking up a long hill, to ease my mare, I was joined by a poor woman, who complained of the times, and that it was a sad country. On my demanding her reasons, she said her husband had but a morsel of land, one cow and a poor little horse, yet he had a *franchar* (42 lb.) of wheat and three chickens to pay as a quit-rent[2] to one Seigneur; and four *franchar* of oats, one chicken and 1 *s.* to pay to another, beside very heavy tailles and other taxes. She had seven children, and the cow's milk helped to make the soup. . . . It was said, at present, that *something was to be done by some great folks for such poor ones, but she did not know who or how, but God send us better, car les tailles et les droits nous écrasent.* This woman, at no great distance, might have been taken for sixty or seventy, her figure was so bent, and her face so furrowed and hardened by labour; but she said she was only twenty-eight. (I, 148)

---

[1] François-René's elder brother. Their father had died in 1786.
[2] A rent paid in lieu of services.

Looking back from the reign of Louis-Philippe on the state of France in his youth, a former *curé* speaks with feeling of the miserable dress and appearance of the poorer peasants, male and female:

> Ils n'avaient souvent que les mêmes [vêtements] pour l'hiver et pour l'été, qu'ils fussent d'étoffe ou de toile; et la paire de souliers très épais et garnis de clous qu'ils se procuraient vers l'époque du mariage, devait, moyennant la ressource des sabots, servir tout le reste de leur vie. J'en ai du moins remarqué plusieurs qui n'étaient pas autrement vêtus pendant toute l'année. Quant à l'usage des bas, il leur était à peu près inconnu; leurs femmes et filles n'en portaient guère que les dimanches, et leur accoutrement des pieds à la tête ne pouvait inspirer que la pitié et le dégoût. (Besnard, *Souvenirs d'un nonagénaire*, I, 31)

We must not, however, imagine the French peasants before the Revolution merely as so many helpless and downtrodden serfs. Their village communities enjoyed a certain measure of self-government, under the close watch, it is true, of the agents of the central government, the *intendant* and his *subdélégué*. On Sundays after Mass the villagers met together to elect their *syndics*, and to discuss such matters as the choice of collectors for the *taille*, the repair of the parish church, the appointment of a schoolmaster (if there was a school), the use of the common lands attached to the village, and, only too frequently, the lawsuits in which the community was engaged. A glimpse of what went on at these village meetings is given by Rétif de la Bretonne in describing life in his native Burgundy:

> La petite paroisse de Sacy ayant des communes,[1] elle se gouverne comme une grande famille; tout s'y décide à la pluralité des voix, dans des assemblées qui se tiennent sur la place publique, les dimanches et fêtes, au sortir de la messe, et qui sont indiquées par le son de la grosse cloche. C'est à ces assemblées qu'elle nomme les syndics, dont les fonctions ressemblent assez à celles des consuls chez les Romains; les collecteurs pour les tailles; les garde-finages[2] pour la sûreté des terres ensemencées et des vignes; enfin

[1] The more usual word was *communaux*.
[2] '*Finage:* terme de pratique. Étendue d'une juridiction ou d'une paroisse jusqu'aux confins d'une autre' (*Dictionnaire de l'Académie Française*, 1798).

les pâtres publics. Le président de ces assemblées est l'homme du seigneur; le procureur fiscal[1] y expose les sujets à traiter; mais chaque particulier a droit de dénoncer les abus qui sont à sa connaissance, ou de proposer les choses utiles qu'il a imaginées. On traite de ces objets sur-le-champ, et s'ils sont de quelque conséquence, on envoie les syndics au subdélégué de l'Intendance, pour se faire autoriser. C'est encore dans ces assemblées qu'on désigne chaque année le *canton* que chacun doit couper dans les bois communs. (*Vie de mon père*, pp. 199-200)

One must not take too literally such an idyllic picture of the workings of these village communities. They were very much under the thumb of the *Intendant,* not without good reason, as they often fell into debt and generally mismanaged their affairs. Yet, especially in those regions where there were common lands, they gave the peasants at least a taste of self-government.

It is easy to paint the life of French peasants before the Revolution as one of unremitting toil and hardship. Yet they had their amusements on Sundays and saints' days (many of the latter were still observed as holidays in the eighteenth century) and at certain other periods of the year. Some notes on village life in Languedoc in the middle of the century, left behind by a very minor lawyer, tell us how in 1754 the young people celebrated May Day:

Le 5 mai la jeunesse de ce lieu, toujours très florissante, ont planté un mai d'une hauteur prodigieuse au son de deux hautbois accompagnés d'un beau tabourin. Ce mai a été magnifiquement arboré devant la porte du château et au bruit éclatant d'une nombreuse mousqueterie. En même temps, l'élite des Messieurs de la jeunesse sur un grand bassin d'argent ont présenté de riches bouquets à Madame la marquise d'Aubais de même qu'à Mr le marquis du Caila.[2] Après s'être acquittés de ce respectueux devoir, ils se sont employés pendant deux jours à la danse et à la bonne chère. (Léonard, *Mon Village sous Louis XV,* p. 160)

Two days of feasting and dancing were devoted to the village's annual fête which took place in September. This is how the

---

[1] 'L'officier qui a soin des intérêts d'un seigneur et des vassaux de sa terre, dans l'étendue de cette terre' (ibid., 1762).
[2] Her son.

same chronicler describes the second day's entertainment in 1753:

> Premièrement le ris, la danse et la bonne chère. L'on dit en proverbe: après la panse, la bonne danse. Les hommes et les femmes y disent assez communément: Vive l'amour pourvu que je dîne. Sur le fait des maîtresses, les jeunes garçons font à l'envi qui pourra avoir ou choisir la plus belle. Les uns et les autres disent qu'ils aiment mieux que leurs yeux dînent que leur bouche.
>
> Cet aimable gala fut en même temps du rampel[1] aux quilles. Mesdemoiselles les filles avaient le leur en particulier comme les jeunes gens. La fille aînée de M. André Delort gagna le prix des quilles qui était une paire [de] bas filoselle ouvrage très fin.
>
> Secondement la course aux chevaux: Mr. Nourry l'aîné, de Congénies.
>
> La course des hommes, gagnée par le sieur Peyronnet, du Caila. Le prix était une écharpe et un mouchoir, le tout de soie.
>
> La course des ânes: celui du sieur Gruvelle surnommé La Treille. Le prix était un bonnet coton rouge et blanc.
>
> La course des enfants, gagnée par Mrs. les enfants du sieur Rebuffat et celui du sieur Arnaud, hôte.
>
> Le prix du saut était un riche mouchoir rouge de soie. Le sieur Théron, fils de Mr le maire de Calvisson, remporta le prix. (p. 162)

Life on the land before 1789 was not then all backbreaking toil, nor was there necessarily bitter animosity between the peasant and his lord.

Yet this rural society was deeply divided not only between the privileged classes and the peasantry, but also between peasant and peasant, between well-to-do landowners or tenant-farmers and landless or nearly landless labourers, with a great mass of middling to poor landowners and *métayers* in between. In 1789, however, the monarchy and the privileged orders succeeded in uniting against them all the plebeian elements of rural society; rich and poor, peasant landowners large and small, tenant farmers and *métayers*, landless labourers, despite all their divergent interests, were unanimous in condemning the system of direct and indirect taxes imposed on them by the

---

[1] Competition.

Crown and the feudal dues and tithes wrung from them by the nobility and clergy. The burning of archives and châteaux, here and there the murder of noblemen and their families, heralded the destruction of a taxation system which had borne with disproportionate weight on the mass of the peasantry and of the feudal dues and tithes which they had paid for so long more and more unwillingly.

# CHAPTER II

# THE TOWNS: TRADE AND INDUSTRY

THE proportion of people in eighteenth century France who lived in the towns is even more difficult to estimate than the total population of the country. If we accept the figure of 26 millions for the total population in 1789, it is probable that not more than 4 million people lived in the towns. This does not mean that there were no towns and cities of a size which, at least by the standards of eighteenth century Europe, was quite considerable. Even though the returns of the 1801 census, the first to be held in England and France, are not entirely reliable, they do furnish a rough notion of the size of the larger cities of the two countries, and they also show that at that date France had more large towns than this country.

London, it is true, was very much larger than Paris, which, with over half a million inhabitants, was far and away the largest French city. Yet if the French capital did not tower over all other towns as London did in England with roughly ten times the population of the next largest city, France possessed several cities larger than the big English provincial towns. Lyons and Marseilles had over 100,000 inhabitants each, a size achieved by no English provincial city, and they, as well as Bordeaux and Rouen, were larger than Manchester, Liverpool, Birmingham or Bristol. The only other English city with over 50,000 inhabitants was Leeds, whereas in France there were also Nantes, Lille and Toulouse. Only six English towns had between 30,000 and 50,000 inhabitants against eight cities of this size in France: Amiens, Angers, Orléans, Besançon and Caen in the north, and in the south Nîmes, Montpellier and Béziers. In the nineteenth century the rate of growth of French provincial towns was to fall far behind those of England; yet in our period they had already reached a very respectable size, a fact which is easily explained by the much larger total population of France.

9   Bouchonnier (*Encyclopédie*)

10   Éperonnier: Étainage des mors (*Encyclopédie*)

11  Coupe et vue générale
d'une mine (*Encyclopédie*)

Yet, not only did the overwhelming majority of the population continue to inhabit the countryside, but the whole economy of the country was still dominated by agriculture. When agriculture flourished, trade and industry flourished; when agriculture went through periods of low prices and stagnation, or when bad grain harvests sent bread prices rocketing, the repercussions on trade and industry were immediate. The reason for this is not far to seek: it was simply that the overwhelmingly agricultural population of the period provided the main market for the trade and industry of the country, while, in addition, a large section of the wealthier classes of the country derived their income from the land in the form of rents, tithes and feudal dues. The upward surge of agricultural prices in the middle period of the century led to an expansion of trade and industry, though even then periods of grain shortage and high prices had an impact on the trading and industrial classes since the decline in their markets brought with it depression and unemployment. Then the last decade or so of the Ancien Régime brought a marked setback to trade and industry; it was a period of agricultural depression which coincided, first, with the War of American Independence and its harmful effect on exports, and then with the Anglo-French trade treaty of 1786 which laid the French market open to the competition of a much more advanced industrial country.

It was not then as in more modern times the degree of industrial activity which determined the prosperity or otherwise of the country; it was the state of agriculture. The effect which high grain prices and the diminished purchasing power of the great mass of the community in country and town had on the textile industry is made perfectly clear in official documents. Thus we find an *inspecteur des manufactures* at Caen declaring in 1753, after four years of high grain prices, that it is 'la cherté des vivres, dont la trop longue durée, en affaiblissant le peuple, a diminué la consommation qui le concerne' (Labrousse, *Esquisse*, p. 534), which has been partly responsible for a fall in production in these industries. On the other hand more moderate grain prices had a stimulating effect on production, as was pointed out by another official writing in 1755 from Aumale, a small town between Dieppe and Amiens:

> On a toujours regardé comme le mobile du commerce intérieur du royaume le juste prix des grains; aussi, depuis les apparences de la récolte abondante qu'il y a eu cette année, les fabricants ont conçu de belles espérances et ils ont enlevé . . . toutes les laines qu'on pouvait mettre en œuvre. (ibid.)

The same official reported in the following year:

> L'expérience démontre tous les jours que rien n'influe davantage sur le commerce à Aumale, que le prix des denrées. C'est, en effet, le seul ressort qui en mette toutes les parties en mouvement. Car aussitôt que l'on voit le blé augmenter de prix, le commerce devient alors languissant et les pièces diminuent en valeur et en nombre. L'augmentation qui est en cet état[1] semble prouver ce raisonnement, puisque depuis un an que le blé s'est maintenu à un prix raisonnable, les pièces ont augmenté en valeur et en nombre. La raison de ces révolutions se conçoit aisément, mais un exemple sera plus sensible. Que l'on suppose qu'un père de famille gagne 6 livres par semaine: encore faut-il qu'il travaille tous les jours, et qu'il lui faille aussi deux boisseaux de blé par chaque semaine. Si le blé ne vaut que 25 s., il lui reste pour acheter de quoi se vêtir lui et sa famille et pour pourvoir aux autres besoins dont elle est susceptible. Mais s'il vaut 50 s. comme depuis environ cinq ans, à l'exception de cette année, il les a presque toujours valus, que peut faire cet homme? Les journées[2] n'augmentent point, les charges ne sont pas moins les mêmes, il ne gagne précisément que ce qui lui est nécessaire pour vivre, il ne saurait acheter. Combien y en a-t-il dans ce cas et, par conséquent, que devient alors la consommation et, par ce contrecoup, le commerce à Aumale? (ibid., pp. 534-5)

The repercussions which high bread prices and the fall in the purchasing power of the mass of consumers had on the market for manufactured goods are also described in documents concerning the grain shortages of the years 1768-70. Thus the *Intendant* of Rouen wrote to the *Contrôleur général* in October 1768:

---

[1] Industry.

[2] 'Le salaire qu'on donne à un ouvrier pour le payer du travail qu'il a fait pendant un ou plusieurs jours' (*Dictionnaire de l'Académie Française*, 1798).

Le pain est devenu si cher que les journaliers, artisans et ouvriers, et artisans des manufactures ont bien de la peine à gagner de quoi en acheter pour vivre et faire vivre leurs familles. Le prix du pain est la boussole des fabriques, elles tombent dans la langueur lorsque le pain est cher. . . . Les fabricants et manufacturiers sont chargés d'étoffes invendues, et pour éviter un plus grand encombrement, ils ont été obligés de mettre bas une grande partie de leurs métiers. Ce parti, qui a été nécessaire, a mis dans l'embarras un très grand nombre d'ouvriers, qui se sont trouvés sans occupation. (ibid. pp. 536-7)

In the following September, when it looked as if grain prices were going to remain high, he reported: 'On ne peut donc s'attendre à voir reprendre aux manufactures de cette généralité l'activité dont elles ont besoin'; and in July 1770 he repeated the warning: 'Le pain restant toujours cher, on ne doit point espérer de voir reprendre sitôt aux manufactures de cette généralité l'activité qui leur est nécessaire; elles y sont cependant une des principales ressources.'

The words of this *Intendant*—'*Le prix du pain est la boussole des fabriques, elles tombent dans la langueur lorsque le pain est cher*'— bring home to us in one striking sentence the dependence of both trade and industry in eighteenth century France on the state of the harvest in any given year and region. Yet undoubtedly both trade and industry shared in the prosperity which agriculture enjoyed for a great part of the eighteenth century. The towns profited not only from the growing wealth of merchants, manufacturers, tax-farmers and bankers, but also —and this was particularly true of Paris—from the swollen rents and feudal dues which the nobility and clergy received from the land. In the second half of the century particularly there was a building boom not only in the capital, but also in the more important commercial cities. 'On bâtit de tous côtés' was the title Mercier gave to one of the opening chapters of his *Tableau de Paris* in the early 1780s:

Les trois états qui font aujourd'hui fortune dans Paris sont les banquiers, les notaires et les maçons ou entrepreneurs de bâtiments. On n'a de l'argent que pour bâtir. Des corps de logis immenses sortent de la terre, comme par enchantement, et des

> quartiers nouveaux ne sont composés que d'hôtels de la plus
> grande magnificence. La fureur pour la bâtisse est bien préférable
> à celle des tableaux, à celle des filles; elle imprime à la ville un air
> de grandeur et de majesté. . . .
>
>    Les remparts se hérissent d'édifices qui ont fait reculer les
> anciennes limites. De jolies maisons s'élèvent vers la Chaussée
> d'Antin, et vers la porte Saint-Antoine que l'on a abattue. Il
> était question de renverser l'infernale Bastille; mais ce monument
> odieux en tout sens choque encore nos regards. (I, 162-3)

Many of the French provincial towns where today the tourist
admires the buildings and general layout—Bordeaux and
Rennes, for instance—owe some of their finest houses and public
buildings to the eighteenth century, while in Paris one thinks
of the Place de la Concorde or such mansions as the Hôtel
Biron (now the Musée Rodin) and the Hôtel de Rohan and
Hôtel de Soubise which today house the Archives de France.

The expansion of trade inside the country and overseas still
had many obstacles to overcome. The road-system was undoubtedly improved in our period, whether by the *corvée* or, in
some parts of France, by means less onerous to the peasants.
The main roads were generally brought up to high standards,
although the secondary roads often remained in a deplorable
state. The importance which was attached to the improvement
of the country's roads is seen in the foundation (in 1747) of a
school for the training of civil engineers—the École des Ponts
et Chaussées. Yet in the pre-railway age the transport of both
persons and goods still remained deplorably slow and expensive.
Although vastly improved, the stage-coaches (*diligences*) still
took two and a half days to go from Paris to Calais, three to
Metz, four to Limoges, five and a half to Bordeaux; these were
for the time rapid journeys and consequently very costly. The
transport of goods by road was, it can well be imagined, proportionately slower and at the same time expensive. One thing
which made grain shortages much worse than they need have
been was that, while near-famine could prevail in some parts
of the country, cereals could be plentiful in others, and yet the
cost and slowness of transporting such bulky produce made it
extremely difficult to relieve the affected provinces, unless there

was access to them by sea, river or canal. Waterways still played an important part in the transport system of the country, even for passengers; the traveller from Paris to the South of France would still go a good part of the way by boat, down the Saône and the Rhône. Other regular boat services ran down the Seine, from Paris to Rouen, and down the Loire, from Orléans to Nantes. Even the Canal du Languedoc was frequently used by travellers between Bordeaux and the Mediterranean coast. It can be imagined therefore that rivers and canals played an important part in the transport of goods.

If today we can grasp, with a certain effort of the imagination, the handicaps imposed on trade by the slow and expensive transport system in the age before the invention of railways and the internal combustion engine, it is less easy to understand the presence of all manner of man-made obstacles to the free passage of goods inside the country. First, there were the tolls (*péages*) paid for the use of the roads, bridges, fords or rivers; while these might well have a quite legitimate origin in the case of roads and bridges, throughout the Ancien Régime the government struggled with little success to reduce the number of illegally levied tolls which added to the heavy cost of transporting goods. But worse still were the customs-barriers not only at the frontiers of France, but inside the kingdom itself, which were set up by the government to levy the so-called *traites*. No doubt it is easy to explain by historical causes how the highly complicated system underlying this tax arose, since the treatment meted out to the different provinces depended, roughly speaking, on the date at which they had been added to the kingdom. One large block of provinces, occupying most of the northern half of France, formed a whole in which all were free to trade with the rest and had at their frontiers a uniform system of dues on the import and export of goods, although duties had, of course, to be paid on goods going to and coming from the rest of France as well as abroad. Outside this large block lay a whole group of provinces, more recently added to the kingdom, such as Brittany, Artois and Flanders in the north, and Lyonnais, Provence and Languedoc in the south, which paid duty on the passage of goods both from each

province to those of the first block and from one province in this group to another, as well as on goods going to or coming from beyond the national frontiers. Finally—this is over-simplifying the whole chaotic arrangement, but its broad outline is sufficient for our purpose—there were the provinces added to France in even more recent times: Alsace, Lorraine and Franche-Comté. These were able to trade freely with foreign countries, but were entirely cut off from the customs point of view from the rest of France. In the administrative jargon of the time they were 'provinces de l'étranger effectif'.

It is true that in the course of the century something was done to mitigate the bad effects which this chaotic system was bound to have on the overseas trade of France, as Necker explains in his *De l'Administration des finances*:

> On demandera d'abord comment, sous l'autorité d'une législation si contraire aux bons principes, le commerce de France a pu atteindre au degré de supériorité dont on a présenté le tableau? C'est que les droits de traite, dans l'état actuel, forment plutôt un imbroglio pour l'administration et une gêne pour les com-merçants qu'un obstacle réel à cette partie des échanges qui importe à la richesse nationale. L'exportation à l'étranger des ouvrages d'industrie et l'importation des matières premières ont été partout affranchies de droit; et peu à peu différents arrêts particuliers, émanés du Conseil, ont réglé d'une manière uniforme les droits d'entrée et de sortie des principaux objets de commerce. C'est par l'effet de ces différentes modifications que depuis longtemps le commerce extérieur a ressenti faiblement l'effet des entraves qui embarrassent encore la circulation intérieure du royaume. (II, 127)

While these modifications no doubt helped the development of overseas trade, there still remained all manner of obstacles in the way of the free circulation of goods inside France. More-over, even goods treated in this way were still liable to customs inspection whenever they crossed any of the barriers inside the country, and all dues continued to be levied in an arbitrary fashion which, given the obscurity and complications of the regulations, it was very difficult to check. On paper each customs-post was required to exhibit a list of the duties which

could be levied. 'Cela est juste et exécuté en partie', wrote a contemporary,

> puisque partout on voit quelques lambeaux d'une pancarte enfumée qui ressemble à quelque chose de pareil. Mais ne devrait-on pas proscrire les pancartes à la main? Tous les changements survenus dans les tarifs ne devraient-ils pas être connus? Enfin la sûreté publique, n'exigerait-elle pas que dans chaque chambre de commerce du royaume il y eût sous la garde des consuls un livre que les négociants pourraient consulter, et où tous les arrêts intervenus sur chaque espèce se trouveraient? C'est le fermier[1] qui propose la loi, qui la rédige, et lui seul en a connaissance! On imprime à la vérité quelques arrêts du Conseil, mais les plus intéressants ne sont pas publiés, surtout lorsqu'ils sont favorables au commerce. Rien n'est plus propre à introduire l'arbitraire dans la perception, police aussi ruineuse pour les revenus publics que pour le contribuable. Cela explique la différence qui se trouve souvent entre les droits perçus dans un port ou dans un autre. Ce cas n'est pas très commun, mais il n'est pas si rare qu'on se l'imagine. (Véron de Forbonnais, *Recherches sur les finances*, II, 26-9)

Such a complicated system could scarcely be regarded as an encouragement to trade.

Despite all these obstacles, the internal trade of France did undoubtedly expand in the eighteenth century, even though there are no statistics by which we can today measure its growth. It is generally agreed, however, that there was relatively greater progress in France's overseas trade for all the frequent setbacks caused by wars which both cut off France from her export-markets and deprived her of a large number of her colonial possessions. We have reasonably reliable statistics to show the progress of her exports and imports between 1715 and 1789.

According to a contemporary source, Arnould's *De la balance du commerce et des relations commerciales de la France dans toutes les parties du monde*, France's trade with other European countries almost quadrupled between 1716 and 1788. Throughout the period the average yearly exports and imports (the years

---

[1] *Fermier général* (see pp. 87-90).

1733-5, 1740-8, 1756-63 and 1777-83 are treated separately as periods of war) show a considerable balance in France's favour:

|  | Exports | Imports |
|---|---|---|
|  |  | (in livres) |
| 1716–20 | 106,216,000 | 65,079,000 |
| 1721–32 | 116,765,000 | 80,198,000 |
| 1733–35 | 124,465,000 | 76,600,000 |
| 1736–39 | 143,441,000 | 102,035,000 |
| 1740–48 | 192,334,000 | 112,805,000 |
| 1749–55 | 257,205,000 | 155,555,000 |
| 1756–63 | 210,899,000 | 133,778,000 |
| 1764–76 | 309,245,000 | 165,164,000 |
| 1777–83 | 259,782,000 | 207,536,000 |
| 1784–88 | 354,423,000 | 301,727,000 |

(Vol. III, Table X)

In other words, exports and imports combined rose in this period from a total of some 171 million livres to 656 millions; even allowing for some decline in the value of money over this period of about seventy years, the growth in France's trade with her European neighbours was certainly impressive.

France's main exports in our period were agricultural products, especially wines and spirits, and all manner of luxury goods, among which silk was particularly important. Her imports consisted largely of raw materials and manufactured goods; her market was flooded with the latter after the trade treaty with England in 1786. If trade with Spain and Holland declined, that with England, Germany and other countries of Northern Europe grew.

In her relations with countries outside Europe, France held he leading place in trade with the Levant, thanks especially to the great Mediterranean port of Marseilles. But more important still to her was trade with her colonies. It is true that, in her long struggle with England, she lost all Canada and most of her possessions in India; by the Treaty of Paris (1763) her Compagnie des Indes was left with only a few trading posts. Yet even the disasters of the Seven Years War left France with rich possessions in the West Indies, the islands of Guadeloupe and Martinique (still today French territories) and especially Saint-Domingue, the western third of the Island of Santo Domingo, corresponding roughly to the modern Haiti. This last territory was the richest sugar-producing region in the world and was the source of great wealth, not only to French traders, but to the French colonists who worked their plantations with slave labour. On the eve of the Revolution these West Indian islands, in addition to importing large quantities of French manufactured goods and wines, exported to France even larger quantities of sugar, coffee, rum, tobacco and cotton. Not all of these goods were for the French market; considerable quantities were re-exported to other European countries. If one adds in the figures for her colonial trade, France's imports and exports in the closing decades of the Ancien Régime become even more impressive. Thus, in the years after the War of American Independence, the period 1784-8, her total overseas trade reached the surprising total of 1,061 million livres.

These figures have often been taken as a sign that the reign of Louis XVI was one of astonishing prosperity. In fact, for the country as a whole, the last dozen years or so of the Ancien Régime were years of economic depression culminating in the *débacle* of 1788-90; yet it is also clear that the depression had spared the big seaports. Arthur Young's impressions of France on the eve of the Revolution bear striking witness to the fact that one sector of the French economy was still doing well. At Bordeaux in 1787 he found every sign of prosperity:

> Much as I had heard and read of the commerce, wealth and magnificence of this city, they greatly surpassed my expectations. Paris did not answer at all, for it is not to be compared to London; but we must not name Liverpool in competition with Bordeaux.

He was struck by the fine new buildings, particularly by the famous theatre, designed by the architect, Victor Louis:

> The *Place-Royale*, with the statue of Louis XV in the middle, is a fine opening, and the buildings which form it regular and handsome. But the quarter of the *Chapeau Rouge* is truly magnificent, consisting of noble houses, built, like the rest of the city

of white hewn stone. . . . The theatre, built about ten or twelve years ago, is by far the most magnificent in France. I have seen nothing that approaches it. . . . The establishment of actors, actresses, singers, dancers, orchestra, etc. speaks the wealth and luxury of the place. I have been assured that from thirty to fifty *louis* a night have been paid to a favourite actress from Paris. Larive, the first tragic actor of that capital, is now here at 500 liv. (£21. 12. 6.) a night, with two benefits. Dauberval, the dancer, and his wife (the Mademoiselle Théodore of London) are retained as principal ballet-master and first female dancer at a salary of 28,000 liv. (£1,255). Pieces are performed every night, Sundays not excepted, as everywhere in France. The mode of living that takes place here among merchants is highly luxurious. Their houses and establishments are on expensive scales. Great entertainments, and many served on plate. High play is a much worse thing; and the scandalous chronicle speaks of merchants keeping the dancing and singing girls of the theatre at salaries which ought to import no good to their credit. (*Travels in France*, I, 59-61)

A similar impression was received by Young when in the summer of 1788 he visited the port of Le Havre. Here again he was struck by the town's air of prosperity and by the wealth of the merchant class:

Inquiries are not necessary to find out the prosperity of this town; it is nothing equivocal; fuller of motion, life and activity than any place I have been at in France. . . . The harbour's mouth is narrow and formed by a mole, but it enlarges into two oblong basins of greater breadth; these are full of ships, to the number of some hundreds, and the quays around are thronged with business; all hurry, bustle and animation.

. . . The next day Mons. Le Reiseicourt, captain of the *Corps Royal du Génie*, to whom I also had letters, introduced me to Messrs. Homberg, who are ranked among the most considerable merchants of France. I dined with them at one of their country houses, meeting a numerous company and splendid entertainment. These gentlemen have wives and daughters, cousins and friends, cheerful, pleasing and well-informed. I did not like the idea of quitting them so soon, for they seemed to have a society that would have made a longer residence agreeable enough. (I, 91-2)

Nantes, which Young visited a month later, also made a deep impression on him. Once again he found every sign of prosperity, and at the same time was struck by the signs of culture among the wealthy middle classes of the town—the theatre and also the *chambre de lecture*, the equivalent of the subscription libraries which sprang up in the great commercial centres of eighteenth century England:

> The town has that sign of prosperity of new buildings, which never deceives. The quarter of the *Comédie* is magnificent, all the streets at right angles and of white stone. I am in doubt whether the *Hôtel de Henri IV* is not the finest inn in Europe. . . . It is, without comparison, the first inn I have seen in France, and very cheap. It is in a small square close to the theatre, as convenient for pleasure or trade as the votaries of either can wish. The theatre cost 450,000 liv. and lets to the comedians at 17,000 liv. a year; it holds, when full, to the value of 120 louis d'or. . . . An institution common in the great commercial towns of France, but particularly flourishing in Nantes, is a *chambre de lecture*, or what we should call a book-club, that does not divide its books, but forms a library. There are three rooms, one for reading, another for conversation, and a third is the library; good fires in winter are provided, and wax candles.

The revolutionary sentiments of the inhabitants of Nantes in September 1788 so struck Young that he indulged in a prophecy, the cautious nature of which was to be mocked by the rush of events in the months which followed:

> Nantes is as *enflammé* in the cause of liberty as any town in France can be; the conversations I witnessed here prove how great a change is effected in the minds of the French, nor do I believe it will be possible for the present government to last half a century longer, unless the clearest and most decided talents be at the helm. (I, 104-5)

Although the prosperity of the great seaports of France, especially in the second part of our period, should not delude us into imagining that the rest of the country was in the same flourishing state in the 1780s, it does constitute one facet of the economic life of the country, and also accounts for some of the wealth and power of the French merchant class on the eve of 1789.

The industrial foundations of France's commerce were, as might be expected in the age before the Industrial Revolution, still for the most part primitive. Large-scale industry, although not unknown, was fairly rare, since a great part of the industry as of the trade of the country was still organized on the guild system, that is, of a master working with the aid of journeymen (*compagnons*) and apprentices. The guilds (*corporations*) did not necessarily include all those engaged in trade and industry in the different towns of France in the eighteenth century, any more than in earlier periods; but modern historians no longer see any great distinction between these trades which were organized in 'métiers jurés' (or 'jurandes') and those which were organized in so-called 'métiers libres', since all forms of guild were in fact controlled in some degree by the local authorities and by the central government.

By our period the guilds had already passed the peak of their long history, and were encountering much hostile criticism which was to lead to Turgot's attempt to suppress them in 1776 and to their final and complete abolition in 1791. They were undoubtedly extremely hostile to all technical improvements and intent on preserving existing methods of manufacture, regardless of the lowering of costs to be achieved by innovations. They were too the very denial of the new liberal principle of free competition, since they stood for the maintenance of a monopoly confined to their members who had served an apprenticeship and, after producing a masterpiece (*chef-d'œuvre*) and paying the necessary fees, had been admitted as members of the guild. The apprenticeship varied considerably in length from town to town and from trade to trade. It might be followed by a period as journeyman, but this was not essential. By the eighteenth century it had become very difficult for anyone who was not the son or son-in-law of a master to become a master in his turn. Admission fees and all sorts of extra expenses, such as providing a banquet for the other members, had become so high that it was difficult, indeed often impossible, for a mere journeyman ever to rise higher in his trade, especially as the sons and sons-in-law of masters were favoured in all sorts of ways. The production of a masterpiece was made a much more difficult test for a mere journeyman than for the son of a master. Take, for instance, what a hostile critic in the *Encyclopédie* has to say of the different treatment which, according to circumstances, could be meted out to candidates:

> S'il est fils de maître, assez ordinairement il est dispensé de chef-d'œuvre; s'il ne l'est pas, fût-il le plus habile ouvrier d'une ville, il a bien de la peine à faire un chef-d'œuvre qui soit agréé de la communauté, quand il est odieux à cette communauté. S'il est agréable au contraire, ou qu'il ait de l'argent, fût-il le plus ignorant de tous les ouvriers, il corrompra ceux qui doivent veiller sur lui tandis qu'il fait son chef-d'œuvre; ou il exécutera un mauvais ouvrage qu'on recevra comme un chef-d'œuvre; ou il en présentera un excellent qu'il n'aura pas fait. (art. *Chef-d'œuvre*)

By the eighteenth century the vast majority of journeymen had no prospect of ever rising to the status of master. Gradually there grew up associations of journeymen (*compagnonnages*) which led a semi-underground existence. As many journeymen indulged in the *tour de France*—that is, moved round the country from town to town exercising their trade—these associations made themselves responsible for finding work for their members when they arrived in a new town. They also took action against journeymen who refused to join the appropriate *compagnonnage*. Now that the journeyman had in many cases a separate organization from that of his master, these associations also fought for the interests of their members so far as wages and conditions of work were concerned. Yet their action tended to be sporadic and local, and although the *compagnonnages* were in a sense the ancestors of modern trade unions, they were the product of a very different economic organization—not of the factory, but of the small workshop where often the master worked alongside his journeymen and apprentices without any very noticeable social gulf.

Undoubtedly the standard of living of the majority of journeymen was extremely low. A contemporary writer tells us that, before 1789,

> les ouvriers, dans toutes les professions mécaniques, alors dans l'usage de faire le tour de France, étaient si peu rétribués par les

maîtres qui les employaient successivement, qu'on les rencontrait sur les routes, à leur sortie de chez eux, vêtus de haillons et portant tout leur bagage dans un très petit sac de toile. La plupart, lorsqu'ils étaient nourris et logés, ce qui avait ordinairement lieu, ne gagnaient que six francs par mois. (Besnard, *Souvenirs d'un nonagénaire*, I, 31 n.)

But then a great many of the masters with whom they lived could scarcely be said to have led a life of luxury, as we see from the same writer's description of the ordinary artisan's household in Angers before the Revolution:

Les artisans étaient alors pour la plupart très étroitement logés. Outre leurs boutiques ou ateliers ils n'occupaient souvent qu'une grande chambre qui leur servait à la fois de cuisine, de salon à manger et de chambre à coucher pour la famille, puis une autre pièce pour les compagnons que l'on était en usage de nourrir et de loger. (I, 200)

Though still important in the economic life of the country, the guilds were soon to be swept away by the Revolution. Moreover, by the eighteenth century they were far from controlling all the commercial and industrial life of the nation. It is a well-known paradox that in France, as in England, in the days before the triumph of the factory system, a great deal of industry was carried on, not in the towns themselves, but in the country where it was outside the control of the guilds. The prosperous merchants of the towns, especially in the north of France, found a large labour force available among the landless or semi-landless peasants of the surrounding countryside. Sometimes the peasants would work independently and merely sell to the merchants the finished or nearly finished product on which they and their families had worked. Such was the position of the peasants of the Rouen region described by the young François de La Rochefoucauld in the early 1780s:

Je vis ensuite les étoffes qu'on appelle cotonnades. Ce sont toutes sortes de fabrications en coton que l'on fait à Rouen et à quinze lieues aux environs. Le paysan qui revient de la charrue, de labourer son champ, se met à son métier de coton et fait soit des siamoises,[1] soit du coutil ou même des toiles de coton blanches et fort fines. Il faut admirer l'activité des Normands. Ce travail ne les dérange pas du tout de leur ouvrage journalier. Les terres sont fort chères et par conséquent bien cultivées. Le fermier les travaille pendant le jour, et c'est le soir, à la lampe, qu'il se met à son métier. Il fait travailler ses valets et sa famille. Quand ils ont travaillé toute la semaine, ils viennent à la ville avec des chevaux ou des charrettes toutes remplies de ces étoffes. (*Voyages en France*, I, 4-5)

More common still, especially in the north of France, was the system whereby the merchants of the towns supplied the peasants of the surrounding country with raw materials and even looms and paid them piece-rates for the articles which they produced. This was, of course, an intermediate stage between the old guild system and the modern factory, when the merchant assembles all his workers in one building, uses power-looms and thus becomes a factory-owner.

Large numbers of peasants, along with their wives and children, thus found a means of eking out their meagre existence with their earnings in domestic industry, and, of course, the merchants employed many workers in the towns in the same way. Only a quarter of a century before the Revolution we find the author of the article *Manufactures* in the *Encyclopédie* so enthusiastically in favour of this system, to which he gives the name of 'manufacture dispersée', that he prefers it to the factory:

Un laboureur, un journalier de campagne, ou autre homme de cette espèce a dans le cours de l'année un assez grand nombre de jours et d'heures où il ne peut s'occuper de la culture de la terre ou de son travail ordinaire. Si cet homme a chez lui un métier à drap, à toile ou à petites étoffes, il y emploie un temps qui autrement serait perdu pour lui et pour l'état. Comme ce travail n'est pas sa principale occupation, il ne le regarde pas comme l'objet d'un profit aussi fort que celui qui en fait son unique ressource. Ce travail même lui est une espèce de délassement des travaux plus rudes de la terre; et, par ce moyen, il est en état et en habitude de se contenter d'un moindre profit.

[1] 'Étoffe de coton fort commune, imitée des toiles de coton fabriquées à Siam' (*Dictionnaire de l'Académie Française*, 1762).

This eulogy shows the importance of domestic industry in our period, particularly in the various textile industries, in what the same writer calls 'les fabriques de draps, de serges, de toiles, de velours, petites étoffes de laine et de soie ou autres pareilles'.

A similar process of merchants controlling industry was to be found in several towns, in particular Lyons, the main centre of the silk industry. Artisans who had formerly worked on their own account with their journeymen and apprentices were now compelled by the pressure of economic forces to obtain their raw materials from a merchant and to accept piece-rates for their work and that of their journeymen and apprentices; the *maîtres ouvriers* in this industry now became subordinated to the wealthier class of *maîtres marchands*.

There was, however, already visible a strong tendency towards the factory system, especially in the cloth industry, where, because of the large number of processes involved, it was in the manufacturer's interest to reduce transport costs by bringing his workers together in one building. This trend was hastened in the closing decades of the century by the introduction of machinery, at least in a limited number of industries. As in England—and indeed with English machines as models and very often Englishmen to work them—the cotton industry led the way. The discoveries of men like Kay, Arkwright and Crompton gradually found their way across the Channel, and although French progress in this field came largely after the Revolution, the beginnings of a large-scale cotton industry were already present by 1789.

Since the time of Colbert the French government had endeavoured to stimulate the development of industry. Factories enjoying government subsidies or interest-free loans bore the title of *manufactures royales*. In addition, they often received support from the local town councils or, in the *pays d'états*, the provincial estates. Some of the *manufactures royales* founded in the time of Colbert—for instance, the famous cloth factory of the Van Robais family at Abbeville—continued to flourish, and a considerable number of new ones were founded in the first half of the century.

The government still kept a strict watch over industry,

12 *J. Vernet*, Construction d'un grand chemin dans un pays montagneux

13  *J. Vernet*, Vue de Bordeaux (1759)

despite the fact that the new doctrines of economic liberalism—
*laissez-faire, laissez-passer*—demanded freedom from all forms of
state intervention. Not only did the *Conseil du commerce* continue,
through its *inspecteurs des manufactures*, to keep a close eye on
industry, but the *Intendants* also played a considerable part in
the supervision of existing industries and the establishment of
new ones. However, in the closing decades of the Ancien
Régime, the new doctrines of *laissez-faire* tended to weaken the
rigid control which, since the time of Colbert, the government
had exercised over industry's choice of raw materials, methods of
manufacture and the quality of the finished product. Although
many of these controls were still in force in 1789, industry
enjoyed ever greater freedom to develop as it wished.

Among the economic developments most significant for the
future which took place in France in the second half of the
century was the expansion of the metal industries. The French
iron industry seems to have developed rapidly, especially in
the closing decades of the century, and although statistics are far
from reliable, it would appear to have had an output nearly
twice as great as that of the corresponding English industry,
even if it was technically much less advanced and tried vainly
to adopt English methods. For instance, William Wilkinson,
the younger brother of the English ironmaster, John Wilkinson,
was persuaded to cross the Channel and in 1777 was appointed
manager of a new iron foundry to be constructed on the island
of Indret, on the Loire, below Nantes. In 1788 Arthur Young
made a trip to the island:

> Messrs. Espivent had the goodness to attend me on a water
> expedition, to view the establishment of Mr. Wilkinson, for boring
> cannon, in an island in the Loire below Nantes. Until that well-
> known English manufacturer arrived, the French knew nothing
> of the art of casting cannon solid, and then boring them. Mr.
> Wilkinson's machinery for boring four cannons is now at work,
> moved by tide wheels; but they have erected a steam engine,
> with a new apparatus for boring seven more. M. de La Motte,
> who has the direction of the whole, showed us also a model of
> this engine, about six feet long, five high, and four or five broad;
> which he worked for us by making a small fire under the boiler

that is not bigger than a large tea kettle; one of the best machines for a travelling philosopher that I have seen. (*Travels in France*, I, 104-5)

Young patriotically stresses the role of John Wilkinson in the establishment of the foundry at Indret, but in reality a more significant part was played by a scion of a famous Lorraine family of industrialists, Ignace de Wendel.

Both men were also associated in the foundation of an even more important undertaking, extended in the nineteenth century by the Schneider family, the famous *fonderie royale* at Montcenis, near Le Creusot. Here by 1785 they had installed the most modern plant on the English pattern; a foundry using not wood but coke, made from the coal of nearby mines, with steam engines, forges, and a horse-drawn railway. Of the 4,000 shares in the company which owned the works, 333 were held by Louis XVI. Arthur Young visited it in 1789.

These are among the greatest iron works in France, and owe their present magnitude entirely to Mons. de Calonne.[1] They were established by Mr. Wilkinson from England in the same expedition into France in which he fixed those on the Loire near Nantes. The iron mine is three leagues off, but those of coal on the spot. They cast and bore cannon on the greatest scale, having five steam engines at work, and a sixth building; they have iron roads for the waggons, make coke of coal à l'anglaise, etc. etc. Here is also a pretty considerable crystal glass works, in which two Englishmen are still left. There is no navigation, as necessary as coals or iron; but the Charolais canal is within two leagues and they hope it will come here. (II, 554)

Here we see clearly the new forces of the Industrial Revolution at work in France on the eve of the Revolution; yet we must not forget that such advanced economic developments were rare before 1789, or that the works at both Le Creusot and Indret proved a failure.

Coal-mining, so important for the future industrial development of the country, was making rapid strides in the eighteenth century. Here as in all other spheres of industry the government exercised control, and in 1783 it set up the École des Mines for

---

[1] The *Contrôleur général* (see pp. 214-19).

the training of mining engineers. A royal decree of 1744 laid it down that all unworked coal was the property of the Crown and that no mine could be operated without permission from the government; this was gradually followed by the formation of a number of joint-stock companies, with considerable capital (some of it furnished by great noblemen), and using such new technical inventions as the steam-engine. In 1789 the largest of these companies, la Compagnie d'Anzin, a small town near Valenciennes, where coal had been discovered in 1734, employed 4,000 workers, and had a dozen steam-engines in use. Yet significant as these companies were for the great economic changes which were to take place in the following century, such large-scale industry, supplied with considerable capital and employing a large labour force, was extremely rare in France before 1789—or even 1830. Moreover, although the output of the French coal industry had been multiplied several times in the course of the century, even in 1789 it was still probably only about one-twentieth of British coal output.

In considering the economic development of France before the Revolution one must bear in mind the limitations on the progress of trade and industry imposed by factors in the social history of the country. As in the previous century, official posts, the purchase of which conferred on the holder social prestige, and often also noble rank with exemption from certain taxes, continued to attract many well-to-do merchants and industrialists, who strove to rise out of bourgeois and despised occupations into a higher social class. No doubt both the development of a different social outlook among the middle classes themselves and the obstacles placed in the way of their rise in status by the existing aristocracy tended to reduce this upward ascent of the wealthy bourgeois. Yet only five years before the Revolution we find Necker repeating the complaint of the bad effects which this desire of merchants and manufacturers for social elevation had on trade and industry:

Cette multitude de charges qui donnent la noblesse et qu'on peut acquérir à prix d'argent, entretiennent un esprit de vanité qui engage à renoncer aux établissements de commerce ou de manufacture au moment où par l'accroissement de la fortune on pourrait y donner la plus grande étendue, époque précieuse où l'on est plus que jamais en situation de lier ses travaux et son industrie à l'avancement de la prospérité de l'état. C'est alors en effet que les négociants peuvent se contenter d'un moindre intérêt de leurs capitaux; c'est alors qu'ils peuvent faciliter le commerce d'exportation par des avances; c'est alors qu'ils peuvent hasarder davantage et ouvrir, par des entreprises nouvelles, des routes encore inconnues . . . Je n'hésite point à dire que ces dispositions arrêtent en France le développement entier des forces et du génie du commerce, et que c'est là une des causes principales de la supériorité que conservent dans plusieurs branches d'affaires les nations où les distinctions d'état sont moins sensibles et où toutes les prétentions qui en résultent ne sont pas un objet continuel d'occupation. (*De l'Administration des finances*, III, 116-17)

Undoubtedly, in comparison with countries like England, economic progress in France was held up throughout our period by the haste with which wealthy merchants and industrialists abandoned their calling and sought for themselves or their sons posts in the legal or administrative world which, while they provided some return for the capital invested in their purchase, gave what was perhaps even more important, social prestige. In addition, as in the previous century, many prosperous bourgeois retired early from business and either invested their money in land or else in government stocks (*rentes*), and spent the rest of their days in idleness, 'vivant noblement' in the revealing phrase of the time, instead of continuing, either for themselves or their sons, the pursuit of wealth through productive economic effort.

More important still in this respect was the fact that the largest fortunes in French society before the Revolution were acquired not by merchants and industrialists, but by all those people, known collectively as 'financiers', who contrived to wax fat on the incessant money needs of the Crown. Bankers in the modern sense of the word still remained relatively unimportant in France before 1789. It is true that in the last decades of the Ancien Régime Paris bankers were enriched by various forms of speculation, both in government stocks and in other fields, but many of these were foreigners.

Large fortunes continued to be made by *financiers* throughout the century. Some idea of the diverse functions of these gentlemen is given in Necker's definition of the term:

> On donne le nom de *financiers* en France aux différentes personnes qui sont chargées du recouvrement des revenus publics, soit comme receveurs, soit comme fermiers, soit comme régisseurs; et l'on comprend encore sous la même dénomination les trésoriers qui paient les dépenses de l'État, les banquiers de la cour qui remplissent le service des affaires étrangères, et les diverses personnes qui, moyennant un droit de commission, font des avances sur la rentrée plus ou moins éloignée des impositions.
> (*De l'Administration des finances*, III, 95)

At the very top came the court bankers and men who assisted the Treasury on a really massive scale. There was, for instance, the famous Samuel Bernard who had already distinguished himself during the reign of the *Roi Soleil* and who, down to his death in 1739 at the age of eighty-eight, continued to astonish his contemporaries by flaunting his colossal wealth. In August 1733 we find the following entry in Barbier's journal:

> Le 16 de ce mois il y a eu ici un grand mariage de la fille du président Bernard de Rieux, petite-fille de Samuel Bernard, avec le marquis de Mirepoix, de la maison de Lévis de Ventadour. Elle n'a que douze ans et demi. Samuel Bernard lui donne huit cent mille livres en mariage. Il y a eu une fête magnifique. Bien des gens blâment le marquis de Mirepoix, qui a près de trente mille livres de rente, de s'allier avec un nom aussi bas et aussi décrié que celui-là. Mais on ne connaît présentement ici que l'argent.
>
> Ce Samuel Bernard est incompréhensible pour la fortune et le bien. Il y a trois mois qu'il a marié la fille de son fils aîné, le maître des requêtes, à M. de Lamoignon, président à mortier, avec huit cent mille livres; et dans un mois on doit faire le mariage de sa propre fille du second lit avec M. Molé, président à mortier, à qui il donne pareille dot.
>
> Il a établi ses fils richement; il a depuis payé leurs dettes qui se montaient à cinq ou six millions; il a donné à Mme Fontaine, sa maîtresse, la seigneurie de Passy, où il a fait faire un bâtiment de plus de trois cent mille livres. Il a marié et bien établi trois filles de Mme Fontaine. Sa table, pour dîner seulement, lui coûte

cent cinquante mille livres par an. Et à quatre-vingt-deux ans, il est à la tête de toute cette famille. Où peut-on trouver des sommes d'argent aussi considérables? (*Chronique de la Régence*, II, 418)

Another famous group of *financiers* who owed part of their wealth to the allied and extremely lucrative occupation of supplying the armies in the field, and who have a tiny place even in the literary history of the century since both Voltaire and Beaumarchais owed to one of them their considerable fortunes, were the four Pâris brothers. The sons of a prosperous bourgeois from the Grenoble region, the two eldest began their career in supplying the armies during the wars of the latter part of the reign of Louis XIV. It was, however, the two youngest brothers, Pâris-Duverney (1684-1770) and Pâris-Monmartel (1690-1766) who were to play a more important part in public affairs, the former mainly as a *munitionnaire* and the latter as court banker. An official document of 1745, in the middle of the War of the Austrian Succession, speaks of the services rendered to the state by the two brothers,

> l'un [Pâris-Monmartel] par son crédit dans les pays étrangers, à la faveur duquel nous pourvoyons à toutes les dépenses que nous sommes obligés d'y faire singulièrement depuis quatre à cinq ans pour nos armées, en conservant nos espèces dans notre royaume, et l'avantage du commerce sur les changes qu'il a jusqu'ici maintenus malgré la difficulté des circonstances, dans le point d'utilité où ils étaient pour nos sujets avant la guerre; et l'autre par ses connaissances et son travail dans les détails infinis de l'approvisionnement et de la subsistance en tout genre de nos armées, en quoi il s'est acquis notre confiance particulière, celle de nos généraux et l'estime de nos troupes. (R. Dubois-Corneau, *Pâris de Monmartel*, p. 257)

There were ups and downs in the careers of the two men, but they finally came out on top, and there is little exaggeration in the words of Saint-Simon:

> Ils sont redevenus les maîtres des finances et des contrôleurs généraux, et ont acquis des biens immenses, fait et défait des ministres et d'autres fortunes, et ont vu la cour à leurs pieds, la ville et la province. (*Mémoires*, XXXVII, 186)

Mme de Pompadour was their protégée, and during her period
of influence at court, they made and unmade ministers, and
from the wings not only controlled the finances of France, but
had their say in such matters as foreign policy and the conduct
of military operations.

Men of such wealth, power and influence were, of course,
exceptional; not all *financiers* rose to such dizzy heights. Apart
from the high Treasury officials at Versailles, there were a
considerable number of wealthy men engaged in the collection
of taxes, direct and indirect—the *receveurs, fermiers* and *régisseurs*
of whom Necker speaks. For example, there were in each
financial district (*élection*) two *receveurs des tailles* who received a
commission on all the taxes they collected; there were some
four hundred of these officials who had to invest a substantial
sum of money in the purchase of their posts and were men of
some wealth and position. But above them came a more select
group of officials—the *receveurs généraux des finances*—to whom the
*receveurs* passed the money which they had collected. These men
numbered altogether forty-eight as there were two in every
*généralité* (their posts had been sold twice over by the government and were exercised in alternate years). These officials had
to invest a very considerable capital in their posts; they also
differed from the tax-collectors of more modern times in that
their functions were not limited to remitting to the Treasury
the money which they received from the *receveurs*; even more
important, they helped the government to borrow money,
since, in addition to their own resources, they enjoyed considerable credit in their region. Given the disorder which reigned in
the finances of the country before 1789, there were plenty of
opportunities for these men to increase their wealth by more or
less legitimate means.

The *fermiers* (tax-farmers) were entrusted with the collection
of such indirect taxes as the *gabelle, aides, traites* and tobacco
duty. From its reorganization in 1726 down to the Revolution
the system was that every six years the collection of the indirect
taxes was farmed out to a company of forty (or, for part of the
period, sixty) *fermiers généraux*. They had to put down a very
considerable sum of money as security, on which they were paid

interest, and in addition they received a salary and expenses; but naturally their main interest was in the profits to be made out of the difference between the sum due to the Treasury and what they actually collected from the taxpayer. In 1780 Necker tried out a new method of collection for some of the indirect taxes such as the *aides*: the *régie générale*. Under this system the *régisseurs*, unlike the *fermiers* who made a profit out of any extra sums they collected beyond the amount due to the Treasury, were paid merely a fixed salary, although in addition they received a commission on any sums collected beyond a fixed amount. Public opinion was on the whole in favour of the new system, but it was tried out only just before the Revolution and affected only some of the indirect taxes.

The tax-farmers were one of the wealthiest sections of the community. Most of them possessed luxurious mansions in Paris and country houses outside; they often indulged in an ostentatious display of their wealth and even ruined themselves by all manner of foolish expenditure. They were never in the nature of things a popular class. The *fermier général* is quite a prominent figure in the satirical literature of the age. At the beginning of the century, in his comedy *Turcaret* (1709), Lesage had pilloried this social class in depicting the downfall of one of its members who is presented as a grasping individual, completely lacking in sense or taste, and concerned only with flaunting his ill-gotten gains. A few years before the Revolution Mercier, in his *Tableau de Paris*, offers a highly satirical picture of the arrogance and ostentation of a *fermier général* and his wife:

> Dans telle maison de fermier général vous trouverez vingt-quatre domestiques portant livrée, sans compter les marmitons, des aides-cuisine, et six femmes de chambre pour Madame . . . Trente chevaux frappent du pied dans l'écurie. Après cela, comment Monsieur et Madame, dans leur magnifique hôtel, prenant l'insolence pour la dignité, n'appelleraient-ils pas *canaille* tous ceux qui n'ont pas cinq cent mille livres de rente? (II, 123)

It was this unpopularity which led to the rounding up and execution of all the surviving tax-farmers during the Terror.

Yet, despite the unpopularity of their profession, individual *fermiers généraux* enjoyed in our period a much greater prestige than in the previous century. Their wealth gained them admission to all but the most exclusive social circles, while large dowries enabled their daughters to marry into the aristocracy, and the wealthy tax-farmer could find for himself a father-in-law of blue blood, but too hard up to provide his daughter with a dowry. Mercier sums up the matter in his usual vivid, if scarcely objective fashion:

> La finance est alliée aujourd'hui à la noblesse, et voilà ce qui fait la base de sa force réelle. La dot de presque toutes les épouses des seigneurs est sortie de la caisse des fermes. Il est assez plaisant de voir un comte ou vicomte, qui n'a qu'un beau nom, rechercher la fille opulente d'un financier; et le financier qui regorge de richesses, aller demander la fille de qualité, nue, mais qui tient à une illustre famille.
>
> La différence est que la fille de condition (qui était menacée de passer dans un couvent le reste de sa vie) se lamente en épousant un homme qui a cinq cent mille livres de rente, croit lui faire une grâce insigne en lui donnant sa main, et crie aux portraits de ses ancêtres *de fermer les yeux sur cette mésalliance*. Le sot époux, tout gonflé de l'avantage de prêter son argent aux parents et aigrefins de sa femme, se croit fort honoré d'avoir fait la fortune de son épouse altière, et il pousse la complaisance jusqu'à se croire bien inférieur à elle. Quelle misérable et sotte logique que celle de la vanité! Comment la comédie de *George Dandin* n'a-t-elle pas guéri les hommes sensés de cette étrange folie? (*Tableau de Paris*, II, 123-4)

Thanks to their wealth, the *fermiers généraux* played an important role in the literary and artistic life of the capital. Architects found in them clients who could afford to pay for handsome new mansions; painters were employed by them to decorate the inside of their houses and found in them customers for their paintings. They acted too as the patrons of musicians and men of letters. On his arrival in Paris in the 1740s, before he had become famous, Rousseau held the post of secretary to a tax-farmer. Marivaux and other writers found a generous patron in Helvétius, the son of a court physician who married into the old aristocracy and gave up his post as *fermier général* to devote himself to philosophy and poetry. The greatest name among the tax-farmers of eighteenth century France was Lavoisier, the founder of modern chemistry, whose career was cut short by the Terror.

The wealthiest section of the *financiers* were, we have seen, on the point of rising out of the middle classes and decorating themselves and their children with titles of nobility. But there were numerous less important posts in the administration which were held by solid bourgeois who joined with the merchants, industrialists and shipowners, the bankers and *rentiers* to form the prosperous section of the middle classes. The liberal professions too were already assuming considerable importance. During the Ancien Régime France was brimming with lawyers, many of them eking out a meagre existence, but others, especially the *avocats* of the Paris bar, often attaining to affluence. Their class was destined to play a remarkable role in the Revolutionary assemblies; one thinks immediately of dozens of famous Revolutionary figures who bore the title of *avocat*— Barnave, Danton, Robespierre to name only three. University teachers and schoolmasters could scarcely be said to belong to the liberal professions, but already doctors, particularly in Paris, often enjoyed both reputation and wealth.

It is less easy to describe the position of the great mass of the inhabitants of the towns—artisans and small shopkeepers, journeymen and workers outside the guilds, the huge numbers of lackeys and women servants who existed in an age of cheap domestic labour. On the whole the wage-earners of the towns seem to have suffered, rather than profited, from the long-term rise in prices which marked the greater part of the century. Wages rose, but failed to keep pace with prices, particularly with the increased cost of food, of which for the poorer classes bread was the most important item. It is true that, unlike the poorer peasants, the lower classes in the towns were shielded against the worst effects of famine and high prices as the government and local authorities controlled the price of bread and prevented it from reaching quite impossible levels. In 1739 Barbier contrasts bread prices in the capital with those in the provinces:

Depuis près de dix mois le pain vaut deux sols six deniers la livre à Paris, et même plus, et s'il n'est pas plus cher, c'est qu'il a été taxé à deux sols six deniers par le grand ordre et la police que l'on fait à Paris, où il est grandement de conséquence d'éviter les suites de la cherté du pain. Mais en Touraine et Anjou, et encore d'autres provinces, il est constant qu'il n'y a pas de blé, que le pain y a valu longtemps plus de quatre à cinq sols la livre et que les paysans mangeaient de l'herbe. (*Chronique de la Régence*, III, 178)

Yet the advantage was only relative, since high prices and low wages or even unemployment led to considerable suffering among the poorer classes of the towns during the periods of grain shortage. Both in Paris and in the provincial towns, these high bread prices led to disturbances and riots which were, of course, mercilessly suppressed.

It was not that the mass of workers in eighteenth century France were entirely defenceless against the economic fluctuations of the day. The journeymen in the guilds had their *compagnonnages* to defend their interests, and we catch occasional glimpses in the documents of the time of other rudimentary forms of industrial organization amongst the workers of the towns. For instance, when in 1724 the government tried to bring down prices by successive reductions in the value of the coinage, it encountered organized resistance from the stocking-knitters of the capital, as Barbier relates in his journal:

Il y a peut-être quatre mille ouvriers en bas. A la première diminution des espèces ils ont voulu gagner cinq sous de plus par paire de bas; il a fallu que le marchand leur accorde. A la seconde diminution le marchand a voulu diminuer ces cinq sols; l'ouvrier n'a pas voulu; le marchand s'est plaint; l'ouvrier s'est mutiné; ils ont menacé de coups de bâton ceux d'entre eux qui prendraient de l'ouvrage à moindre prix, et ils ont promis un écu par jour à ceux qui n'auraient point d'ouvrage, et qui ne pourraient pas vivre sans cela. Pour cet effet ils ont choisi entre eux un secrétaire, qui avait la liste des ouvriers sans travail, et un trésorier qui distribuait la pension; ceux-là demeuraient dans le Temple; ils profitaient du besoin qu'on a d'eux et faisaient les séditieux. On s'est plaint au contrôleur général, et on en a fait mettre une douzaine, ces jours-ci, en prison, et au pain et à l'eau. C'est pour faire voir qu'il ne faut pas laisser déranger le peuple, et la peine qu'on a à le réduire. (I, 351)

Yet such attempts at industrial combination were extremely rare. It was not merely that they were always liable to encounter the united resistance of masters, municipal authorities and the government; there was as yet no class consciousness amongst the industrial working class, still relatively small in numbers and scattered for the most part in small workshops spread over the country. Trade unions and political parties to defend the interests of the urban working class still lay far ahead in the nineteenth century.

The social class which in our period was seeking its place in the sun was the bourgeoisie. Inevitably a class which included so many different social groups and so many different degrees of wealth was not entirely united in outlook; nor did its outlook on the world suddenly change overnight at any period of the century. For centuries its members had been the strongest supporters of monarchy, indeed of absolute monarchy, in which they saw a guarantee of law and order and an obstacle to feudal anarchy. Whole generations of prosperous bourgeois had had as their aim to emerge from a social status and a calling such as that of merchant which were despised in the aristocratic society in which they lived; they had grasped every opportunity, legal or otherwise, to rise up into the aristocracy— buying official posts which conferred noble rank, purchasing *lettres de noblesse* or estates which carried titles with them, or sometimes merely assuming noble rank without anyone's permission. This ascent of the wealthiest section of the middle classes up the social ladder is well summed up by Sénac de Meilhan:

Rien ne fut de tout temps plus facile à franchir que la ligne qui séparait la noblesse d'avec le tiers état. Il a suffi, jusqu'à la fin du seizième siècle, d'entrer dans le service militaire ou de posséder un fief noble, pour être au rang des gentilshommes. . . . Les lettres d'anoblissement et la possession des charges ont été substituées à ces moyens d'acquérir la noblesse. Lorsqu'on parle des avantages de la noblesse, on ne peut se dispenser de les regarder comme étant en grande partie communs au Tiers état, puisque l'origine connue d'une partie de la noblesse se trouve, dans des temps peu reculés, venir de cet ordre. Si, dans un espace de trois cents ans, les grands emplois de l'État ont été accordés à des hommes dont les pères ou grands-pères étaient nés dans la bourgeoisie; si de degré en degré, de génération en génération, l'homme du Tiers s'élevait successivement à un rang supérieur à celui de ses pères, il est indispensable de regarder comme du tiers ordre tous ceux qui en descendent, à quelque élévation qu'ils soient parvenus. Il fallait, à la vérité, que le tiers ordre passât lentement par divers degrés ce que les nobles anciens franchissaient d'un seul pas; mais il avait enfin la faculté de s'élever avec le temps aux mêmes emplois. Il n'existait pas de barrière insurmontable qui lui en fermât l'accès, et de génération en génération la vitesse du mouvement était pour lui accélérée. (*Le Gouvernement, les Mœurs et les Conditions en France avant la Révolution*, pp. 111-12)

These aspirations towards a higher social class did not suddenly fade out in the eighteenth century; on the contrary they persisted until the Revolution. And yet gradually a subtle change came over at least a section of the wealthy middle class. Many of its members began gradually to shake off their old feeling of inferiority in face of the aristocracy, to ask whether after all their contribution to the economic life of the country did not make them more useful members of society than the court nobles who spent their days dancing attendance on the King and extracting from him favours which in the end had to be paid for out of the taxes wrung from the Third Estate. Over fifty years before the Revolution, Voltaire gives expression to this new point of view in his *Lettres philosophiques* when he compares the respect accorded to the merchant in England with the state of affairs in France:

En France est marquis qui veut, et quiconque arrive à Paris du fond d'une province avec de l'argent à dépenser et un nom en *ac* ou en *ille*, peut dire: 'Un homme comme moi, un homme de ma qualité', et mépriser souverainement un négociant. Le négociant entend lui-même parler si souvent avec dédain de sa profession, qu'il est assez sot pour en rougir. Je ne sais pourtant lequel est le plus utile à un État, ou un seigneur bien poudré qui sait récisément pà quelle heure le roi se lève, à quelle heure il se he, et qui se donne deoucsc airs de grandeur en jouant le rôle d'esclave dans l'antichambre d'un ministre, ou un négociant qui enrichit son pays, donne de son cabinet des ordres à Surate et au Caire, et contribue au bonheur du monde. (Letter X)

This feeling of inferiority which Voltaire endeavours to combat soon gave way to what becomes in the literature of the age a positive commonplace: praise of trade and the role of the merchant class in society. A *philosophe* like Baron d'Holbach reaches almost lyrical heights in his praise of the merchant:

> Dans les pays les plus lointains des milliers de bras s'empressent à satisfaire ses désirs ; l'océan gémit sous le poids des navires qui des climats les plus éloignés viennent apporter à ses pieds des richesses, et l'abondance à ses concitoyens. Le comptoir du négociant peut être comparé au cabinet d'un prince puissant, qui met tout l'univers en mouvement. (*La Morale universelle*, II, 253)

The same theme invades the theatre in the 1760s, in the new genre of the *Drame*. Into the mouth of the hero of *Le Philosophe sans le savoir* (1765) Sedaine puts words which glorify the role of the merchant and exalt his outlook and virtues:

> Quel état, mon fils, que celui d'un homme qui, d'un trait de plume, se fait obéir d'un bout de l'univers à l'autre! Son nom, son seing n'a pas besoin, comme la monnaie d'un souverain, que la valeur du métal serve de caution à l'empreinte, sa personne a tout fait; il a signé. Cela suffit... Ce n'est pas un peuple, ce n'est pas une seule nation qu'il sert; il les sert toutes, et en est servi; c'est l'homme de l'univers. . . . Quelques particuliers audacieux font armer les rois, la guerre s'allume, tout s'embrase, l'Europe est divisée; mais ce négociant anglais, hollandais, russe ou chinois n'en est pas moins l'ami de mon cœur; nous sommes, sur la superficie de la terre, autant de fils de soie qui lient ensemble les nations, et les ramènent à la paix par la nécessité du commerce. Voilà, mon fils, ce qu'est un honnête négociant. (Act II, Sc. 4)

Five years later Beaumarchais produced his *drame*, *Les Deux Amis ou le Négociant de Lyon*, of which he wrote: 'Je souhaite qu'elle plaise aux négociants, cette pièce qui a été faite pour eux et en général pour honorer les gens du tiers état.' The

praise of the merchant in this play is even more fulsome and
detailed than that in *Le Philosophe sans le savoir*:

> Je fais battre journellement deux cents métiers dans Lyon. Le
> triple de bras est nécessaire aux apprêts de mes soies. Mes
> plantations de mûriers et mes vers en occupent autant. Mes
> envois se détaillent chez tous les marchands du royaume; tout cela
> vit, tout cela gagne, et, l'industrie portant le prix des matières
> au centuple, il n'y a pas une de ces créatures, à commencer par
> moi, qui ne rende gaiement à l'Etat un tribut proportionné au
> gain que son émulation lui procure . . . Et tout l'or que la guerre
> disperse, qui le fait rentrer à la paix? Qui osera disputer au
> Commerce l'honneur de rendre à l'État épuisé le nerf et les
> richesses qu'il n'a plus? Tous les citoyens sentent l'importance
> de cette tâche: le négociant seul la remplit. Au moment que le
> guerrier se repose, le négociant a le bonheur d'être à son tour
> l'homme de la patrie. (Act II, Sc. 10)

Praise of the merchant in the literature of the age is only one
sign of a change in outlook among the members of the middle
class. Gradually in the course of the century they threw off their
old feeling of inferiority in face of the aristocracy. Their outlook
became an expansionist one as the growth of trade and industry,
as material and intellectual progress opened up fresh horizons.
Increasingly the prosperous members of the middle classes saw
in the political and social condition of the France of their day
an obstacle to further economic progress. Absolutism which
neither gave the well-to-do members of their class a say in the
running of the country nor showed itself capable of introducing
the necessary reforms in the administration and in the taxation
system against the resistance of the privileged orders, ceased
to appear to them a tolerable form of government. Moreover,
in the very decades which preceded the Revolution, the nobility
was striving its hardest both to regain something of its former
political power and to give itself a monopoly of all the highest
posts in the state—in the government and administration, in
the law courts and the Church, and finally in the army. The
privileges of the nobility in the matter of taxation were a further
grievance of the middle classes on the eve of the Revolution.
There is a famous passage in the memoirs of the Marquis de

Bouillé—no friend of the Third Estate, since it was he who organized the royal family's flight from Paris in 1791—in which he contrasts the growing wealth and prosperity of the middle classes before the Revolution with their inability to rise to any of the more important posts in the state, despite their often superior qualifications:

> Ils avaient reçu, en général, une éducation qui leur devenait plus nécessaire qu'aux gentilshommes, dont les uns, par leur naissance et par leur richesse, obtenaient les premières places dans l'État sans mérite et sans talents, tandis que les autres étaient destinés à languir dans les emplois subalternes de l'armée. Ainsi, à Paris et dans les grandes villes, la bourgeoisie était supérieure en richesses, en talents et en mérite personnel. Elle avait dans les villes de province la même supériorité sur la noblesse des campagnes; elle sentait cette supériorité, cependant elle était partout humiliée; elle se voyait exclue, par les règlements militaires, des emplois dans l'armée; elle l'était en quelque manière, du haut clergé, par le choix des évêques parmi la haute noblesse, et des grands vicaires en général parmi les nobles; elle l'était de plusieurs chapitres de cathédrale. La haute magistrature la rejetait également, et la plupart des cours souveraines n'admettaient que des nobles dans leur compagnie. Même pour être reçu maître des requêtes, le premier degré dans le Conseil d'État qui menait aux places éminentes d'intendant, et qui avait conduit les Colbert et les Louvois et tant d'hommes célèbres aux places de Ministres d'État,[1] on exigeait dans les derniers temps des preuves de noblesse. (*Mémoires*, p. 123)

The struggle of the French middle classes which began in 1787 with the summoning of the first Assemblée des Notables was to be waged in two directions: against a monarchy which denied them political rights and appeared more and more as an obstacle to material and intellectual progress; against the privileged orders, above all the nobility, which had striven successfully throughout the century to maintain and extend its privileges and which was now endeavouring, in face of a failing monarchy and the as yet untried masses of the Third Estate, to secure for itself a dominant position in the political

---

[1] *Ministres d'État* were the members of the highest (and smallest) royal council.

14   Bordeaux, Le Grand Théâtre (1775–1780)

15   Paris, L'École Militaire (1768–1773)

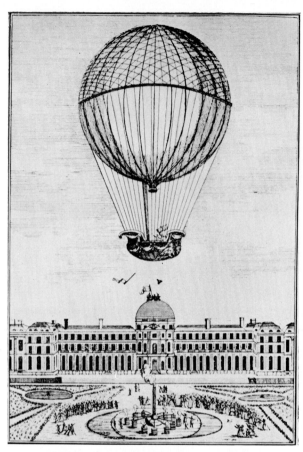

16   First ascent of a hydrogen balloon
(from the Tuileries, 1 December 1783)

17   The steam carriage of Nicolas Cugnot (1771)

life of the country. The answer of the Third Estate is summed up in a famous pamphlet which appeared in print in January 1789—*Qu'est-ce que le Tiers État?* The opening words of Abbé Sieyès sum up the whole work:

> Le plan de cet écrit est assez simple. Nous avons trois questions à nous faire:
>
> 1° Qu'est-ce que le tiers état? Tout.
> 2° Qu'a-t-il été jusqu'à présent dans l'ordre politique? Rien.
> 3° Que demande-t-il? A y devenir quelque chose.

# CHAPTER III

# THE PRIVILEGED ORDERS: THE CLERGY AND THE NOBILITY

FRENCH society before the Revolution was divided into three orders: at the top came the two privileged orders, the clergy and the nobility, and beneath them the great mass of the *Tiers État* or *roturiers*. These social divisions were, however, in all sorts of senses theoretical. As Talleyrand put it, with particular reference to the position of the clergy to which he had once belonged: 'L'État, quoique divisé en trois ordres, ne l'était réellement qu'en deux classes: la classe noble et la classe plébéienne; une partie du clergé appartenait à la première, et l'autre partie à la seconde de ces deux classes' (*Mémoires*, I, 116). The clergy was in fact what it had always been: a mirror of the society which it served; the highest posts had become more and more a monopoly of the great noble families who left the more modest and less well-paid functions to men of bourgeois or peasant origins. This state of affairs was to have important consequences in the social and political life of France.

Considered as a whole, the clergy was an immensely wealthy body. It owned a considerable proportion of the agricultural land of the country, even though its property was not as widespread as was once believed. Its holdings in the west of France were on the whole slight, and, broadly speaking, became less and less as one moved southwards. In certain regions of the north-east, around Cambrai and Laon for instance, the Church owned as much as 30 or 40 per cent. of the land, but this was altogether exceptional. Even if in other regions of the country the Church owned fairly substantial amounts of land, modern historians seem to agree that the average for the whole country cannot have been more than about 6 per cent.

However, the clergy's interest in the countryside was not limited to drawing rents from its agricultural land. As in previous centuries, it continued to exercise feudal rights, exactly like the nobility, over a much larger area of the country. A vivid account of this aspect of the clergy's ownership of land is contained in the memoirs of a man whose father farmed not only the land of a priory, but also 'les rentes nobles dues audit prieuré, lequel rendait les religieux de l'abbaye de Saint-Aubin d'Angers seuls seigneurs de toute la paroisse, avec droit de haute, moyenne et basse justice'.

The feudal dues which his father collected for the monks are described in the following terms:

> Ces rentes consistaient en 500 boisseaux de blé, poids de 30 livres, soit 100 hectolitres, 648 boisseaux de seigle, soit 65 hectolitres, 1,025 boisseaux d'avoine, soit 200 hectolitres, 24 boisseaux d'orge, soit 5 hectolitres, 10 charrois à bœufs des Alleuds à Angers, 40 journées de faneurs et vendangeurs, 15 couples de chapons et poules, et 25 francs de cens en argent.
>
> Les lods et ventes produisaient 250 francs par an, attendu l'usage de faire remise du tiers et même de moitié du droit. Ces deux articles étaient censés produire environ 3,000 francs, et les dîmes à peu près la même somme.

The burden which feudal dues represented for the peasants is described by the same writer:

> Pour les rentes féodales, le seigneur ou son fermier, ayant fait publier au prône de la messe paroissiale qu'à tels jours (on en indiquait trois consécutifs pour celles dues aux Alleuds), il les recevrait, les débiteurs étaient tenus d'en faire le paiement auxdits jours, sous peine d'être poursuivis judiciairement après leur expiration. Comme, lors de l'acensement des domaines qui en étaient grevés, ils l'étaient pour lors au nom d'un seul individu, lorsque dans le laps des temps ils avaient été divisés entre plusieurs propriétaires par succession ou vente, le seigneur avait droit . . . d'exiger la totalité de la rente créée par ledit acensement, du plus solvable des codébiteurs, sauf son recours contre chacun d'eux, ce qu'il ne manquait pas de faire et ce qui donnait lieu à des frais considérables. De plus, ces grains devaient être les plus nets possible, et de la meilleure qualité; aussi se vendaient-ils sur le marché un cinquième ou un sixième plus cher que les autres.
>
> Pour les lods et ventes, non seulement l'acquéreur d'un immeuble était obligé de payer au seigneur le douzième du prix

de son acquisition, mais il devait lui remettre une copie authentique de son acte, et celui-ci avait droit de la garder pendant un an et jour; pendant lequel intervalle de temps il pouvait se décider ou à recevoir les lods et ventes, ou à exercer le retrait, c'est-à-dire, prendre l'immeuble pour lui-même, aux charges seules de rembourser l'acquéreur de ses loyaux coûts.[1] Il avait aussi celui de céder son droit de retrait à qui bon lui semblait.

We see here how the monks in question, in addition to rents from such land as they owned in the parish, drew considerable sums in feudal dues, particularly from those paid in kind, and often in a manner vexatious to the peasants. In addition to their feudal dues they drew roughly the same amount in tithes.

The levying of tithes in this parish had features which were scarcely likely to make them any more agreeable to the peasants:

> Pour les dîmes, le cultivateur ne pouvait enlever ses produits avant d'avoir averti le décimateur, qui envoyait un de ses agents les compter, et mettre de côté son douzième; et le premier ne pouvait encore enlever ce qui lui appartenait, avant d'avoir transporté gratuitement sur l'aire ou dans les granges du prieuré ce qui était dû au décimateur, obligation exorbitante, que je n'ai vue imposée en aucune autre commune que dans celle des Alleuds. (Besnard, *Souvenirs d'un nonagénaire*, I, 2-3)

The burden which tithe imposed on the peasants, though everywhere considerable, varied enormously; the twelfth of which this writer speaks seems to have been the average; all cereal crops were everywhere subject to it, but usage varied greatly so far as other agricultural products, even wine, were concerned. In addition to such vexations as those just described, the peasants had also the grievance that the tithe was seldom used for its original purpose: the maintenance of their *curé* and of the parish church. Very often, as in the case described above, the tithe was collected on behalf of monasteries and convents, bishops and cathedral chapters, who merely paid a small amount to the *curé* and contributed relatively little to the proper upkeep of the church. Tithes also gave rise to endless litigation,

---

[1] 'Expenses genuinely incurred.'

and there was a general demand, if not for their abolition, at least for the reduction of the burden and for their return to their original use.

In *L'Homme aux quarante écus* Voltaire puts into the mouth of the principal character of his *conte*, a peasant, the following reflections on the subject:

> Il est triste, disait-il, qu'un curé soit obligé de disputer trois gerbes de blé à son ouaille, et qu'il ne soit pas largement payé par la province. . . . Le malheureux cultivateur qui a déjà payé aux préposés son dixième, et les deux sous pour livre, et la taille, et la capitation, et le rachat du logement des gens de guerre, après qu'il a logé des gens de guerre, etc., etc., etc.; cet infortuné, dis-je, qui se voit encore enlever le dixième de sa récolte par son curé, ne le regarde plus comme son pasteur, mais comme son écorcheur, qui lui arrache le peu de peau qui lui reste. Il sent bien qu'en lui enlevant la dixième gerbe de droit divin, on a la cruauté diabolique de ne pas lui tenir compte de ce qu'il lui en a coûté pour faire croître cette gerbe. Que lui reste-t-il, pour lui et pour sa famille? Les pleurs, la disette, le découragement, le désespoir; et il meurt de fatigue et de misère. Si le curé était payé par la province, il serait la consolation de ses paroissiens, au lieu d'être regardé par eux comme leur ennemi. (*Œuvres complètes*, XXI, 346-7)

It was sentiments like these which caused the National Assembly to abolish tithes outright in 1789.

In addition to what it derived from rents from its agricultural land, from feudal dues and from tithes, the clergy also drew a large income from its valuable urban properties. Yet, despite its great wealth, the clergy enjoyed considerable privileges in the matter of direct taxation. It is true that even at the time various writers (including Necker) argued that, in one form or another, the clergy paid something approaching its share of direct taxation. It was argued, for instance, that though the clergy was nominally exempt from the *taille*, it did in fact, like the nobility, pay its share indirectly—through the reduced rents paid by its farmers.

The *clergé de France*, as distinct from the so-called *clergé étranger* of such recently annexed provinces as Alsace, Lorraine and

Flanders, enjoyed the peculiar privilege of holding regular assemblies which negotiated with the government the amount of their contribution to the national exchequer, which was known as the *don gratuit*. The *Assemblées du Clergé* were held in principle every five years, but there were occasionally extra meetings in periods of emergency. It has been calculated that for the period from 1715 to 1788 the *clergé de France* paid to the government in the form of *dons gratuits* an average amount of some three to three and a half millions, scarcely a large sum in proportion to its vast income. If it had in fact to pay more than this, that was its own fault, for it insisted on raising loans to pay these sums, which meant in the course of time a large debt and heavy interest payments. In practice, the attempt to argue that the clergy really made a fair contribution to the national exchequer breaks down.

In addition to these privileges the clergy also enjoyed exemption or partial exemption from a great many indirect taxes. It was not only the free-thinking *philosophes* who in eighteenth century France argued th at the clergy should be made to pay its fair share of taxation. From the first half of the century onwards successive French governments attempted, but always in vain, to reduce these privileges, which were defended with great vigour right down to 1789. In 1726, after it had been compelled to abandon a first attempt to make the clergy contribute at least something in the way of direct taxes, the government was forced to issue in the King's name a declaration containing a solemn renunciation of all attempts, present and future, to extract such tributes from the clergy. Fortified with this clear and unambiguous statement of its immunities, the clergy successfully staved off an attempt to take them away in 1750, and at the very last *Assemblée du Clergé*, which met in the fateful year 1788, extracted yet another confirmation of its immunities from the government, and proceeded to give less than a quarter of what it had been asked for in the way of *don gratuit*. Its resistance to all attempts to whittle away its exemption from taxation down to the very end of the Ancien Régime was indeed one of the features of the aristocratic revolt which brought absolute monarchy to its ruin.

The privileges of the clergy in the matter of taxation were all the more unpopular with the general public because a small minority of its members enjoyed tremendous wealth and were at the same time a closed caste. The eighteenth century continued the process, already marked in the previous age, whereby the great majority of the highest posts in the Church were the preserve of the sons of the aristocracy. Indeed, by the second half of the century all archbishops and bishops were of noble birth, and in addition other lucrative posts of abbot, prior and canon were virtually a monopoly of the aristocracy. In his *Tableau de Paris* Mercier commented on this situation in vigorous terms:

A qui donne-t-on les évêchés? Aux nobles. Les grosses abbayes? Aux nobles. Tous les gros bénéfices? Aux nobles. Quoi, il faut être gentilhomme pour servir Dieu? Non. Mais la cour s'attache ainsi la noblesse; et l'on paie les services militaires, de même que d'autres moins importants, avec les biens de l'Eglise. (IV, 145)

If we do not believe Mercier, we can turn to the memoirs of Talleyrand, a scion of an old noble family who held important posts in the Church and began the Revolution as Bishop of Autun: 'Dans l'Église et l'épiscopat les dignités les plus lucratives étaient devenues le partage presque exclusif de la classe noble' (*Mémoires*, I, 117).

Quite a number of these clerical dignitaries entered the Church, not from a sense of vocation, but simply because they were younger sons or were prevented by some disability from following a career in the army, and perhaps already had an uncle in a high post to which they could hope to succeed. Talleyrand's uncle was Archbishop of Rheims; what finally decided his family to send him into the Church was that, although he was the eldest son, an accident to his foot, which caused him to limp, made it impossible for him to take up a career in the army.

Cet accident a influé sur tout le reste de ma vie; c'est lui qui, ayant persuadé à mes parents que je ne pouvais être militaire, ou du moins l'être sans désavantage, les a portés à me diriger vers une autre profession. Cela leur parut plus favorable à l'avancement de la *famille*. Car dans les grandes maisons, c'était la *famille*

que l'on aimait, bien plus que les individus, et surtout que les
jeunes individus que l'on ne connaissait pas encore. . . . Tous
les soins dont on m'environnait tendaient à m'inculquer pro-
fondément dans l'esprit que le mal que j'avais au pied m'empê-
chant de servir dans l'armée, je devais nécessairement entrer dans
l'état ecclésiastique, un homme de mon nom n'ayant point
d'autre carrière. (*Mémoires*, I, 7, 19)

The army or the Church were the only two careers open to the
sons of great noblemen; if they had to choose the Church, they
often remained in outlook and way of life *grands seigneurs*. Many
were addicted to hunting or even more worldly pursuits; more
still spent the minimum of time with their flock, and instead of
being overcome with boredom in their diocese, spent as much
time as they could at Paris or Versailles. A great cleric would
brave anything, even a most disagreeable lodging in the garrets
of Versailles, to be within reach of the society he loved and of
the intrigues of the court. Take, for instance, the vivid picture
of the sordid apartments at Versailles allotted to the Archbishop
of Paris, given by Mme Roland who visited the château in 1774
with her family:

Nous logeâmes dans le château. Mme Legrand, femme de la
Dauphine . . . n'étant pas de quartier, nous prêta son apparte-
ment. Il était sous les combles, dans un même corridor que celui
de l'archevêque de Paris, et tellement rapproché qu'il fallait que
ce prélat s'observât pour que nous ne l'entendissions pas parler;
la même précaution nous était nécessaire. Deux chambres,
médiocrement meublées, dans la hauteur de l'une desquelles
on avait ménagé de quoi coucher un valet, dont l'abord était
détestable par l'obscurité du corridor et l'odeur des lieux
d'aisances, telle était l'habitation dont un duc et pair de France
s'honorait d'avoir la pareille pour être plus à portée de ramper
chaque matin au lever des Majestés. (*Mémoires*, II, 103-4)

The attractions of Paris and Versailles had long created the
scandal of the non-residence of French bishops. For men of
their noble birth and aristocratic connections the social life of
Paris and the amusements and intrigues of the court had too
often an irresistible appeal. Moreover, they were men of substance, drawing large incomes not only from their diocese, but

also from the possession of wealthy abbeys and priories, and often too from clerical sinecures at court. Their total income could reach quite princely proportions and allowed of a most luxurious standard of living. To take only one example out of dozens, here is Barbier's account of the posts which were left vacant by the Cardinal de La Rochefoucauld when he died in 1757:

> Le roi a, par cette mort, de grandes places à donner: 1. celle de grand aumônier de France; 2. la feuille des bénéfices, place importante dans les circonstances présentes;[1] 3. l'archevêché de Bourges; 4. l'abbaye de Cluny, qui a une nomination considérable et de cinquante mille livres de rente; celle d'Aisne, diocèse de Lyon, de trente-trois; de Beaulieu, diocèse de Rhodez, de quatorze mille livres; de Saint-Vandrille, diocèse de Rouen, de quarante mille livres. En sorte qu'indépendamment de la place de grand aumônier et de la feuille des bénéfices, qui fait une place de ministre, M. le Cardinal de La Rochefoucauld avait pour cent soixante mille livres de bénéfices, suivant la taxe de l'*Almanach royal*.[2] (*Chronique de la Régence*, VI, 526)

Even those who lacked the pretext of a post at court, given their social connections and wealth, could not be expected to bury themselves in their diocese. To quote Mercier once again:

> Les évêques violent facilement et sans remords la loi de la résidence, en quittant le poste qui leur est assigné par les saints canons. L'ennui les chasse de leurs diocèses, qu'ils regardent comme un exil. Ils viennent presque tous à Paris pour y jouir de leurs richesses, et, mêlés dans la foule, y trouver cette liberté qu'ils n'ont pas dans le séjour où la bienséance les force à la gêne de la représentation. . . .
>
> L'ambition, qui s'alimente par ce qu'elle a déjà obtenu, les pousse à la cour et dans les bureaux des ministres. Là ils attendent le fruit de leurs intrigues et de leurs complaisances, et ils tentent de porter sourdement la main à l'administration. (*Tableau de Paris*, I, 169-70)

[1] As Barbier goes on to explain, this post was almost as important as a minister's, since the holder's functions were to advise the King about the conferment of the Church appointments in his gift.

[2] The official handbook of the government in the eighteenth century; the figures which it gave for the value of Church posts are generally considered to be far too low.

Among eighteenth century bishops there was a pious minority, who resided faithfully in their dioceses, but often displayed a fanatical zeal in persecuting Jansenists, or free-thinkers, or Protestants, which was out of keeping with the tolerant spirit of the age. At the other end of the scale came a minority who remained first and foremost *grands seigneurs*, enjoying as often as they could the pleasures of Paris and the court; they led wordly lives and enjoyed, thanks to their wealth, a luxurious existence. If their attitude to their religion was generally one of indifference, there were some high clerics who were on friendly terms with the *Philosophes* and even scorned the religion which brought them a handsome living. Some of the most distinguished archbishops and bishops of the period were primarily administrators; in the *pays d'états* they had an important political role to play as intermediaries between the central government and the estates of the province, and some of them even aspired to play a role in national politics—for example, at the end of the Ancien Régime, Loménie de Brienne, the Archbishop of Toulouse. The hold of the aristocracy over the high posts of the Church was not limited to bishoprics. There were all manner of posts for the younger sons of the nobility, as canons and *grands vicaires*, and for such of their daughters as they were not in a position to marry off, both in convents and as *chanoinesses*. For the religious orders of both sexes the eighteenth century was a period of decline, after the upsurge of the previous century. The number of monks and nuns dwindled, and in the 1760s the government intervened in their affairs, fixing the minimum age for vows at twenty-one for men and eighteen for women, and closing down some 1,500 monasteries and convents. It can be imagined that in the aristocratic society of the day posts of abbots and abbesses were normally the preserve of members of the nobility. In addition, several hundred posts as abbot and prior were held *en commende* by noblemen who were only nominally clerics and who, although they drew a third of the incomes of the monastery of which they were titular head, continued to live quite worldly lives and seldom went near the source of their income, as they had no functions to fulfil. Large numbers of the younger sons and daughters of the aristocracy could thus be found comfortable posts in the Church. As most religious orders were wealthy, even the monks and nuns could lead fairly comfortable lives, a fact which did not increase their popularity with the general public. To take one example out of thousands, the author of an official report, writing in 1780 of a wealthy Cistercian monastery in the province of Haute-Guyenne, speaks of

> l'excès des dépenses qui se font dans cette maison pour recevoir sensuellement une foule d'étrangers oisifs et aisés; qu'on retranche de la table les vins, liqueurs, un service et les nombreux domestiques qui l'entourent, on pourra aisément soulager et encourager la misère de plus de 20 paroisses et la contrée ne sera plus scandalisée de voir des religieux passer le jour à table et la nuit au jeu. (Richeprey, *Journal des voyages en Haute-Guyenne*, I, 354-5)

If the regular clergy had on the whole a bad press in the eighteenth century, the secular clergy, the *curés* and *vicaires*, were generally popular. In contrast to their wealthy aristocratic superiors whose pride of rank often prevented them from having contact with such lowborn fellows, they were frequently ill-paid and not very different in outlook from the peasants whom they served. The majority of the parish clergy seem to have been *curés* and *vicaires à portion congrue*, that is to say, they did not collect the tithes in their parish themselves, but received merely a small salary from an abbey or other titheholder. *Congru*, according to the 1798 edition of the *Dictionnaire de l'Académie Française*, means: 'Suffisant, convenable. En ce sens il n'est guère d'usage qu'en cette phrase, *Portion congrue*, qui se dit de la pension annuelle que les gros décimateurs sont tenus de payer aux curés.' Littré adds the following definition of the term: 'Par extension, portion congrue, rente, traitement fort exigu.' The amount of the *portion congrue* had been fixed at the end of the previous century at 300 l. for *curés* and 150 l. for *vicaires*. Despite the steep rise in prices in the eighteenth century it was not until 1768 that their salaries were raised to 500 and 200 l. They were further raised to 700 and 350 l. in 1786. Even the 1786 figures were far below the 1,200 l. which many of the *Cahiers* of 1789 considered the minimum necessary for a decent living for a *curé*.

The fantastic disproportion between the stipends of the mass of *curés* and *vicaires* and those of their superiors was made worse by the inequality with which the clergy levied its taxes on its members—the so-called *décimes*—which were raised to cover the payment of the *don gratuit* to the Treasury. Theoretically this tax was progressive and fell most lightly on the smallest incomes; in practice it placed a heavy burden on the worst paid section of the clergy. Like the gross disparities in income, the often shocking inequalities in taxation made for bad relations between the higher clergy and the mass of their humbler brethren.

Not all the parish clergy were badly off. In the towns they often enjoyed a reasonable standard of living, and this was also true of a privileged minority in the countryside. A former *curé*, who was appointed to a country parish in Le Maine in 1780, speaks with enthusiasm in his memoirs of his first impressions of his lot:

> Revenu plus que suffisant, liberté et indépendance, presbytère vaste, grand et bon jardin, à moitié entouré de pièces d'eau empoissonnées, une exploitation agricole toute montée, une population peu nombreuse, dont tout l'extérieur annonçait l'aisance et les mœurs douces, une contrée fertile et plantée comme un jardin, tout concourait à satisfaire mes goûts et mes besoins.
> (*Souvenirs d'un nonagénaire*, I, 287)

And well it might; even when he had paid his *décimes* and the salary of his *vicaire*, he was left with over 3,000 l. a year, which allowed him to lead quite a gentlemanly existence until the Revolution put an end to it:

> Loin d'avoir fait des économies, j'avais des dettes. Supprimer toute espèce de dépenses superflues et les payer furent deux points adoptés immédiatement; vendre les chevaux et la voiture, ainsi que quelques articles inutiles de mobilier, et renvoyer le domestique de service, furent les premiers moyens employés. . . . Je résolus de supprimer ou de rendre très rares les dîners soit avec mes confrères soit avec les autres voisins que j'avais habitude de fréquenter, de m'accoutumer à une vie frugale et dure, comme par exemple de me contenter d'un plat . . . et de vivre en ermite.
> (II, 33)

Yet the lot of this prosperous and cultured *curé*, who was able to afford a cabriolet and to make regular visits to Paris and other parts of France, and was invited to the châteaux of the region, was very different from that of his humbler colleagues. His first contacts with them are described in vivid terms:

> Le premier abord fut un peu froid, parce qu'ils me prenaient pour une manière d'abbé de cour; mon costume était plus soigné que le leur, j'étais arrivé au pays en chaise de poste, et aussi j'avais vécu longtemps au château, dont ils n'aimaient pas les propriétaires, par lesquels j'avais été à même de reconnaître qu'ils étaient traités avec dérision, pour ne pas dire avec mépris. . . .
>
> Sans doute cette société n'offrait point d'attraits séduisants; mais tout simples et rustiques qu'ils parussent dans leur manière de vivre et dans leur costume, il y avait généralement chez eux un fonds de bon cœur et de franchise, qu'on doit toujours être satisfait de rencontrer. . . .
>
> J'avais d'abord été surpris, mais je ne fus pas fâché dans la suite de voir que l'habit ecclésiastique ne se portait guère qu'à l'église, où il restait suspendu à la sacristie, et je me fis insensiblement à la rusticité de manières, de mise et de conversation, dans laquelle on se servait souvent—et même à l'église—de mots tout à fait triviaux, ou seulement usités parmi les paysans, et meme très grossiers, tels que les f . . ., les b . . . et autres familiers aux charretiers. C'est ainsi que le curé de Meurce, lorsqu'il publiait les bans de deux pauvres hères ou tout à fait mal assortis, disait en chaire: 'Il y a promesse de mariage . . .'; puis il s'arrêtait en pouffant de rire, et reprenait, 'entre tel et telle'. C'est ainsi que le vieux curé de Dissé, prêt à donner la bénédiction et ayant en vain demandé l'encensoir à l'enfant de chœur, lui dit un jour, en élevant la voix: 'Baille-moi l'encensoir, f . . . bête'. (I, 311-13)

Such *curés*, underpaid and lacking in refinement, often ignorant and uncouth, were none the less close to the peasants around them, whose speech and outlook they frequently shared.

The gulf between the aristocratic minority installed in the high posts of the Church and the plebeian mass of the secular clergy had its repercussions on the stormy events of 1789. In the electoral assemblies which chose the deputies of the clergy to the *États généraux*, the *curés* used their voting power to prevent all but a minority of liberal-minded bishops from representing their order. When, in June of that year, the Third Estate called upon the two privileged orders to join it in one assembly, sixteen *curés* answered the summons; and two days after the Third Estate resolved to call itself the *Assemblée nationale*, the clergy decided, by a narrow majority, to join it. Their abandonment of the cause of the privileged orders was the result of the treatment meted out to so many *curés* over the past centuries by their aristocratic superiors.

The nobility in France before 1789 was far from being a homogeneous class. 'Au lieu d'une noblesse,' wrote Talleyrand in his memoirs (I, 117-18), 'il y en avait sept ou huit: une d'épée et une de robe, une de cour et une de province, une ancienne et une nouvelle, une haute et une petite.' Over against the relatively small number of descendants of the old feudal families, the *noblesse d'épée*, came all manner of nobles of more recent origin, the sons, grandsons and great-grandsons of well-to-do bourgeois. There was the *noblesse de robe*, which owed its rank to the purchase of official posts in the law courts and in the higher civil service. There was the *noblesse de cloche* whose members had acquired noble rank by purchasing posts in the town councils. There were the *anoblis*, men who had purchased *lettres de noblesse* which raised them up from the middle classes into the lower ranks of the aristocracy. The situation was further complicated by the process of intermarriage which had long been going on between all the different sections of the nobility; the members of the old *noblesse d'épée* had long married into the families not only of the less ancient *noblesse de robe*, but also of the wealthy tax-farmers who had even more recently secured noble rank.

Moreover, there was not only the obvious difference between the older nobility and the members of their caste of more or less recent noble origins. There was also the gap, within the more or less exclusive families of the nobility, between a *duc et pair* and a mere *comte* or *marquis*, though very often the latter might belong to older and more illustrious families. There were also great differences in wealth between families of more or less ancient noble rank; the descendants of a once great noble family might vegetate in their half-ruined château in the depths of the provinces while more recent and less illustrious families shone at court. There was a great gulf between the poor provincial *hobereau*, often left without any land and subsisting as best he could on what feudal dues remained to him, little different except for his pride in rank from the peasants in whose midst he lived, and the wealthy nobleman with a mansion in Paris and the entrée at court. The different categories of the old feudal nobility which still survived before 1789 are well described by the Marquis de Bouillé:

> Il y avait en France à peu près 80,000 familles nobles . . . Dans cette nombreuse noblesse il existait environ mille familles dont l'origine se perdait dans les temps reculés de la monarchie. Parmi celles-ci on en voyait à peine deux ou trois cents qui avaient échappé à la misère et à l'infortune. On remarquait encore quelques grands noms à la cour qui rappelaient le souvenir des grands personnages qui les avaient illustrés, mais qui, trop souvent, étaient avilis par les vices de ceux qui en avaient hérité. On voyait quelques familles, dans les provinces, dont l'existence et la considération avaient surnagé, en conservant le patrimoine de leurs pères, par des alliances avec des familles plébéiennes. Le reste de cette ancienne noblesse languissait dans la pauvreté, et ressemblait à ces chênes antiques mutilés par le temps, dont il ne reste que le tronc dépouillé. (*Mémoires*, p. 121)

The right to be presented at court was confined to a small number of noble families, who might or might not be prosperous. Chateaubriand's family belonged to the latter category, but in 1787 his elder brother insisted that he should be presented:

> Le jour fatal arriva; il fallut partir pour Versailles plus mort que vif. Mon frère m'y conduisit la veille de ma présentation et me mena chez le maréchal de Duras,[1] galant homme dont l'esprit était si commun qu'il réfléchissait quelque chose de bourgeois par ses belles manières; ce bon maréchal me fit pourtant une peur horrible.
> Le lendemain matin je me rendis seul au château.... Lorsqu'on

---

[1] *Premier gentilhomme de la chambre.*

annonça le lever du roi, les personnes non présentées se retirèrent; je sentis un mouvement de vanité; je n'étais pas fier de rester, j'aurais été humilié de sortir. La chambre à coucher du roi s'ouvrit; je vis le roi, selon l'usage, achever sa toilette, c'est-à-dire prendre son chapeau de la main du premier gentilhomme de service. Le roi s'avança allant à la messe; je m'inclinai; le maréchal de Duras me nomma: 'Sire, le chevalier de Chateaubriand'. Le roi me regarda, me rendit mon salut, hésita, eut l'air de vouloir m'adresser la parole. . . . Le roi, plus embarrassé que moi, ne trouvant rien à me dire, passa outre. Vanité des destinées humaines! ce souverain que je voyais pour la première fois, ce monarque si puissant était Louis XVI à six ans de son échafaud! . . . (*Mémoires d'outre-tombe*, I, 203-5)

It can thus be seen that among the persons who enjoyed noble rank—a quite considerable number since whereas in England only actual peers and peeresses are noble, their children being legally commoners, in France all members of titled families were numbered among the nobility—there were the most striking differences both in wealth and social standing. It is difficult to generalize about a class which included such varied social types as the great nobleman, deriving a large income from the rents and feudal dues of his estates and from favours picked up at Versailles; the well-to-do member of the *noblesse de robe* with his official post, inherited from father or uncle, and large estates and other investments; and the miserably poor provincial *hobereau* in his tumble-down château.

The old *noblesse d'épée* had declined in the previous century or so in both economic and political power. Even the minority which continued to draw a substantial income from landed property, in both rents and feudal dues, was often in a sorry financial plight, as it lived beyond its income, was burdened by debts and interest payments, and sometimes became involved in scandalous bankruptcies. Frequently such noble families had been able to keep themselves afloat by intermarriage with the newer *noblesse de robe* and especially with the wealthy class of tax-farmers and bankers. Yet, as in the age of Louis XIV, they depended to a considerable extent on the pensions and other favours which they could wring from the King and his ministers.

Comme les Negres rament de bout

Commerce des Esclaves

18 Le Commerce des Esclaves
à la Martinique

19 Nancy, Grille de la Place
Stanislas

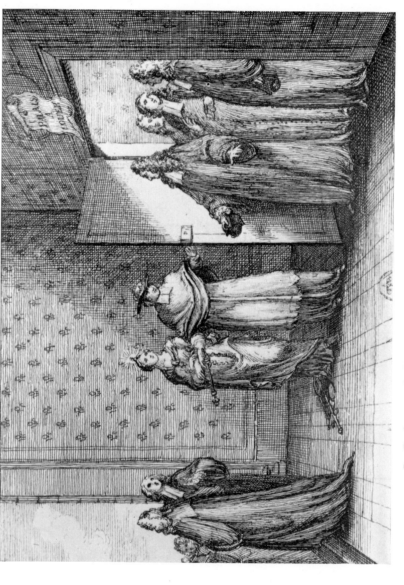

20  Le Parlement de Paris opprimé, exilé, dans les fers (September 1732)

'Un grand seigneur', wrote Montesquieu in the *Lettres persanes*, 'est un homme qui voit le roi, qui parle aux ministres, qui a des ancêtres, des dettes et des pensions. S'il peut, avec cela, cacher son oisiveté par un air empressé, ou par un feint attachement pour les plaisirs, il croit être le plus heureux de tous les hommes' (p. 226).

In his *Compte rendu au roi* (1781) Necker speaks in scathing terms of the way in which the court nobility battened on the Treasury, looking upon it as the providence which should solve all its financial problems, and, not content with drawing large sums in pensions and gifts, even expecting to be given a commission in the financial operations of the government:

> Des mélanges d'état par des alliances, l'accroissement du luxe, le prix qu'il oblige de mettre à la fortune, enfin, l'habitude, ce grand maître de toutes choses, avaient fait des grâces qui peuvent émaner du trône la ressource générale; acquisitions de charges, projets de mariages et d'éducations, pertes imprévues, espérances avortées, tous ces événements étaient devenus des occasions de recourir à la munificence du souverain; on eût dit que le trésor royal devait tout concilier, tout aplanir, tout réparer; et comme la voie des pensions, quoique poussée à l'extrême, ne pouvait ni satisfaire les prétentions, ni satisfaire assez la cupidité honteuse, l'on avait imaginé d'autres tournures, et l'on en eût inventé chaque jour: les intérêts dans les fermes, dans les régies, dans les étapes, dans beaucoup de places de finance, dans les pourvoiries, dans les marchés de toute espèce, et jusque dans les fournitures d'hôpitaux, tout était bon, tout était devenu digne de l'attention des personnes souvent les plus éloignées par leur état de semblables affaires. (pp. 28-9)

Such avidity for money rewards of all kinds is explained by the often desperate financial straits to which an extravagant mode of living drove noblemen. Some thirty years earlier the Marquis d'Argenson had written in his journal:

> Observons qu'à mesure que la noblesse devient plus pauvre en revenus, elle augmente en magnificence de luxe, tables, maisons, ameublement, boîtes et maîtresses: la dépense ancienne et ordinaire, quand on s'y tient, déshonore aujourd'hui. (VIII, 278)

Some insight into the extravagance of the court nobility is given by the accounts of a wealthy family with large estates in Burgundy. In 1763 the total property of the head of the family, who was military governor of the province, was valued at 1,239,953 *l*. 3s. 7d.—a tidy sum. But the debts came to 1,287,456 *l*. 5s. 6d. In 1790 the annual income of the then duke came to 231,039 *l*., but his expenditure was 245,119 *l*. Even large incomes could not suffice for the luxurious mode of living which kept such noble families constantly in debt. Some idea of the way the great nobles lived in their Paris mansions is given in the chapter 'Fournisseurs' in Mercier's *Tableau de Paris*:

> On ne voit qu'à Paris de ces intrépides *fournisseurs* qui avancent pendant des années entières le pain, la viande, le vin, les meubles, l'épicerie, l'apothicairerie, à M. le Marquis, à M. le Comte, à M. le Duc. C'est le privilège de la noblesse. On ne prêterait pas de même au bourgeois; on le presserait; mais on attend, lorsqu'il s'agit d'un homme titré.
>
> Telle maison noble doit au boucher six années de fournitures, à l'épicier cinq, au boulanger quatre; les domestiques eux-mêmes font crédit de leurs gages, tandis que toute maison roturière solde au bout de chaque année. . . .
>
> Quand les fournisseurs, impatients d'attendre, sollicitent enfin leur payement, l'intendant vient au lever de M. le Duc et lui dit: Monseigneur, votre maître-d'hôtel se plaint que le boucher ne veut plus fournir de viande, parce qu'il y a trois ans qu'il n'a reçu un sol; votre cocher dit que vous n'avez qu'une seule voiture en état de servir, et que le charron ne veut plus avoir l'honneur de votre pratique, si vous ne lui donnez un accompte de dix mille francs; le marchand de vin refuse de remplir votre cave, le tailleur de vous donner des habits. . . . *Les impertinents!* s'écrie le maître, *qu'on aille chez d'autres. Je leur retire ma protection.*
>
> Il trouve d'autres fournisseurs, quoique les premiers n'aient pas été payés. Le soir il risque cinq cents louis d'or au jeu; et s'il en perd cinq cents autres, il les paye le lendemain. Un créancier de cartes l'emporte toujours sur un créancier de pain ou de viande. (IV, 126-7)

How the extravagant mode of living of many members of the court nobility led them into debt is well illustrated by a courtier's pun. At a court reception in 1782 'le roi remarqua le marquis de G—— comme ayant l'habit le plus riche et le plus élégant; il l'en complimenta. Ce seigneur, fort endetté, lui répondit avec un sérieux comique: 'Sire, cela se doit!' (Mme d'Oberkirch, *Mémoires*, I, 247).

The army remained *the* career for a member of the *noblesse d'épée*. Although a minority of wealthy nobles sought to increase their income either by introducing agricultural improvements on their estates or by investing capital in new industrial undertakings, trade—even wholesale trade—was still regarded as beneath the dignity of a nobleman, who feared above all to 'déroger.' Since the seventeenth century when the royal policy had been to attract all noblemen of importance to the court, there remained for the member of the old noble family under an absolute monarchy only the choice, as Mirabeau scornfully put it, between 'porter les armes ou valeter à la cour' (*Mémoires*, I, 30).

Yet for the nobles who sought a career in the army, there was nothing approaching equality of opportunity, since the scales were heavily weighted in favour of the courtier. The contrast between the *noblesse de cour* and the provincial *hobereau* is well brought out in the following passage:

Les provinces différentes du royaume sont remplies d'une infinité de noblesse pauvre chargée d'enfants que les pères et mères n'ont pas le moyen de faire élever dans une éducation convenable, encore moins de les faire entrer au service. Les enfants de cette noblesse passent leur jeunesse avec des paysans dans l'ignorance et dans la rusticité, servent le plus souvent à l'exploitation de leurs biens, et ne diffèrent au vrai des paysans que parce qu'ils portent une épée et se disent gentilshommes; ce sont des sujets perdus pour l'État.

D'un autre côté la noblesse riche qui habite Paris, les grandes villes ou la cour mettent leurs enfants au collège, de là à l'académie pour monter à cheval et à faire des armes, ensuite mousquetaire, capitaine de cavalerie, et les plus en crédit ont à dix-huit ou vingt ans un régiment sans avoir aucune pratique du militaire. Ils passent leur jeunesse dans le luxe, les plaisirs, et la débauche auprès des femmes; ils ont plus de politesse et d'éducation, mais ils n'ont aucune des sciences nécessaires, point de détails, beaucoup de valeur pour se battre, mais peu capables de commander;

c'est ce qui fait que nous avons si peu de bons généraux et même de bons officiers généraux. (Barbier, *Chronique de la Régence*, V, 14-15)

This was written in 1751, before the disasters of the Seven Years War had provided still further evidence of the sorry effects of the system of recruiting and training army officers. A successful general could retrieve his fortunes out of the pensions and other favours granted him by the court. When the Duc de Croÿ lost his father-in-law in 1750, he lists the considerable spoils to be divided up among the courtiers: 'Le duc d'Harcourt était maréchal de France (8,000 livres), capitaine des Gardes (36,000), gouverneur de Sedan (20,000), cordon bleu (3,000), et avait 8,000 livres de pension, ce qui lui faisait 71,000 livres de rente, de bienfaits du roi' (*Journal inédit*, I, 138). But for many officers the extravagance of army life meant only debts and financial ruin. Some idea of the expensive way in which the nobles set out for the wars is given in the following passage from Barbier, written in 1733 at the beginning of the War of the Polish Succession:

> On se pique assez pour avoir des équipages magnifiques. Le duc de Richelieu, . . . qui n'est pas encore officier général a, à ce qu'on dit, soixante-douze mulets, trente chevaux pour lui, grand nombre de valets, et il a fait faire des tentes sur le modèle de celles du roi. La guerre n'est que superficielle; il peut y avoir de la politique à laisser faire cette dépense aux seigneurs, ce qui les abaisse toujours et les met dans la dépendance du gouvernement; mais si la guerre est sérieuse, il paraîtrait plus sage d'empêcher cette émulation, de prescrire une façon de vivre moins délicate et moins somptueuse. Les officiers généraux, qui sont riches, mènent des aides de cuisine et des aides d'office, comme si c'était pour célébrer quelque fête. Et ceux qui ne sont pas également riches se ruinent et se mettent hors d'état de soutenir plusieurs campagnes. (II, 428-9)

The *noblesse d'épée* represented only a small minority among the nobility as a whole. For generations fresh blood had been admitted to the order as wealthy bourgeois bought themselves titles or acquired hereditary noble rank by the purchase of official posts. In 1784 Necker listed some 4,000 posts which

conferred 'la noblesse héréditaire, soit dès l'instant qu'on en est revêtu, soit à la seconde ou à la troisième génération, soit au bout d'un certain nombre d'années de possession':

> 80 charges de maîtres des requêtes.[1]
>
> 1000 charges environ dans les Parlements, en retranchant celles qui sont possédées par les conseillers-clercs.[2]
>
> 900 charges environ dans les Chambres des comptes et les Cours des aides.[3]
>
> 70 dans le Grand Conseil.
>
> 30 dans la Cour des monnaies.
>
> 20 au Conseil provincial d'Artois.
>
> 80 au Châtelet de Paris.
>
> 740 dans les bureaux des finances.[4]
>
> 50 charges de grands baillis, sénéchaux, gouverneurs et lieutenants généraux d'épée.
>
> 900 charges de secrétaires du roi.
>
> Enfin on peut fixer à 200 environ les offices en commission au parlement de Nancy et au Conseil souverain d'Alsace, plusieurs charges tenant au second ordre au Conseil et à la Chancellerie, celles aux tribunaux de la table de marbre, et quelques autres encore.

A great many of these official posts, as Necker goes on to point out, no longer in fact conferred hereditary nobility as many of the highest law-courts were reluctant to admit any but nobles to their ranks:

> Il faut observer cependant qu'entre ces différentes charges il en est un grand nombre qui, par le fait, ne deviennent pas une source de nouveaux nobles, car depuis que le royaume en est rempli, plusieurs cours souveraines n'admettent que difficilement dans leurs compagnies les familles bourgeoises qui n'ont pas encore acquis cette petite illustration. (*De l'Administration des finances*, III, 115-16)

In the eighteenth century, wealthy bourgeois more frequently rose into the nobility by acquiring posts which gave them the high-sounding title of *Secrétaires du roi*; these were in fact pure sinecures which none the less conferred hereditary nobility as

---

[1] Judges and administrators, from whose ranks most *Intendants* were chosen.
[2] Because the holders of these posts were clergymen.
[3] See p. 120.
[4] Boards of civil servants which dealt with matters of taxation.

well as many other privileges upon their holders. Mercier does not fail to introduce a portrait of the *Secrétaire du roi* into his *Tableau de Paris*:

> Le nouvel ennobli qui vient d'acheter cette charge, tout étonné de sa régénération, est presque honteux d'avoir été roturier. Il s'éloigne de toutes ses forces de la classe dont il sort. Il a si peur qu'on ne se souvienne de sa roture décédée qu'il emploie ses richesses à capter la bienveillance des hommes nobles. Il aime à se frotter contre eux; on dirait du fer qui cherche à s'imprégner de l'aimant.
>
> Il ne sort pas du nouveau tourbillon où il est entré; il se persuade bientôt qu'il y a toujours vécu. Ayant passé la ligne de démarcation, il ne regarde plus en arrière qu'avec effroi, et sa conduite est constamment en garde contre un roturier.
>
> Oh, comme il voudrait faire boire de l'eau du fleuve Léthé à tous ceux qui l'environnent! Comment se rappeler que l'on tenait l'aune, le marteau il y a six mois; que l'on courait tout crotté négocier aux quatre coins de la ville rescriptions, billets des fermes, actions des Indes?
>
> Le fils d'un secrétaire du roi sera plus noble que son père; aussi l'acheteur de la charge n'envisage-t-il qu'avec un certain respect ce fils qui, épurant la race, devient la tige d'une famille de gentilshommes. Son imagination ravie se prosterne devant ses petits-fils, qui seront décorés de titres et n'auront rien de commun avec la souche originelle. (VII, 180)

All these nobles—whether they belonged to the *noblesse d'épée* or the *noblesse de robe*, or were new *anoblis*, often drawn from the ranks of the tax-farmers—were inextricably mingled in the course of the eighteenth century by intermarriage. In his journal for 1752, Barbier gives a list of recent marriages based on considerations of wealth:

> Il y a eu des mariages de conséquence dont le bien a été le principe. M. le vicomte de Rohan-Chabot, maréchal de camp, a épousé mademoiselle de Vervins, fille d'un conseiller au Parlement, lequel était fils de M. de Bonnevie, fermier général; et M. Bonnevie de Vervins avait épousé la fille de M. Moreau de Nassigny, président des requêtes du Palais, lequel est fils d'un marchand de drap, rue Saint-Denis; il a eu un fils maître des requêtes et intendant de province, qu'on nomme Moreau de

Beaumont, lequel a épousé une fille de M. de La Rivière, fermier général. M. Parat de Montgeron, receveur général des finances, d'une très basse origine, vient de marier sa fille à un M. le chevalier de Breteuil, officier de gendarmerie. (*Chronique de la Régence*. V, 153-4)

The members of the *noblesse de robe*, who belonged to families which one, two or more generations back had been of bourgeois stock, had acquired or inherited posts in which a good deal of capital was invested. They also held positions of power in the country. The *maîtres des requêtes* provided many future ministers and even more *Intendants* who, as the representatives of the central government in the provinces, dominated the whole life of the *généralité* under their control. When the Scottish adventurer John Law fled the country in 1720, after the collapse of his famous System, he was held up at Valenciennes by the *Intendant* who at that moment was the young Marquis d'Argenson:

Ce fut alors que j'eus avec lui une conversation assez longue, dont voici ce que j'ai retenu de plus digne de remarque. Law me dit: 'Monsieur, jamais je n'aurais cru ce que j'ai vu pendant que j'ai administré les finances. Sachez que ce royaume de France est gouverné par trente intendants. Vous n'avez ni parlements, ni comités, ni États, ni gouverneurs. J'ajouterai presque ni rois, ni ministres; ce sont trente maîtres des requêtes, commis aux provinces, de qui dépend le bonheur ou le malheur de ces provinces, leur abondance ou leur stérilité, etc.' (*Journal*, I, 43 n. 2)

In addition to the high civil servants, who served the central government in the councils at Versailles or scattered over the provinces in the different *intendances*, the *noblesse de robe* contained another important section of the community—the judges of the Parlements and the other *cours souvéraines*.

Among the thirteen Parlements of France in 1789,[1] that of Paris stood out above all others as the area of its jurisdiction included nearly half of the kingdom. The members of these

---

[1] Paris (founded in 1302), Toulouse (1443), Grenoble (1451), Bordeaux (1462), Dijon (1476), Rouen (1499), Aix-en-Provence (1501), Rennes (1553), Pau (1620), Metz (1633), Besançon (1674), Douai (1686), Nancy (1775).

courts (Necker estimated their number at about a thousand) not only possessed important judicial functions; they also had a say in the administration of the country and, as we shall see, wielded considerable political power. From the Regency of Philippe d'Orléans down to the Revolution, they used this power to limit the authority of the Crown and ultimately destroyed not only absolutism, but themselves. Of similar social standing were the judges of the other so-called *cours souveraines*: the Chambre des Comptes of Paris and various provincial towns, charged with the supervision of the royal finances and the king's domain; the Cour des Aides of Paris and three other towns in the provinces, which mainly heard appeals in cases arising out of the collection of indirect taxes; the Cour des Monnaies which tried cases of counterfeiting; and the Grand Conseil which dealt with cases which the King had chosen to take out of the hands of the other courts. Posts in these courts were either acquired by purchase or, more frequently in our period, were inherited from a father or uncle. Their holders had large amounts of capital locked up in their official posts, and often other money invested in *rentes* and various government securities; many of them were big landowners and also, like the old nobility, drew feudal dues from the peasants on their estates. The various branches of the nobility still owned a high proportion of the land, although the amount varied from region to region, from somewhere near half down to less than 10 per cent. Its holdings appear to have been largest in the west of France, but they were also very considerable around the larger towns like Paris, Toulouse or Dijon, where there was a Parlement.

If since the end of the Middle Ages a great many old noble families had lost a considerable part of their landed property, the new men from the towns had based their new noble rank on a substantial holding in land, especially in the sixteenth century. It was they above all who reconstituted and even increased, between the fifteenth century and the Revolution, the nobility's share of the land. To this task and to the allied task of exploiting to the full the income from feudal dues with which their estates furnished them, they brought the methodical attitude of business men, determined to squeeze every penny out of their investment. If they seized every opportunity to increase the land under their direct control which they could cultivate themselves or more frequently let out to *métayers* or tenant-farmers, they also were mainly responsible for the onslaught on the common lands and such communal grazing rights as *la vaine pâture* which took place in the eighteenth century. They were also behind the *réaction seigneuriale*—the attempt to derive from feudal dues every penny that they could be made to yield.

The long-term price movements of agricultural products favoured the large landowner, who saw his rents rise to keep pace with the general rise in prices and his feudal dues, especially those levied in kind, swollen by the same process. This was especially the case in the second half of the century when prices rose more steeply—both as a general trend and in periods of grain shortage. The depression of the last decade or so of the Ancien Régime when the burden of high rents and of feudal dues bore heavily on the peasantry could scarcely be expected to add to the popularity of noble landowners.

Another cause of the nobility's unpopularity lay in the privileges which it enjoyed in the matter of taxation. If there were limits to their exemption from the *taille*,[1] a tax which was regarded essentially as a plebeian one, such privileges as the nobles possessed 'établissaient une distinction', wrote Talleyrand, 'dans laquelle la classe plébéienne voyait moins une faveur pour les nobles, qu'une injure pour elle' (*Mémoires*, I, 119). It was also notorious that they generally managed to avoid paying anything like their fair share of the other direct taxes, the *capitation* and *vingtième*. Take, for instance, what Turgot has to say about the *capitation*, a tax designed to fall on all classes of society, according to their wealth, and to exempt only the very poor:

> La capitation même, qu'on a eu l'intention de faire supporter à tous et pour laquelle la noblesse n'a point de privilège de droit, tombe dans le fait presque uniquement sur les taillables. . . .
> Si l'on compare la capitation que paye un gentilhomme avec

---

[1] See pp. 51-3.

celle que paye un paysan au marc la livre de la taille,[1] on verra
que le gentilhomme est taxé dans une proportion si différente
qu'elle tient lieu dans le fait d'un vrai privilège sur une imposition
que la loi a cependant voulu rendre commune à tous les sujets
du roi. (*Œuvres*, II, 611)

The same thing happened with the *vingtièmes*; the nobles managed to avoid paying anything like their fair share, and the
Parlements, whose members were naturally zealous in defence
of the privileges, real or usurped, of the aristocracy, successfully
resisted the attempts of various *contrôleurs généraux* to secure a
fairer assessment of the tax. The nobles were, of course, also
exempt from the hated *corveé*, and when Turgot attempted, in
1776, to replace it by a small tax on all landowners, noble or
otherwise, he met with bitter resistance from the privileged
orders. The Paris Parlement fought desperately—and in the
end successfully—to preserve this privilege. Most indirect taxes
had to be paid by nobles and *roturiers* alike; yet even here many
nobles enjoyed important exemptions or reductions.

The privileges of the nobility before 1789 were not limited to
matters of taxation. Their hated *droit de chasse* gave them a
monopoly of the favourite sport of the age. There was no such
thing as equality before the law; in civil cases the nobleman
enjoyed various privileges, and if accused of a crime, he had
the right to be tried by a special court. If found guilty, he could
be neither hanged nor whipped, since such degrading punish-
ments were reserved for the *roturier*. In the still profoundly
aristocratic society of eighteenth century France there was a
gulf between the aristocracy and the rest of the community.
The unpopularity of the nobles on the eve of the Revolution is
brought out in a bitter passage in Mercier's *Tableau de Paris*:

Les châteaux hérissent nos provinces, englobent une partie des
grandes possessions, ont des droits abusifs de chasse, de pêche,
de coupe de bois; et ces châteaux recèlent encore de ces fiers
gentilshommes qui se séparent réellement de l'espèce humaine,
qui joignent des impôts particuliers à ceux du monarque, et qui
oppriment trop facilement le paysan pauvre et abattu, s'ils ont
perdu le privilège de le tuer en mettant dix écus sur sa fosse.

[1] Proportionally to the amount of *taille* which he had to pay.

L'autre portion de la noblesse environne le trône, les mains sans cesse ouvertes pour mendier éternellement des pensions et des places. Elle veut tout pour elle, dignités, emplois, préférences exclusives; elle ne permet aux roturiers ni élévation ni récompense, quels que soient leur génie et les services rendus à la patrie; elle leur défend de servir sur terre, de servir sur mer; puis elle veut des évêchés, des abbayes, des bénéfices, etc., pour tout ce qui ne veut pas servir. (VIII, 154)

We have already come across the paradox that, at the approach of the Revolution which was to destroy for ever its whole position in society, the French nobility was increasing its hold on all the important posts in the state. Saint-Simon could no longer have applied to the governments of France under Louis XV and Louis XVI, as he had done to that of Louis XIV, the contemptuous description of 'règne de vile bourgeoisie'. Gone were the days when bourgeois like Colbert or Louvois could rise up into the highest offices in the state. It was not merely that in the eighteenth century the great nobles occupied a place among the King's ministers which Louis XIV had deliberately denied them; one thinks, for instance, of the long years of power enjoyed by the Duc de Choiseul towards the end of the reign of Louis XV. Ministers and secretaries of state continued to be drawn largely from the ranks of the upper civil servants—the *conseillers d'état* and *maîtres des requêtes*; but such administrators, originally with rare exceptions of bourgeois origins, belonged to families which had risen several generations back into the aristocracy. To become a high civil servant of the status of a *maître des requêtes* noble birth was by the second half of the century practically essential. Under Louis XVI all the *Intendants* were noblemen, although their titles did not necessarily go far back; if a few belonged to the old feudal nobility, most of them came from families ennobled in the previous hundred to a hundred and fifty years. The majority of them belonged to families which had enjoyed noble rank for at least four generations. Thus government and administration were monopolized by the aristocracy.

Again in the Parlements and other *cours souveraines*, although, almost without exception, the judges were originally of bourgeois stock, most posts had been kept in the same family for several generations, and the family was by the eighteenth century of respectable nobility. As the century wore on, the different Parlements did their best to keep out bourgeois candidates, and although for various reasons they did not always succeed in doing so, the tendency was all in the direction of making it difficult for any but sons of noblemen to be admitted. We have already seen how all the high posts in the Church were monopolized by the nobility in eighteenth century France.

If the government, the high civil service, the law courts and the Church were by now all virtually closed to the bourgeois, however talented or rich, a similar effort was made in 1781— only eight years before the Revolution—to keep the aristocratic career *par excellence*, the army, a preserve of the aristocracy, above all of the court nobility. A royal decree required that in future candidates for commissions should present certificates proving that they possessed four generations of noble birth. While this decree could be got round, it did have the effect either of keeping out of the army altogether a number of *roturiers* or else preventing them from rising to the rank of officer; this was the fate of several great generals of the Revolutionary and Napoleonic wars. The decree was certainly badly received by the general public. Take, for instance, the observations of a great nobleman like Talleyrand on its repercussions:

> Une foule d'écrits s'élevèrent contre une disposition qui fermait à tout ce qui n'était pas noble une carrière que Fabert, que Chevert, que Catinat et d'autres plébéiens comme eux avaient parcourue avec gloire.
> Les professions lucratives étant interdites à la noblesse pauvre, on avait cru devoir lui ménager ce dédommagement. On n'avait vu que ce côté de la question. Mais cette mesure, substituant évidemment la naissance au mérite personnel dans ce qui était le domaine propre du mérite, choquait et la raison et l'opinion. Car, pour dédommager les nobles d'avoir perdu les avantages que la classe plébéienne regardait déjà comme un préjugé humiliant pour elle, on faisait à cette dernière une injustice et un affront.
> (*Mémoires*, I, 120-1)

Inequality before the law and the quasi-monopoly of the

highest posts in the state enjoyed by the nobility before 1789 receive a laconic condemnation in article 6 of the *Déclaration des droits de l'homme*; the law, it declares,

> ... doit être la même pour tous, soit qu'elle protège, soit qu'elle punisse. Tous les citoyens étant égaux à ses yeux, sont également admissibles à toutes dignités, places et emplois publics, selon leur capacité et sans autre distinction que celles de leurs vertus et de leurs talents.

Similar treatment is meted out to the fiscal privileges of the nobility and clergy in article 13:

> Pour l'entretien de la force publique, et pour les dépenses d'administration, une contribution commune est indispensable: elle doit être également répartie entre tous les citoyens, en raison de leurs facultés.

Today such principles seem to us self-evident; yet it required a revolution to establish them in France.

One of the paradoxes of eighteenth century French history is that the Revolution which was to sweep away the privileges of the nobility and to destroy its political power was largely precipitated by that very section of the community. When it actually broke out in 1789, the middle classes and, behind them, the peasants were to destroy the power and privileges of the aristocracy; the long-term causes of the Revolution lay both in the unsatisfactory conditions on the land and especially in the obstacles—economic, social and political—which the Ancien Régime presented to the rise of the middle classes, enriched by the expansion of trade and industry. Yet, in the aristocratic society which existed in France down to 1789, it was the privileged orders and particularly the nobility which alone could challenge the power of the Crown and seek to impose limits on the absolute monarchy established by Louis XIV. The revival of the nobility as a political force after its eclipse in the seventeenth century and its long struggle against the monarchy, both to maintain its privileges and to achieve a dominant position in the state, are striking features of the reigns of Louis XV and Louis XVI—of the whole period between the death of the *Roi Soleil* and the fall of the Bastille.

Richelieu, Mazarin and Louis XIV had destroyed the power of the old feudal nobility. After the collapse of the Fronde in 1653 the great nobles were to become domesticated, to be kept engaged in harmless occupations under the eye of their master, first in Paris and then at Versailles. Stern economic necessity contributed to their obedience, since it was only by keeping themselves under the King's eye at Versailles that they could obtain the pensions and other favours which allowed them to keep up a luxurious standard of living. The attractions of the court were such that to be exiled to his estates in the provinces was an almost unbearable punishment for a nobleman; and so it continued to be to the end of the Ancien Régime. In the 1750s, when his son-in-law was allowed to return to Paris from his exile but not to appear before Louis XV, d'Argenson wrote in his journal: 'La privation de la vision intuitive[1] du roi est une peine quasi capitale pour le courtisan. Il faut que la famille sollicite tout de nouveau' (VII, 240).

Under Louis XIV the great nobleman was confined to the career of soldier or courtier. He was deliberately excluded from all part in the central government; the King preferred bourgeois ministers who owed everything to him. On his estates the nobleman was under the eye of the *Intendant*, the representative of the central government; he had no part to play in local affairs. Even in those provinces where there were still provincial estates (*pays d'états*), his functions were purely decorative, as resistance to the will of Louis XIV was unthinkable. Elsewhere in France everything was controlled by the *Intendant* and his agents, the *subdélégués*.

Similar obedience was demanded from the *noblesse de robe* in the Parlements. After throwing their weight about in the Fronde, they were reduced to submission by Louis XIV. Traditionally the Parlements possessed the right to make remonstrances (the famous *droit de remontrance*) before registering royal edicts and giving them force of law. In the reigns of Louis XV and Louis XVI they were to hold up new taxes or necessary reforms by refusing to register the necessary edicts,

---

[1] 'Vision béatifique, dite aussi vision intuitive et faciale, vue de Dieu face à face par les justes aussitôt après la mort' (Littré).

or by the threat of a refusal, and in the long run their actions had a most crippling effect on the power of the Crown. However, under a monarch as absolute as Louis XIV, registration was reduced to a mere formality; he insisted that they must register his edicts first and produce their remonstrances afterwards, which meant in effect that the Parlements were stripped of all political power.

Long before Louis XIV disappeared from the scene, there had been signs of growing restlessness among the nobility. M. le duc de Saint-Simon, for instance, was disgruntled with the absolutism of Louis XIV which had stripped the nobility, and particularly its most exalted members, the *ducs et pairs*, of all power in the state. His ideal was a government in which the caste to which he belonged—its members were, he declared, 'les conseillers nés et naturels du roi et de l'état'—would play a leading part and from which the bourgeois ministers and secretaries of state of Louis XIV would be excluded in favour of the old nobility. There was Fénelon, a *grand seigneur* and archbishop, whom people expected to be the real ruler of France when at last his pupil, the Duc de Bourgogne, succeeded to the throne; he and the group of great nobles with whom he was in contact were also opposed to absolutism because they sought above all to restore the power of the old feudal nobility.

Another nobleman whose writings, when they saw the light of day after his death in 1722, were to exercise a considerable influence was Henri de Boulainvilliers. Delving back into the distant past of France, he worked out the theory that the members of the *noblesse d'épée* were the descendants of the Franks who had conquered Gaul, and that the members of the *tiers état* (in which he included those families which had been ennobled by the King) were the descendants of the conquered Gauls. On this theory he based the claim of the nobles both to their privileges and to the political power which had been wrested from them through the centuries by the monarchy. He was, of course, furiously opposed to absolutism and denounced the high priest of the doctrine of the Divine Right of Kings, Bossuet, in indignant terms. For the *Intendants*, the agents of the hated absolute monarchy whom he holds largely responsible for the degradation of the nobility, he has nothing but bitter scorn:

> La noblesse voyait en général qu'elle allait être éclairée de trop près; . . . mais cette même noblesse ne voyait pas qu'elle allait être dégradée, jusqu'au point d'être réduite à prouver son état devant ces juges nouveaux, qu'elle allait perdre son autorité naturelle sur ses propres sujets jusqu'au point d'être non pas confondue avec eux (car on a bien voulu que la distinction demeurât), mais tellement avilie que les paysans, lesquels originairement ne sont libres et propriétaires de leurs biens que par la grâce des seigneurs, auraient à l'avenir le droit d'imposer les nobles à la taille, eux et leurs possessions, et qu'à jamais ils demeureraient exclus de leur droit naturel de diriger et de conduire cette populace aveuglée. (*État de la France*, I, 38-9)

The history of the reigns of Louis XV and Louis XVI is thus in part foreshadowed in the discontent with absolutism and the yearning for an aristocratic reaction which are clearly visible in the closing years of the despotic reign of the *Roi Soleil*.

In practice, in the three-quarters of a century which were to elapse between 1715 and the Revolution, the shrewdest blows directed against absolutism came not from the old *noblesse d'épée*, but from a section of the aristocracy which men like Saint-Simon, Fénelon and Boulainvilliers had all affected to despise as mere bourgeois upstarts—the judges of the Parlements. When they regained from the Regent in 1715 their right of remonstrance, they gradually made more and more devastating use of this weapon as the century wore on. The Parlements had been bourgeois in origin and had helped the Crown in its long struggle to subdue the feudal aristocracy; now in the eighteenth century they became aristocratic in outlook. Their members intermarried with the old *noblesse d'épée*; and they clung tenaciously to all the privileges which their more or less recently acquired noble rank conferred upon them. The French judiciary had been made independent of the Crown by the selling of official posts (*la vénalité des charges*). 'Elle avait été bourgeoise et royaliste', wrote Barnave, one of the chief spokesmen of the *tiers état* in 1789, 'elle devint noble, féodale, réfractaire.' The consequences of this change he sums up thus:

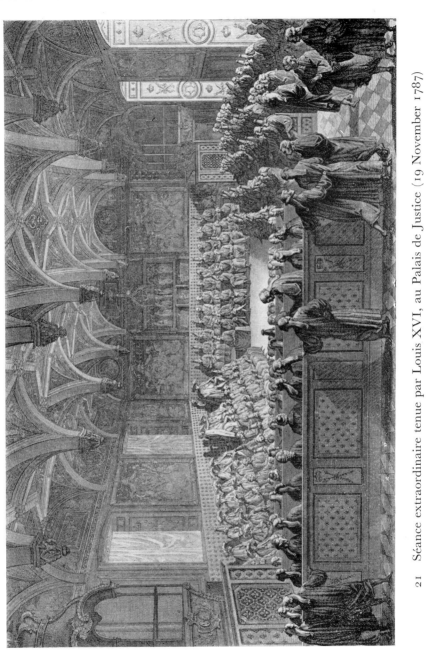

21 Séance extraordinaire tenue par Louis XVI, au Palais de Justice (19 November 1787)

22   *Ollivier*, Thé à l'anglaise chez la Princesse de Conti

Il en résulta une combinaison extrêmement défavorable au pouvoir, celle où l'ordre judiciaire est en opposition contre lui; car alors il a à combattre la force qui devrait le soutenir, et il est obligé d'y suppléer par des moyens irréguliers qui ont toujours plus de scandale que d'efficacité, et qui conduisent aux plus grands abus, les cassations d'arrêts, les tribunaux extraordinaires, les commissions, les lettres de cachet. (*Œuvres*, I, 78)

In their struggle against the Crown the Parlements were able to enlist the support of public opinion. Though their underlying aims—the maintenance of the privileges of the nobility and the exercise of political power in its interests—were thoroughly selfish, in the absence of the *États généraux* which had not met since 1614, they could claim to speak for the nation. The reactionary outlook of the *Parlementaires* is well brought out in a famous passage in which Mme de Staël characterizes the Paris Parlement, the most important of all the *cours souveraines*:

Aucun corps ne s'est jamais montré plus ardemment défenseur des anciens usages que le parlement de Paris; toute institution nouvelle lui paraissait un acte de rébellion, parce qu'en effet son existence ne pouvait être fondée sur les principes de la liberté politique. Des charges vénales, un corps judiciaire se prétendant en droit de consentir les impôts, et renonçant pourtant à ce droit quand les rois le commandaient; toutes ces contradictions, qui ne sauraient être que l'œuvre du hasard, n'admettaient point la discussion; aussi était-elle singulièrement suspecte aux membres de la magistrature française. Tous les réquisitoires contre la liberté de la presse partaient du Parlement de Paris; et s'il mettait des bornes au pouvoir actif des rois, il encourageait en revanche ce genre d'ignorance, en matière de gouvernement, qui, seul, favorise l'autorité absolue. (*Considérations sur les principaux événements de la Révolution française*, I, 173)

Yet such was their popularity, at least down to the year 1788, that in their struggle against the Crown the Parlements could mobilize behind them the great weight of public opinion.

If it was the Parlements who in the eighteenth century played the leading part in the defence of the interests of the nobility as a whole, it must not be imagined that the *noblesse d'épée* had no ambition to assume a more active political role.

With the development of what was derisively known as *anglo-manie*, interest grew in what was happening on this side of the Channel; French nobles cast envious eyes on the part played in national and local affairs by the English aristocracy and squires. If French noblemen were no longer, as under Louis XIV, entirely excluded from any part in the government, the great majority of courtiers could only compare their futile lives with the power enjoyed by English peers in the government of their country, in the House of Lords and as ministers, and by the English squires in the House of Commons and naturally too in the government. Again they were filled with frustration when, on their estates, they found themselves deprived of all say in local affairs unless they happened to live in a province like Brittany, which still had its Estates. There, it is true, the noblemen could use their power to preserve their considerable privileges in the matter of taxation and join with the Parlement at Rennes in resisting the power of the Crown and its agents in the province. But few provinces still had Estates, and nowhere else did the aristocracy assert itself so vigorously as in Brittany. Over the greater part of the country local affairs were entirely in the hands of the agents of the central government—the *Intendant* and his *subdélégués*.

The ambition of the provincial nobleman to take some part in local affairs was matched by the desire of the court nobility to play a role on a national level. The envy with which they looked at the role of the English nobles and gentry is well expressed in the memoirs of the Comte de Ségur:

Ce qui aiguillonnait encore notre vive impatience, c'était la comparaison de notre situation présente avec celle des Anglais. Montesquieu nous avait ouvert les yeux sur les avantages des institutions britanniques; les communications entre les deux peuples étaient devenues beaucoup plus fréquentes; la vie brillante, mais frivole, de notre noblesse, à la cour et à la ville, ne pouvait plus satisfaire notre amour-propre lorsque nous pensions à la dignité, à l'indépendance, à l'existence utile et importante d'un pair d'Angleterre, d'un membre de la Chambre des Communes, et à la liberté, aussi tranquille que fière, de tous les citoyens de la Grande-Bretagne. (*Mémoires*, I, 89)

It was such political ambitions among the aristocracy—a hatred of absolutism combined with a desire to play a part in national affairs and at the same time to preserve as far as possible the privileges of their order—that lay behind the aristocratic revolt at the end of the Ancien Régime.

Two strands are interwoven in the history of eighteenth century France. On the one hand, thanks to the growing importance of trade and industry, the middle classes continued their ascent and were assuming an ever more important part in the life of the nation. Gradually, but only very gradually—traditionally they were loyal supporters of absolutism—they were becoming dissatisfied with a political machine which showed itself increasingly inefficient and out of date, and hoping to see set up a new form of government in which they would have their share and which would allow them room for expansion. A similar hatred of absolutism underlay the struggle of the aristocracy, led by the Parlements, to impose limits on the power of the Crown. For the greater part of our period it was this aristocratic movement which held the centre of the stage; the middle classes and their desire for a new order only appear in clear and unmistakable fashion on the very eve of 1789. Up till then it was the aristocracy, headed by the Parlements, which led the struggle against absolutism.

In her *Considérations sur les principaux événements de la Révolution Française* Mme de Staël wrote:

> Il existe une lettre de Louis XV, adressée à la duchesse de Choiseul, dans laquelle il lui dit: 'J'ai eu bien de la peine à me tirer d'affaire avec les parlements, pendant mon règne; mais que mon petit-fils[1] y prenne garde, ils pourraient bien mettre sa couronne en danger'. En effet, il est aisé de voir, en suivant l'histoire du dix-huitième siècle, que ce sont les corps aristocratiques de France qui ont attaqué les premiers le pouvoir royal. (I, 43)

In the slow work of undermining absolutism which it carried on between 1715 and 1789, the French nobility had the support of the mass of the nation, which was becoming increasingly

---

[1] Louis XVI.

dissatisfied with the old order. It is possible to speculate on what might have happened if, when the crisis of the Revolution began in 1787, the privileged orders and the Third Estate had remained united; but such speculation is idle. By their refusal to help the monarchy out of its financial mess, the privileged orders forced the summoning of the *États généraux*; but now they had to face the Third Estate, which was not content to allow the first two orders either to maintain their privileges intact or to have the lion's share of political power. In the struggle which followed, the privileged orders succumbed to the power of the Third Estate. Mme de Staël sums up neatly the outcome of the struggle, when she writes of the role of the privileged orders in the critical years which began in 1787:

> Le parti des aristocrates, c'est-à-dire, les privilégiés, sont persuadés qu'un roi d'un caractère plus ferme aurait pu prévenir la révolution. Ils oublient qu'ils ont eux-mêmes commencé les premiers, et avec courage et raison, l'attaque contre le pouvoir royal . . . Doivent-ils se plaindre d'avoir été les plus forts contre le roi, et les plus faibles contre le peuple? Cela devait être ainsi. (*Considérations*, I, 46-7)

In the words of another contemporary, Barnave, it was the fate of the aristocracy of eighteenth century France to 'provoquer une révolution, dont elle est devenue la victime' (*Œuvres*, I, 84).

# CHAPTER IV

# THE REGENT AND FLEURY, 1715-1743

THE seventy-two years' reign of Louis XIV came to an end in September 1715. Louis XV, his great-grandson, was a delicate child of five, who had somehow survived the ravages of disease which had removed from the scene in the last years of the reign his grandfather, father and elder brother. The new king was also to enjoy a long reign—fifty-nine years—but not only did he require a regent until he attained his legal majority in 1723; he left power in the hands of his former tutor, Cardinal Fleury, until the latter's death in 1743. Only then did he at long last take (or claim to take) the reins of power into his own hands. For almost the first half of his reign he remained a more or less negligible figure on the political scene.

In 1715 power fell into the hands of Philippe, Duc d'Orléans, the nephew of the late king and first prince of the blood. Mistrusting his nephew, Louis XIV had so arranged things in his will that while he was to be head of the Conseil de Régence, he was left little power. However, the duke, urged on by his supporters, went in person to the Paris Parlement and invited it to quash the will and to give him full powers as Regent. To secure its support he had to offer a *quid pro quo*— the restoration of the right of making remonstrances which Louis XIV had so long denied them. Out of this concession was to come the long conflict between the Crown and the Parlements which was to rage until the Revolution and proved so damaging to the power and prestige of the monarchy.

The Regent was a man of considerable intelligence with a wide knowledge of politics, music, painting and chemistry (it was even whispered—though the accusation was quite unfounded—that he had poisoned those princes who stood between him and the throne and who had died with mysterious rapidity in the closing years of Louis XIV). In many ways he was an attractive character, especially in contrast to his uncle. Yet for all his undoubted gifts he was utterly lacking in moral sense; he was too absorbed in a life of debauchery to pursue a coherent policy which could solve the many problems which faced France in 1715. Throughout the Regency he and his circle led a wild life in his Paris home, the Palais Royal, where he lived surrounded by depraved noblemen ('ses roués' as he himself called them) and aristocratic ladies of equally low morals. Night after night the Palais Royal was the scene of scandalous parties. His early death at forty-nine was brought on by this sort of life.

It was more or less inevitable that effective power should gradually fall into other hands. Abbé Dubois, the son of a provincial doctor, had been the Regent's tutor and had continued to exercise a great influence on his pupil. A highly ambitious and none too scrupulous man, though he was not as black as Saint-Simon painted him, he began his ascent to power by exercising his considerable diplomatic talents, and by 1718 he had had himself appointed secretary of state for foreign affairs. In the five years which he still had to live he made himself more and more powerful both at home and abroad. Although he was of modest bourgeois origins and had never been actually ordained, he got himself appointed to the aristocratic see of Cambrai and succeeded in wangling a cardinal's hat, while in 1722 he became prime minister of France. Less than a year later, at the very height of his power, he died, only a few months before the Regent was struck down by apoplexy.

Though this period was far from being the only regency in French history, 'la régence', used on its own, is normally taken in France to apply to it; and the word is even used, as in 'des mœurs régence', to signify what Littré calls 'dignes des roueries galantes de la cour du régent'. Yet this period of French history is interesting for rather different reasons. It was a period of reaction against the iron rule of Louis XIV, an age of experiment and of violent change which is faithfully mirrored in the greatest literary work of the period, the *Lettres persanes* of the youthful Montesquieu, which appeared anonymously in 1721.

In persuading the Paris Parlement to quash the will of

Louis XIV, the Regent had promised not only to restore its right of remonstrance, but also to introduce important reforms in the machinery of government by setting up a series of councils to manage affairs. To the Parlement he declared

> qu'outre le conseil de régence où se rapporteraient toutes les affaires, il était nécessaire d'établir un conseil de guerre, un conseil de finance, un conseil de marine, un conseil pour les affaires étrangères et un conseil pour les affaires du dedans du royaume; qu'il jugeait même important de former un conseil de conscience . . . et qu'il espérait que la compagnie ne lui refuserait pas quelques-uns de ses magistrats qui, par leur capacité et leurs lumières, pussent y soutenir les droits et les libertés de l'Église Gallicane. (Flammermont, *Remontrances du Parlement de Paris*, I, 20)

In this form, the scheme was dressed up to appeal to the *noblesse de robe*, but its main appeal was to the great nobles. As a matter of deliberate policy, Louis XIV had excluded princes of the blood and great noblemen from all share in the government. Under him power was exercised by bourgeois *secrétaires d'état* like Colbert and Louvois, who might also be called as *ministres d'état* to serve in the highest and extremely exclusive royal council, presided over by the King—the *conseil d'état* or *conseil d'en haut*. Naturally the great nobles had never taken kindly to their exclusion from political power and, in the last part of the reign of Louis XIV, one of the main aims of men like Saint-Simon and Fénelon had been to put an end to this 'règne de vile bourgeoisie' and to restore the power of the great nobles. Their aim was to take away power from such members of the recently elevated *noblesse de robe* as the *contrôleur général* and the *secrétaires d'état* and to have their functions taken over by a series of councils in which the great nobles would have a preponderant position.

In his memoirs Saint-Simon sets forth clearly both these aims and the difficulties in the way of their realization—the incapacity of the great nobles who lacked both a general education and administrative training:

> Mon dessein fut donc de commencer à mettre la noblesse dans le ministère, avec la dignité et l'autorité qui lui convenait, aux

dépens de la robe et de la plume,[1] et conduire sagement les choses par degrés et selon les occurrences, pour que peu à peu cette roture perdît toutes les administrations qui ne sont pas de pure judicature . . . pour soumettre tout à la noblesse en toute espèce d'administration. L'embarras fut l'ignorance, la légèreté, l'inapplication de cette noblesse accoutumée à n'être bonne à rien qu'à se faire tuer, à n'arriver à la guerre que par ancienneté, et à croupir du reste dans la plus mortelle inutilité, qui l'avait livrée à l'oisiveté et au dégoût de toute instruction hors de guerre, par l'incapacité d'état de s'en pouvoir servir à rien. Il était impossible de faire le premier pas vers ce but sans renverser le monstre qui avait dévoré la noblesse, c'est-à-dire le contrôleur général et les secrétaires d'état. (*Mémoires*, XXVII, 8-9)

The purpose of the whole scheme is made brutally clear in the last sentence.

The Regency provided an opportunity to try out these plans. Above all the other councils came the *Conseil de Régence*, presided over by the Regent, and consisting mainly of princes of the blood and great noblemen (among them Saint-Simon), although, as in the other councils, a small place was still found for experienced bourgeois administrators of the previous reign. Beneath the *Conseil de Régence* came altogether seven councils: for internal affairs, religious matters, war, navy, finances, foreign affairs, and, as an afterthought, commerce. All these councils were presided over by great noblemen, and members of the old nobility occupied a prominent place in them; yet, as put into practice by the Regent, the system rested on a compromise. The high civil servants of the *noblesse de robe* were still strongly represented on all these bodies. Being experienced administrators, they could not but be impatient of the ineptitude of the aristocratic amateurs who had at last succeeded in regaining a place in the machinery of government.

The experiment was to break down within three years. It was warmly defended by a prominent writer of the time, Abbé de Saint-Pierre, whose *Discours sur la Polysynodie* was published in 1718 and got him into hot water for his attacks on the despotism of Louis XIV; he was expelled from the Académie

---

[1] The high civil servants.

Française for this misdemeanour. In the same year most of the Councils were wound up and replaced by *secrétaires d'état*; the rest gradually faded out and by the end of the Regency the form of government which had obtained under Louis XIV was restored. The attempt to bring back the great nobles into the government proved a failure, very largely because of their inability to govern. Yet the experiment was interesting, both because it was the last time under the Ancien Régime that the great nobles had a chance to play a part in the government and because it formed one part of the aristocratic reaction which was such an important feature of the history of eighteenth century France.

Another aspect of the same movement—and one which was later to become of crucial importance—was the attempt made during the Regency by the more recently ennobled branch of the aristocracy, the *noblesse de robe*, established in the Parlements of France, to make use of the political power which, in restoring its right of remonstrance, the Regent had bestowed upon it. The memory of another Regency—that of Anne of Austria, during which the Paris Parlement had played a prominent part in the Fronde—was not yet dead; it was indeed traditional for the Parlements to re-assert their power under such conditions. A royal declaration of September 1715 gave 'notre cour de Parlement' permission

de nous représenter ce qu'elle jugera à propos, avant que d'être obligée de procéder à l'enregistrement des édits et déclarations que nous lui adresserons, et nous sommes persuadé qu'elle usera avec tant de sagesse et de circonspection de l'ancienne liberté dans laquelle nous la rétablissons, que ses avis ne tendront jamais qu'au bien de notre état et mériteront toujours d'être confirmés par notre autorité. (Flammermont, *Remontrances du Parlement de Paris*, I, vi)

These expectations were not to be fulfilled. Within two years of the death of Louis XIV, the Paris Parlement was already on its high horse. When asked to register a financial edict, it was bold enough to vote to

rejeter l'édit, faire des représentations et demander communication des états des revenus du roi, de sa dépense et de l'emploi qui

en a été fait depuis la régence. . . . Les députés ont été nommés, et M. le premier président à la tête ayant rendu compte à M. le Régent et fait des représentations, M. le Régent les a très mal reçus, et a dit que c'était une cabale et un attentat à l'autorité du roi, qu'il était le dépositaire de cette autorité, qu'il ne la laisserait point avilir tant qu'elle serait entre ses mains, et que le Parlement avait excédé son pouvoir en voulant connaître des affaires de l'État. (Marais, *Journal*, I, 230)

Despite his anger at such unheard-of insolence, the Regent finally had to give way and, what was almost unbelievable in an absolute monarchy, to produce a detailed account of the national income, expenditure and debts to a group of commissioners nominated by the Parlement.

The clash with the Regent became more acute in 1718 when the Parlement presented repeated remonstrances against the financial policy of the government. Matters came to a head in August when the Parlement intervened in financial affairs with a series of edicts. There is some truth, despite the hostile exaggerations of the author, in Saint Simon's words:

Après ce coup d'essai il n'y avait plus qu'un pas à faire pour que le Parlement devînt en effet, comme de prétention folle, le tuteur du roi et le maître du royaume, et le Régent, plus en sa tutelle que le roi, et peut-être aussi exposé que le roi Charles I^er d'Angleterre. Messieurs du Parlement ne s'y prenaient pas plus faiblement que le parlement d'Angleterre fit au commencement et, quoique simple cour de justice, bornée dans un ressort comme les autres cours du royaume à juger les procès entre particuliers, à force de vent et de jouer sur le mot de parlement, ils ne se croyaient pas moins que le parlement d'Angleterre, qui est l'assemblée législative et représentative de toute la nation. (*Mémoires*, XXXV, 18)

The government was obliged to have recourse to a *lit de justice*, that is the King appeared in person in the Palais de Justice and commanded the Parlement to register the edicts. The spokesman of the government reaffirmed with brutal clarity the claim of absolute monarchy to possess complete legislative power. Laws, new and old, he declared,

ne subsistent que par la volonté du souverain et n'ont besoin que
de cette volonté pour être loi; leur enregistrement dans les cours,
à qui l'exécution en est confiée, n'ajoute rien au pouvoir du
législateur; c'en est seulement la promulgation, et un acte
d'obéissance indispensable dont les cours doivent tenir et tiennent
sans doute à honneur de donner l'exemple aux autres sujets.
(Flammermont, *Remontrances du Parlement de Paris*, I, 86)

Having thus reduced the registration of new laws by the
Parlements to a mere formality, he went on to impose severe
restrictions on the *droit de remontrance*. When the Parlement
protested, three of the judges were arrested and it was silenced,
at least for a time.

Two years later, in 1720, came another clash with the
Regent over financial matters. When the Parlement repeatedly
refused to register a financial edict, the Regent ordered the
whole body to be exiled *en bloc* outside Paris, to Pontoise; this
was the first time that such a thing had happened in French
history, but it was not to be the last. The disagreement was
made worse by a religious conflict which added to the confusion of the Regency period and was to embitter relations
between the Parlement and the Crown for the next forty years.
The Jansenist controversy had flared up again in the closing
years of the reign of Louis XIV, when fresh persecutions led in
1709 to the dispersal of the nuns of Port Royal des Champs and
in the following year to the demolition of this famous Jansenist
stronghold. Three years later, at the instigation of Louis XIV,
the Pope issued a bull, known from its opening word as the
Bull *Unigenitus*[1] in which he condemned a hundred and one
propositions from a book originally published some forty years
earlier by a fervent Jansenist, Father Quesnel.

This condemnation of the basic doctrines of Jansenism was
intended to settle the controversy once and for all; in practice
it gave rise to a bitter dispute between the Jansenists and their
opponents which lasted for half a century until its surprising
conclusion: the suppression in France of the Society of Jesus,
the principal supporters of the bull, in 1764.

---

[1] It was also known as *la constitution*; hence its supporters are frequently referred
to as *constitutionnaires* and its opponents as *anti-constitutionnaires*.

Neither the French episcopate nor the Parlements, Louis XIV found to his angry disgust, were willing to accept the bull without all sorts of reservations, and he died without seeing the matter finally settled. The dispute over Jansenism had shifted from the theological to the political plane, because it revived the ancient controversy between the Ultramontanes, those who held that the Pope had absolute authority in matters of faith and discipline, and the Gallican party which endeavoured to maintain for the French Catholic Church a certain independence of Rome. Traditionally the Parlements were strongholds of Gallicanism and could not but view with suspicion the Pope's condemnation of the 91st proposition in Quesnel—'La crainte d'une excommunication injuste ne doit jamais nous empêcher de faire notre devoir'. To condemn this proposition as heretical seemed to imply that there could be no such thing as an 'unjust' excommunication, i.e. that the Pope was infallible. The opponents of the bull could thus argue that not only were they maintaining the rights of the French Catholic Church, but also that they were defending the rights of the Kings of France against the papal claim to release peoples from their oath of obedience and to depose kings.

Few of the judges of the Parlements were Jansenists, but as Gallicans they supported the Jansenists in their struggle against the Ultramontane party. This point is well brought out by the lawyer Barbier's somewhat ironical account of their position:

D'ailleurs ils ne s'embarrassent pas pour le fond de la Constitution, pour savoir à quel carat doit être l'amour de Dieu, ni combien de sortes de grâces Dieu a fait faire pour ceux qui habiteront ce bas monde. Cela ne les regarde pas, c'est de la théologie; mais ce qui les lanterne,[1] c'est la quatre-vingt-onzième proposition qui est condamnée et qui porte: *Que la crainte même d'une excommunication injuste ne nous doit jamais empêcher de faire notre devoir.* La cour de Rome prétend que quand elle excommunie, même à tort et à travers, l'on doit suivre ses volontés à la lettre, et que par là elle peut excommunier les rois et dégager les peuples du serment de fidélité. . . . C'est ce qui révolte le Parlement et lui

---

[1] bothers.

fait prendre parti pour l'intérêt du Roi, car ceci ne regarde que les têtes couronnées et les souverains. (*Chronique de la Régence,* II, 115-16)

Thus the paradoxical situation arose that while the government strove to get the bull accepted as a 'loi de l'Église et de l'État', its chief opponents argued that they were defending the rights of the French Church as well as those of the King against the Papacy. The Jansenists had the support not only of the Parlements, but also, especially in Paris, of a considerable section of the middle and lower classes. The controversy between Jansenists and Jesuits was inextricably mixed up with the discontent of the lower and middle classes of the capital can with the political claims of the Parlements. Hence the heat which it engendered in the next fifty years.

On the death of Louis XIV the Regent made up his mind, after some hesitation, to get the Bull *Unigenitus* accepted in France. However, it encountered stiff resistance from the Sorbonne, the Faculty of Theology of the University of Paris, and many members of the regular and secular clergy of the Paris diocese. In 1717, after the breakdown of negotiations, four French bishops appealed to a general council against the bull, that is, rejected the Pope's decisions on the hundred and one propositions. The Sorbonne, the great majority of the Paris clergy and two more bishops associated themselves with this step, as did the Archbishop of Paris, although he kept his own appeal secret for a year. The ranks of the *appelants*, as they were called, were further swollen by the adhesion of all four faculties of the University of Paris, several provincial universities and faculties of theology and many more members of the secular clergy.

The Regent, however, went ahead with his policy of securing the acceptance of the bull, assisted by Abbé Dubois who hoped for a cardinal's hat as a reward. In 1720 Dubois worked out an ingenious compromise between the two parties which was embodied in a royal declaration; this needed to be registered by the Parlement, then in exile at Pontoise, but the Parlement refused. It was forced into submission only by the threat of exile to Blois, and the creation of two new courts at Tours and

Poitiers, which would have greatly diminished the area of its jurisdiction. Then the controversy died down for a number of years, but before long it was to flare up again in a more violent form and to lead to a head-on collision between Louis XV and his Parlements. Thus both in the conflict between the Crown and the Parlements and in the controversy between Jansenists and Jesuits, Gallicans and Ultramontanes, the Regency offers a foretaste of what was to come later in the century.

The most spectacular and best-known episode of the Regency period was provided by a Scotsman, John Law, and his famous *Système*.[1] The financial legacy bequeathed by Louis XIV to his successor was a frightening one. The *Conseil des Finances* set up at the beginning of the Regency had to struggle with a heavy burden of debt, a large budget deficit and the additional difficulty that the revenues of several future years had been used up in advance. Recourse was had to all manner of expedients including the setting up of a *Chambre de Justice* to make the wealthy *financiers* disgorge their ill-gotten gains, but it yielded relatively little and was suppressed after a year. Attempts were made to reduce the burden of debt by cutting down the value of government bills issued by Louis XIV, reducing the interest on the *rentes* from 5 to 4 per cent. and sometimes even the capital, and by tinkering with the coinage. Yet none of these measures solved the problem.

It was here that Law appeared upon the scene. The son of an Edinburgh goldsmith and banker, he was born in 1671. He was a very handsome and well-educated man who had inherited a considerable fortune. In 1691 he took the road south to London; there he led a gay life until he was sentenced to death for killing a man in a duel. He escaped, and took refuge in Holland. While in England and Holland he studied the workings of the newly founded Bank of England and of the Bank of Amsterdam, which was a century older. After various travels which included a sojourn in Italy, he returned to Scotland and in 1705 put before the Parliament in Edinburgh proposals for the establishment of a trading corporation and

---

[1] The French transformed the outlandish name of Law (or Laws) into 'Lass' and generally speak even today of 'le système de Lass'.

the use of paper money. However, his canny compatriots would
have nothing to do with the scheme.

The imminence of the Union with England where he was
still under sentence of death, drove Law back to the Continent
and finally, in 1707, to France. In Paris, where he gambled on
a grand scale, he made the acquaintance of the future Regent.
Before long Louis XIV had him expelled for his gambling
activities, and he did not return until the end of 1713, not long
before the death of the old king.

Law's theories on banking and credit were the culmination
of a whole movement of ideas in Western Europe at the end of
the seventeenth century. Law gathered these ideas together
into a coherent whole and gave them a bolder form than
anyone else. The foundation of his system was his conviction
that the primary factor in the wealth of a nation was the ease
and rapidity with which money circulates; this explained the
superiority, in his eyes, of paper money over gold and silver.
Backing for paper money, whether in gold or anything else, he
held to be relatively unimportant, since he considered that the
real guarantee of its value lay in the expanding prosperity
which it promoted. By a proper organization of credit, he held,
the state could liquidate its debts and at the same time bring
unheard-of prosperity to the country.

After the death of Louis XIV, Law put before the Regent
a plan for the economic regeneration of the country. This was
turned down by the government, but in the following year the
Regent allowed him to set up a bank known as the Banque
Générale. In theory this was a private affair, but as 75 per cent.
of the capital consisted of government bills, the operations of
the bank were from the beginning linked with the liquidation
of the national debt. Tax-collectors were instructed to accept
the bank's paper money and to make payments in it. Thus the
bank soon became a semi-State enterprise.

Law's next step was to set up, in 1717, a trading company
known as the Compagnie d'Occident (or the Compagnie du
Mississipi) which was given a monopoly of trade with the
French colony of Louisiana. The company was linked with
his bank, and at the same time with the Treasury since govern-

ment bills were accepted for the purchase of shares in it. Gradually he achieved a monopoly of all French overseas trade, changed the name of his company to that of Compagnie des Indes, and in addition took over the collection both of the *taille* and of indirect taxes.

An enormous amount of capital was invested in the bank and the Compagnie des Indes. By accepting government bills in the payment of shares they made a considerable contribution to the reduction of the national debt; and in 1718 the bank was transformed into a state bank. The *Système* reached its height at the end of 1719 and the beginning of 1720. In January 1720 Law, a foreigner (now naturalized) and a Protestant (now hastily converted), was raised to the most important post in a French Government under the Ancien Régime—that of *Contrôleur général*—with control over the finances and the economic life of the country. In one of the numerous defences of his system which he wrote in these years, he painted the following picture of the prosperity which he had brought to France:

> En effet, quelle condition, quelle profession ne s'est sentie des richesses écloses du nouveau système? Les terres et les maisons sont montées au double et au triple de leur prix pour le vendeur, et croîtront considérablement en revenu pour l'acquéreur; l'officier d'épée ou de robe touche ses pensions ou ses gages, auxquels il ne fallait plus penser; le marchand et l'ouvrier ne peuvent suffire aux demandes des acheteurs; le menu peuple, ceux mêmes qui, par la bassesse de leur fortune, ne sont, pour ainsi dire, d'aucune classe; tous enfin trouvent à vivre, à gagner, à s'enrichir. Parmi les défiants mêmes, les déclamateurs ou aveugles ou malintentionnés, combien de débiteurs se sont tirés de l'oppression de leurs créanciers! combien de créanciers ont recueilli de dettes désespérées! (*Œuvres complètes*, III, 101-2)

The result of all his financial juggling had been to create a colossal wave of speculation, like that unleashed in England by the South Sea Bubble in the very same period. The company's 500 *l.* shares soared up to 10,000 *l.* and even touched for a moment 18,000. Vast fortunes were made by people drawn from all sections of society, from the lackeys of yesterday to the princes of the blood. In October 1719 a contemporary wrote:

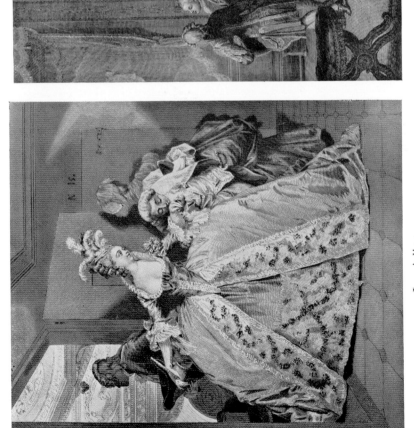

23  Les Adieux

24  Dame du Palais

25  La Partie de Wisch (i.e. Whist)

On assurait que M. le duc de Bourbon avait profité de vingt millions sur les actions de la Compagnie des Indes, ce qui avait mis ce prince en état d'acquitter ses dettes et d'acquérir une terre considérable qui lui avait coûté huit cent mille livres; que M. le Prince de Conti y avait aussi gagné quatre millions cinq cent mille livres; M. le duc d'Antin, douze millions; M. le marquis de Conflans, cinquante mille écus; M. Le Riche, cinquante mille livres; M. l'abbé de Tavannes, douze cent mille livres; M. l'abbé Prot, neuf cent mille livres. Mademoiselle Angletorp, Anglaise, fille d'un colonel, âgée de vingt-deux ans, y avait aussi gagné de quoi acquérir en son pays une terre de douze cents livres sterling de rente. Un seigneur anglais y avait gagné deux millions qui lui valaient cinquante mille livres sterling de rente. Le secrétaire du comte de Stair, ambassadeur d'Angleterre, y gagna deux cent mille livres. (Buvat, *Journal de la Régence*, I, 450)

The inevitable crisis of the *Système* began in February 1720. Shortly before, a dividend of 40 per cent. had been declared on the shares of the company; but, if their holders had paid 10,000 *l.* for them, the net interest they received was only 2 per cent. It was clear to those in the know that the shares were bound to fall and they began to realize their holdings; moreover, they also presented their paper money at the bank and demanded gold in return. The result was panic; in a few days the shares fell by 50 per cent.

Until December 1720 Law fought to save what he could from the wreck of his *Système*. But all his desperate measures failed to avert the inevitable catastrophe. He had to reckon with the hostility of other ministers, especially the powerful Dubois, and of rival bankers like the Pâris brothers who were probably responsible for starting the rot. A similar catastrophe overcame the South Sea Company in England in these very months. In December Law gave up the struggle and fled to Brussels. He had arrived in France with a large fortune; he left it a ruined man.

It took some three years to clear up the financial mess which he left behind him. The Treasury undoubtedly profited from the *Système* as the national debt had been halved since the beginning of the Regency; but its collapse had long-term effects which were less favourable. It frightened both the government and the general public. To the very end of the Ancien Régime the idea of a national bank was looked upon as too dangerous; the Banque de France was thus not founded until 1800—over a century after the Bank of England.

The immediate economic consequences of the *Système* were mixed. On the one hand thousands of people were ruined (it is perhaps to the *Système* that we owe the plays and novels of Marivaux who was driven by his losses in it to seek a living with his pen), and the violent inflation which caused a steep rise in the cost of living brought suffering to the lower classes, especially in the towns. Yet it did give a considerable fillip to trade and industry, and the seaports in particular profited from the boom in the colonial trade.

The social and moral effects of the *Système* were undoubtedly striking. They are clearly brought out by Montesquieu, a bitterly hostile critic, whose *Lettres persanes* appeared in the year following its collapse. Enormous fortunes were made almost overnight; the lackeys of yesterday became the masters of today.

> Tous ceux qui étaient riches il y a six mois sont à présent dans la pauvreté, et ceux qui n'avaient pas de pain regorgent de richesses. Jamais ces deux extrémités ne se sont touchées de si près. . . . Quelles fortunes inespérées, incroyables même à ceux qui les ont faites! Dieu ne tire pas plus rapidement les hommes du néant. Que de valets servis par leurs camarades, et peut-être demain par leurs maîtres! (pp. 351-2)

Many great noblemen, even princes of the blood like the Duc de Bourbon who was to succeed Philippe d'Orléans as prime minister of France, discredited themselves by their rapacious behaviour; they took advantage of their position and were among the first to change their paper money into coin when the crash finally came. The *Système* gave rise to all sorts of fraud and swindling, not to mention crimes of violence: a scion of a very aristocratic family in the Austrian Netherlands, the Comte de Horn, was broken on the wheel for a particularly brutal murder. Montesquieu's indignation was aroused not only by the mingling of social ranks brought about by the *Système*, but also by the moral corruption it produced:

J'ai vu naître soudain, dans tous les cœurs, une soif insatiable des richesses. J'ai vu se former, en un moment, une détestable conjuration de s'enrichir, non par un honnête travail et une généreuse industrie, mais par la ruine du prince, de l'état et des concitoyens. . . .
Quel plus grand crime que celui que commet un ministre, lorsqu'il corrompt les mœurs de toute une nation, dégrade les âmes les plus généreuses, ternit l'éclat des dignités, obscurcit la vertu même, et confond la plus haute naissance dans le mépris universel? (*Lettres persanes*, pp. 388-9)

Such are the blistering comments on Law and all his works which Montesquieu put into the mouth of his Persian travellers.

As far as foreign affairs were concerned, after the almost continuous war which had raged from 1688 to the Treaty of Utrecht in 1713, the Regency was a relatively tranquil period. There was a curious lull—one which was to last indeed until the outbreak of the War of the Austrian Succession in the 1740s —in the bitter commercial and colonial conflict which so often set England and France at one another's throats for more than a century, from 1688 down to Waterloo.

The lull was partly due to the uncertain position of the two rulers who had newly been installed in both countries. In France the Regent was faced with a constant threat from his nephew, Philip V of Spain, who, as a grandson of Louis XIV, had not abandoned his claims to the throne of France and would certainly have tried hard to wrest the succession from the Regent if the young Louis XV had died. In England George I was by no means sure of keeping the throne which he had ascended in 1714. After the failure of the Jacobite rising in the following year, the two countries were drawn together by the skilful secret diplomacy of Dubois, and in 1717 a Triple Alliance was signed between England, France and Holland. In the following year the Emperor joined the alliance, and the discovery of a plot inside France to drive the Regent from power (a conspiracy named after the Spanish ambassador, Cellamare, who was involved in it) led finally in 1719 to France joining England in a declaration of war against Spain.

French troops entered Spain, but did not penetrate very

deeply. Seeing their country invaded and their plans to cause trouble inside France brought to nothing, the Spaniards sought peace, and in 1721 relations had so far improved that Dubois was able to sign an alliance between the two countries. As a result of this it was agreed that the Spanish Infanta, a child of three, should marry the young Louis XV, who had now reached the age of eleven. Thanks largely to the diplomatic skill of Dubois, the Regency had given France a scarcely broken period of peace which was much needed after nearly a quarter of a century of war.

The Regency came to an end in February 1723 when the King achieved his legal majority. Cardinal Dubois who was confirmed in his position as prime minister, died in August; and Philippe d'Orléans, who took his place, was struck down by apoplexy in December. The post then passed to the Duc de Bourbon, who remained in power till 1726. The chief event of his ministry was the marriage of Louis XV, in the year before his dismissal. As the Spanish Infanta to whom he was betrothed was only six when the Duc de Bourbon came to power, France would have had to wait too long for an heir to the throne; if Louis died without an heir, the King of Spain would be certain to lay claim to the throne and this would precipitate a European crisis. So the Infanta was sent off home (much to the indignation of the Spaniards), and finally in 1725, after long lists of marriageable princesses had been examined, the government's choice fell on Marie Leczinska, the daughter of ex-King Stanislas of Poland, who was living in exile in a modest château in Alsace. The Queen was seven years older than her husband, still a mere boy of fifteen. After twelve years of marriage, she had borne him ten children; after that she was to be neglected by her husband and played no part at all in affairs of state.

In the following year the Duc de Bourbon was ousted from power by Fleury, who, as the King's former tutor, had already wormed his way into the *Conseil d'en haut*. In 1726 he was a very old man (he was born in 1653), yet he clung to power until his death in 1743, at the age of ninety. Appointed Bishop of Fréjus in 1698, he had been made tutor to the future Louis XV in 1714. In this capacity he had had ample opportunity of getting to know the young king and had pandered to his pupil's indolence in order to win his confidence and affection. On his appointment he flattered Louis XV by using the argument that the King was now old enough to govern by himself, and refusing the title of prime minister, contented himself with that of *ministre d'état*, that is, a member of the select group of ministers who formed the *Conseil d'en haut*. Such apparent modesty did not prevent Fleury from being the real ruler of France for the next seventeen years.

In his foreign policy Fleury's main aim was the maintenance of peace. In this he was aided by the fact that his period in office coincided roughly with that of Sir Robert Walpole with whom he got along well. On the other hand he was handicapped, until he dismissed his secretary of state for foreign affairs, Chauvelin, in 1737, by the latter's anti-Austrian sentiments, which were popular at court as Austria was France's traditional enemy on the Continent. Nevertheless, he managed to keep the peace of Europe until 1733, when France became involved in the War of the Polish Succession on the side of Stanislas, the father-in-law of Louis XV, against a candidate supported by Austria and Russia. After the failure of Stanislas's attempt to regain the throne of Poland, the main result of this war, which lasted in rather desultory fashion until 1738, was that Austria ceded to him the Duchy of Lorraine which, after his death in 1766, was incorporated into France.

The considerable success which Fleury had achieved in his foreign policy did not last to the very end of his career. In 1739 English trading interests compelled Walpole to declare war on Spain, and in the following year the death of the Emperor Charles VI opened the crisis of the Austrian succession which was to involve Europe in a general war. France had adhered to the so-called Pragmatic Sanction which assured the succession to the late Emperor's daughter, Maria Theresa, but Fleury allowed himself to be pushed into a war to put the Elector of Bavaria on the imperial throne. As England came to the assistance of Maria Theresa, this meant the end of friendly relations between them, and a war both on the Continent and at sea. France's invasion of Bohemia led to a military set-back when Frederick the Great, who had seized Silesia, made peace with Maria Theresa, and left his French allies in the lurch. Several thousand French troops, trapped in Prague, were forced into submission, while the main French army made its escape in a battered condition. When Fleury died in 1743, the war still had another five years to go.

At home, after the upheavals of the Regency period, Fleury's policy was one of retrenchment. It was scarcely, however, one of reform, as in many respects France reverted to the state of affairs before the death of Louis XIV. One excellent measure which contributed to the prosperity of the country was the definite fixing of the value of the coinage in 1726. What was probably a retrograde step was the return in the same year of the old system of collection of indirect taxes by means of *fermiers généraux* who had been suppressed by Law.

The arrival in power in 1730 of a new *contrôleur général*, Orry, who kept his post for the record period of fifteen years, produced some noteworthy changes. He was compelled by the War of the Polish Succession and then once again by the War of the Austrian Succession to revive the *dixième*, a direct tax instituted to finance the later wars of Louis XIV and abolished by the Regent. Orry could scarcely be said to have reformed the French financial system, always the weak spot of the monarchy, since he had recourse to such familiar expedients as loans and the sale of offices in order to raise money; but it would appear that at least in time of peace—and this was something almost unheard of under the Ancien Régime—he succeeded in keeping expenditure slightly below revenue.

One of the main features of Orry's administration was the putting on a regular basis, in 1738, of an institution which was not altogether new—the *corvée* for the building and upkeep of the roads. Although this tended to weigh most heavily on those least able to bear the burden, the peasants, the system organized by Orry did help to give France what was then the finest road-system in Europe.

On the whole the period in which Fleury was at the head of the government was one of moderate prosperity. After the stabilisation of the coinage in 1726 there began to set in the long-term rise in prices which covered the middle part of the century. Yet it was a slow process and its effects were offset, at least so far as considerable parts of the country were concerned, by the distress of the famine years, 1739 and 1740. Fleury himself had the sufferings of the masses brought to his notice in no uncertain fashion when in 1740 his carriage was held up in Paris by a mob of starving women shouting: 'Du pain! Du pain! nous mourons de faim'.[1]

Fleury's administration saw another flare-up of the Jansenist controversy and a violent clash between the Paris Parlement and the Crown. The trouble started in 1727 when a bishop who was one of the most stubborn opponents of the Bull *Unigenitus* was haled before a provincial council, suspended from his functions and exiled by a *lettre de cachet* to a monastery where he died in 1740. This treatment was regarded as persecution by many clerics and laymen, and caused intense indignation. Then, in 1729, the Archbishop of Paris, who had been a very wavering supporter of the Jansenist position, died and was replaced by a fanatical *constitutionnaire* who immediately created uproar by suspending some 300 priests of his diocese who were suspected of Jansenism.

Resistance then spread to the Parlements, which had played a very modest part in public affairs for the previous decade. In 1730 the King sent to them for registration a royal declaration ordering all clergymen to accept the Bull *Unigenitus* without reservations. The Paris Parlement was compelled to register this declaration in a *lit de justice*, but it took its revenge, as did some of the provincial Parlements, by all sorts of obstructive acts. For instance, it decreed that all priests who had been suspended by their bishops for Jansenist views should resume their functions. The Parlements, particularly the Paris courts, continued their opposition during the years 1731 and 1732, supported by the great body of public opinion, while the government continued in its determination to enforce obedience to the bull and to the King's will. The Chancellor, in a speech at Versailles to the deputies of the Paris Parlement at the beginning of 1732, rejected the argument that in opposing the

[1] See p. 34.

bull the Parlements were upholding the King's power against
the Pope and re-affirmed in full the powers of the Crown in all
matters of legislation:

> Au surplus le pouvoir de faire des lois et de les interpréter est
> essentiellement et uniquement réservé au roi. Le Parlement n'est
> chargé que de veiller à leur exécution; il doit se renfermer exacte-
> ment dans les bornes de l'autorité qu'il plaît à Sa Majesté de lui
> confier pour l'administration de la justice. Le roi connaît toute
> l'étendue des droits de sa suprême puissance, et il n'a pas besoin
> d'être excité à maintenir les maximes du royaume.[1] Il a toujours
> empêché et empêchera toujours qu'elles ne souffrent la moindre
> atteinte. Mais la plus inviolable des maximes qui regardent
> l'autorité royale est qu'il n'est jamais permis de manquer à
> l'obéissance qui lui est due. Le devoir le plus essentiel et le plus
> indispensable des magistrats est d'en donner l'exemple aux autres
> sujets du roi, et de prouver leur soumission personnelle par les
> effets[2] beaucoup plus que par les paroles. (Barbier, *Chronique de
> la Régence*, II, 238)

Such a scolding did not make the Parlement any more docile,
and in May 1732 two of the boldest opponents of the bull among
its members were arrested. The Parlement's retort was to make
use of a device which it was frequently to employ in the next
fifty years; its members downed tools and ceased the administration of justice. When ordered by the King to resume their
duties, they returned to the Palais de Justice, but only to take
action against a pastoral letter of their enemy, the Ultramontane Archbishop of Paris. More judges were then arrested,
and when the King summoned a deputation to court to warn
the Parlement that he expected immediate obedience, all but
two or three of the judges signed a collective letter of resignation. The delivery of this document to the Premier Président
of the Parlement was an impressive scene, described in vivid
detail by Barbier who, as an *avocat*, followed these events with
passionate interest.

> Quand cela a été fait, toutes les sept chambres sont sorties en
> même temps, se sont jointes dans la grande salle, et ont été, par

[1] The Gallican principles limiting the power of the Pope in France.
[2] Deeds.

l'escalier de la Sainte-Chapelle et la cour du Palais, chez M. le premier président. Ils marchaient deux à deux les yeux baissés, au nombre de plus de cent cinquante, passant au milieu d'un monde infini dont le Palais[1] était plein. Dans leur chemin, le public disait: 'Voilà de vrais Romains et les pères de la patrie!' Ceux qui ont vu cette marche disent qu'elle avait quelque chose d'auguste et qui saisissait. Arrivés chez M. le premier président, les présidents de chaque chambre lui ont présenté les démissions pour les lui remettre. M. le premier président a reçu cette compagnie avec des lamentations sur le parti violent qu'ils prenaient, les suppliant d'y faire de nouvelles attentions, les assurant qu'il était très attaché à sa compagnie et qu'il était prêt à se sacrifier pour elle. Les présidents ont persisté à lui offrir ces démissions; il n'a pas voulu les recevoir; il a reconduit messieurs du Parlement, et on a dit qu'il a été effrayé du monde qui était dans sa cour. Messieurs du Parlement ont repassé dans la cour du Palais dans la même marche, et ont remonté dans leurs chambres. (II, 296)

The resignations, which the Premier Président had refused to accept, were sent to the Chancellor. The government's reply was a mild one; the judges were persuaded to withdraw their resignations, but when the King held a *lit de justice* to secure the registration of a royal edict, the Parlement retorted by declaring the registration null and void. The government answered this challenge to its authority by exiling to the provinces 139 judges. Yet two months later all were recalled and the government withdrew the edict which had caused the clash with the Parlement.

For the next twenty years or so the Parlements were to give the government relatively little trouble, but we already see revealed the weakness of the Crown in its handling of them. Fleury's policy of alternating severity and weakness was to prove typical of the government's behaviour towards the Parlements for most of the reign. In this same year, when the clash between the Crown and the Parlements was at its height, there appeared a short pamphlet, the famous *Mémoire touchant l'origine et l'autorité du Parlement de France*, generally known as the *Judicium Francorum*, which summed up the political claims

---

[1] Palais de Justice.

of the Paris Parlement. For the sake of appearances the Parlement had to condemn the work, but there is no doubt that it faithfully reflected the outlook of its members.

The author of the *Judicium Francorum*—as the spokesman of the Paris Parlement, he speaks slightingly of the upstart provincial Parlements—traces back the origins of the Paris court to the assemblies held by the Franks. 'Du temps de Philippe Auguste', he declares, 'ces sortes d'assemblées, par le jugement desquelles tout était résolu, changèrent de nom et non pas d'autorité: on commença de les appeler *Parlement*.' When, under Philip the Fair, this body began to hear appeals, even those in which only private individuals were concerned, it did not lose its original function of deliberating on new laws:

> Le Parlement ne perdit pas pour cela la connaissance des affaires publiques. Il n'avait garde de renoncer à un droit si avantageux et si nécessaire pour le bien de la nation; il représentait toujours cette assemblée générale des Francs; pour être sédentaire, il conserva toujours sa dignité et son pouvoir.

The Parlement, he continues, has always represented the three orders in the state. Even today the clergy is represented by a number of *conseillers clercs* (ecclesiastical judges); the nobility by the princes of the blood and *ducs et pairs*. Here the argument becomes a little confused, because, despite their more or less recent bourgeois origins, the judges of the Parlement, who were ennobled by the possession of their posts, could not relish being called the representatives of the third estate; but the author forges ahead with his argument in the vague formula: 'Enfin le corps entier, qui est un corps mixte, y représente tous les ordres du royaume.'

The Parlement, he goes on, still deals with the same matters as the assemblies of the Frankish kings. No government measures can be legal without its consent:

> Les étrangers ne croient pas la paix conclue avec nous qu'après que le traité y a été vérifié; le roi y envoie aussi les motifs qu'il a de faire la guerre. C'est une loi fondamentale que rien ne peut être imposé sur les sujets du roi et qu'on ne peut faire aucun officier en France, donner aucun titre nouveau, que par le consentement

du Parlement, qui représente le consentement général du peuple. Telle est la forme essentielle du gouvernement français.

The claim that the Parlement represents the nation is summed up in the formula: 'Le roi ne peut contracter avec ses peuples que dans le Parlement, ni détruire rien de ce qu'il a fait que dans le même lieu.' Such an attitude, based on the pseudo-historical argument that the Parlement 'se trouve aussi ancien que la couronne, il est né avec l'État', was frequently to be adopted in the violent collisions between Crown and Parlement which took place after 1750.

Another aspect of the Jansenist controversy in the period of Fleury is important because of its influence on public opinion in these years—particularly, but by no means, exclusively, on the outlook of the *Philosophes*. In 1731 the sober *avocat* Barbier, whose profession of faith in these clashes between the government and the Parlements is summed up in the cautious bourgeois formula: 'Je crois qu'il faut faire son emploi avec honneur sans se mêler d'affaires d'État sur lesquelles on n'a ni pouvoir ni mission' (*Chronique de la Régence*, II, 32), complained of the effects which the bitter controversy aroused inside the French Catholic Church by the Bull *Unigenitus* must inevitably have on the faith of the masses:

> Le seul inconvénient que je trouve dans toutes ces disputes, très amusantes pour les gens d'esprit, qui n'ont que faire et qui trouvent par là des ouvrages très bien travaillés, c'est que l'on creusera trop ces matières, et cela ôtera dans l'esprit du peuple la soumission et la subordination à l'Église, qui sont les enfants de l'ignorance, mais qui sont nécessaires pour la police d'un grand état. (II, 148)

Stranger things still were to follow. In this very year 1731 numerous miracles began to be performed on the tomb of a pious Jansenist, François de Pâris, who had died four years earlier. The son of a wealthy judge of the Paris Parlement, he had entered the Church, but had been too humble to go beyond the status of deacon (hence his name of 'le diacre Pâris'); he had published a number of theological works, but his main occupation was relieving the poor in his parish of Saint-Médard, a plebeian quarter of Paris. The miraculous healing of all sorts of diseases on his tomb led to a tremendous rush of spectators, drawn from all classes, to the cemetery. The ecclesiastical authorities did not look with favour on these Jansenist miracles, and finally, in January 1732, the government ordered the closing of the cemetery, whereupon, it is alleged, a wag put up the following notice on the gate:

> De par le roi, défense à Dieu
> De faire miracle en ce lieu.

Just before the closing of the cemetery, Barbier notes in his journal with open-eyed astonishment 'le concours et le culte qu'on rend au tombeau de M. Pâris':

> On comptait que cette dévotion se ralentirait d'elle-même dans les mauvais temps (il en fait actuellement de très mauvais); cela n'y fait rien. On a dans ce petit charnier de Saint-Médard de la boue par-dessus le soulier; on y est mouillé quand il pleut, le quartier fort mauvais et fort éloigné de la ville, cependant il y a du monde depuis cinq heures du matin jusqu'à cinq heures du soir, et très souvent des personnes de considération. On y psalmodie toujours avec grande dévotion; la tombe est toujours remplie de malades; les convulsions y sont encore plus fréquentes, et on publie de temps en temps des miracles nouveaux et considérables. (*Chronique de la Régence*, II, 231-2)

The closing of the cemetery inspired in him sceptical thoughts about all miracles:

> Quoi qu'il en soit, on n'y entend rien. S'il n'y avait point eu ici deux partis, les miracles de M. Pâris auraient passé doux comme miel; au lieu que la cour de Rome et la cour de France le regardent comme un homme mort hors le sein de l'Église. Cela nous fait voir ce que nous devons penser de tous les miracles de l'antiquité, qui n'ont d'autre autorité que la simplicité et la cabale. (II, 244)

Needless to say, the comments made by the *Philosophes* later in the century were even more pointed. In 1746, in his *Pensées philosophiques*, Diderot devoted to these miracles one of his most trenchant paragraphs:

> Un faubourg retentit d'acclamations: la cendre d'un prédestiné y fait, en un jour, plus de prodiges que Jésus-Christ n'en fit en toute sa vie. On y court; on s'y porte; j'y suis la foule. J'arrive à peine que j'entends crier: miracle! miracle! J'approche, je regarde, et je vois un petit boiteux qui se promène à l'aide de trois ou quatre personnes charitables qui le soutiennent; et le peuple qui s'en émerveille, de répéter: miracle! miracle! Où donc est le miracle, peuple imbécile? Ne vois-tu pas que ce fourbe n'a fait que changer de béquilles? Il en était, dans cette occasion, des miracles, comme il en est toujours des esprits. Je jurerais bien que tous ceux qui ont vu des esprits, les craignaient d'avance, et que tous ceux qui voyaient là des miracles, étaient bien résolus d'en voir. (LIII)

When, with the closing of the Cimetière Saint-Médard, this movement was driven underground, odder things still were to happen. The Jansenist miracles continued in the secret assemblies of the *convulsionnaires* who were drawn from all ranks of society and included Voltaire's own brother. Men and women were hit with logs, pierced with swords or nails, even crucified; they then proceeded to prophecy and their wounds were miraculously healed. The *convulsionnaires* split into various sects with all sorts of strange beliefs to match their strange practices. In the meantime the conflict between Jansenists and Jesuits continued. Among a minority at any rate all this bitter strife between different parties inside the Catholic Church produced only scepticism. In 1734, in discussing one of the innumerable controversies of the time, Barbier wrote:

> Plus on creuse ces matières, soit sur les prophéties, soit sur les anciens miracles reçus par l'Église, et plus on voit l'obscurité des unes et l'incertitude des autres qui se sont établis dans ces temps reculés avec autant de fondement que ce qui se passe aujourd'hui sous nos yeux. (*Chronique de la Régence*, II, 501)

Such views were soon to be made commonplace in the writings of the *Philosophes*.

The long period in which Fleury managed to cling to power,

despite the increasing infirmities brought on by extreme old age, is not one of the most absorbing periods of French history. Yet, despite the denigrations of contemporaries like the Marquis d'Argenson, historians today tend to see in his work, both at home and abroad, solid achievements which contrast favourably with what was to come in the second half of the reign of Louis XV.

# CHAPTER V

# THE PERSONAL REIGN OF LOUIS XV
## 1743-1774

WITH the death of Fleury, Louis XV, at the age of thirty-three, was at last free to take over the reins of power. The period of thirty years or so in the middle of the eighteenth century, in which he was the nominal ruler of France was not a glorious one in her history. Despite the general prosperity of the country these three decades were a period of disasters abroad, particularly in the Seven Years War in which France lost most of her colonial empire, and at the same time they saw a great decline in the power and prestige of the monarchy.

In recent years a determined effort has been made to 'whitewash' Louis XV. Yet when we have accepted that he did not say, 'Après moi le déluge', or, as Mme de Pompadour's funeral procession started on its way, 'Elle n'aura pas le beau temps pour son voyage'; when we have conceded that other French kings before him had flaunted a succession of mistresses and that he was a good father, it still remains that he was a poor and indolent ruler who in the latter part of his reign brought absolutism into contempt.

His greatest asset as a king was a magnificent presence; from childhood to premature old age he was strikingly handsome. Yet even as a child he was both lazy and bored, and already took pleasure in inflicting pain on other people. He always remained timid, afraid of new faces and a bad public speaker. A far from edifying life did not prevent him from being extremely pious and attending all the religious services required of him; he loathed the *Philosophes* for their attacks on religion. If he was not unintelligent, he lacked that devotion to the *métier de roi* which Louis XIV had possessed. He showed his courage on the field of battle, yet hated war for humanitarian reasons. At the beginning of his personal reign he enjoyed considerable popularity; the news of his serious illness at Metz, when he was with his armies in 1744, aroused consternation among the general public. At this period of the reign his title of 'Louis le Bien-Aimé' did not have the satirical ring which it was later to acquire. His chief weaknesses as a ruler were indolence, shyness and irresolution; he often allowed himself to be persuaded, against his better judgment, into following disastrous policies.

Above all, he was the victim of boredom; he had constantly to be amused. He was fond of the pleasures of the table and delighted in *petits soupers* served without valets and in the midst of a few intimates of both sexes. His great passion in life—apart from the fair sex—was hunting. Historians have often commented on the strange diary kept by his grandson, Louis XVI, in which on the dates of some of the most important events of his reign one finds the word 'rien'—meaning simply that there was no hunting that day. Yet the expression was already current in the reign of Louis XV. When Mme Campan first appeared at court in 1768, 'le roi,' she tells us, 'ne pensait plus qu'au plaisir de la chasse; on aurait pu croire que les courtisans se permettaient une épigramme quand on leur entendait dire sérieusement, les jours où Louis XV ne chassait pas: "Le roi ne fait rien aujourd'hui" ' (*Mémoires*, p. 47). Another important ingredient in the King's life was his incessant journeyings from Versailles to the palaces, large and small, which he possessed in the Paris region, from Compiègne to Fontainebleau. 'Le premier jour de l'an', Mme Campan adds, 'il marquait sur son almanach les jours de départ pour Compiègne, pour Fontainebleau, pour Choisy, etc. Les plus grandes affaires, les événements les plus importants, ne dérangeaient jamais cette distribution de son temps' (pp. 47-8).

The government of France in the years after the death of Fleury was chaotic. The King himself was unable or unwilling to govern, nor did he have a prime minister to govern for him. The affairs of the country were run by the *Contrôleur général* and the *secrétaires d'état*, some of whom, along with two or three high personages without departmental responsibilities, were also members of the *conseil d'en haut*, which met under the chairmanship of the King. But Louis seldom exercised any real control

26 *Anon.*, Le Régent Philippe d'Orléans et son neveu, le roi Louis XV

27
*A. S. Belle*, John Law

28
*Rigaud*, Cardinal Fleury

over the policy of his government; instead of co-ordinating the activities of his ministers, he allowed them to go their separate ways. France was governed by a small group of independent ministers, more or less equal in power, who did not agree on any common policy and who did their best to get in one another's way. The Duc de Croÿ wrote in his journal in 1747 on the King's relations with his ministers:

Il paraissait que, quoi qu'il fît beaucoup par lui-même, ses ministres prenant aisément un grand crédit sur son esprit, il s'en rapportait à eux sur presque tout. Ainsi, sans qu'il eût de premier ministre, chacun l'était dans son département, où il faisait faire presque tout ce qu'il voulait, cependant avec ménagement et crainte des rapports de leurs ennemis au roi qui cherchait le bien et aurait voulu être instruit. Il se donnait même quelques soins pour cela, mais peut-être pas assez, ou ne s'y prenait-il pas bien. (*Journal inédit*, I, 92)

His ministers owed their position to court intrigue, and strove their hardest to keep it by the same methods. Something of the atmosphere of the court and of the motives behind the cabals formed there for or against ministers is conveyed in the following passage from d'Argenson:

On a beau se moquer à la cour de la personne des ministres, cependant tout roule sur eux, sur leur déplacement ou élévation. Ce sont là les guerres de cour, les conquêtes, les défaites, les batailles et les sièges, la cabale qui déplace, l'intrigue qui avance vers le ministre, et tout cela se fait en vue de l'argent: car on ne doute pas qu'un ministre placé de votre main, ou bien auquel vous avez contribué, ou, si vous avez nui au disgrâcié dont il occupe la place, on ne doute pas, dis-je, que celui-ci ne vous fasse faire des affaires et ne serve injustement à votre fortune par des grâces iniques et passe-droits, et ces places et grâces rapportent de l'argent. (*Journal*, II, 344)

Yet, although he proved a weak ruler, Louis was not completely uninterested in what was going on in the world around him. He went to immense trouble to organize what is known as 'le secret du roi'—an information service with his own secret agents to keep him informed on foreign affairs and even to carry out a policy of his own. But 'le secret du roi' never produced any worth-while results.

The situation was further complicated by the favour enjoyed by Mme de Pompadour from her presentation at court in 1745 to her death in 1764. Jeanne Poisson, who received the title of Marquise de Pompadour when she was installed at court, was born in 1721. She was the daughter of a *commissaire aux vivres*, a supplier of food to the armies, who was a protégé of the great *financier*, Pâris-Duverney. At twenty she had married the nephew of a *fermier général*. She thus belonged, not to the court aristocracy, but to the world of wealthy tax-farmers. Some of her unpopularity derived from the fact that she was looked upon in court circles as a 'gate-crasher', for the illustrious position which she occupied had hitherto been regarded as a monopoly of the wives and daughters of the aristocracy.

The new favourite was an intelligent and well-read woman, who was on friendly terms with the *Philosophes* (including, at any rate for a time, Voltaire) and with men of letters in general. She was lively and witty, fond of singing, music and amateur theatricals, and was thus able to keep the bored King amused. Her position at court was strengthened by her connections with the Pâris brothers, the big bankers and *financiers* who enjoyed immense power.

She amused the King with plays and ballets and also with new buildings (architecture was one of his few more intellectual interests), and indulged his passion for being constantly on the move between Versailles and his other palaces. The expense of the court and all the different royal households was already a heavy burden; as d'Argenson put it in a famous phrase which describes very vividly, if not without exaggeration, the high cost of the splendours of Versailles and the other royal palaces, 'la cour est le tombeau de la nation' (*Journal*, VII, 46). The cost of the new buildings put up to suit the whim of the favourite, the lavish entertainments and the gifts showered upon her, all these were badly received by the general public. Her unpopularity naturally reflected on the King too, as we see from the opening verses of a *chanson* of the time:

Les grands seigneurs s'avilissent
Tous les financiers s'enrichissent,
Tous les Poissons s'agrandissent:
C'est le règne des vauriens.
On épuise la finance
En bâtiment, en dépense;
L'État tombe en décadence,
Le roi ne met ordre à rien, rien, rien.

Une petite bourgeoise,
Élevée à la grivoise,
Mesurant tout à la toise,
Fait de la cour un taudis.
Le roi, malgré son scrupule,
Pour elle follement brûle;
Cette flamme ridicule
Excite dans tout Paris ris, ris, ris.

It is true that her reign as mistress was relatively short-lived; she was given a respectable position at court in 1756 when she was appointed—somewhat incongruously—Dame du Palais de la Reine; but Louis's affection and his reliance upon her did not cease until her death in 1764. Even if her political role was not as great as has sometimes been made out—she was not a kind of prime minister—she certainly exercised a considerable influence on public affairs through her part in ministerial intrigues. She played an important role in foreign affairs: during the negotiations which led up to the reversal of alliances in 1756, she was assiduously courted by the Austrian ambassador. Again she made and unmade ministers and, in time of war, even generals. Inevitably she was blamed by the general public both for the extravagance of the court and for the disasters of the Seven Years War.

We have seen how the period of relative peace had come to an end in 1740 with the outbreak of the War of the Austrian Succession. Whereas England backed the claims of Maria Theresa, France supported those of the Elector of Bavaria, and thus found herself at war with the traditional enemy, Austria; she was compelled by the claims of the continental struggle to neglect the more important colonial war with England, on whom she declared war in 1744. The war had begun badly for France with the fiasco of the Bohemian expedition, but a new complexion was put on events by the series of brilliant campaigns conducted in the Austrian Netherlands by the great general Maurice de Saxe, half-German, half-Swedish in origin. In 1745 he defeated the Anglo-Dutch-Austrian forces at Fontenoy, a victory which Voltaire celebrated in a famous poem, and captured a large number of towns, including Ghent, Bruges and Ostend. Though the Young Pretender's expedition came to a disastrous end at Culloden at the beginning of 1746, Maurice de Saxe continued his advance in the Austrian Netherlands and occupied Brussels; in the following year he penetrated into Holland and won a costly victory at Lawfeld.

The war against England at sea and in the colonies went less well. Although the French navy had been greatly improved since the Treaty of Utrecht, it was still only about one-third of the size of its English rival; it continued to be sacrificed to the land forces. The English navy was thus able to inflict several defeats on the French and even to land troops on French soil. In North America the port of Louisbourg on Cape Breton Island was seized by New England colonists, supported by the English fleet. In India, despite overwhelming English sea power, the French did somewhat better than this; in 1746 they seized the English settlement at Madras, and succeeded in repulsing the English land and sea forces which besieged Pondicherry.

The Treaty of Aix-la-Chapelle which brought the war to an end in 1748 was highly unpopular in France; 'bête comme la paix' the populace of Paris is reported to have said. England and France agreed to hand back their respective conquests in the war; thus while France regained Cape Breton Island, she lost not only Madras, but all the territory occupied by Maurice de Saxe in the course of his brilliant campaigns in the Low Countries.

So far as Anglo-French rivalry was concerned, the War of the Austrian Succession ended more or less in a stalemate. Such was not the case with the Seven Years War which followed after a few years of uneasy peace; it had calamitous results for

France, since it was to cost her both Canada and her chances
of an empire in India. Hostilities between the two countries
in North America and at sea, broke out before the declaration
of war in 1756. The opening of the war in Europe was preceded
by the famous reversal of alliances. In order to protect Hanover,
the English government allied itself with Frederick the Great
by the Treaty of Westminster in January 1756. When news of
this treaty reached Versailles, it gave a fillip to the secret
negotiations which had already been going on for some time
between the two traditional enemies, France and Austria.
Before more than a preliminary treaty had been signed between
the two countries, Frederick opened the war by invading
Saxony. The second treaty of Versailles, signed in May 1757,
went much further than the first; in addition to furnishing
troops and subsidies, France agreed not to make peace until
Austria had wrested back Silesia from Frederick, and in return
was to receive a certain number of towns in the Austrian
Netherlands. By this unequal bargain France found herself
committed to a war on the Continent while she was already
engaged in the much more important struggle with England.
In the event, she suffered disastrous defeats at sea and in her
colonial possessions while absorbed in the land war in Europe.

There Frederick the Great managed, as if by a miracle, to
resist the combined but disunited armies of France, Austria and
Russia. After some initial successes, the French army under a
court general, Soubise, along with an Austrian army, suffered
a crushing defeat at the hands of Frederick at Rossbach, a
village in Thuringia, in 1757. In the following year a French
army operating in Western Germany suffered a humiliating
defeat at Crefeld. In the next three years, from 1759 to 1761,
further campaigns were fought in Western Germany, but they
were all a failure, partly because the French generals fell out
with one another. Altogether the performance of the different
French armies in the continental war caused shame and alarm
in France.

The war at sea and in the colonies had even more unfortunate
results. France began the war with a relatively small, but still
respectable navy; outnumbered and outmanœuvred by the

English fleets, French ships were soon swept from the seas. English troops were landed at various points along the coasts of France to do what destruction they could, although the 13,000 men landed in Brittany were repulsed. The French plans for an invasion of England in 1759 ended disastrously; the Mediterranean fleet was defeated at Lagos on the Portuguese coast, while the Brest fleet was destroyed at Quiberon. Henceforth her navy was negligible and her colonies defenceless.

The consequences for French possessions in North America, the West Indies and India were calamitous. After seizing Cape Breton Island in 1758, British forces cut off the French colony of Louisiana from Canada. In the following year Wolfe arrived before Quebec and forced the city to capitulate; its fall, and that of Montreal a year later, settled the fate of the colony. In the West Indies the French islands of Guadeloupe and Martinique were also captured. In India where, thanks to Dupleix, France had shortly before been on the point of founding a vast empire on the ruins of the Mogul monarchy, all her possessions were lost.

France was compelled to pay the price for these humiliating defeats in the Treaty of Paris which, in 1763, brought to an end the war with England. She lost all her possessions in North America, except for the tiny islands of Saint-Pierre and Miquelon to the south of Newfoundland, and the western half of Louisiana (the eastern half was ceded to her ally, Spain, to compensate her for the loss of Florida). Canada and its approaches were lost for ever. In the West Indies she had to cede several islands, though she managed to keep Martinique, Guadeloupe and St. Lucia, as well as the rich colony of Saint-Domingue. In India her possessions were reduced to the trading-posts which she had possessed at the time of the Treaty of Aix-la-Chapelle. Thus English sea power had destroyed French influence both in India and North America. In the war on the Continent, thanks to Frederick the Great's victories Prussia had clearly emerged as the strongest power in Germany.'

Out of the Seven Years War arose an alliance between the Bourbon rulers of France, Spain, Parma and Naples, who signed in 1761 the so-called *Pacte de Famille*. Spain had joined in the war against England in 1762, but with results which were hardly helpful to her French ally. However, the alliance was to work better during the War of American Independence. In 1770 the two allies were almost involved in a war against England by a dispute over the Falkland Islands, but at the last moment, in view of her internal difficulties, France drew back and succeeded in restraining the ardour of Spain.

The last part of the reign of Louis XV did nothing to arrest the decline of French influence in Europe. France had to stand helplessly by while Austria, Prussia and Russia took part in the first partition of Poland. The Austrian alliance, newly cemented in 1770 by the marriage between the Dauphin, the future Louis XVI, and the Archduchess Marie Antoinette, had brought France no advantages and was still unpopular. The last part of the reign filled Frenchmen with a feeling of humiliation at the decline of their country's prestige in Europe.

In internal affairs during the second half of the reign the first outstanding event was the attempt of Machault, who succeeded Orry as *Contrôleur général* in 1745, to put through important reforms in the taxation system. So long as the war lasted he was compelled to resort to such expedients as loans in order to keep the French armies in the field, and when it ended in 1748, the finances of France were in a critical state, as the King had promised that the *dixième* imposed during the war would end with it, and this left no means of coping with the large debt incurred during these years. Machault's attention was mainly directed towards redressing the inequalities in France's system of direct taxation. He aimed at effecting a slight reduction in the *taille* and at forcing both the inhabitants of those provinces with estates (the *pays d'états*) and the privileged orders to make a larger contribution to the Treasury. In 1749 two government edicts appeared, one to raise a loan to cover the war debt and the other to establish a new tax, the *vingtième*, the revenue from which was to be used to create a sinking fund to secure the repayment of the national debt. Unlike the *dixième* which had been imposed in periods of war and then allowed to drop until a fresh emergency arose, the *vingtième* was to be a permanent tax. Moreover, it was to be paid by all persons without distinction of rank and it was to be collected directly by the government, even in the *pays d'états* which in the past had managed to secure *abonnements* for such taxes as the *capitation* and *dixième*, with the result that they paid far less per head of the population than the provinces without estates.

Such a tax was unlikely to be popular with either the privileged orders or the *pays d'états*. The Paris Parlement made remonstrances against the two edicts, masking its anger at a tax which would fall on the nobility as well as the *tiers état* by hypocritical lamentations about the sufferings which it would bring to the poor;

> Qu'il nous soit permis d'ajouter, Sire, que cette espèce d'imposition ne doit être employée que dans les besoins les plus pressants.
>
> Que, comme elle se répartit indistinctement sur tous vos sujets, qu'elle frappe également sur le pauvre et sur le riche, qu'elle est de telle nature que le pauvre, quelque retranchement qu'il fasse, même sur son nécessaire, ne peut en adoucir la charge, sa rigueur et son étendue portent trop loin pour qu'on doive en faire usage dans de simples vues de précautions et d'arrangement. (Flammermont, I, 400)

However, the Parlement's resistance was shortlived and it finally registered the two edicts.

Stiffer opposition was encountered from the *pays d'états* which would have preferred, failing the withdrawal of the new tax, to have had an *abonnement* under which they would have escaped paying their fair share. The Estates of Languedoc, finding their attempts to wriggle out of all or part of the new tax were vain, refused to vote their usual contribution (*don gratuit*) to the Treasury and had to be dissolved. For two years, from 1750 to 1752, the Estates were not summoned and the *vingtième* was levied directly by the *Intendant*. Even sharper resistance was encountered in Brittany, where the nobility played the leading role in the Estates. Some of its leaders were imprisoned, but the Estates succeeded in sabotaging the collection of the new tax.

The stiffest resistance of all was put up by the clergy. Machault calculated that, leaving aside the 30 millions of the *clergé étranger*, the total income of the *clergé de France* came to 220 million livres. After allowance had been made for the stipends of the *curés* and the cost of schools, hospitals and other charitable institutions, there still remained a taxable income of 114 millions. While one-twentieth of this represented some five and a half million livres, the average annual contribution made by the clergy since the beginning of the century in the form of the *don gratuit* amounted to only 3,655,000 livres. When the *Assemblée du Clergé* met in 1750, Machault did not mention the possibility of applying the *vingtième* to the incomes of the clergy, but asked instead for a sum of 7½ million livres, payable in five annual instalments, as a contribution towards the repayment of the national debt. As this contribution was to be based on declarations of incomes by the clergy, the Assembly felt that this was merely the first step in subjecting it to the new tax.

Barbier gives a very clear account of the situation in his journal:

> Dans le discours des commissaires et dans la déclaration du roi il n'est pas dit un mot de l'imposition du vingtième sur les biens ecclésiastiques, pour ne point effaroucher le clergé; mais il prévoit bien que toutes les déclarations particulières étant une fois données, vérifiées et arrêtées, la perception du vingtième ou du dixième, dans les cas pressants, sera aussi facile que sur tous les autres biens du royaume. Et c'est ce titre d'imposition égale et commune à tous les autres sujets que le clergé ne veut point entendre, prétendant ne contribuer aux charges de l'État que volontairement et par don gratuit, et n'être point assujetti de droit à une imposition, par le privilège des biens ecclésiastiques.

Barbier vigorously rejects this claim to privilege in the matter of taxation (his reference to England throws interesting light on the penetration into France of a knowledge of conditions in this country):

> Mais, dans le fond, ce privilège prétendu, ainsi que tous les autres, ne sont que de pures visions. La taxe des impositions sur les biens doit être proportionnelle et répartie également sur tous les sujets du roi et membres de l'État, à proportion des biens que chacun possède réellement dans le royaume. En Angleterre, les

terres du clergé, de la noblesse et du tiers état payent également, sans distinction; et pour les bestiaux chaque tête paye une somme. Rien n'est plus juste. (*Chronique de la Régence*, IV, 469-70)

This view was not shared by the clergy; they complained to the King about this measure, and when the Assembly was ordered to reach a decision on the matter, it protested and was dissolved.

A considerable number of pamphlets—one of them was contributed by Voltaire—attacked the clergy's claim to exemption; but the government was divided and finally Louis gave way to the resistance of the privileged orders. At the end of 1751 the demand for an annual payment of 1½ million livres from the clergy was withdrawn, and when Machault ceased to be *Contrôleur général* in 1754, his successor allowed the Estates of Brittany and Languedoc to compound for a lump sum by way of their *abonnement*. The attempt to reduce the inequalities in the taxation system had been successfully resisted by the privileged orders, and the financial position of the monarchy remained precarious.

In the early 1750s, after a lull of nearly twenty years, the Jansenist controversy and the clash between the Parlements and the Crown flared up again with renewed vigour. The quarrel between Jansenists and Jesuits, Gallicans and Ultramontanes, now reached its height though, when it was disposed of by the suppression of the Jesuits in 1764, the struggle between the King and his Parlements was to become even more violent.

In 1749, in order to stamp out Jansenism, certain bishops who supported the Bull *Unigenitus* began to order their clergy to refuse the sacraments to people suspected of Jansenist sympathies, if they did not produce what was called a *billet de confession*, a certificate that they had made their confession to a priest who accepted the bull. Naturally great scandal was caused when sick Jansenist sympathisers were refused the sacraments, particularly as some died without the consolations of religion. The answer of Jansenist families subjected to this form of persecution was to denounce to the Parlements the priests who had refused the sacraments.

The Parlements were, of course, delighted to take action. They fined the priests and ordered them to administer the sacraments; if they refused to obey, they issued a warrant for their arrest and sold up their property. The new Archbishop of Paris, Christophe de Beaumont, against whom Rousseau was to employ his eloquence in the controversy aroused by his *Émile*, was among the clerics who had ordered priests to refuse the sacraments to persons suspected of Jansenist sympathies. After dealing with *curés* of his diocese, the Paris Parlement finally took proceedings against the Archbishop himself and threatened to sell up his property.

In this quarrel between Gallicans and Ultramontanes, the Parlements and the higher clergy, the King naturally tended to side with the clergy as he considered it less dangerous to the authority of the Crown. Mme du Hausset, the *femme de chambre* of Mme de Pompadour, gives in her memoirs a vivid account of the King's dislike and fear of the Parlements when she reproduces the following conversation between Louis and his mistress:

> Un jour le maître entra tout échauffé. Je me retirai; mais j'écoutai dans mon poste. 'Qu'avez-vous? lui dit madame.—Ces grandes robes et le clergé, répondit-il, sont toujours à couteaux tirés; ils me désolent par leurs querelles. Mais je déteste bien plus les grandes robes. Mon clergé, au fond, m'est attaché et fidèle; les autres voudraient me mettre en tutelle.' . . . M. de Gontaut entra, et, voyant qu'on parlait sérieusement, ne dit rien. Le roi se promenait agité; puis tout d'un coup il dit: 'Le régent a eu bien tort de leur rendre le droit de faire des remontrances; ils finiront par perdre l'État.—Ah! sire, dit M. de Gontaut, il est bien fort pour que de petits robins puissent l'ébranler.—Vous ne savez pas ce qu'ils font et ce qu'ils pensent, reprit le roi; c'est une assemblée de républicains. En voilà, au reste, assez . . .' (pp. 71-2)

When in February 1753 the King ordered the Paris Parlement to stop all proceedings in cases arising out of refusals of the sacraments, the judges drew up lengthy remonstrances in which they not only defended their conduct in this dispute, but also spoke haughtily of their role as *pouvoirs intermédiaires* between the King and his subjects.

Louis declined to receive these bold remonstrances, and in May, when the Parlement decided to refuse to carry on the

administration of justice, he exiled most of its members to their estates or to various provincial towns and had four judges arrested. The Grand'Chambre, the court containing the most senior judges, was not touched, but when it protested against the exile of the other sections of the Parlement, it was transferred to Pontoise outside Paris. Meanwhile the government was having trouble with the provincial Parlements and was compelled to take extreme measures, particularly against the Rouen Parlement which had taken drastic action against the Bishop of Évreux and a *curé* who had refused the sacraments to a sick person without a *billet de confession*. This is how Barbier describes the action taken by the government at Rouen:

> M. le marquis de Fougères est arrivé au Parlement, accompagné de tous les officiers d'un régiment de dragons qui est à Rouen, lesquels sont restés dans la Grand'Chambre. . . .
> M. de Fougères a présenté la lettre de cachet à M. le premier président pour en faire lecture, qui portait d'obéir en tout à M. de Fougères; défenses au Parlement de délibérer; et ordre au Parlement de faire rayer et bâtonner en sa présence tous les arrêts rendus par le Parlement, au sujet de l'évêque d'Évreux et du curé de Verneuil; et de transcrire sur les registres, à la marge, l'ordre du roi.
> Messieurs du Parlement de Rouen, attendu la défense de délibérer, se sont tous levés sur-le-champ et se sont retirés, malgré les représentations de M. de Fougères qu'ils ont laissé seul.
> Le greffier voulait aussi se retirer, mais M. de Fougères l'a arrêté et lui a présenté un ordre du roi, particulier pour lui; sur quoi il a été obligé de représenter les registres sur lesquels M. de Fougères a fait biffer tous les arrêts et transcrire l'ordre du roi, par un petit clerc qu'il avait, dit-on, avec lui. (*Chronique de la Régence*, V, 404-5)

Meanwhile the conflict between the King and the Paris Parlement dragged on. The judges at Pontoise refused to deal with ordinary cases and in November they were sent still further from Paris to exile at Soissons. To take the place of the Parlement the King was obliged to set up a new court, made up of *conseillers d'État* and *maîtres des requêtes*; neither the lower courts nor the lawyers would recognize these judges, who were

thus left with nothing to do. In May 1754 Barbier wrote in his journal:

> Le 5 de ce mois, il y a un an que le Parlement fit son arrêté de cesser leurs fonctions pour les affaires du Palais, dont le public, peu prévoyant en général, fut si content que l'on claqua des mains dans la grande salle et que l'on cria: Vive le Parlement!
>
> Le 9, il y a un an que Messieurs des Enquêtes et Requêtes sont partis de Paris pour aller au lieu de leur exil. Le 11, il y a un an que le Parlement fut transféré à Pontoise, où Messieurs de la Grand'Chambre se rendirent le lendemain.
>
> A cette joie inconsidérée du 5 mai 1753 a succédé une grande misère parmi les gens du Palais (ils ne s'attendaient pas à de si longues vacances), et beaucoup d'ennui à tous messieurs les magistrats. On ne croit pas qu'en pareille occasion ils quittent une seconde fois leurs fonctions, ni que le public les y excite par les applaudissements. (*Chronique de la Régence*, VI, 27)

Two months later, however, negotiations between the government and the leaders of the Parlement were brought to a successful conclusion, and the government gave way to the extent of recalling the exiled judges for 1 September.

On its return the Parlement registered by a narrow majority a royal declaration which, while reproaching the judges for their past disobedience, imposed absolute silence in the dispute about the Bull *Unigenitus*.

> Par cet arrangement [wrote Barbier] le Parlement obtient tacitement tout ce qu'il a toujours prétendu; car le roi imposant ce silence et défendant toute innovation, défend les billets de confession, les refus de sacrements, les questions sur la Constitution; non seulement permet, mais enjoint au Parlement de procéder contre les ecclésiastiques contrevenants. M. l'archevêque de Paris et le clergé ne sont pas contents de cette déclaration. (*Chronique de la Régence*, VI, 54-5)

The so-called *Déclaration de silence* failed to restore peace. Acting on the orders of their bishops, priests continued to refuse the sacraments to persons without a *billet de confession*. The Paris Parlement took action against a recalcitrant *curé*, and to satisfy public opinion, the King exiled the Archbishop of Paris to his country house. The provincial Parlements continued to join in the conflict by taking proceedings against various bishops, and the King, much against his will, was compelled to back the Parlements up by exiling several of them.

The Paris Parlement, intoxicated with its triumph, went so far, in March 1755, as to declare solemnly that the Bull *Unigenitus* did not possess 'le caractère . . . et les effets de règle de foi'. This declaration, Barbier tells us, was greeted with enthusiasm by the large number of people present in court when it was made:

> Toute l'audience a claqué des mains à cette prononciation; c'était une joie publique dans la grande salle, et on a regardé cet arrêt comme l'extinction et l'anéantissement de la constitution Unigenitus. . . . Tout le public, qui en général est janséniste, triomphe et est charmé de cet arrêt. (*Chronique de la Régence*, VI, 144-5)

The King was far from pleased: an *arrêt du conseil* annulled this decree, yet the Parlement went on taking proceedings against priests who refused the sacraments to suspected Jansenists.

At this point the Parlement's conflict with the Crown became merged in a new conflict with the rival court of the *Grand Conseil*. In remonstrances presented in November 1755, the Parlement stated publicly its claim to be as old as the monarchy:

> Sire, il y a treize cents ans que la monarchie subsiste, il y a treize cents ans que votre parlement, sous quelque dénomination qu'il ait été connu, forme toujours le même tribunal et exerce les mêmes fonctions dans l'État. Son administration, quant à la manutention des lois, n'a jamais cessé d'être la même jusqu'à ce moment; et il a toujours conservé le glorieux avantage d'être la vraie *Cour de France*, parce qu'il est né avec l'empire des Français pour être une branche de la forme essentielle du gouvernement. (Flammermont, *Remontrances*, II, 26)

After declaring that no royal edict could have force of law unless registered by the Parlement and that it was 'dépositaire des lois du royaume', it went on to vaunt the advantages of a monarchy in which the will of the sovereign was tempered by the advice of the highest courts in the land:

C'est dans cette vue, sire, que pour éclairer et tempérer le pouvoir absolu de la souveraineté par la prudence des conseils, la bonté de nos souverains a communiqué de tout temps à leurs premiers magistrats cette puissance établie pour soumettre la licence des hommes à l'équité des princes; ils ont senti, ils ont reconnu, sire, que de tels ministres de leur autorité ne servent qu'à faire régner justement les monarques et à leur concilier de plus en plus les peuples. . . .

Et quels avantages n'ont pas résulté, sire, depuis la naissance de la monarchie jusqu'à ce jour, de ce mélange heureux de souveraineté et de prudence, et de cette sage modération de l'une par l'autre! Harmonie constante et essentielle, aussi ancienne que l'empire français; c'est à elle qu'il est redevable de ces progrès et de sa grandeur; elle est le principe et le gage de sa conservation; elle maintient sans effort l'autorité; elle assure la souveraineté par la justice. (Flammermont, *Remontrances*, II, 86-7)

This quarrel with the *Grand Conseil*, which was favoured by the King, dragged on into 1756. In February the Parlement played its trump card; it decided to invite the princes of the blood and *ducs et pairs* to assist it in its deliberations to defend the honour of the 'cour des pairs'. The significance of this move lay in the fact that this was the first time in the eighteenth century that the Parlement had appealed to the highest members of the aristocracy to come to its aid in its struggle with the Crown. On this occasion the King's order forbidding them to appear at the Parlement was obeyed, but, later in the century, their part in events was to add to the discomfiture of the monarchy. Already in 1756 they were only too eager to play their part in the struggle against the Crown. As d'Argenson put it, 'les pairs sont plus ardents que les magistrats; ils grillent d'entrer dans les affaires publiques, et bientôt ils seront plus aigrement et plus hautement parlementaires que les robins même' (*Journal*, IX, 229).

In the meantime the struggle over the Bull *Unigenitus* went on, and now the outbreak of the Seven Years War increased the tension between the Crown and the different Parlements by compelling the government to seek the registration of edicts to raise the taxes needed to carry on the war. When, in July 1756, the Paris Parlement was asked to register edicts prolonging existing taxes and creating new ones, it made representations which compelled the King to hold a *lit de justice*, the first since 1732. Matters were further complicated by the conflicts in progress between the government and various provincial Parlements. As in recent struggles they had supported the Paris Parlement, the latter returned the compliment by supporting their provincial colleagues and protested to the King against various acts of the government, which it alleged, tended to destroy 'la sûreté des offices des différentes classes de son parlement, la dignité de leur caractère et la liberté de leurs suffrages' (Flammermont, *Remontrances*, II, 133).

This was the first time that the Paris court had publicly maintained the doctrine that all the Parlements of France formed one body, the individual members of which were, to use its expression, 'les différentes classes' of the Parlement of France. Contemporaries were quick to seize on the importance of this expression. 'Voilà, ce me semble,' wrote d'Argenson, 'la première fois que le Parlement déclare à Sa Majesté et au public son système foncier que tous les parlements n'en font qu'un seul, mais distribués en différentes quadrilles ou *classes*' (*Journal*, IX, 293). The importance of this claim is brought out even more clearly by Barbier when he stresses the limitations which, if accepted, it would impose on the power of the Crown.

> On suppose que les douze Parlements du royaume ne forment qu'un même corps dans l'État, qu'il n'y a en France qu'un seul Parlement, dont celui de Paris est le chef et les autres les membres, une émanation, un démembrement, cela suivant l'ancienne constitution de l'État. Cette proposition, jointe au système général déjà établi, qu'aucune loi ne peut être publique et assujettir les sujets, qu'autant qu'elle aura été vérifiée, reçue et consentie et enregistrée dans les parlements, limiterait essentiellement l'autorité royale et le pouvoir du souverain, dans le cas d'une union bien entendue entre tous les parlements du royaume.
> (*Chronique de la Régence*, VI, 330)

At this time the provincial Parlements were showing themselves even bolder than the Paris court; as d'Argenson put it: 'Le plus difficile pour l'autorité royale sera de soumettre les parlements provinciaux qui sont plus résistants et plus révoltés

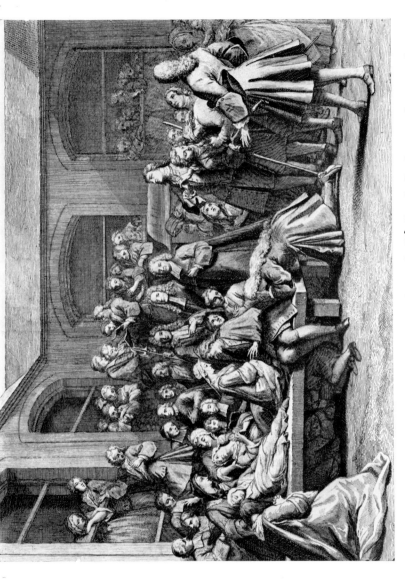

29  Le Tombeau du B. François de Pâris, Diacre de l'Église de Paris, mort le 1$^{er}$ mai 1727.
Illustré par des miracles sans nombre et des conversions éclatantes

30
*L. M. Vanloo*, Louis XV

31
*Boucher*, Mme de Pompadour

que celui de Paris. Ils sont tous complotés pour dépouiller les intendants de leur autorité' (*Journal*, IX, 372).

The last months of 1756 and the beginning of 1757 were a period of near-anarchy in France. In November, a pastoral letter of the Archbishop of Paris which a lower court, acting during the Parlement's vacation, held to infringe the King's declaration of silence on the bull, was burnt by the hangman. In December, the Parlement suppressed as published without permission a papal brief, solicited by the French government, which, while instructing the clergy to refuse the sacraments to persons known for their rejection of the Bull *Unigenitus*, forbade the use of *billets de confession*. The King's answer was to hold another *lit de justice* in which the Parlement was compelled to register a royal declaration which confirmed the Bull *Unigenitus* as a 'règle de foi', that is, destroyed the Parlement's claim that it was not, and at the same time a royal edict which abolished two sections of the Parlement. Thereupon nearly all the judges resigned their posts, and as the *avocats* refused to plead, those who remained could only petition the King for the return of their colleagues.

The internal state of France at the end of 1756, when she had a fresh European war on her hands, is summed up in one of the last entries of d'Argenson's journal which, even allowing for the author's tendency to exaggerate, gives an alarming picture of the disintegration of the King's authority:

Le roi a tenu ce discours: 'Il faut qu'il n'y ait plus de roi, s'il subsiste encore en France un parlement, comme il était avant le lit de justice que j'ai tenu le 13 décembre . . .' Aussi se répand-il un sérieux triste et profond sur cet événement; le peuple est en rage muette, et qu'on ne croie pas qu'il manque de canaux multipliés pour faire passer dans les masses *l'idée de la résistance*. Les gens de justice sont partout, agents supérieurs ou inférieurs, leurs innombrables suppôts, les plaideurs, une estime générale pour la magistrature, qui est réellement la portion la plus estimable aujourd'hui de la nation par ses mœurs, son savoir et ses lumières; tout le second ordre de l'Église opposé à la bulle *Unigenitus* et leurs dévots, ce qui va encore plus loin; toutes les provinces, leurs cours supérieures, la misère qui prêche, les magistrats qui consolent, un sourd mécontentement contre la cour, une fureur non déguisée contre l'avidité des hommes de finance, une révolte ouverte contre les intendants, l'envie, la pauvreté, la faim. (*Journal*, IX, 377-8)

Critical as the situation looked at the beginning of 1757, matters were slightly eased by a diversion: the attempt on Louis XV's life by a certain Damiens. This gave the Parlement an important criminal case to try. By September of that year, seeing that it was impossible to overcome the resistance of those members of the Parlement who had resigned their posts, the King gave way and accepted a compromise.

The financial difficulties which arose in the course of the Seven Years War led to fresh conflicts between the Crown and the different Parlements. In 1759 Louis XV was obliged to hold another *lit de justice* to compel the Paris Parlement to register edicts creating new taxes; but the matter did not end there, as the Parlement presented remonstrances at the beginning of 1760 against the manner in which the registration had been secured. It maintained that no law could be valid unless it was freely discussed before it was registered:

Toute administration dans l'État est fondée sur les lois. Il n'en est aucune sans un enregistrement libre, précédé de vérification et d'examen. Cette vérification, nécessaire pour donner à toutes les lois le caractère d'authenticité auquel les peuples reconnaissent l'autorité qui doit les conduire, n'est pas moins intéressante pour les sujets, ni moins utile aux vues du souverain, lorsque la loi a pour objet de procurer des secours à l'État par la voie des impositions. (Flammermont, *Remontrances*, II, 274)

Barbier brings out in his journal the boldness of these principles and also shows that they had the support of a considerable section of the community:

Cela porte un furieux coup à l'autorité souveraine, et le ministère est obligé de souffrir toutes ces réserves et protestations, par le besoin d'argent et les circonstances malheureuses où l'État se trouve réduit par la mauvaise administration et encore plus par la trop grande bonté du roi, qui souffre autour de lui un nombre infini de gens qui ne cherchent que pillage. Le Parlement a raison de profiter des circonstances pour étendre son autorité, d'autant plus que les peuples, accablés d'impôts et prévenus par les bruits et les plaintes sur l'administration, comptent trouver quelque adoucissement par le moyen de la résistance du Parlement. (*Chronique de la Régence*, VII, 237)

The Parlement kept up its resistance to all new taxes, and in the following year the King had to hold yet another *lit de justice* before new financial edicts were registered. In the speech which he made on the King's behalf, the Chancellor upbraided the judges for their unpatriotic attitude in resisting new taxes in the middle of a war.

Meanwhile the provincial Parlements were offering the same opposition to new taxes. The Rouen Parlement showed itself particularly bold. In 1760, after denouncing in its remonstrances all the new taxes introduced since the last meeting of the *États généraux* in 1614, it demanded the restoration of the Estates of the province:

Rendez-nous, sire, notre liberté précieuse; rendez-nous nos États. Il est de l'essence d'une loi d'être acceptée; le droit d'accepter est le droit de la nation; ce droit vainqueur du temps et des préjugés, ce droit, autrefois l'âme du gouvernement français, subsiste encore, malgré les efforts conjurés des passions intéressées à l'anéantir. Ce droit subsiste, et V.M. le reconnaît en adressant ses édits aux magistrats qui peuvent suppléer à la nation en les vérifiant. Exercé, pendant l'interstice des États, par ceux que la nation regarde comme dépositaires de la législation, ce droit sacré et imprescriptible ne saurait l'être que par eux. (Floquet, *Histoire du Parlement de Normandie*, VI, 371)

It was not a far cry from this demand for the restoration of provincial estates to what was soon to become the slogan of the Parlements: 'Summon the *États généraux*!'

The most important minister in this part of the reign was the Duc de Choiseul who, in 1758, was appointed secretary of state for foreign affairs. He remained in office until 1770, and although not formally prime minister, wielded considerable power, especially as he also came to hold two other secretaryships of state, those for war and the navy. His main achievements lay in the realm of foreign policy where he had the task of liquidating the Seven Years War; he also signed the *Pacte de*

*Famille* among the Bourbon rulers and annexed Corsica in 1768. In home affairs he was responsible for general policy, but the divisions inside the government showed up the increasing weakness of the monarchy.

Nowhere was this seen more clearly than in the way the Paris Parlement and most of the provincial Parlements carried through the dissolution of the Society of Jesus, almost without the government daring to intervene. This surprising conclusion to the long controversy between Jansenists and Jesuits arose out of a curious cause, the unsuccessful commercial enterprises of Father La Vallette, a Jesuit missionary on the island of Martinique in the West Indies. This father was ruined by the capture of various French vessels in the hostilities with England which raged even before the outbreak of the Seven Years War. A Marseilles firm to which he owed 1½ million livres went bankrupt as a result, and decided to sue for the debt, not the Society in Martinique, but the main body in France. The firm won its case, and the Jesuits were rash enough to appeal to their old enemy, the Paris Parlement.

In 1761 they lost their case, were ordered to pay damages as well as their debt, and were forbidden to engage in any commercial transactions in future. The verdict was received with enthusiasm by the general public. This was only the beginning of their misfortunes. The Parlement rapidly took further steps. It ordered distraint upon all the property of the Society in France in order to secure the payment of its debt to the Marseilles firm. Worse still, it decided to examine the statutes of the Society, and its commissioners proceeded to rake over all the more dubious aspects of its past history—its theories of regicide and the murder of Henry III, the resistance to Henry IV under the Ligue, the recent attempt to assassinate the King of Portugal, not forgetting the Gunpowder Plot. Despite the government's efforts to take the affair into its own hands, the Parlement went ahead; in August 1761 it condemned twenty-four books written by Jesuits to be burnt by the hangman and ordered all pupils in Jesuit schools and seminaries to leave them before 1 October.

At this point Louis XV intervened and postponed the closing

of Jesuit schools for a year. The Parlement, however, registered this edict only on condition that the delay should be limited to 1 April 1762. Before the fatal date came round, the King issued a declaration which would have regularized the position of the Jesuits in France, but the Parlement played out time until 1 April. The Jesuit schools were then closed, and in August the Parlement suppressed the Society in France, sequestrated its property and dispersed its members. In the next two years most of the provincial Parlements also condemned the Society. Given the general unpopularity of the Jesuits, Louis XV dared not intervene on their behalf. However, when in 1764 the Paris Parlement ordered the ex-Jesuits to leave the country, the King at last acted, and while decreeing the dissolution of the Society, allowed its members to remain in France and quashed all legal proceedings against them.

The closing of the Jesuit schools raised many educational problems, both administrative—the schools had to be controlled by someone, and teachers were needed to staff them—and theoretical. There had long been dissatisfaction with the state of secondary education in France. The Jesuit curriculum, which consisted mainly of Latin and scholastic philosophy, was considered quite unsuited to the needs of the educated classes. There was a widespread demand for a more modern education, one which would include French and French literature, modern languages, history, geography and, of course, the sciences in which the age was passionately interested. Some effort was in fact made to introduce a more modern curriculum into schools in the last decades of the Ancien Régime.

The judges of the Parlements, one of the best educated sections of the community, naturally took a considerable part in these discussions about the reorganization of secondary education. One of the most important educational works to appear in these years was the *Essai d'éducation nationale*, published in 1763 by La Chalotais, *procureur général* (attorney general) of the Rennes Parlement, who, as we shall see, was to play a prominent part in the struggles between the Parlements and the Crown in the years which followed.

The end of the war in 1763 at once led to a new conflict over taxes. A second and a third *vingtième* were both due to disappear with the coming of peace; but the Treasury was overwhelmed with debts, and although the government abolished the third *vingtième*, it was compelled to retain the second for a further six years, and, what annoyed the privileged orders including the judges of the Parlements most of all, it began to take measures to carry out a proper land survey which would gradually wipe out the grosser inequalities in the assessment of the tax. The Parlements resisted with all their might. The King had to hold a *lit de justice* in Paris to secure the registration of the edicts concerning this and other fiscal matters, The opposition of the provincial Parlements was even stiffer, as Barbier explains:

> Il y a eu jusqu'ici une grande fermentation dans la plus grande partie des parlements du royaume, sur le refus d'enregistrer l'édit et les déclarations du mois d'avril dernier, au sujet des impôts, et surtout à Grenoble, contre le marquis Dumesnil; à Besançon, contre le duc de Randan; à Rouen, contre le duc d'Harcourt; à Toulouse, contre le duc de Fitzjames, tous lieutenants généraux pour le roi dans les provinces et porteurs des ordres du roi pour faire enregistrer forcément ces édits et déclarations du mois d'avril, jusque-là que le Parlement de Rouen a donné la démission de ses charges, au nombre de plus de quatre-vingts; qu'il y a eu des décrets de prise de corps contre ces messieurs porteurs des ordres, en sorte qu'on n'a point perçu les droits nouveaux dans ces provinces. (*Chronique de la Régence*, VIII, 112)

Once more the King gave way and dismissed the *Contrôleur général*, replacing him by a judge from the Paris Parlement, whom he allowed to lay down the condition that, so long as the *vingtièmes* continued to be levied, it must be on the existing assessments. This meant both that the present inequalities would continue and that the Treasury would be unable to profit from any increase in the national wealth; the problem of reducing the deficit was thereby made more difficult.

The weakness of the government came out most clearly in this period of the reign in its handling of the conflict between the Duc d'Aiguillon, the *commandant* of Brittany (that is the representative, along with the *Intendant*, of the central government) and the Parlement and the Estates of the province.

D'Aiguillon was on bad terms with La Chalotais, the *Procureur général* of the Parlement of Rennes. When in 1764 this Parlement was called up to register a financial edict, it did so with all manner of restrictions and made various violent criticisms of the administration of the province by d'Aiguillon. The government thereupon summoned to Versailles the chief members of the Parlement and after the King had addressed a stinging rebuke to the deputation, he took La Chalotais aside and said to him: 'Conduisez-vous avec plus de modération; c'est moi qui vous le dis, ou vous vous en repentirez.'

When the deputation arrived back in Rennes, the Parlement, far from showing remorse, drew up new remonstrances to justify those which had given offence. In the light of events some twenty years later, this document has a sinister ring, for in defending the rights of their province, the judges put forward the principle that only the *États généraux* could give their consent to taxes:

> L'Établissement de Saint-Louis, les décisions des États généraux au commencement du treizième siècle, les ordonnances de 1355, 1560 et 1576 ne permettent pas de douter que dans le droit commun de la France le consentement des trois ordres dans l'assemblée des États généraux ne soit nécessaire pour l'établissement ou la prorogation des impositions. (Le Moy, *Remontrances du Parlement de Bretagne*, p. 86)

Although these remonstrances were received less brutally than the first, trouble was to arise later in the same year when the Estates of Brittany met. Down to our own day this province has been noted for its particularist tendencies, and until 1789 it was dominated by the nobility. An edict increasing the indirect taxes of the province had been registered, though with reservations, by the Parlement; but when the Estates met, they protested to the vacation court of the Parlement which promptly forbade the levying of the extra taxes. When the full Parlement met after the vacation, it had torn down copies of the government edict quashing the vacation court's decision, returned to the King his letters patent containing this edict, and suspended the administration of justice. Finally, in May 1765, encouraged in their resistance by the other Parlements, all the judges except twelve resigned their posts.

Thereupon the government ordered the arrest of a number of members of the Parlement, including La Chalotais. A special court was set up to try him and a new Parlement formed. This produced indignant protests from both the Paris and the provincial Parlements. In accordance with the doctrine that the different Parlements of France were merely branches of one body, the Paris Parlement drew up repeated remonstrances protesting against the treatment of their Breton colleagues. Finally the King's patience gave out, and in March 1766 he went in person to the Palais de Justice and held a *séance royale*, known as 'la séance de la flagellation' because of the scathing terms in which he spoke of the political claims of the Parlements. In the declaration which he had read out he dismissed as pernicious innovations the following catalogue of their political claims:

> . . . que tous les parlements ne font qu'un seul et même corps, distribué en plusieurs classes; que ce corps, nécessairement indivisible, est de l'essence de la monarchie et qu'il lui sert de base; qu'il est le siège, le tribunal, l'organe de la nation; qu'il est le protecteur et le dépositaire essentiel de sa liberté, de ses intérêts, de ses droits; qu'il lui répond de ce dépôt, et serait criminel envers elle s'il l'abandonnait; qu'il est comptable de toutes les parties du bien public, non seulement au roi, mais aussi à la nation; qu'il est juge entre le roi et son peuple; que, gardien respectif, il maintient l'équilibre du gouvernement, en réprimant également l'excès de la liberté et l'abus du pouvoir; que les parlements coopèrent avec la puissance souveraine dans l'établissement des lois; qu'ils peuvent quelquefois par leur seul effort s'affranchir d'une loi enregistrée et la regarder à juste titre comme non existante; qu'ils doivent opposer une barrière insurmontable aux décisions qu'ils attribuent à l'autorité arbitraire et qu'ils appellent des actes illégaux, ainsi qu'aux ordres qu'ils prétendent surpris, et que, s'il en résulte un combat d'autorité, il est de leur devoir d'abandonner leurs fonctions et de se démettre de leurs offices, sans que leurs démissions puissent être reçues.

Against these absurd pretensions Louis maintained—only two

decades before 1789—the absolutist principle that the monarch was the source of all power, including legislative power.

... c'est de moi seul que mes cours tiennent leur existence et leur autorité; la plénitude de cette autorité, qu'elles n'exercent qu'en mon nom, demeure toujours en moi, et l'usage n'en peut jamais être tourné contre moi; c'est à moi seul qu'appartient le pouvoir législatif sans dépendance et sans partage; c'est par ma seule autorité que les officiers de mes cours procèdent, non à la formation, mais à l'enregistrement, à la publication, à l'exécution de la loi, et qu'il leur est permis de me remontrer ce qui est du devoir de bons et utiles conseillers; l'ordre public tout entier émane de moi et les droits et les intérêts de la nation, dont on ose faire un corps séparé du monarque, sont nécessairement unis avec les miens et ne reposent qu'en mes mains. (Flammermont, *Remontrances du Parlement de Paris*, II, 557-8)

The clash between two viewpoints is brought out here with dramatic clarity.

For the moment, at any rate, these bold words did not lead to any decisive action. The Paris Parlement continued to protest against the imprisonment and trial of La Chalotais and their other Breton colleagues. When the government quashed the proceedings against the Breton judges, but exiled them to different parts of France, the Paris Parlement continued to bring pressure on the King to secure their complete pardon and the restoration of the Parlement at Rennes. Finally in 1768 d'Aiguillon resigned his post as *Commandant* of the province, and in the following year the Parlement of Rennes was reinstated. All might have been quiet in Brittany, but the King obstinately refused to reinstate La Chalotais and five of his colleagues.

In the meantime the Paris Parlement continued to oppose the government's financial measures, and to voice its criticisms in stronger and stronger language. At the end of 1768, when the government presented new financial edicts for registration, its remonstrances offered the most biting criticism of the government's policy. After listing the various sums of money which had entered the Treasury in recent years, it scolded: 'Tant d'impôts, tant d'emprunts, tant d'avances, tant de sommes touchées n'ont cependant pas encore, sire, comblé le vide de votre trésor royal.' In sarcastic terms it preached to the King the virtues of a new policy of economy: 'Il est une ressource d'autant plus abondante qu'elle n'a point encore été mise en usage: l'économie.' After pointing out the increase in the pensions paid by the Treasury since the reign of Louis XIV, it summed up its criticisms in insolent terms:

Depuis le retour de la paix,[1] tous les édits contenant emprunts ou imposition ont annoncé, sire, le même motif, la nécessité.

Toutes les très humbles et très respectueuses remontrances de votre parlement ont présenté à V.M. la même ressource, l'économie.

Toutes les réponses de V.M. ont donné à votre parlement les mêmes espérances, celles de la réforme dans les dépenses.

Néanmoins, sire, la dépense paraît toujours avoir augmenté et, par conséquent, la nécessité devenue plus grande a exigé de plus amples secours.

V.M. a la bonté d'assurer de nouveau votre parlement qu'elle s'occupe des moyens de rétablir l'économie dans les dépenses et que ses vues en cette partie ont déjà commencé à s'effectuer utilement.

Votre parlement, sire, plein de confiance dans la bienveillance paternelle de V.M. envers vos peuples, ne balance point à croire qu'elle n'ait donné des ordres à cet égard.

Mais l'exécution de vos ordres, sire, loin d'être manifeste et publique, et les retranchements, loin d'être amples et efficaces, laissent encore douter si les dépenses ne sont pas augmentées. . . .

L'économie bien entendue et bien décidée ne souffre point, sire, de retard; elle coupe dans le vif. (Flammermont, *Remontrances du Parlement de Paris*, III, 45-6, 52-3)

Clearly the warnings of the 'séance de la flagellation' had had no effect. Yet another *lit de justice* had to be held.

In 1769 and 1770 the Paris Parlement continued to harry the government over its financial policy; but the immediate cause of the great event of 1771—the bold reforms of a new chancellor, Maupeou—was the continued controversy over the Duc d'Aiguillon. When the King curtly rejected the petition of the Parlement of Rennes for the recall of La Chalotais and his exiled colleagues, it opened proceedings against d'Aiguillon.

[1] In 1763.

These were quashed by the government, but the duke insisted that he should be tried. For a peer the appropriate tribunal was the Paris Parlement—or rather the most august form of that court, the *cour des pairs*, which required the presence of the princes of the blood and the *ducs et pairs*. The trial of d'Aiguillon opened at Versailles in April 1770 and dragged on until the end of June, when the King held a *lit de justice* and quashed the whole proceedings. The Parlement was furious and, declaring that since d'Aiguillon's honour was compromised, it ordered him 'de ne point venir prendre sa séance en icelle cour et de s'abstenir de faire aucune fonction de pairie jusqu'à ce que par un jugement rendu en la cour des pairs, dans les formes et avec les solennités prescrites par les lois et ordonnances du royaume, que rien ne peut suppléer, il se soit pleinement purgé des soupçons qui entachent son honneur' (Flammermont, *Remontrances du Parlement de Paris*, III, 216-17). When the King quashed these proceedings also, the Parlement did not give way. It went straight on towards its doom and that of all the other Parlements; a new government team was being formed which would take a much stronger line with the recalcitrant judges than Choiseul had done.

Since the installation, in 1768, of a new chancellor, René-Nicolas Maupeou, and the presentation at court of a new mistress, Mme du Barry, in the following year, the days of Choiseul's ministry had been numbered, especially as in 1769 Maupeou was joined in the government by a new *Contrôleur général*, Abbé Terray, who was also hostile to the chief minister. Not only did Choiseul and his wife and sister attempt to pour ridicule on Mme du Barry; he also brought France to the very brink of another war with England. In December 1770 he was relieved of all his offices and exiled to his estates. Though he was to retain a powerful party at court well into the next reign, he never returned to power. With his dismissal the way for an all-out attack on the Parlements was open.

The Paris Parlement continued to intervene in the dispute between the Crown and the Parlement of Rennes. At the end of November, Maupeou sent for registration a royal edict forbidding the Parlements to claim to act as one body, to correspond with one another and to cease the administration of justice, under penalty of confiscation of their posts. The Parlement was placed in an awkward dilemma; either it obeyed and renounced all its political claims, or else it disobeyed and risked a headlong collision with the government. When the Parlement met on 3 December, it decided to make representations to the King against the edict. In face of this resistance the King held a *lit de justice* at Versailles. The Chancellor declared that once the King had rejected the remonstrances of the Parlement on a new edict, the matter was finished.

S'il commande alors, vous lui devez la plus parfaite soumission.

Si vos droits s'étendaient plus loin, si votre résistance n'avait pas un terme, vous ne seriez plus ses officiers, mais ses maîtres; sa volonté serait assujettie à la vôtre; la majesté du trône ne résiderait plus que dans vos assemblées; et, dépouillé des droits les plus essentiels de la couronne, dépendant dans l'établissement des lois, dépendant dans leur exécution, le roi ne conserverait que le nom et l'ombre vaine de la souveraineté. (Flammermont, *Remontrances du Parlement de Paris*, III, 164-5)

The Parlement's answer was to suspend the administration of justice and to offer fresh remonstrances. The King refused to receive these until the Parlement had resumed its functions, but the latter repeatedly declined to obey this command. Maupeou then acted. During the night of 19-20 January 1771, every judge received a *lettre de cachet* ordering him to resume his functions and to state in writing 'par simple déclaration de *oui* ou de *non*' whether he was prepared to do so. Over a hundred refused, and several who had at first consented withdrew their agreement. On the afternoon of the 20th the judges met in the Palais de Justice and reaffirmed their position. The scene which followed is vividly described in the journal of the bookseller, Hardy. His words bring out the impression which Maupeou's attack on the Parlement made on the ordinary citizens of Paris.

Entre 9 et 10 heures du soir, l'assemblée étant terminée, les portes de la Grand'Chambre s'ouvrent et l'on en voit sortir d'abord les huissiers frappant de la baguette devant le doyen, comme ils ont coutume de faire devant le premier président; ensuite le doyen, âgé de quatre-vingt-deux ans, s'appuyant sur un secrétaire de la cour, et tenant dans ses mains tremblantes la déclaration ci-dessus transcrite, puis tous les présidents et conseillers des Enquêtes et Requêtes, en ordre de cour et marchant très posément deux à deux, éclairés par des flambeaux que portaient les domestiques, lesquels se rendent en l'hôtel de M. le premier président, où se trouvent pour lors les présidents à mortier, et remettent la déclaration susdite à ce magistrat qui leur fait l'accueil le plus distingué. Les personnes qui furent les témoins de cette cérémonie, triste et fort ressemblante à des funérailles, ne purent s'empêcher d'être attendries jusqu'aux larmes. On était pénétré de la plus vive douleur de voir l'affreuse inquisition que la Chancellerie s'efforçait d'établir et l'on était singulièrement frappé de l'horreur du tableau d'événements funestes qui se présentaient comme dans un lointain, et dont il ne paraissait pas possible de se garantir, à moins d'un miracle de la toute-puissance de Dieu. (*Mes Loisirs*, I, 234-5)

After this last meeting each judge received a *lettre de cachet*, declaring his post confiscated and exiling him to the provinces.

To take the place of the Parlement, one of the royal councils, the *Conseil des Parties*, was installed in the Palais de Justice; but the *avocats* and *procureurs* refused to recognize the new court, and justice was at a standstill. The brutality of the measures taken by Maupeou aroused resistance in all sections of society. The other *cours souveraines* in Paris and the provincial Parlements protested with the utmost violence against the treatment meted out to their colleagues. The indignation of the other courts led them to put forward the argument that, if the King would not allow the Parlements to protect the interests of the nation, then the only thing left was to summon the *États généraux*. In the most famous protest of all, the Paris Cour des Aides argued that since the King had reduced to silence all the natural intermediaries between himself and his people, the summoning of the *États généraux* now was the only solution: 'Interrogez donc, sire, la nation elle-même, puisqu'il n'y a plus qu'elle qui puisse être écoutée de Votre Majesté' (*Recueil des Réclamations*, I, 27).

The Chancellor went ahead with his plans for a reform of the whole judicial system. As the area of jurisdiction of the Paris Parlement was notoriously too large, new courts were set up at Blois, Châlons, Clermont-Ferrand, Lyons and Poitiers to judge all the civil and criminal cases previously dealt with by the Parlement. The Paris Parlement was kept, but restricted to judging cases concerning the Crown and the peers of the realm; its right to register laws and present remonstrances on them was also preserved. The same edict contained two further reforms —the abolition of the buying and selling of judicial posts and of all charges to litigants. In April, at another *lit de justice*, the King installed a new Parlement in Paris, and when the provincial Parlements renewed their protests, they too were reformed. Two of them were replaced by lesser courts, and although they kept the title of Parlement, the rest were diminished in size, and both the sale of their posts and the charging of fees to litigants were abolished. Very often a great many of the existing judges refused to continue to serve, and had to be exiled and replaced by new men.

The furious opposition encountered by Maupeou's reforms offered a kind of dress rehearsal for the aristocratic revolt of the years 1787 and 1788. The princes of the blood, who since the Fronde had been kept silent by the Crown, won popularity by their protests against these arbitrary acts. The nobility, especially in those provinces which had estates, proclaimed its solidarity with the judicial members of its caste; in Normandy demands were voiced for the restoration not only of the Parlement of Rouen, which had been one of the two courts reduced in rank, but also of the provincial estates abolished in 1655. Some insight into the outlook of the aristocracy in this period is furnished by a memoir sent by two noblewomen to Gustavus III of Sweden. To them the destruction of the Paris Parlement seemed an act of naked despotism which endangered the monarchy itself, since by removing the last barrier to arbitrary government Maupeou had opened people's eyes to the fundamentally despotic nature of the régime and produced a demand for the *États généraux*:

> Nos rois se sont servis de ce parlement pour appuyer et consacrer leur autorité aux yeux du peuple, en laissant dans l'ombre et

l'oubli les États généraux; le peuple s'accoutuma donc à le considérer comme son organe, et la puissance du souverain s'en accrut d'autant; devenue aujourd'hui sans bornes, elle voudrait briser même ce léger frein. Combien ne lui est-il pas utile cependant? Combien d'hommes à qui ce simulacre de liberté faisait croire qu'ils n'étaient pas soumis à une autorité arbitraire? La ruine du parlement n'est pas faite pour augmenter la puissance du roi. . . . Un roi habile, en détruisant tout pouvoir qui peut mettre un obstacle au sien, se gardera bien d'avertir ses sujets qu'il les a rendus esclaves de sa seule volonté, car cette idée effrayante les fait discuter sur l'injustice d'une autorité si grande, et leur fait examiner sur quel droit on se l'attribue. M. le Chancelier, depuis six mois, a fait apprendre l'histoire de France à des gens qui seraient peut-être morts sans l'avoir sue. (Geffroy, *Gustave III et la cour de France*, I, 235-6)

Opposition to Maupeou's reforms was by no means confined to the aristocracy. No doubt many of the changes brought about by him were just in themselves. Under the old Parlements justice had been slow and costly; heavy fees were exacted from litigants and the area of jurisdiction was far too large. The buying and selling of judicial offices was an obvious scandal. Yet, except among the Jesuits and their supporters, the reforms were extremely unpopular. The *Philosophes* in general, while hating the Parlements for their intolerance and their resistance to all reforms, looked upon their abolition as an act of despotism. It is true that Voltaire gave wholehearted and public support to Maupeou. In a series of witty pamphlets he denounced the old Parlements, which he detested for their banning of the works of the *Philosophes* and for such judicial murders as those of Calas and the Chevalier de La Barre. For instance, in a pamphlet entitled *Les Peuples aux Parlements*, he speaks ironically of the protests against such desirable reforms as the abolition of *épices* (payments by litigants to their judges) and the splitting up of the enormous area of jurisdiction of the Paris Parlement:

On sonne le tocsin pour nous alarmer; on nous répète que nous allons devenir esclaves dès le moment que les juges ne recevront plus d'épices. Tremblez, nous dit-on, les impôts vont pleuvoir, quand le parlement de Paris ne jugera plus les procès de Châlons-sur-Marne. (*Œuvres complètes*, XXVIII, 419)

Certainly other *Philosophes* like Diderot and D'Holbach had no illusions about the selfish aims of the Parlements, or their intolerance and obscurantism. Yet the events of 1771 appeared to them to mean the destruction of the last barrier against despotism. Diderot, for instance, wrote to a Russian lady in April of that year:

> Nous touchons à une crise qui aboutira à l'esclavage ou à la liberté; si c'est à l'esclavage, ce sera un esclavage semblable à celui qui existe au Maroc ou à Constantinople. Si tous les parlements sont dissous, et la France inondée de petits tribunaux composés de magistrats sans conscience comme sans autorité, et révocables au premier signe de leur maître, adieu tout privilège des états divers formant un principe correctif qui empêche la monarchie de dégénérer en despotisme. (*Œuvres complètes*, XX, 28)

Yet despite the outcry aroused by the reforms of Maupeou things soon settled down; the new Parlements and other courts got into their stride fairly rapidly, and if all these changes had not been undone after the death of Louis XV only three years later, they might have had good results. They had many advantages from the point of view of the general public, however much they might be contrary to the interests and political claims of the former judges and their allies among the nobility.

Yet the precariousness of the whole reform was demonstrated in the last year of the reign when the prestige of the new Paris Parlement—known as the 'Parlement Maupeou'—was gravely compromised by Beaumarchais, the future author of *Le Barbier de Séville* and *Le Mariage de Figaro*. Beaumarchais owed his considerable fortune largely to his dealings with the *financier*, Pâris-Duverney. Before the latter died in 1770, he signed a document which showed that he owed Beaumarchais 15,000 livres, but his nephew and heir refused to pay up, alleging that the account was forged. Beaumarchais won his case, but his opponent appealed to the new Parlement; in order to win the good graces of the judge in charge of his case, Beaumarchais paid his wife 100 louis for an interview with the husband whom he found dead set against him. The next day he paid for a

34 *Duplessis*, Louis XVI

35 *Mme Vigée-Lebrun*,
Marie-Antoinette

second interview with an expensive watch and also fifteen louis which were, so the judge's wife said, for her husband's secretary. When the second interview could not be arranged, the judge's wife returned the 100 louis and the watch, but not the other 15 louis. In April 1773 he lost his case.

This was a highly discreditable story, both for Beaumarchais and for the judge whose wife was taking money to arrange interviews with litigants. Beaumarchais's answer to the judgment which both ruined him and gave him the reputation of a forger was to ask the judge's wife for the return of the 15 louis which he knew the judge's secretary had never received; and to spread the story in the Paris *salons*. The judge decided to accuse Beaumarchais of attempted corruption, a crime for which there were the heaviest penalties. Between September 1773 and February 1774 Beaumarchais proceeded to defend himself in a brilliant series of *mémoires* in which he set forth his case. He succeeded in winning over public opinion to his side and in discrediting both the individual judge and the whole of the Parlement Maupeou. He was the hero of the hour.

The government of these last years of the reign—the so-called *Triumvirat* of the Chancellor, Maupeou, the *Contrôleur général*, Abbé Terray, and the Duc d'Aiguillon, who became secretary of state for foreign affairs in June 1771—was very far from popular. Terray, a man of considerable intelligence who had specialized in financial matters as a judge of the Paris Parlement, had to face an extremely difficult situation when he entered the government in 1769. The expedients to which the deficit and the heavy national debt drove him were not likely to endear him either to the taxpayer or to the investor in government stocks. On the other hand, his attempt to make the assessment of the *vingtième* less arbitrary did bear fruit and made it the least unsatisfactory of the direct taxes levied under the Ancien Régime. Yet, although his expedients did something to improve the state of the Treasury in the last years of the reign, they did not otherwise change fundamentally the unsatisfactory financial situation. And that was, as we shall see, to weigh heavily on the whole reign of Louis XV's successor.

The long reign came to a sudden end in May 1774, when the

King was carried off by an attack of smallpox at the age of sixty-four. In the last thirty years his earlier popularity had gradually turned into indifference or contempt. The prestige of the monarchy had been gravely impaired by unsuccessful wars, the long conflict with the Parlements and the weakness and extravagance of the government. Public opinion was increasingly eager for reform; and although Maupeou's onslaught on the Parlements had demonstrated that the government was not entirely incapable of vigorous action, it had not been well received, as it appeared to bring out the fundamentally despotic character of absolutism.

Though historians have rightly regarded it as the inglorious reign of a weak and incompetent monarch, a contemporary, looking back in 1774 on events in France since 1715, could still compare the age of Louis XV favourably with that of Louis XIV. It had been, on the whole, a period of rising prices, of relative prosperity for a considerable section of the community, despite many lamentable episodes in the political and military spheres. Abbé de Véri denied that the reign of Louis XIV was the greatest in French history; for him it was the reign of his great-grandson which had been 'l'époque la plus heureuse de notre histoire.'

> Ce n'est sûrement pas à ses talents que ce bonheur est dû . . . Ses qualités étaient plutôt bonnes que vicieuses, mais, ne sachant pas gouverner par lui-même, il ne voulut pourtant pas avoir de principal ministre depuis le cardinal de Fleury, et il ne sut pas donner de la consistance, de la force et de l'union au ministère en corps auquel il s'en remit. Cette seule circonstance fut la source des reproches légitimes qu'on put lui faire les trente dernières annees de son règne; elle ternit l'éclat que le gouvernement mâle et facile du duc d'Orléans, pendant sa minorité, et la direction sage et modérée du cardinal de Fleury donnèrent à ses premières annees. Jamais la France n'a été si riche et si abondante en toutes sortes de manufactures, si ornée par la foule de ses savants, si bien cultivée dans les campagnes et si peuplée en habitants que sous le règne de Louis XV. (*Journal*, I, 82-3)

His grandson who succeeded him was not to enjoy the same good fortune; the greater part of his reign was to be a period of economic depression which helped to sharpen the existing tensions in society and contributed to the upheaval of 1789.

Yet, even at this stage in the century, only fifteen years before the Revolution, although demands for reform were becoming louder, there was no notion of trying to dispense with a powerful monarchy. Although he had brought contempt on himself, Louis XV had not finally succeeded in discrediting the Crown. On his accession the new king could count on an extraordinary amount of good will, provided he used his power to achieve some at least of the reforms now demanded by public opinion. But in the early years of his reign he was to show that the monarchy was incapable of reforming itself and society; after that a revolution became inevitable. Its outbreak was only a question of time.

# CHAPTER VI

# LOUIS XVI AND MARIE ANTOINETTE

THE new king was in his twentieth year at his succession. Heavy and unpleasing in appearance, he completely lacked the handsome presence of his grandfather. He was almost pathetically well-meaning and full of good intentions, but thoroughly weak, vacillating and of very mediocre intelligence. His brother-in-law, the Emperor Joseph II, wrote of him in 1777, after a visit to Versailles:

Cet homme est un peu faible, mais point imbécile; il a des notions, il a du jugement, mais c'est une apathie de corps comme d'esprit. Il fait des conversations raisonnables et il n'a aucun goût de s'instruire ni curiosité, enfin le *fiat lux* n'est pas encore venu, la matière est encore en globe. (*Marie-Antoinette, Correspondance secrète*, III, 74n.)

Two years earlier Abbé de Véri had described the somewhat unregal occupations of the young king and summed up his character in the following words:

On voit le roi passer les matinées dans son cabinet à regarder dans son télescope ceux qui arrivent à Versailles. Il s'y occupe souvent à balayer, clouer, déclouer, etc. Un sens assez droit, des goûts simples, un cœur honnête, une âme vraie, voilà son bon côté. Un penchant à l'indécision, une volonté faible, des lumières bornées dans sa manière de voir et de sentir: voilà le contraste. (*Journal*, I, 244)

Louis XVI satisfied his urge for outdoor exercise in the traditional manner of the French kings, by hunting, a sport in which he indulged with a positive passion. In his diary the word 'rien', meaning that there was no hunting on that particular day, takes on a burlesque effect when contrasted with the events going on in the world around him, particularly in the critical days of 1789. Thus, when on 20 June the deputies of the *Tiers État* swore their solemn oath in the Jeu de Paume at Versailles never to separate until they had given France a constitution, and the whole future of the monarchy was at stake, we find the word 'rien' in the diary; and on 5 October, the day on which the mob of Paris women arrived at Versailles (they were to forcibly remove the King and his family to Paris the next day), Louis was out hunting, as we see from the entry in his diary: 'Tiré à la porte de Châtillon, tué 81 pièces, interrompu par les événements' (*Journal*, pp. 136-8).

With this passion for hunting went an enormous appetite for both food and drink. Two years before the Revolution a contemporary wrote:

> La constitution physique de Sa Majesté exige qu'elle prenne beaucoup d'exercice. Douée d'une force prodigieuse, son appétit est en raison de ses facultés. Voici le menu d'un de ses déjeuners[1] ordinaires. A six heures le roi sonne, et demande ce qu'il y a pour déjeuner. 'Sire, un poulet gras et des côtelettes'.—'C'est bien peu de chose, qu'on me fasse des œufs au jus!' Le roi préside lui-même aux préparatifs, mange quatre côtelettes, le poulet gras, six œufs au jus, une tranche de jambon et boit une bouteille et demie de vin de Champagne; il s'habille, part pour la chasse, et revient dîner avec un appétit incroyable. (*Correspondance secrète inédite*, II, 151)

It was this well-meaning, but weak and apathetic monarch, lacking every quality of leadership, who was to face the terrible crisis in French history which began in 1787. How he ought to have met it no one, even among historians, is bold enough to say; the way in which he faced it and the humiliations and ultimate death which he encountered can arouse even among his most devoted apologists no more than pity.

Marie Antoinette, who was only nineteen at the beginning of the reign, possessed a much stronger character, and inevitably exercised a strong influence over the King. Indeed, she was to play a role very different from that of the general run of French queens, whose life, except when they were called upon to act as regent, was one of political self-effacement behind a display of regal pomp. Marie Antoinette had arrived at

[1] Breakfast; dinner was the midday meal.

Versailles as Dauphine at the tender age of fifteen; from the first she had no one around her to give her the guidance which a girl of her rather frivolous and empty-headed nature required. The last person to whom she could turn for help was her husband. Like him she hated the strict etiquette and perpetual life of ceremony at court; instead of leading the public existence expected of a queen, she spent her days in a narrow circle of favourites, with the result that the court at Versailles was frequented less and less by the great ladies, who preferred their mansions in Paris. The letters written to her mother, Maria Theresa, by her mentor, the Austrian Ambassador, Mercy-Argenteau, are full of lamentations on this score. In 1776 he reported to Vienna:

S.M. s'ennuie du séjour de Versailles, elle le trouve triste et désert; je lui ai fait observer que cet inconvénient tenait beaucoup aux arrangements de la reine, parce que ses déplacements continuels, et qui remplissent des journées entières, mettent tout le monde dans l'incertitude du moment où l'on pourrait faire sa cour. Le soir il n'y a que très rarement jeu chez la reine, encore ces soirées ne sont-elles pas décidément marquées; il n'y a que les soupers dans les cabinets, mais c'est le hasard qui décide du choix des femmes qui y sont appelées, et cela ne procure point aux autres l'occasion de se montrer. Il s'ensuit de là que journellement il arrive moins de monde à Versailles, et que cela ira toujours en empirant, à moins que la reine ne se décide à tenir sa cour d'une façon plus stable et plus réglée. (*Marie-Antoinette, Correspondance secrète*, II, 443)

The consequences of this desertion of Versailles by the court nobility were to be serious for the monarchy, as it became more and more isolated from the rest of the community, and more particularly from that part which, in the aristocratic society of the Ancien Régime, was still extremely important. The point is well put in the memoirs of the Duc de Lévis:

Excepté quelques favoris, que le caprice ou l'intrigue désigna, tout le monde fut exclu; le rang, les services, la considération, la haute naissance ne furent plus des titres pour être admis dans l'intimité de la famille royale; seulement, le dimanche, les personnes présentées pouvaient pendant quelques instants voir les princes. Mais elles se dégoûtèrent, pour la plupart, de cette inutile corvée, dont on ne leur savait aucun gré; elles reconnurent à leur tour qu'il y avait de la duperie à venir de si loin pour n'être pas mieux accueillies, et s'en dispensèrent ou ne vinrent que de loin en loin. . . . Ainsi Versailles, ce théâtre de la magnificence de Louis XIV, où l'on venait avec tant d'empressement, de toute l'Europe, prendre des leçons de bon goût et de politesse, n'était plus qu'une petite ville de province où l'on n'allait qu'avec répugnance et dont on s'enfuyait le plus vite possible. Mais tout se tient dans une monarchie; la cour, naturellement composée de ce qu'il y a de plus considérable dans la nation, est le lien nécessaire entre le peuple et le trône. Lorsque cet intermédiare fut détruit, le roi et sa famille se trouvèrent isolés et privés de leur appui naturel. (*Souvenirs et portraits*, p. 333)

The Queen spent all her days in the narrow circle of the friends and families of two favourites—the Princesse de Lamballe, for whom she revived the post of *surintendante de la maison de la reine* at a salary of 150,000 *l.*, and especially the Comtesse de Polignac, on whose family all sort of favours were showered. In this company Marie Antoinette, relieved of the burden of perpetual court ceremony, was able to indulge in her favourite amusements—playing for high stakes, music, dancing and amateur theatricals (she played the part of Rosine in the *Barbier de Séville*), when she was not at the Petit Trianon, with its 'jardin anglais' and its imitation farm.

There is no doubt that the family and friends of the Comtesse de Polignac ruthlessly exploited the Queen's favour, as Joseph II put it in a letter to Mercy-Argenteau in 1786:

Le maudit besoin de s'amuser et de tuer le temps, quand on ne trouve pas en soi-même des ressources à s'occuper, rend la reine esclave de sa favorite et de sa soi-disant société, car, pour peu qu'elle se refuse à leurs désirs, ils savent bien s'en venger par l'ennui, l'uniformité et la tristesse qu'ils lui font éprouver, et par ce moyen ils engagent à plusieurs démarches qu'elle-même trouve déraisonnables et outrées. (*Correspondance secrète du Comte de Mercy-Argenteau*, II, 7)

Yet, even when she was not egged on by her circle to demand favours for them and for their families and friends, Marie

Antoinette herself was extravagant. Ten years earlier Mercy had reported to Maria Theresa:

> Parmi les bruits qui s'élèvent contre la gloire et la considération essentielle à une reine de France, il en est un qui paraît plus dangereux et plus fâcheux que les autres. . . . On se plaint assez publiquement que la reine fait et occasionne des dépenses considérables. . . .
>
> Le public a vu d'abord avec plaisir que le roi donnât Trianon à la reine; il commence à être inquiet et alarmé des dépenses que S.M. y fait. Par son ordre on a culbuté les jardins pour y faire un jardin anglais, qui coûtera au moins cent cinquante mille livres. La reine a fait faire un théâtre à Trianon; elle n'y a encore donné qu'un spectacle suivi d'un souper, mais cette fête a été très dispendieuse. . . .
>
> La pension de la reine a été plus que doublée; cependant la reine a contracté des dettes. . . .
>
> Le principe des dettes de la reine est connu et n'excite pas moins de cris et de plaintes. La reine a acheté beaucoup de diamants, et son jeu est devenu fort cher; elle ne joue plus aux jeux de commerce, dont la perte est nécessairement bornée. Le lansquenet est devenu son jeu ordinaire, et parfois le pharaon, lorsque son jeu n'est pas entièrement public. Les dames et les courtisans sont effrayés et affligés des pertes auxquelles ils s'exposent pour faire leur cour à la Reine. (*Marie Antoinette, Correspondance secrète*, II, 493-7)

Such complaints, it must be remembered, came not from some obscure pamphlet, but from the letters of the Austrian Ambassador to her mother.

Given her attitude to money and that of her circle, Marie Antoinette could scarcely be expected to support a policy of rigid economy which the state of the Treasury demanded, especially as it affected the cost of the court and of pensions to courtiers. Hence the nickname 'Madame Déficit' which she acquired as 1789 approached. Again, given the weakness of her husband—she almost openly despised him and once referred to him in a letter as 'le pauvre homme', to the indignation of her mother—it was inevitable that she should intervene in political matters, and here her actions were often unfortunate. Acting through the Austrian Ambassador, her mother and brother exploited her position to secure French support for various Austrian actions which were no concern of France or even conflicted with her interests. Here she was often far from getting her own way, but the fact that she was driven into supporting at Versailles purely Austrian interests rapidly earned her another derogatory nickname, that of 'l'Autrichienne'.

The fate which overcame her in the Revolution has tended to earn for Marie Antoinette sympathy and even a dazzled admiration. As early as 1790 Edmund Burke began the tradition in the famous passage in his *Reflections on the French Revolution*:

> It is now sixteen or seventeen years since I saw the queen of France, then the dauphiness, at Versailles; and surely never lighted on this orb, which she hardly seemed to touch, a more delightful vision. I saw her just above the horizon, decorating and cheering the elevated sphere she had just begun to move in,— glittering like the morning-star, full of life, and splendour, and joy. Oh! what a revolution! and what a heart must I have to contemplate without emotion that elevation and that fall! Little did I dream that I should have lived to see such disasters fallen upon her in a nation of gallant men, in a nation of men of honour and of cavaliers. I thought ten thousand swords must have leaped from their scabbards to avenge even a look that threatened her with insult.—But the age of chivalry is gone.—That of sophisters, economists and calculators has succeeded; and the glory of Europe is extinguished for ever. (pp. 112-13)

Yet, tragic as was her situation, Marie Antoinette was undoubtedly a liability to the French monarchy in its decline; her frivolity did considerable harm to her personal reputation, and her irresponsibility in political matters only made the situation worse. It is difficult to realize with what enthusiasm the new king and queen were greeted on their accession to the throne, after the long and inglorious reign of Louis XV, and how steadily all this good will was dissipated until within fifteen years absolute monarchy was destroyed and the royal family were virtually prisoners in the Tuileries.

Foreign affairs were relatively unimportant down to 1789, apart from the War of American Independence which had considerable repercussions at home. With the new reign came a new Foreign Minister, Vergennes, who enjoyed a long spell of office from 1774 to his death in 1787. He refused to allow France to be dragged into supporting Austrian policies on the Continent, despite all the pressure brought upon him by the pro-Austrian party at court, led by Marie Antoinette. When the American Revolution broke out in 1775, France at first limited its support for the rebels to supplying them with arms and munitions by secret agents, the most important of whom was Beaumarchais. It was only in 1778 that France signed a treaty of alliance with the United States; in the hostilities which followed she was supported by Spain, who declared war on England in the following year.

This time the French navy did very much better against the English than in the earlier wars of the century, and on land the French expeditionary force played a decisive part in the defeat of the English armies in North America. France had her revenge for the humiliations of the Seven Years War, and in the Treaty of Versailles, which was signed in 1783, she received a number of small consolation prizes, such as Tobago in the Windward Islands and the trading stations in Senegal which she had lost in 1763.

Yet, despite the gain in prestige, the cost of the war was very heavy for so small a return, and undoubtedly the loans raised to finance the war made the monarchy's unsolved financial problems still worse and thus helped to precipitate the Revolution. Moreover, the popularity of Franklin who represented the new republic in Paris and the contact of young aristocratic officers like La Fayette with the American people fighting for their liberty, had an enormous influence on the outlook of educated Frenchmen. There was indeed something paradoxical in the support which, out of motives of *Realpolitik*, the greatest monarchy in Europe gave to the American insurgents. The impact on France of the subversive ideas engendered by the American Revolution and its declaration of rights is clearly revealed in the writings of a man like Condorcet and in the newspapers and memoirs of these years.

At home the early part of the reign of Louis XVI saw the

failure of attempts at important reforms. The impulse for thes did not come from the rather cynical old man, Maurepas, who was recalled from his twenty-five years' exile by the young king, and although technically only *ministre d'état*, was in fact prime minister until his death in 1781 at the age of eighty. Soon the ministers of Louis XV were pushed out of the government, and the reform of the judicial system was undone by the recall of the Parlements.

This step, although on the whole popular, was to have disastrous consequences for the authority of the monarchy. The Parlements had learned nothing and forgotten nothing. When, in November 1774, the Paris Parlement was reinstated in a solemn *lit de justice*, the King imposed severe restrictions on its powers. Although it regained its *droit de remontrances*, its representations against an edict had to be made within a month and only after the edict had first been registered; again, severe penalities were provided for mass resignations and interruptions to the administration of justice. Annoyed by such scurvy treatment the Parlement, within two months of its reinstatement, was already presenting remonstrances against the very edicts governing its reinstatement. The princes of the blood and peers took part in the drawing up of these remonstrances. Next the Parlement drew up a declaration in which it mingled protestations of fidelity and gratitude with a haughty reaffirmation of its right to deliberate freely on the edicts presented to it:

> Considérant en outre ladite cour que, dans le lit de justice du 12 novembre dernier, la publication des édits et ordonnances qui y ont été portés a été ordonnée et faite sans être précédée d'un examen où le concours des lumières, la réflexion et la maturité nécessaires à la vérification des nouvelles lois eussent pu mettre les membres de ladite cour en état de discerner le vœu qu'ils devaient former pour l'acquit de leur devoir envers le roi, l'état et eux-mêmes. . . .
>
> Déclare ladite cour, selon ce qui s'est pratiqué en semblables conjonctures, qu'elle n'a pu, ni dû, ni entendu consentir à ce qui pourrait en être induit au préjudice des lois, maximes et usages du royaume, du bien du service dudit seigneur roi et des

droits essentiels des sujets, (Flammermont, *Remontrances du Parlement de Paris*, III, 266-7)

The King meekly tolerated this just as he allowed the Parlements up and down the country to drive out all those judges who had served in the courts set up by Maupeou. Worse was soon to follow when the Parlements put all their weight into obstructing reforms and into making the financial position of the monarchy impossible.

Among the ministers brought into the government by Maurepas in 1774 was Turgot. His appointment as *Contrôleur général* aroused great hopes among the *Philosophes*, with many of whom he was on friendly terms. In his enthusiasm Condorcet dashed off the following lines to Voltaire:

Vous savez sans doute la nomination de M. Turgot. Il ne pouvait rien arriver de plus heureux à la France et à la raison humaine. Jamais il n'est entré dans aucun conseil de monarque d'homme qui reunît à ce point la vertu, le courage, le désintéressement, l'amour du bien public, les lumières et le zèle pour les répandre. (*Œuvres*, I, 36)

Turgot was a man of forty-seven who had followed the usual career of a high civil servant, first as *conseiller* in the Paris Parlement, then as *maître des requêtes* and, for the last thirteen years, as *Intendant* of Limoges. There he had introduced reforms into the assessment and collection of the *taille*, replaced the *corvée* by a tax, and developed roads, education and public assistance. His ideal was an enlightened despot who would carry out, through his ministers, the reform of abuses and at the same time take into account the desires of his subjects by instituting representative assemblies on a local and a provincial basis. In economic affairs he was a thorough-going liberal who believed with passionate fervour in the principles of *laissez-faire*.

The enthusiasm of the *Philosophes* was further increased when in 1775 he was joined in the government by Malesherbes, the new secretary of state for the King's Household, who, as *Directeur de la Librairie* in the 1750s, had made it possible for them to publish many of their works, including the *Encyclopédie*.

To many of the *Philosophes* and their supporters the millennium seemed just round the corner.

Unfortunately for these hopes the difficulties which Turgot had to face were immense. He was not the head of a united government bent on carrying through an agreed programme of reforms. In the midst of the constant intrigues to bring about his downfall, he needed the backing of the King, and as the King was weak, he needed the support of the Queen. But Marie Antoinette was opposed to his policy from the first.

On his appointment in August 1774 Turgot expounded his policy to the King in a long letter the conclusion of which ran:

> Point de banqueroute;
> Point d'augmentation d'impositions;
> Point d'emprunts. . . .
> Pour remplir ces trois points, il n'y a qu'un moyen. C'est de réduire la dépense au-dessous de la recette, et assez au-dessous pour pouvoir économiser chaque année une vingtaine de millions, afin de rembourser les dettes anciennes. Sans cela le premier coup de canon forcerait l'État à la banqueroute. (*Œuvres*, IV, 109-10)

The last remark was prophetic; we have seen the effect which France's part in the War of American Independence was to have on her finances.

The policy of rigorous economy which he here outlined inevitably led to a head-on clash with such vested interests as the tax-farmers and the court nobles who battened on the Treasury. In his short period of office Turgot had no time to completely recast the complicated system for the assessment and collection of direct taxes like the *taille* and the *vingtième*, but he did attempt some reforms. He took a much tougher line than his predecessors with the tax-farmers, handing over the collection of some indirect taxes to *régisseurs* who were mere agents of the government. By cutting out useless officials he reduced the cost of tax-collection by six million livres.

In economic matters, particularly in the very important grain trade, Turgot attempted to apply the liberal principles of the economists of his day. Abbé Terray had reverted to the

traditional policy of strict government control over the movement, price and method of sale of grain, which, in accordance
with the new liberal principles, had been relaxed in the 1760s
to permit free trade in grain inside France and even a certain
amount of export. One of Turgot's first acts was to issue a
decree allowing the free circulation of grain inside the country;
this was a typically liberal measure, based on the fervent belief
that, left to its own devices and to the operation of the law of
supply and demand, private enterprise would deliver the goods.
However, Turgot continued the old policy of regulating the
grain trade in order to ensure that Paris did not go short, nor
did he dare to authorize exports.

Unfortunately for his liberal principles the harvest of 1774
was a poor one, and imports of grain were insufficient to make
up the deficiency. Bread prices rose very high in the critical
period, the late spring of 1775. There were disturbances in
various parts of the country; in May crowds even invaded the
château at Versailles and on the following days there were
serious riots in Paris. Order was rapidly restored, but Turgot's
position in the government was shaken.

He had come into office with various projects of reform, but
the only ones of importance which he had time to try to carry
out were the abolition of the *corvée* and of the guilds. These were
the two most important projects contained in six edicts which
he brought forward early in 1776. In abolishing the *corvée* and
replacing it by a tax on all landowners, privileged as well as
*roturiers*, one of his clearly stated aims was to reduce inequalities
in the matter of taxation, to shift part of the burden from the
poorest section of the community on to the shoulders of the rich.
The edict abolishing the guilds threw open all forms of trade
and industry, except such professions as those of chemist, goldsmith, printer and bookseller which were controlled by the
government. This was again a typically liberal measure; the
guilds had long been under attack as monopolies which impeded
the free development of trade and industry. In the preamble to
the edict they were denounced as being responsible for the
present high prices of bread and meat, and their suppression
was demanded in the name of the liberal principle of free com-

petition. The only way to bring down food prices was, it was argued, to abolish these monopolies: 'Ce n'est que par la concurrence la plus libre qu'on peut se flatter d'y parvenir.' Such measures aroused fears of the imminence of other reforms, such as the abolition of feudal dues, with compensation. The opposition inside and outside the government redoubled its efforts to get rid of Turgot. The Paris Parlement entered the lists as the champion of the privileged orders against the abolition of the *corvée*, and it also opposed the abolition of the guilds for quite selfish reasons, since, to quote the British Ambassador in Paris, the judges had 'a personal interest in supporting these *communautés*, which find them such constant employment, and open so large a field for chicane' (P.R.O. State Papers, 78/297). In its remonstrances against the edict abolishing the *corvée* the Paris Parlement revealed quite blatantly its selfish interest in the maintenance of the privileges of the nobility. 'What we have we hold' was the principle underlying such criticisms as these:

La première règle de la justice est de conserver à chacun ce qui lui appartient, règle fondamentale du droit naturel, du droit des gens et du gouvernement civil, règle qui ne consiste pas seulement à maintenir les droits de propriété, mais encore à conserver ceux qui sont attachés à la personne et qui naissent des prérogatives de la naissance et de l'état.

De cette règle de droit et d'équité il suit que tout système qui, sous une apparence d'humanité et de bienfaisance, tendrait, dans une monarchie bien ordonnée, à établir entre les hommes une égalité de devoirs et à détruire ces distinctions nécessaires, amènerait bientôt le désordre, suite inévitable de l'égalité absolue, et produirait le renversement de la société civile, dont l'harmonie ne se maintient que par cette gradation de pouvoirs, d'autorités, de prééminences et de distinctions qui tient chacun à sa place et garantit tous les états de la confusion. . . .

Quels ne sont point les dangers d'un projet produit par un système inadmissible d'égalité, dont le premier effet est de confondre tous les ordres de l'État en leur imposant le joug uniforme de l'impôt territorial? (Flammermont, *Remontrances du Parlement de Paris*, III, 278-9)

The remonstrances did not confine themselves to defending the exemption of the nobility from the *corvée*; they went further and defended all its privileges and prerogatives. This was in 1776— only thirteen years before the Revolution which was to sweep away all such privileges.

C'est à son antique constitution que la monarchie doit son lustre et sa gloire; c'est la noblesse qui en a posé les fondements, qui les a élevés, qui les a soutenus; c'est elle qui a porté la couronne dans la maison royale, c'est elle qui l'y a maintenue; sans elle, les rois sont sans force, les peuples sans défenseurs. . . .

Si l'on dégrade la noblesse, si on lui enlève les droits primitifs de sa naissance, elle perdra bientôt son esprit, son courage et cette élévation d'âme qui la caractérise.

Ce corps, inaltérable dans sa valeur et dans sa fidélité, ne peut souffrir de changement, de diminution dans les honneurs et les distinctions dues à la naissance et au service de ceux qui le composent.

Ces distinctions, sire, ou plutôt ces droits, n'ont été méconnus dans aucun âge de la monarchie. (III, 288)

The judges of the Parlement saw clearly that to yield on the question of the *corvée* would be to endanger the whole edifice of their privileges in the matter of taxation:

Assujettir les nobles à un impôt pour rachat de la corvée, au préjudice de la maxime que *nul n'est corvéable s'il n'est taillable*, c'est les décider corvéables comme les roturiers; et ce principe une fois admis, ils pourraient être contraints à la corvée personnelle aussitôt qu'elle serait rétablie. . . .

Qui pourrait même répondre aux nobles qu'après les avoir rendus corvéables, on ne prétendît pas, dans la suite, les rendre taillables? (III, 290-1)

The edicts were registered only after the King had held a *lit de justice*. Turgot had won a Pyrrhic victory; he had succeeded in persuading the King to force through his reforms, but the Parlement was determined to get rid of him. As a contemporary put it a few years later: 'Les Parlements ne pardonnent jamais, et l'on n'a pas d'exemple qu'un ministre en guerre avec eux ait pu faire plus que se débattre pendant quelque temps' (*Correspondance secrète inédite*, I, 388). His position in the government was weak; the courtiers, threatened by his economy

measures, were endeavouring to undermine his position. Marie
Antoinette was so furious that Turgot should support Vergennes
in demanding the recall from London of her protégé, the Comte
de Guines, that, according to a letter of the Austrian Ambassador to Maria Theresa, 'le projet de la reine était d'exiger du
roi que le sieur Turgot fût chassé, même envoyé à la Bastille le
même jour que le comte de Guines serait déclaré duc; il a fallu
les représentations les plus fortes et les plus instantes pour
arrêter les effets de la colère de la reine' (*Marie-Antoinette,
Correspondance secrète*, II, 446).

All this opposition undermined Louis XVI's support for
Turgot; in May 1776 he was dismissed. No doubt he had his
faults; he was not good at getting on with other people, he was
always convinced that he alone was right, and he was not the
sort of man to maintain his position by the intrigues which
flourished at Versailles under the Ancien Régime. As his friend,
Abbé de Véri, put it on receiving the news of his fall:

> M. Turgot, inébranlable dans la poursuite de ses plans quand il
> les a bien approfondis, n'a aucune flexibilité pour savoir se prêter
> aux opinions des autres. Il est rempli de maladresses à l'égard
> d'une foule de gens dans les cours, qu'il faut savoir ne pas révolter
> Comme il voit ordinairement ses projets avec la plus grande
> évidence (fruit du travail et de son talent naturel), il ne peut
> pas concevoir qu'on voie différemment que lui, et ses études
> solitaires du cabinet ne lui ont pas donné l'art de faire passer sa
> conviction dans l'âme de ceux qui n'y sont pas préparés. La
> droiture de ses intentions, qu'il croit aussi évidente aux yeux
> d'autrui qu'aux siens, jointe à une disposition naturelle, l'a
> toujours éloigné des tournures de souplesse, de condescendance
> et de prévenance qui sont un si grand ressort dans les cours.
> (*Journal*, I, 432-3)

Yet his fall, after less than two years in the government and
before he had had a chance to carry out more than a fraction
of his extremely moderate programme of reforms, was a mis-
fortune for the monarchy. The attempt to institute an enlightened despotism and to bring about reforms by peaceful
methods had failed, owing to the weakness of the King and the
opposition of the privileged orders.

His fall was followed by a period of reaction. The *corvée* was revived; though the parishes were given the choice between the old system and paying a money tax, based on the *taille*, this meant that the privileged orders were still exempt. The guilds were restored, though their numbers were reduced and various reforms were laid down. Both these edicts were promptly registered by the Paris Parlement. The new *Contrôleur général* died before the year was out, and his place was taken by Jacques Necker, a banker from Geneva, who was not only a foreigner, but a Protestant. Because of this he could not hold the post of *Contrôleur général*, but for four years, from 1777 to his resignation in 1781, he bore the title of *Directeur général des finances*.

When he was brought into the government in 1776, Necker was a successful banker of forty-eight. He had built up a large fortune, and his wife was well known through her *salon* in which their daughter, the future Mme de Staël, was soon to show off her precocious talents. He had made for himself a reputation as a financial and economic expert by his books in which he attacked the fashionable liberal doctrines, arguing against free trade and for government control of the all-important grain trade. He was a somewhat vain man; he was a successful banker, but lacked administrative experience. He was in favour of some degree of reform, but fondly imagined that changes could be brought about without a clash with vested interests.

The outbreak of the War of American Independence in 1778 brought fresh financial difficulties. Necker managed to finance the war without imposing new taxes, although he had to renew the second *vingtième* in 1780. The edict was registered without any serious resistance by the Paris Parlement, but two years earlier it had kicked up a tremendous fuss about the way in which government officials were steadily improving the assessment of this tax. In its remonstrances it put forward the astonishing proposition that, in the absence of any system of representative government, the declarations of individual tax-payers must be accepted without further investigation:

Tout propriétaire a droit d'accorder les subsides, ou par lui-même, ou par ses représentants; s'il n'use pas de ce droit en corps

de nation, il faut bien y revenir individuellement; autrement il n'est plus maître de sa chose, il n'est plus tranquille propriétaire. ... Le seul moyen de rendre les impôts légitimes est d'écouter la nation; au défaut de la nation, le seul moyen de les rendre supportables est d'écouter les individus, en sorte que la déférence aux déclarations soit du moins une image, un vestige, un dédommagement conservatoire du droit national. (Flammermont, *Remontrances du Parlement de Paris*, III, 404)

Again, when in order to meet the increased expenditure occasioned by the general rise in prices since the middle of the century, the government argued that the increasing income from the land should gradually bear a heavier tax, the Parlement protested:

Que la progression des vingtièmes doive suivre la progression des revenus, c'est une théorie arbitraire qui doit céder aux dispositions expresses des édits et déclarations dont votre parlement vient de mettre la chaîne sous les yeux de V.M.; la disposition est donc illégale. ... Elle verra que cette maxime de la progression proportionnelle des vingtièmes est contraire non seulement aux édits, non seulement à la justice, mais encore à la sage politique d'une administration prévoyante. (III, 406-7)

Such was the attitude adopted by the Parlement as the spokesman of the nobility in face of the financial needs of the government; new taxes, however necessary, would obviously have encountered fierce resistance.

Necker, however, did not risk his popularity by such methods. Indeed it was with him a matter of deliberate policy to cover the extra expenditure necessitated by the war by means of loans. Money flowed in, from abroad as well as from France, but financing the war by borrowing was bound to throw a disastrous burden on the Treasury. However, this popular policy was accompanied by certain minor reforms in the taxation system. Necker abolished a number of posts in his department, continued Turgot's policy of substituting *régisseurs* for tax-farmers in the collection of certain indirect taxes, and made some reforms in the *ferme générale*. His attempts to improve the system of public accounts and to reduce the amount of pensions and the cost of the court led to little practical result. The

verdict of Abbé de Véri in 1780 on his financial administration is not altogether unjust: 'Je ne puis m'empêcher de comparer ce qu'il a fait jusqu'à ce jour à la dextérité de l'intendant d'un homme riche, qui, laissant dépenser son maître au delà de ses facultés, a le secret de lui faire trouver des emprunts faciles moyennant l'apparence de quelques légères économies de pure parade' (*Journal*, II, 352).

Necker did not confine his activities to the finances; he also planned to set up provincial assemblies which would concern themselves with such matters as the assessment and levying of direct taxes, the building of roads and economic affairs. In 1778 the experiment was tried out in one province, Le Berry. The provincial assembly was to consist of 48 members: 12 drawn from the clergy, 12 from the nobility and 24 (half from the towns and half from the country) from the *tiers état*. One-third of the members of the assembly, which was presided over by the Archbishop of Bourges, were chosen by the King, and the rest were co-opted. It met for a month every two years; all the members sat and voted together, irrespective of their order.

The new assembly got under way, but Necker's plans to extend the system to other provinces encountered resistance from both the *Intendants* and the *Parlements* who were anxious not to see their power diminished. The reform was in fact a timid one, and the Berry assembly's plea that its members should be elected, fell on deaf ears.

Necker also carried out a number of humanitarian reforms, such as the abolition of the use of torture to extract confessions (*la question préparatoire*) and the ending of serfdom on the royal domain, although he was powerless to abolish it on the estates of the nobility and clergy. For a time, by a cautious policy of being all things to all men, he enjoyed great popularity. Yet he had powerful enemies, even inside the government. Finally, in February 1781, to answer his critics Necker published his *Compte rendu au roi*. Under the Ancien Régime the ordinary citizen had no idea how the Treasury's revenue and expenditure were made up and how they were related to one another; that was simply not his business. But now Necker told anyone who cared to buy a copy of his *Compte rendu* (the work had a tremendous success, as over 100,000 copies are said to have been sold); or rather Necker professed to tell him. At the end of the detailed tables of revenue and expenditure there appeared a reassuring little sum:

RÉSULTAT

| | |
|---|---|
| Les revenus montent à . . . . | 264,154,000 livres. |
| Et les dépenses à . . . . . | 253,954,000 |
| Les revenus excèdent les dépenses de | 10,200,000 |

*Nota.*—Cet excédent est indépendant des 17,326,666 livres, employées en remboursement, et dont le détail suit ci-après.

The creditors of the state could sleep in peace; there was a nice little surplus of revenue over expenditure, and an even larger sum had been applied to the reduction of existing debts.

Though it is impossible to state precisely what was the true state of the Treasury in 1781, there is no question that these figures gave an unduly optimistic view of the situation. One of Necker's successors estimated the true deficit for that year at some 70 million livres, and that, of course, included no allowance for over 200 millions of extra expenditure on the war.

Necker did not confine himself to giving figures in his *Compte rendu*; he offered a detailed defence of his financial policy, and included not only criticisms of such existing taxes as the *gabelle* and the *corvée*, but also a scathing attack on the courtiers who battened on the Treasury.[1] Although the *Compte rendu* was a best-seller, Necker's position in the government was weakened and the courtiers and Parlements were hostile. A contemporary wrote at the end of April:

Le directeur général des finances est on ne peut pas plus chancelant. Ce sont les parlements qui le renverseront, s'il ne résiste pas à l'orage. On a remis à des membres de ces corps plusieurs lettres de lui, où, en parlant des administrations provinciales qu'il voulait établir peu à peu dans tout le royaume, il disait que son but était de réduire les parlements aux fonctions de juges. Là-dessus grande rumeur. Le parlement de Paris vient de refuser

[1] Quoted above, p. 113.

l'enregistrement d'un édit portant établissement d'une administration provinciale dans le Bourbonnais. (*Correspondance secrète inédite*, I, 387-8)

To strengthen his position in the government, Necker asked the King for wider powers; when Louis refused, he resigned. Public opinion was shocked by the disappearance of a popular minister who at least held out promise of reforms. By 1781, after the dismissal of Turgot and the resignation of Necker, very little was left of the good will which had greeted Louis XVI on his accession; hopes of serious reforms seemed to have vanished.

Necker's successor, Joly de Fleury, who remained a bare two years in power, not only had recourse to loans, but also was compelled to raise new taxes, including, in 1782, a third *vingtième*. This roused considerable opposition from the Parlements. It is true that, after protesting, the Paris Parlement registered the decree, but tougher resistance came from the Besançon Parlement. After its members had been summoned to Versailles and compelled to accept the new tax, it issued on its return in February 1783 a furious declaration, accusing the government of destroying its right to make remonstrances and demanding the summoning of both the estates of Franche-Comté and the *États généraux*. This was a cry which was often to be repeated by the Parlements in the next few years.

Joly de Fleury was dismissed in March 1783, and his successor did not last out the year. His place was taken by Calonne, a very controversial figure who enjoyed a low reputation with his contemporaries, especially after his fall in 1787, but is nowadays rated higher by historians. Fifteen years as *Intendant* had given him considerable administrative experience by the time he entered the government at the age of forty-nine. A handsome appearance, polished manners and a brilliant mind made him a most impressive figure; but he was at bottom an unstable and somewhat unprincipled character.

In order to restore confidence in the Treasury, he pursued an expansionist economic policy, splashing money around, and giving people the impression that all was well with the country's finances. For some three years he pleased nearly everybody; the Queen and the other members of the royal family, along with the courtiers, were found the money they wanted; important public works were carried out all over France; he even doubled the value of the *jetons* which the members of the Académie Française received for attending its meetings. All this was made possible by a succession of loans. Calonne was on good terms with the bankers and, despite the opposition of the Parlements, succeeded in floating loans which, to begin with at any rate, were over-subscribed. But by 1786 he was already in a tight corner and had to offer exorbitant terms in order to raise money.

It was in August of that year that Calonne finally put before the King a sweeping programme of reforms to deal with the critical financial situation. These reforms were not merely fiscal; they affected the whole administration and the economic life of the country. In order to meet the annual deficit which he estimated at 112 million livres for 1786, he proposed to make economies and to raise extra revenue, mainly by a new land tax, a *subvention territoriale*, which would replace the existing *vingtièmes*. This tax would be borne by all land, whether it belonged to the nobility, the clergy or the Third Estate, and the *pays d'états* would no longer be let off with an *abonnement*, but would have to pay their full share. To make the clergy pay the new tax, Calonne proposed that it should be compelled to repay the huge debt which it had contracted to provide its *don gratuit*, by selling its feudal dues and such rights as the *justice seigneuriale* and the *droit de chasse*. The other main source of extra revenue which he proposed was a raising and extension of the stamp duty.

With these changes in taxation was combined a system of assemblies at the level of the parish, the district and the *généralité*. The parish assemblies were to be responsible for the classification of land for the *subvention territoriale*, and were also to assess local taxes, supervise public works and distribute poor relief. The district assemblies were to have such functions as apportioning the royal taxes between the different towns and villages in their area. Finally in the *pays d'élection* (Calonne did not propose to touch the existing provincial estates) there was to be an assembly which met for about a month each year, but which was to possess a permanent committee to deal with business out of session. Although these assemblies were to have power to deal with such questions as the apportionment of the royal taxes among the different districts, they were to remain under the strict control of the *Intendant*. Another feature of these assemblies was that their members were to be chosen without distinction from all three orders.

Calonne's reforms also covered the economic field. He wished to liberate French trade, industry and agriculture from many of the restrictions imposed upon them, by abolishing internal customs-barriers, by further relaxing government control over the grain trade, and by a reform of the *taille, gabelle* and the *corvée*. He proposed to limit the liability of an individual who was subject to the *taille personnelle* to one-twentieth of his income and not to allow the tax of artisans and day labourers to exceed one day's wages a year; the total amount of the *taille* over the country as a whole was to be reduced by one-tenth. His reform of the *corvée* was limited to commuting it for a money payment; he did not attempt, as Turgot had done, to make the privileged orders pay their share. His reform of the *gabelle* was to be a relatively minor one, but would at least have done something to reduce the extraordinary differences in the price of salt between different regions.

Apart from the necessity of persuading both the King and his colleagues in the government of the desirability of this programme, Calonne also had to find a means of putting it into practice. To summon the *États généraux* was unthinkable in 1786; to present the necessary edicts straight to the Parlements was to invite a bitter conflict and endless delays; the situation was too urgent for that. He hit upon an expedient which had last been used in the reign of Louis XIII, in order to avoid summoning the *États généraux*: to summon an *Assemblée des Notables*. Calonne hoped that it would accept his programme and thus make registration by the Parlements easier; he also considered that if it proved obstructive, it could simply be dissolved, and the battle with the Parlements could then be faced. Events, unfortunately for him, did not turn out quite that way.

For a variety of reasons the opening session of the *Assemblée des Notables* did not take place until February 1787. Its 144 members consisted of 14 archbishops and bishops, 7 princes of the blood, 36 great noblemen, 37 judges of the Parlements, along with 4 *Intendants* and 8 *conseillers d'état*, 12 representatives (four from each order) of the provincial estates, and 26 representatives of the towns. The members were thus drawn mainly from the privileged orders. In his opening speech, after justifying the financial policy which he had followed since he came to power and carefully explaining that the deficit (of unspecified amount) which France was facing had a long history, Calonne gave a brief account of his programme of reforms. After declaring that further borrowing was ruled out and that economies alone would be insufficient, he stated bluntly where the solution to France's financial problems lay:

> Que reste-t-il pour combler un vide effrayant et faire trouvet le niveau désiré?
> Que reste-t-il qui puisse suppléer à tout ce qui manque, et procurer tout ce qu'il faudrait pour la restauration des finances?
>
> LES ABUS.
>
> Oui, messieurs, c'est dans les abus même que se trouve un fonds de richesses que l'État a droit de réclamer et qui doivent servir à rétablir l'ordre. C'est dans la proscription des abus que réside le seul moyen de subvenir à tous les besoins. C'est du sein même du désordre que doit jaillir une source féconde, qui fertilisera toutes les parties de la monarchie . . .
> Les abus qu'il s'agit aujourd'hui d'anéantir pour le salut public, ce sont les plus considérables, les plus protégés, ceux qui ont les racines les plus profondes et les branches les plus étendues.
> Tels sont les abus dont l'existence même pèse sur la classe productive et laborieuse; les abus des privilèges pécuniaires; les exceptions à la loi commune, et tant d'exemptions injustes qui ne peuvent affranchir une partie des contribuables qu'en aggravant le sort des autres;
> L'inégalité générale dans la répartition des subsides, et l'énorme disproportion qui se trouve entre les contributions des différentes provinces, et entre les charges d'un sujet d'un même souverain;

La rigueur et l'arbitraire de la perception de la taille;
La crainte, la gêne et presque le déshonneur imprimés au
commerce des premières productions;
Les bureaux des traites intérieures, et ces barrières qui rendent
les diverses parties du royaume étrangères les unes aux autres;
Les droits qui découragent l'industrie, ceux dont le recouvre-
ment exige des frais excessifs et des préposés innombrables; ceux
qui semblent inviter à la contrebande, et qui tous les ans font
sacrifier des milliers de citoyens. . . .
Enfin tout ce qui altère les produits, tout ce qui affaiblit les
ressources du crédit, tout ce qui rend les revenus insuffisants, et
toutes les dépenses superflues qui les absorbent. (*Discours prononcé
dans l'Assemblée des Notables*, pp. 22-4)

The next day, in presenting to the assembly the first section
of his reforms (these included the *subvention territoriale*, as well
as measures for dealing with the debts of the clergy and the
setting up of the various provincial assemblies), Calonne was
even more brutally frank, whether he was speaking of the
administrative chaos and such blatantly unjust taxes as the
*gabelle*, or reminding the privileged orders of their duty to
contribute their full share to the needs of the state. Before the
representatives of the clergy and nobility he openly denounced
their claim to exemption from certain taxes; in the name of
the King he put forward

ces vérités incontestables, que tous les membres d'un État, ayant
un besoin égal de la protection du souverain, ont aussi des devoirs
égaux à remplir; que la contribution aux charges de l'État est la
dette commune de tous; que toute préférence envers l'un est une
injustice envers l'autre. . . . Ces vérités sont inébranlables, puisqu'elles ont pour fondement la raison, la justice et l'intérêt
national. (*Mémoire sur l'imposition territoriale*, pp. 12-13)

All this hardly went down well with the high clerics and
noblemen to whom he was speaking, though they were too
cunning openly to oppose his taxation plans. They accepted
the principle of equality with the secret intention of sabotaging
the new tax when it came to the discussion of details. But what
equally concerned them was to assert their claims to political
power; refusing to confine themselves to the modest role which

had been assigned to them, the mere discussion of detailed methods of implementing the reforms, they insisted on dealing with much wider questions, and indeed pressed for the communication of the detailed accounts of the Treasury. They also tried to ensure that the new assemblies would secure a predominant position for the privileged orders in local government.

When the discussions between Calonne and the assembly ended in deadlock, the *Contrôleur général* took the bold step of appealing to public opinion by having circulated large numbers of copies of a pamphlet, written by a well-known lawyer, explaining the aims of the *subvention territoriale*. The pamphlet stressed in particular that the increase in the total amount of taxes to be paid would fall, not on the ordinary taxpayers, but on those who had hitherto enjoyed unjustified exemptions. The appeal to public opinion was a failure; at this stage it favoured resistance to the government's plans, especially as they involved new taxes, and in any case Calonne had a bad reputation as a spendthrift and a charlatan. As Mme de Staël later wrote of the assembly's opposition to Calonne's reforms:

> Cette assemblée, presque en entier composée de nobles et de prélats, n'était certainement pas, à quelques exceptions près, de l'avis d'établir l'égale répartition des taxes; mais elle se garda bien d'exprimer son désir secret à cet égard; et se mêlant à ceux dont les opinions étaient purement libérales, elle fit corps avec la nation, qui craignait tous les impôts, de quelque nature qu'ils fussent. (*Considérations*, I, 117)

On 8 April Calonne was dismissed. A few days later a contemporary observer wrote: 'On sait que M. de Calonne a succombé bien plus à la cabale des privilégiés et du clergé qu'à l'impression que devaient faire ses vices et ses prodigalités' (*Correspondance secrète inédite*, II, 129). What was at stake for the monarchy was clearly brought out in a passage in a letter from Joseph II to his ambassador in Paris:

> Je suis bien curieux d'apprendre l'issue de la fameuse Assemblée des Notables. Si le roi mollit et abandonne le contrôleur général, son autorité est perdue pour jamais, et le clergé, la noblesse et

les parlements feront une espèce de coalition, de manière qu'il
ne trouvera en tout que de l'opposition et sera à la fin obligé
d'accepter comme en Angleterre les ministres qu'ils voudront lui
donner ou renvoyer ceux qui leur déplairont. (*Correspondance
secrète*, II, 92)

Calonne's successor lasted less than a month, and power
then passed to one of his main critics in the *Assemblée des Notables*,
Loménie de Brienne, Archbishop of Toulouse, who enjoyed a
considerable reputation as an administrator and was Marie
Antoinette's choice to meet the crisis. Before his appointment
the King had been compelled to make important concessions
to the assembly, and even to produce the national accounts so
that its members could verify the existence of the deficit.

Despite his earlier criticisms of Calonne's programme, Brienne
was compelled to adopt it in a modified form and thus he, in
his turn, found himself up against the intransigence of the
assembly. The meetings came to an end when it finally rejected
Brienne's revised plans for a land-tax. The government was
thus left to face the resistance of the Parlements to its programme of reforms.

When in July Brienne's proposal for the stamp-tax and the
*subvention territoriale* came before the Paris Parliament, it adopted
new and, in view of its past history, surprising tactics; it declared that it was not competent to discuss new taxes and that
only the *États généraux* could deal with the financial situation.
In remonstrances presented on 26 July 1787 it boldly demanded
the summoning of the *États généraux*:

Louis le Grand, se croyant obligé de percevoir le dixième, douta
qu'il en eût le droit, et si le parlement crut alors avoir celui de
l'enregistrer, ce fut parce que l'impôt ne devait avoir qu'une
courte durée, ce fut surtout parce que la position de l'État
semblait s'opposer à tous délais; sans cela, il eût dit que la nation
seule, réunie dans ses États généraux, pouvait donner à un impôt
perpétuel un consentement nécessaire, que le parlement n'avait
pas le pouvoir de suppléer ce consentement, encore moins celui
de l'attester quand rien ne le constatait; et que, chargé par le
souverain d'annoncer sa volonté aux peuples, il n'avait jamais
été chargé par ces derniers de les remplacer. C'est ce que votre

parlement prend aujourd'hui la respectueuse liberté de dire à V.M. Pénétré de cette vérité, alarmé d'un déficit qui semble monter à une somme énorme, frappé des désordres qui l'ont produit, et qui pourraient le perpétuer, il a formé le vœu de voir la nation assemblée préalablement à tout impôt nouveau. Elle seule, instruite de la véritable position des finances, peut extirper de grands abus et offrir de grandes ressources. (Flammermont, *Remontrances du Parlement de Paris*, III, 673-4)

A few days later, in a petition to the King, it demanded in even more categorical terms the summoning of the *États généraux*. The petition ended with the following words:

... Considérant en outre que la nation, représentée par les États généraux, est seule en droit d'octroyer au roi les secours nécessaires, que la nation peut sans partialité délibérer sur les moyens de vous procurer, sire, les secours dont le besoin sera évidemment démontré; a arrêté, persistant dans son arrêté du 16 de ce mois, de supplier très humblement V.M., en se rendant aux vœux portés audit arrêté, d'assembler les États généraux de votre royaume, préalablement à tout impôt nouveau. (III, 676)

When, on 6 August, the King held the customary *lit de justice* to force through these two new taxes, the Premier Président repeated this demand to his face. The importance of the Parlement's demand for the summoning of the *États généraux* is brought out in a famous sentence of Mme de Staël: 'Les castes privilégiées commencèrent l'insurrection contre l'autorité royale, et le parlement prononça le mot dont devait dépendre le sort de la France' (*Considérations*, I, 123).

The following day, the Parlement assembled in the Palais de Justice and declared 'nulles et illégales les transcriptions ordonné s être faites sur ses registres', and a week later, it declared illegal the government's publication of the new edicts. *Lettres de cachet* were then issued ordering the members of the Parlement to retire into the provinces to Troyes, but on its arrival there, the court made on 27 August yet another demand for the *États généraux*. Excitement ran high in Paris where public opinion was behind the Parlement's demands. It was supported in its stand by the Paris Cour des Aides and Chambre des Comptes and by the provincial Parlements and other courts.

For several days riots and all manner of disturbances took place in Paris. Then suddenly, when excitement was at its height, Loménie de Brienne, now decorated with the title of *principal ministre*, worked out a compromise; the government withdrew the *subvention territoriale* and the stamp-duty in return for which the Parlement registered an edict prolonging the two existing *vingtièmes*. Thereupon it was recalled to Paris, and returned to the capital in triumph.

This reconciliation proved short-lived. In November the King held a *séance royale*—a less solemn occasion than a *lit de justice*, but one which he intended to have the same effect—to register an edict covering loans spread over the next five years on the understanding that the *États généraux* would be summoned before 1792. The edict encountered outspoken opposition from certain of the judges, one of whom demanded the summoning of the *États généraux* for 1789. When the King brought the long proceedings to an end by ordering the registration of the edict without a vote, the Duc d'Orléans, the first prince of the blood after the King's two brothers, protested that the proceedings were illegal. The government retorted by exiling the duke to his estates and arresting two judges. As usual, the provincial Parlements supported their Paris colleagues and also came into conflict with the government on their own account.

The affair dragged on during the winter until finally a fresh crisis, one which was graver than any of its predecessors during the century because it involved not only the Parlements, but the whole power of the privileged orders in revolt against the monarchy, was unleashed by the drawing up in April 1788 of the Paris Parlement's remonstrances against the *séance royale* of the previous November. When these were presented to the King, he replied to the deputation which he had summoned to Versailles in terms which exposed the political claims of the courts: 'Si la pluralité dans mes cours forçait ma volonté, la monarchie ne serait plus qu'une aristocratie de magistrats, aussi contraire aux droits et aux intérêts de la nation qu'à ceux de la souveraineté' (Flammermont, *Remontrances du Parlement de Paris*, III, 735).

When it demanded the summoning of the *États généraux* which, given the power enjoyed by the nobility and clergy in previous assemblies, were likely both to defend their interests and to allow them considerable scope for the exercise of political power, the Parlement had not renounced its own claims to a share in the running of the country. In remonstrances which it drew up on 30 April, it hinted broadly that it expected to share power with the King and the *États généraux*:

C'est précisément parce qu'il n'est pas donné aux rois d'être sans cesse en garde contre l'erreur et la séduction, c'est pour ne pas abandonner la nation aux malheureux effets des volontés surprises, que la constitution exige, en matière de lois, la vérification des cours; en matière de subsides, l'octroi préalable des États généraux, pour être sûr que la volonté du roi sera conforme à la justice et ses demandes aux besoins de l'État. (Flammermont, *Remontrances du Parlement de Paris*, III, 740)

Before these remonstrances could be presented, the Parlement got wind of the severe measures which the government intended to take against it and, on May 3, proceeded to draw up a list of the fundamental laws of the monarchy, which included the following:

Le droit de la nation d'accorder librement les subsides par l'organe des États généraux régulièrement convoqués et composés;
Les coutumes et les capitulations des provinces;
L'inamovibilité des magistrats;
Le droit des cours de vérifier dans chaque province les volontés du roi et de n'en ordonner l'enregistrement qu'autant qu'elles sont conformes aux lois constitutives de la province ainsi qu'aux lois fondamentales de l'État. (III, 746)

The government annulled this declaration and attempted to arrest two of the judges, who took refuge in the Palais de Justice. When the Parlement assembled on the morning of 5 May, it sent a deputation to Versailles to protest against the attempt to arrest two of its members and decided to remain in session until a reply was received. At midnight an officer and a detachment of soldiers arrived to arrest the two judges; after an all-night session they finally gave themselves up.

On the 8th the King held one final *lit de justice* at Versailles at which he announced a complete reform of the judicial system:

> L'ordre que je veux établir n'est pas nouveau: le Parlement était unique quand Philippe le Bel le rendit sédentaire à Paris; il faut à un grand état un seul roi, une seule loi, un seul enregistrement; des tribunaux d'un ressort peu étendu, chargés de juger le plus grand nombre des procès; des parlements, auxquels les plus importants sont réservés; une cour unique, dépositaire des lois communes à tout le royaume, et chargée de leur enregistrement; enfin des États généraux assemblés non une fois, mais toutes les fois que les besoins de l'État l'exigeront. Telle est la restauration que mon amour pour mes sujets a préparée et consacrée aujourd'hui pour leur bonheur. (III, 751)

This programme, a revised version of the reforms of Mauopeu which had been undone at the beginning of the reign, was far-reaching. The first edict created 47 *grands-bailliages*, courts of appeal whose competence was sufficiently wide to leave the Parlements very little work, either in criminal or civil cases. Another edict reduced the number of judges of the Paris Parlement, a measure which was to be extended to the other Parlements. Finally, after other reforms such as the abolition of the last form of torture still practised in criminal cases (the *question préalable*, which was used to make condemned criminals reveal their accomplices), another edict ordered that in future all royal edicts were to be registered only by one court, the *cour plénière*, which would be presided over by the King and have as its members the princes of the blood, peers, senior judges of the Paris Parlement, and a great number of dignitaries, lay and ecclesiastical.

After the *lit de justice* of 8 May 1788 the so-called aristocratic revolt entered upon its most violent phase. The Paris Parlement had been sent on holiday, but the provincial Parlements now joined in the battle, supported by many great nobles and also by the clergy. When the *Assemblée du Clergé* met in June, it refused to come to the aid of Brienne in the desperate financial situation beyond offering a ridiculously small *don gratuit*, and protested against the treatment meted out to the Parlement. The clergy combined the demand for the maintenance of its

36　Versailles, Le Petit Trianon

37　Versailles, Le hameau de Marie-Antoinette

38  *Duplessis*, Necker                    39  Turgot

40  *Heinsius*, Calonne

fiscal privileges with a call for the summoning of the *États généraux.*

Meanwhile the provincial Parlements were stirring up trouble; before the events of May 1788 their actions had been rapidly reducing the country to a state of chaos:

> Un commandant, un commissaire du roi entraient dans une de des cours pour faire enregistrer un édit; le tribunal tout entier disparaissait, et laissait le commandant seul avec le greffier et le premier président. La loi enregistrée, le commandant parti, tout le tribunal accourait pour déclarer l'enregistrement nul. Les routes étaient couvertes de *grandes députations* des parlements, qui allaient à Versailles voir biffer leurs registres de la main du roi, et qui retournaient dans leur ville couvrir une nouvelle page d'un nouvel arrêté plus audacieux que celui qui venait d'être annulé. Plus ces actes étaient incendiaires, plus ils respiraient la révolte, et plus on s'empressait de leur donner une publicité effrayante. L'impossibilité de gouverner arrivait rapidement. (Weber, *Mémoires,* pp. 123-4)

Now up and down the country they sought the support of the nobility and of all the members of the huge legal profession, and in several places turned resistance to the edicts of 8 May into riots and disorder. In his memoirs Marmontel describes what dangerous examples of disorder the Parlements set, first in Paris and then in the provinces:

> La magistrature se fit protéger par la populace, et sous les yeux de la grande police furent impunément commis tous les excès de la plus grossière licence: pernicieux exemple, que l'on n'a que trop imité! Ce fut donc par le Parlement que fut d'abord provoquée l'insurrection et la révolte. . . .
> Dans les provinces, le despotisme des parlements chacun dans son ressort, la sécurité dont jouissaient leurs membres dans les vexations qu'ils exerçaient sur leurs voisins, leur arrogance, leur orgueil n'étaient pas faits pour rendre leur cause intéressante; mais, par leurs relations et leurs intelligences dans la classe privilégiée, ils formaient avec elle un parti nombreux et puissant. Le peuple même s'était laissé persuader que la cause des parlements était la sienne. (III, 148-9)

At Dijon and Toulouse there were riots when the *grand-bailliage* took the place of the Parlements; while in the provinces of

Béarn, Brittany and Dauphiné the execution of the May edicts led to open revolt. In Béarn the rebels used force to reinstate the Parlement. In Brittany the Parlement was supported by the nobility, which occupied a dominant position in the provincial estates and sent deputation after deputation to Versailles. In Dauphiné resistance to the edicts united all three orders who revived their provincial estates which had not met for over 150 years and there demanded the summoning of the *États généraux*.

These disorders made the financial situation even more desperate. At the beginning of July the government issued an edict announcing its intention to summon the *États généraux* in the near future and inviting all and sundry to state their views as to the form they should take. On 8 August another decree fixed the date of their meeting for 1 May 1789. On the 16th Brienne suspended all payments from the Treasury for six weeks; on the 25th he resigned. Necker took his place as *ministre d'état*, in fact as prime minister.

A month later the Parlements were recalled. The Paris Parlement was reinstated on 23 September and in the following month the provincial courts. Yet in the very moment of their triumph they suddenly forfeited all their popularity. Their resistance to the government, and especially their demand for the summoning of the *États généraux* had secured for them the support of the great majority of the nation. But there was a complete misunderstanding between the Parlements, representing the privileged orders, and the mass of the nation over the form in which the Estates should meet and consequently over their aims. For the Parlements and indeed for most of the members of the privileged orders it was understood that their form would be the same as when they last met in 1614, that is to say that the three orders would meet and vote separately. This would have meant that the first two orders would have had a permanent right of veto over the *Tiers État*. The Parlements also expected that, even with periodical meetings of the Estates, their political role would not by any means be over. Their attitude is well described by Marmontel:

Les exemples du temps passé pour la composition des États généraux étaient inconstants et divers; mais le plus grand nombre de ces exemples étaient favorables à la classe privilégiée, et, si celui de 1614 était suivi, comme le Parlement le demandait et croyait l'obtenir, l'ordre de la noblesse et celui du clergé s'assuraient la prépondérance. Leurs droits, leurs privilèges leur seraient conservés et garantis pour l'avenir; et, en échange du service que le Parlement leur avait rendu, il serait constitué lui-même, dans l'intervalle des assemblées, leur représentant perpétuel. (*Mémoires*, III, 157)

What the Third Estate meant by the *États généraux* was something very different—an assembly in which due weight would be given to the new importance of the middle classes in society by greatly increasing the number of representatives of the Third Estate, and replacing the system under which the three orders voted separately (the *vote par ordre*) by allowing the representatives of the three orders to vote together (the *vote par tête*).

The Parlements destroyed their popularity when they made it clear that what they had in mind was the old form of the Estates. When, on 24 September, the Paris Parlement registered the royal declaration announcing the summoning of the *États généraux* for January 1789, it added the condition that they should be summoned and composed 'suivant la forme observée en 1614'. The provincial Parlements followed this example. Thus the Parlement of Rennes in the following month specified the same condition: 'Déclare la cour remercier très respectueusement S.M. du rapprochement de la tenue des États généraux, dont la cour continuera de demander la convocation suivant les formes légales et constitutionnelles' (Le Moy, *Le Parlement de Bretagne*, p. 548). The effect on public opinion was tremendous; in the midst of the agitation for the doubling of the number of the deputies of the *Tiers état* and for the *vote par tête*, the Parlements finally cast aside their pretence of representing the nation, and by revealing their selfish class interests finally lost their popularity and their influence over events. A contemporary wrote:

Jamais révolution dans les esprits ne fut plus prompte, jamais al malédiction ne remplaça plus subitement l'enthousiasme. Je vis ce même parlement reçu en triomphe le 22 septembre,[1] parce qu'il avait provoqué les états généraux; couvert d'outrages le 24, parce que, scrupuleux observateur des formes, il voulait que leur convocation eût lieu d'après le mode de 1614. (Weber, *Mémoires*, p. 158)

The meeting of the *États généraux* which the Parlements had done so much to bring about was soon to destroy their very existence.

The question of the form of the *États généraux* was the one which occupied public opinion in the closing months of 1788. 'Si la noblesse et le clergé viennent à réussir dans leurs prétentions', wrote an observer in November, 'nos publicistes présagent l'anéantissement du pouvoir monarchique, la misère et la servitude pour le tiers état, et la conversion de notre forme de gouvernement en triple aristocratie, noble, magistrale et sacerdotale. Tel sera, disent-ils, l'effet d'États modelés sur ceux de 1614' (*Correspondance secrète inédite*, II, 304). Necker was in favour of doubling the number of deputies of the Third Estate, but he decided to summon another meeting of the *Assemblée des Notables*. When it met in November and December, it too came out strongly in favour of the practice followed in 1614; of the seven sections (*bureaux*) of the assembly, only one voted for the doubling of the number of deputies of the Third Estate. This intransigence increased still further the unpopularity of the privileged orders.

At last, on 27th December, the government was persuaded by Necker to come down on the side of the Third Estate by satisfying at least the first of its demands about the composition of the *États généraux*, and to declare: 'Le nombre des députés du Tiers État sera égal à celui des deux autres ordres réunis.' The other question—whether the deputies of each order should meet and vote separately or in one national assembly—had still to be decided when the Estates met at Versailles in May 1789.

The events of these two crucial years 1787 and 1788 repay detailed analysis, not only in their own right, but also for the

---

[1] This should read 'le 23 septembre'.

light which they throw on'French history for the whole period from 1715 to 1789. In them we see clearly revealed the antagonism between the Crown and the privileged orders which underlay the struggle of the monarchy with the clergy, the provincial estates and especially the Parlements during the reigns of Louis XV and Louis XVI; and in the last months before the Revolution we see revealed another conflict, one which was now to dominate the scene, that between the privileged orders and the Third Estate. In 1787 and 1788 the attempt of the privileged orders to wrest political power from the monarchy and their refusal to make any sacrifice of their privileges, coming on top of a financial crisis which could only be solved by such sacrifices, precipitated the Revolution. By the end of 1788 the united front of privileged orders and Third Estate to break the power of absolutism had cracked, as the divergent interests of the two parties had been brought to light by events. The determination of the clergy and nobility to wield political power and to preserve their privileges came up against the resolve of the Third Estate, not only to have a share in the government of France, but also to remould society and to sweep away aristocratic privilege. At the end of 1788 and the beginning of 1789 the struggle took on a different appearance. 'Le débat public a changé de face,' wrote an observer in January 1789. 'Il ne s'agit plus que très secondairement du roi, du despotisme, de la constitution; c'est une guerre entre le tiers état et les deux autres ordres' (Mallet du Pan, *Mémoires et correspondance*, I, 163). The privileged orders were now to change their tune, to forget their struggle against absolutism and to endeavour to join with the monarchy in propping up the old order against the onslaught of the Third Estate. In the famous pamphlet *Qu'est-ce que le tiers état?* published at the beginning of January 1789, Sieyès wrote:

> La peur de voir réformer les abus inspire aux deux premiers ordres plus d'alarmes qu'ils ne sentent de désirs pour la liberté. Entre elle et quelques privilèges odieux, ils ont fait choix de ceux-ci. Leur âme s'est identifiée avec les faveurs de la servitude. Ils redoutent aujourd'hui ces États généraux qu'ils invoquaient naguère avec tant d'ardeur. Tout est bien pour eux; ils ne se

plaignent plus que de l'esprit d'innovation; ils ne manquent plus de rien; la crainte leur a donné une constitution. (p. 78)

The fact that the privileged orders were, like the monarchy, the victims of the Revolution should not be allowed to hide their part in the slow but continuous disintegration of absolutism between 1715 and 1789, a process which began under the Regency of Philippe d'Orléans with the sudden reappearance of the aristocracy on the political scene, first in the short-lived experiment of the *Conseils* and then in the infinitely more dangerous revival of the power of the Parlements.

# CHAPTER VII

# THE WRITER AND HIS PUBLIC

Both the economic position of men of letters and their status in society underwent a vast improvement in the course of the eighteenth century in France. At the beginning of our period it was still impossible for a writer to make a living with his pen. Unless he had private means or a job which left him sufficient leisure to write, he could not manage to live on what he earned from publishers and, if he was a playwright, from the theatre; the smallness of the reading public and the restricted number of people able and willing to support a new play during its first run made this inevitable. If the writer lacked private means or a job, he was compelled, in order to eke out a living, to depend on the patronage of great noblemen, wealthy tax-farmers or the King and other members of the royal family. Gradually in the course of the century the lot of the writer improved considerably with the growth in the size of the reading public. In the last decades of the Ancien Régime it became possible for an author, once he had made a name for himself, to earn a comfortable living with his pen and thus to make himself independent of patronage.

This development away from dependence on a patron to having at least the possibility of living on what he earned from publishers or the theatre was not confined to France. Indeed, the process began earlier in England and went further than it did on the other side of the Channel; rather paradoxically, seeing that the population of England was considerably less than half that of France throughout our period. Yet there seems no doubt at all about the facts; independence of patronage was achieved considerably earlier here than in France. Pope led the way; his translations of the *Iliad* (1715-20) and the *Odyssey* (1725-1726) brought him in some £9,000 and allowed him to proclaim his independence of patronage:

> But (thanks to Homer) since I live and thrive,
> Indebted to no Prince or Peer alive.

Pope's position was exceptional. 'I take myself,' he wrote in 1723, 'to be the only scribbler of my time, of any degree of distinction, who never received any places from the establishment, any pension from a court, or any presents from a ministry. I desire to preserve this honour untainted to my grave.' Other English writers of the first half of the century continued to depend on patronage; yet by about 1760 the growth in the reading public began to make it possible for a man of letters to live by his pen alone. Shortly before that date Samuel Johnson had produced the famous definition in his dictionary: 'Patron. One who countenances, supports or protects. Commonly a wretch who supports with insolence, and is paid with flattery.' In 1773 he could declare: 'We have done with patronage.' Goldsmith summed up the writer's new independence when he wrote in 1760:

> At present the few poets of England no longer depend on the great for subsistence; they have now no other patrons but the public, and the public, collectively considered, is a good and generous master. . . .
> A man of letters at present, whose works are valuable, is perfectly sensible of their value. Every polite member of the community, by buying what he writes, contributes to reward him. The ridicule, therefore, of living in a garret, might have been wit in the last age, but continues such no longer, because no longer true. A writer of real merit now may easily be rich, if his heart be set only on fortune. . . . He may now refuse an invitation to dinner, without fearing to incur his patron's displeasure, or to starve by remaining at home. He may now venture to appear in company with just such clothes as other men generally wear, and talk even to princes with all the conscious superiority of wisdom. Though he cannot boast a fortune here, yet he can bravely assert the dignity of independence.

The difference in the position of English and French writers at this period of the century is well brought out by the advice which Hume gave to Rousseau in 1765 to take refuge in London. His own *History of England*, the sixth volume of which had appeared three years earlier, had brought him in well over £3,000. He wrote to Rousseau: 'Les libraires de Londres offrent aux auteurs plus d'argent que ceux de Paris; ainsi vous pourrez sans peine y vivre frugalement du fruit de votre propre travail' (Rousseau, *Correspondance générale*, XIV, 218). The more favoured position of writers on this side of the Channel often aroused the envy of their French colleagues in the course of the century. There is the famous chapter in the *Lettres philosophiques* of Voltaire, with the challenging title 'De la considération[1] qu'on doit aux gens de lettres', in which he speaks enthusiastically of the lot of English writers and scientists and contrasts it with the lowly state of their French counterparts. The account of conditions in England which he gives here is not strictly accurate, as the political patronage which conferred all manner of official posts and sinecures on English writers had faded out long before Voltaire wrote, and the improvement in the status of the man of letters was to derive from the independence conferred by substantial payments from publishers. The following lines are perhaps truer, despite their obvious exaggeration, of conditions in France than of those in England in the 1730s:

M. Addison, en France, eût été de quelque académie, et aurait pu obtenir, par le crédit de quelque femme, une pension de douze cents livres, ou plutôt on lui aurait fait des affaires, sous prétexte qu'on aurait aperçu, dans sa tragédie de *Caton*, quelques traits contre le portier d'un homme en place. En Angleterre, il a été secrétaire d'État. M. Newton était intendant des monnaies du royaume. M. Congreve avait une charge importante. M. Prior a été plénipotentiaire. Le docteur Swift est doyen d'Irlande, et y est beaucoup plus considéré que le primat. Si la religion de M. Pope ne lui permet pas d'avoir une place,[2] elle n'empêche pas au moins que sa traduction d'Homère ne lui ait valu deux cent mille francs. J'ai vu longtemps en France l'auteur de *Rhadamiste*[3] prêt de mourir de faim; et le fils d'un des plus grands hommes que la France ait eus, et qui commençait à marcher sur les traces de son père, était réduit à la misère sans M. Fagon.[4] (Letter XXIII).

---

[1] In the sense of 'respect, esteem'.
[2] As a Catholic, he was excluded from all public offices.
[3] Crebillon *père*, whose tragedy *Rhadamiste et Zénobie* was performed in 1711.
[4] Louis Racine, the son of the famous dramatist. He was compelled to take a post in the provinces in the *fermes*.

In the second half of the century, when English writers had achieved independence of patronage, and, when once established, could earn large sums of money with their pen, French men of letters cast envious glances across the Channel. In 1766 we find Grimm complaining about the meagre rewards obtained by Diderot and his collaborators from a vast undertaking like the *Encyclopédie* and comparing them with the large profits made by the publishers. 'Je ne connais guère de race plus franchement malhonnête', he exclaims, 'que celle des libraires de Paris. En Angleterre l'*Encyclopédie* aurait fait la fortune des auteurs' (*Correspondance littéraire*, VII, 45). Four years later, shortly after William Robertson's *History of Charles V* brought him the stupendous sum of £4,500 (the equivalent of over 100,000 livres in French money), we find Voltaire writing to a young author: 'Je voudrais que chacune de vos lignes vous fût payée comme aux Robertson' (*Œuvres complètes*, XLVII, 541). Another French writer declared: 'Si un libraire de Paris en avait donné la huitième partie de cette somme, il aurait cru faire encore à l'auteur un traitement bien généreux' (Fenouillot de Falbaire, *Avis aux gens de lettres*, pp. 40-1).

Nevertheless, if English writers were in our period in a more favourable position than their French colleagues, this must not blind us to the fact that the same process was at work on both sides of the Channel; in France, too, at any rate in the closing decades of the Ancien Régime, it was becoming possible for a writer to earn a living with his pen and to make himself independent of patronage. Yet literary patronage retained down to 1789 an importance which it had lost before that date in England.

The reason for this state of affairs is obscure. Given the much larger population of France, one would have expected the Paris book trade to be in a flourishing state, and although contemporary evidence on this point is conflicting, there is an interesting remark on the comparative size of the book trade in London and Paris in a French periodical a few years before 1789. 'Les Anglais évaluent le commerce de l'imprimerie de Paris à près de deux millions sterling, c'est-à-dire, à quarante-cinq millions de livres tournois environ, et ils confessent que celui de Londres ne monte guère qu'au quart' (Bachaumont, *Mémoires secrets*, XXIX, 139). What is more, French books had a European market, as the French language was familiar to the cultured classes everywhere. Unfortunately for the native Frenchman, a considerable part of that market was lost to him by the absence of an international copyright agreement. Not only did he earn nothing from the translation of his works into foreign tongues, but publishers abroad were quite free to produce pirated editions in French. All over Europe—in Germany, Switzerland, England and especially Holland— publishers brought out unauthorized editions (*contrefaçons*) of his works without even thinking of paying him a penny for them. If, because of the censorship or for any other reason, he sold his manuscript to a foreign publisher, he generally received less for it than if he had had it published in Paris, and once again pirated editions appeared all over the place, in France and abroad. Rousseau's publisher, Rey of Amsterdam, wrote to him in 1764 the somewhat astonishing sentence: 'Si vos ouvrages étaient moins recherchés, j'en vendrais davantage, parce qu'on ne les contreferait pas si souvent' (*Correspondance générale*, XI, 136). Some notion—a very rough one, of course—of the loss in which pirated editions might involve a writer is given in the following lines, written in 1770:

> J'ai vu l'an passé la lettre d'un libraire qui, ayant acheté mille écus une pièce de théâtre, représentée avec succès à la Comédie Italienne, écrivait à l'auteur qu'il lui en donnerait dix mille francs, s'il voulait lui garantir les contrefactions.[1] Voilà sept mille livres que les contrefacteurs volent à cet homme de lettres.
> (Fenouillot de Falbaire, *Avis aux gens de lettres*, p. 42)

Moreover, even inside France a considerable proportion of the population could not read and therefore did not either buy or borrow books. The degree of illiteracy in France in the eighteenth century can only be roughly measured; the only method so far used has been to examine the parish registers of a large number of different regions in order to discover how

---

[1] 'Contrefaction, il ne se dit qu'en parlant de livres, dans le sens de contrefaçon' (*Dictionnaire de l'Académie Française*, 1762).

many people were able to sign their names when they were married. At the end of the seventeenth century the figures for men and women were 28·74 per cent. and 13·97 per cent. respectively. The situation improved considerably in the eighteenth century, since the corresponding figures for the period 1786-90 had risen to 47·45 per cent. and 26·88 per cent. Even so, at the end of the Ancien Régime over half the men and nearly three-quarters of the women were still incapable of signing their names in the marriage register.

Certainly at the beginning of our period the reading public was a small one, and the publisher who acquired a manuscript was faced with the certainty that if the book was a success, the sales of his edition would be greatly reduced by pirated versions produced both at home and abroad. If the book had only a modest success, its sales would be small, and therefore he would generally only risk a small printing. Then, as now, publishers were not always the soul of generosity and it would be possible to accumulate many pages of extremely rude eighteenth-century references to the tribe, who incidentally, as the functions of publishing and bookselling had not yet been separated out, were known in our period, not as 'publishers' and 'éditeurs', but as 'booksellers' and 'libraires'. It was of publishers that Voltaire wrote in his best English in 1752: 'Booksellers are the hell of writers' (*Correspondence*, XX, 263). Then, as now, publishers did sometimes make money out of an author's books. With engaging frankness Rousseau's publisher, Rey, wrote to him at the end of 1760, shortly before he put on the market the first edition of *La Nouvelle Héloïse*, that he expected to make 10,000 livres out of the book—approximately five times the lump sum which he had given Rousseau for his manuscript (*Correspondance générale*, V, 224-5).

Although disputes frequently arose about the respective rights of author and publisher in our period, it seems to have been generally accepted that, in deciding what lump sum he should pay an author for his manuscript (a royalty system seems to have been unknown), the publisher was entitled to calculate it on the returns which he could expect from the first edition and that he had a right to produce further editions without necessarily paying the author anything more, although he might often make a token payment. Inevitably most payments received by authors were small. Our information on this point, especially for the first half of the century, is somewhat scrappy, but is sufficient to give us a general picture of the situation. If the exiled poet, Jean-Baptiste Rousseau, known as 'le grand Rousseau' until his fame was eclipsed by that of his more famous namesake Jean-Jacques, could collect 800 guineas from a subscription edition of his works published in London in 1723, and if Voltaire's friend, Thieriot, could obtain 200 guineas for the London edition of the *Lettres philosophiques*, payments made by Paris publishers were much more modest, at this period in the century. For most literary works they seem to have come within the range of 1,000 to 1,500 or 2,000 livres. Thus in 1748 Diderot received 1,200 *l.* for his somewhat disreputable novel, *Les Bijoux indiscrets*, while in 1737 Destouches was given 700 *l.* for a new play, *L'Ambitieux et l'Indiscrète*. In the latter year Voltaire received 1,200 *l.* from the same publisher for his comedy, *L'Enfant prodigue*, and La Chaussée obtained 1,600 *l.* for *L'École des Amis*. A decade or so later, prices for plays seem to have risen rather higher; in 1749 a Paris publisher gave Crébillon 3,600 *l.* for his tragedy, *Catalina*, while in the following year Mme de Grafigny received 2,000 *l.* for her *Cénie*.

Although we do not have as much information as we could wish about the amount of money which writers received from publishers in the first half of the century, it is clear from these examples that the general level was still low. In comparison, at any rate in this period of the century, writing for the theatre still seems to have been a relatively paying proposition, provided one could produce a box-office success, or better still, a series of such plays. Throughout our period a successful play still remained the passport to fame for a young and unknown writer. In 1734 a contemporary wrote: 'Tous nos beaux esprits ne s'occupent plus que du théâtre, l'unique carrière en effet où il y ait quelque gloire à acquérir. . . . Aujourd'hui un jeune rimeur n'a pas plus tôt fait une petite épître en vers qu'il entreprend une comédie. Celui qui a fait deux odes, veut donner une tragédie' (Monod-Cassidy, *Abbé Le Blanc*, p. 197). A decade later, on his arrival in Paris, the young Marmontel had, he tells us in his memoirs, the following dialogue with the more experienced Voltaire:

> En attendant, voyons, à quoi allez-vous travailler?—Hélas, je n'en sais rien, et c'est à vous de me le dire.—Le théâtre, mon ami, le théâtre est la plus belle des carrières; c'est là qu'en un jour on obtient de la gloire et de la fortune. Il ne faut qu'un succès pour rendre un jeune homme célèbre et riche en même temps; et vous l'aurez, ce succès, en travaillant bien. (I, 143)

Unfortunately the playwright's career was still bestrewn with obstacles. In Paris, right down to the Revolution, there was only one theatre to which the young playwright with serious literary ambitions could take his play. Since 1680, when Louis XIV had put an end to competition between French companies of actors by amalgamating them in the Comédie Française, this theatre had enjoyed a virtual monopoly of all plays with literary pretensions. It is true that the return of the Italian actors in 1716 had provided a mild amount of competition, but although so great a playwright as Marivaux gave the majority of his works to them, the plays produced in their theatre throughout the century contributed very little to French drama.

The monopoly which the actors of the Comédie Française enjoyed made them haughty, overbearing and oppressive to the authors who brought them new plays. Lesage, who knew at first hand all their little ways, inserted a blistering passage on their behaviour towards playwrights in the first volume of his novel, *Gil Blas*, published in 1715. His hero, who at one stage in the novel has entered the service of an actress named Arsénie, describes the following scene:

> Notre petit laquais vint dire tout haut à ma maîtresse: Madame, un homme en linge sale, crotté jusqu'à l'échine,[1] et, qui, sauf votre respect, a tout l'air d'un poète, demande à vous parler. Qu'on le fasse monter, répondit Arsénie. Ne bougeons, messieurs, c'est un auteur. Effectivement c'en était un dont on avait accepté

[1] A traditional expression to convey the poverty of the writer; cf. Boileau, *Satire I*: . . . Tandis que Colletet, crotté jusqu'à l'échine, S'en va chercher son pain de cuisine en cuisine.

une tragédie, et qui apportait un rôle à ma maîtresse. Il s'appelait
Pedro de Moya. Il fit en entrant cinq ou six profondes révérences
à la compagnie, qui ne se leva, ni même ne le salua point.
Arsénie répondit seulement par une simple inclination de tête aux
civilités dont il l'accablait. Il s'avança dans la chambre d'un air
tremblant et embarrassé. Il laissa tomber ses gants et son chapeau.
Il les ramassa, s'approcha de ma maîtresse, et lui présenta un
papier plus respectueusement qu'un plaideur ne présente un
placet à son juge: Madame, lui dit-il, agréez de grâce le rôle que
je prends la liberté de vous offrir. Elle le reçut d'une manière
froide et méprisante, et ne daigna pas même répondre au compliment. (Book III, Chap. xi)

The playwright not only had to deal with haughty actors and
temperamental actresses before he could get his play accepted
and performed; he also had to put up with unfavourable
financial conditions. In those days he did not receive a penny
in fees for performances of plays given either in the provinces
or abroad; however successful his play might have been, once
it was published anyone was free to perform it anywhere without paying a fee to the author. All he could count on in the way
of receipts, even if his play passed the test of public performance,
was a modest payment from his publisher and what the actors
deigned to give him for his play. Theoretically, once certain
expenses had been paid, he was entitled to a fixed share of the
proceeds from each performance, a share which naturally
varied according to the length of his play. In practice, as it was
in their interest to stop paying him as soon as possible, the
actors had all sorts of little dodges to reduce the royalties to the
smallest figure they could. They would inflate their expenses
to keep down in the books the profits from each day's performance; and they used all manner of devices to make the first run
of the play as short as possible since, once the play had been
taken off, it became their property and the author had no
further claim on them.

Even so, the author of a really successful play in the first half
of the century could earn fairly respectable sums of money;
although the first run of the most popular play did not normally
exceed twenty to thirty performances, it did bring a good

amount of money as well as fame to an impecunious young writer. In 1748 the young Marmontel, who had taken Voltaire's advice, received nearly 3,000 *l.* from the Comédie Française for his first tragedy. That was the average sum for a successful comedy or tragedy in the first half of the century, though somewhere in the neighbourhood of 4,000 *l.* was reached by such highly successful plays of the period as Voltaire's *Zaïre*, Destouches's comedy, *Le Glorieux*, and Mme de Grafigny's *Cénie*. The record for the period was achieved by Voltaire's tragedy, *Mérope*, which in 1743 brought its author over 6,000 *l.* during its first run of twenty-nine performances.

Naturally such plays were altogether exceptional. The degree of success enjoyed by most new plays—even those which were very far from being a failure—was much more modest; and so were the author's earnings from them. Marivaux, the only playwright of the first half of the eighteenth century whose works still live on the stage today, fared very differently. It is true that none of the best-known of his plays had its first performance at the Comédie Française; but although we do not know exactly what they earned for their author, it is clear that plays like *Le Jeu de l'amour et du hasard* and *Les Fausses Confidences* were far from achieving a sensational success during their first run at the Théâtre Italien. At the Comédie Française his two most successful plays—*Les Serments indiscrets* and the second *Surprise de l'amour*—earned royalties only during a first run of nine performances and each brought him about 300 *l.*

In fact, no playwright or any other kind of writer of this period in the century could succeed in making a career with his pen. Biographers of Lesage and Prévost sometimes claim that each of these men was the first French writer to make a living with his pen; but their success could only be described as moderate. Each of them had to have at least some recourse to patronage during his career, and neither could be said to have earned a satisfactory living from writing. Lesage abandoned the Comédie Française shortly after the semi-failure of his great comedy of manners, *Turcaret*, and devoted a considerable part of his life to producing mere hackwork for the Théâtres de la Foire. In the novel as in drama he was compelled to produce a

41 La Petite Loge

42   La Sortie de l'Opéra

great many 'pot-boilers' in order to keep the wolf from the door. A contemporary wrote of him in 1733:

> Lesage, auteur de *Gil Blas*, vient de donner la *Vie de M. Beauchêne*, capitaine de flibustiers. Ce livre ne saurait être mal écrit, étant de Lesage; mais il est aisé de s'apercevoir par les matières que cet auteur traite depuis quelque temps qu'il ne travaille que pour vivre et qu'il n'est pas le maître par conséquent de donner à ses ouvrages du temps et de l'application. (Claretie, *Lesage*, pp. 41-2)

Though astonishingly little is known of the life of one of the greatest French writers of the period, it is quite clear that even all this hackwork did not provide him with anything approaching a reasonable living. Abbé Prévost lives today in one short masterpiece, *Manon Lescaut*; but as he was driven to trying to earn a living with his pen, this one novel is merely a tiny fraction of his enormous output of novels, translations and all manner of compilations which necessity drove him to produce.

A writer like Marivaux, who was not so prolific as either Lesage or Prévost, fared even worse. His earnings from his plays, novels and other writings appear to have been meagre, and although he received assistance from such patrons as Louis XV (through the good offices of Mme de Pompadour) and the tax-farmer, Helvétius, he appears to have led a poverty-stricken existence in the last part of his life, when he had virtually ceased to produce new novels or plays. Literary patronage was certainly needed in these years to supplement the modest sums which a writer could count on receiving from publishers or the theatre. Even the young Voltaire, although he quickly realized that to secure independence the only thing for him to do was to make money outside literature, eagerly sought for pensions at the beginning of his career, and successfully tapped such patrons as the Regent, Louis XV and his Queen. However, although he continually lamented the good old days of Louis XIV and Colbert when, he fondly imagined, pensions and favours of all kinds were showered on writers (this was an almost complete delusion), he never sought these after the beginning of his career except as a token of his literary reputation and as a kind of protection against persecution. His appointment as Historiographer Royal and Gentleman of the Bedchamber in 1745 was not to prove one of his happiest experiences, and he soon abandoned Versailles for Potsdam, with even more disillusioning results. As for the money which he was entitled to receive from publishers and the theatre, as soon as he had used his connections in the right places to build up for himself a comfortable income and eventually to make himself an extremely rich man, he regarded them as so much small change. He frequently gave his earnings from the theatre to actors and actresses with whom he wished to remain on good terms; the payments which he received from his books were often handed over at his request to struggling young writers. Voltaire was in fact an altogether exceptional figure in his age: the man of letters who was at the same time a man of substance. But he owed his wealth hardly at all to his literary work.

Another outstanding writer of the first half of the century, Montesquieu, did not disdain to accept money for his books, but he was a large landowner and for a time a *Président à mortier* of the Bordeaux Parlement; he could not be regarded as a professional writer. He clearly considered himself as more than a cut above such fellows, who were driven to eke out their meagre earnings from publishers or the theatre by accepting the pensions and gifts of the King, other members of the royal family, great noblemen and wealthy tax-farmers.

Some idea of the gradual progress of the writer towards independence is to be obtained from a consideration of the careers of two other great writers of the age, Rousseau and Diderot, men of a slightly later period since they came to maturity between roughly 1750 and 1760. From Rousseau's *Confessions* and correspondence we can form a fairly precise idea of his earnings as a writer. He entered the field fairly late, in 1750, with his First *Discours*; for this he received nothing at all from his publisher. His second *Discours* brought him only 600 *l.*, but in the meantime he had done quite well out of his opera, *Le Devin du Village*, since, in addition to 1,200 *l.* from the Opéra and 500 from his publisher, he received gifts of 2,400 *l.* and 1,200 *l.* from Louis XV and Mme de Pompadour for court performances, i.e. a total of over 5,000 *l.* The *Lettre à d'Alembert* brought him only 720 *l.*, and even his novel, *La Nouvelle Héloïse*, probably the record best-seller of the whole of the eighteenth century, earned him just over 2,000 francs from the Amsterdam publisher who brought out the first edition. From the incredible number of pirated editions of his novel he received, of course, nothing at all, except that Malesherbes insisted that the Paris publisher who brought out the first pirated edition in France should pay him 1,000 *l.* The *Contrat social* brought him 1,000 *l.*, but he did better with *Émile*, for Malesherbes saw to it that his Paris publisher paid him 6,000 *l.* His polemical work, the *Lettres écrites de la Montagne*, brought him 1,500 *l.* and his *Dictionnaire de musique*, 2,400, plus an annuity of 300 *l.* Towards the end of his career he made an arrangement whereby, in return for an annuity of 1,600 *l.*, he sold the rights in an edition of his complete works (to include among other unpublished writings his *Confessions*); this arrangement ultimately came to nothing and after his death the edition of his complete works brought his heirs 24,000 *l.*

Given the enormous popularity of his writings, Rousseau could scarcely be said to have obtained his due. He was, of course, almost savagely independent (though this did not prevent him from accepting patronage, for instance a small annuity from 'Milord Maréchal', George Keith) and he endeavoured to eke out a living by copying music. Even his warmest admirers are compelled to admit that Jean-Jacques was an extremely odd fellow, and although it is interesting to know in some detail what he actually received from his writings, his cannot be regarded as a typical case. Nor unfortunately can that of Diderot, since, although he struggled for the greater part of his career, unaided by any form of patronage, to earn a living with his pen, a very considerable proportion of his work appeared posthumously, and in many cases long after his death. He certainly began his career by working for publishers at such routine tasks as translating, and then graduated to the editorship of the *Encyclopédie*, a task which was to absorb most of his energies for over twenty years of his life. In 1767 when his work on the *Encyclopédie* was virtually over, he wrote—in a work

composed, it is true, to represent the interests of publishers!—
of his own and other writers' earnings:

> Il y a des hommes de lettres, à qui leur travail a produit dix,
> vingt, trente, quatre-vingt, cent mille francs. Moi, qui ne jouis
> que d'une considération commune et qui ne suis pas âgé, je crois
> que le fruit de mes occupations littéraires irait bien à quarante
> mille écus. (*Œuvres complètes*, XVIII, 47)

A hundred and twenty thousand francs, spread over some
twenty-five years, was a modest, but fairly comfortable and
steady income. Although there is no question that Diderot
earned nothing like his due for his herculean labours on the
seventeen volumes of text and eleven volumes of plates of the
*Encyclopédie*, it would seem, so far as one can get at the truth
from the accounts of the enterprise and from his correspondence, that contemporary and more recent writers have tended
to exaggerate the parsimonious treatment which he received
from his publishers. As the work grew to ever greater proportions, so his agreements with the publishers were altered in his
favour, and it would seem as if something like half the sum
which he gave for his total earnings from his writings came from
his work on the *Encyclopédie*. Yet although Diderot did draw a
fair amount of money from this work and his other writings, the
fact that he was able to enjoy a comfortable old age and to
provide his daughter with a substantial dowry was due to two
factors outside his earnings as a professional writer. The share
of his father's estate when the latter died in 1759 brought him
a small but secure income; and if the authorities in France
would not lift a finger to help a writer of such suspect views, he
secured a generous patron in Catherine the Great who paid
him over 60,000 *l.* in one form or another for his library and his
manuscripts. Once again true independence with a modest
affluence was not wholly achieved by one of the greatest
writers of the age.

None the less, there seems no doubt that in the closing
decades of the Ancien Régime the economic position of the
writer was steadily improving; it was slowly becoming possible
to achieve some measure of independence of patronage. The

gradual reduction in illiteracy was steadily increasing the reading public, and although books remained dear, they could be borrowed as well as bought. There were *cabinets littéraires* where books could be read in return for a small payment, as Mercier points out in his *Tableau de Paris*:

> N'avez-vous point de bibliothèque? Pour quatre sols vous vous enfoncez dans un *cabinet littéraire*, et là, pendant une après-dînée entière vous lisez depuis la massive *Encyclopédie* jusqu'aux feuilles volantes. (IV, 3)

Marmontel, a man of most modest origins, describes how at Clermont-Ferrand, about 1740, he and his fellow schoolboys borrowed books from a circulating library kept by a bookseller of the town:

> A frais communs, et à peu de frais, nous étions abonnés pour nos lectures avec un vieux libraire; et comme les bons livres sont, grâce au ciel, les plus communs, nous n'en lisions que d'excellents. Les grands orateurs, les grands poètes, les meilleurs écrivains du siècle dernier, quelques-uns du siècle présent, car le libraire en avait peu, se succédaient de main en main; et dans nos promenades chacun se rappelant ce qu'il avait recueilli, nos entretiens se passaient presque tous en conférences sur nos lectures. (*Mémoires*, I, 62)

A less stilted description of the workings of a Paris circulating library is given forty years later by Mercier in the chapter of his *Tableau de Paris* entitled 'Loueur de livres':

> Usés, sales, déchirés, ces livres en cet état attestent qu'ils sont les meilleurs de tous; et le critique hautain qui s'épuise en réflexions superflues, devrait aller chez le *loueur de livres*, et là voir les brochures que l'on demande, que l'on emporte, et auxquelles on revient de préférence. . . .
>
> Les ouvrages qui peignent les mœurs, qui sont simples, naïfs ou touchants, qui n'ont ni apprêt, ni morgue, ni jargon académique, voilà ceux que l'on vient chercher de tous les quartiers de la ville et de tous les étages des maisons. . . .
>
> Il y a des ouvrages qui excitent une telle fermentation que le bouquiniste est obligé de couper le volume en trois parts afin de pouvoir fournir à l'empressement des nombreux lecteurs; alors vous payez non par jour, mais par heure. . . . (V, 36-7)

As the century wore on, there were more and more signs of a widening of interest in literature. Though Paris still retained its dominant position in the theatrical life of France, it no longer entirely dwarfed the provinces as it had done for the greater part of the seventeenth century. In the second quarter of the century there had begun, both in the great commercial centres and in the garrison towns, a considerable revival of theatrical activity. We have seen how on the eve of the Revolution Arthur Young found large and prosperous theatres in such towns as Bordeaux and Nantes.[1] Again, the number of provincial academies roughly doubled between about 1750 and 1770; it was from the Dijon Academy that Rousseau received the stimulus to compose his two early works, the *Discours sur les sciences et les arts* and the *Discours sur l'inégalité*. More important was the encouragement which academies of this kind gave, in the different regions of France, to an interest in literary and intellectual matters.

Perhaps the clearest sign of a broadening of the public interest in literature is furnished by the Paris theatres, in particular the two privileged theatres, the Comédie Française and the Théâtre Italien. Since the seventeenth century the cultured sections of the middle classes had formed an important section of the audiences which frequented the leading Paris theatres, alongside the more aristocratic members of the community, male and female, who occupied the *premières loges* and —at least down to 1759 at the Comédie Française—disported themselves on the seats on the stage. Down to about 1760 the audience of the Comédie Française remained small in numbers and was drawn from a restricted section of society, from the cultured middle class upwards. Round about that date various contemporaries noted a new and even somewhat alarming phenomenon—the infiltration into the theatre of people of more modest rank and education. In 1762 a contemporary critic could still speak as if the great mass of spectators were drawn from the middle and upper ranks of society:

> Ce n'est point le peuple qui fréquente chez nous les spectacles; c'est une coterie particulière de gens du monde, de gens d'arts et

---

[1] See above, pp. 73-5

de lettres, de personnes des deux sexes à qui leur rang ou leur fortune a permis de cultiver leur esprit: c'est l'élite de la nation à laquelle se joint un très petit nombre de gens qui tiennent au peuple par leur état ou par leur profession. (Grimm, *Correspondance littéraire*, VI, 171)

A dozen years later his successor speaks contemptuously of the new spectators who in recent years have found their way into the cheapest part of the theatre—the *parterre*—which furnished standing room only to male spectators:

En effet, le parterre était composé, il y a quinze ans, de l'honnête bourgeoisie et des hommes de lettres, tous gens ayant fait leurs études, ayant des connaissances plus ou moins étendues, mais en ayant enfin. Le luxe les a tous fait monter aux secondes loges, qui ne jugent point, ou dont le jugement, au moins, reste sans influence; c'est le parterre seul qui décide du sort d'une pièce. Aujourd'hui cet aréopage est composé de journaliers, de garçons perruquiers, de marmitons; qu'attendre de pareils sujets? et peut-on se méprendre à la cause des disparates de leurs jugements? (ibid. X, 341)

One must not take such exaggerations literally, but this and other contemporary evidence does show that, while throughout the eighteenth century the vast majority of the occupants of the cheapest part of theatres like the Comédie Française and the Théâtre Italien were lawyers, schoolmasters, writers, students, in a word 'intellectuals' and members, present or future, of the liberal professions, in the last two or three decades of the Ancien Régime the *parterre* of these theatres did begin to attract a certain proportion of the lower classes. No doubt as illiteracy decreased, reading also attracted an ever-wider section of the community, even if it was from circulating libraries that their books generally came. Mercier, we have seen, speaks of the customers of circulating libraries coming 'de tous les quartiers de la ville et de tous les étages des maisons'.

The growth in the reading public in the second half of the century no doubt meant larger editions of works and more frequent reprints, and therefore better payments from publishers. In addition, fresh sources of income were opened up by the expanding demand for reading matter. There was, for instance, a considerable growth in the periodical press. To the established reviews which went back to the seventeenth century —the *Gazette de France*, the *Journal des Savants* and, most important of all from the literary point of view, the *Mercure de France*—were added new periodicals, published outside as well as inside France. From these writers could obtain fresh sources of income as editors and reviewers. In 1779 the capital acquired its first daily newspaper, *Le Journal de Paris, ou La Poste du soir*, seventy-five years after the first London daily. Writers, especially the young and unknown, might continue to obtain very small returns from their books; it is characteristic in 1782 that Laclos, the author of the *Liaisons dangereuses* which is held in some quarters to be the greatest French novel of the century, obtained only 1,600 *l.* for his book. Yet other writers of the time were drawing substantial sums from literary journalism in addition to what they might earn from their plays, novels or other writings. La Harpe apparently drew 6,000 *l.* a year as editor of the *Mercure*, while Rivarol received 150 *l.* a month for writing reviews for the same journal. Another writer, Suard, is alleged to have obtained up to 20,000 *l.* a year as editor of the *Journal de Paris* in the 1780s.

Another source of income for writers was provided by the contemporary demand for works of popularization, for dictionaries, encyclopaedias, works of reference and the like. The compilation of such works could help struggling authors to pay their rent and even provide them with a comfortable income. An obscure *abbé* named De La Porte, whose writings are known today only to specialists in the period, was earning a considerable annual income by helping publishers to satisfy this demand; in the words of a contemporary:

> L'abbé de La Porte, employé par les libraires, gagne tous les ans cinq ou six mille livres à ce métier-là, et les libraires gagnent des capitaux, car le débit de toutes ces compilations est étonnant, et il ne se passe pas une semaine qu'il ne s'en publie une nouvelle.
> (Grimm, *Correspondance littéraire*, VIII, 274)

A precise example of the earnings of a writer from casual jobs of this kind is furnished by a contract signed in 1779 between the writer, Suard, and the publisher, Panckoucke. In return for some three months' work revising and, where necessary, adding to the relevant articles in the *Encyclopédie* of Diderot and D'Alembert to make them into the two quarto volumes on literature and grammar of the new *Encyclopédie méthodique*, which Panckoucke was bringing out, Suard was to receive for a total of 180 or 190 sheets 'la somme de vingt-quatre livres pour chaque feuille de copie nouvelle et . . . quinze livres pour toutes les feuilles tirées du *Dictionnaire encyclopédique*, soit que ces dernières soient copiées en entier, soit qu'il y ait du retranchement ou des additions. . . . Il sera remis en outre au Sr Suard un exemplaire complet de ladite *Encyclopédie méthodique*, plus six exemplaires du *Dictionnaire de grammaire et de littérature*.'

In the closing decades of the Ancien Régime writers were no longer inclined to take what publishers and actors cared to offer them. A vigorous attack on the sordid avarice of publishers was made, for instance, in 1770 by an obscure writer called Fenouillot de Falbaire in his *Avis aux gens de lettres*. He contrasts the rapid fortunes made by publishers with the poverty of the majority of writers:

> Les libraires engloutissent chez nous tout le produit des livres qui s'y composent. Aussi font-ils presque tous des fortunes rapides et prodigieuses, dont l'on ne doit plus s'étonner. Tel qui n'avait rien en commençant ce commerce, se trouve, au bout de dix ou quinze ans, riche de sept à huit cent mille francs; et ces exemples ne sont point rares parmi eux. La plupart ont un train de maison très considérable, des ameublements chers, des campagnes charmantes, tandis qu'ordinairement l'écrivain aux ouvrages duquel ils doivent cette opulence, est relégué sous les toits, à un troisième, à un quatrième étage, où une simple lampe éclaire sa pauvreté et ses travaux. (pp. 38-9)

The copyright law of France was extremely unsatisfactory from the author's point of view in the eighteenth century. For a book to appear legally (there were in practice other methods available) it required a licence (*privilège*), issued by the King for a limited number of years, generally not more than ten; when it expired, the publisher to whom the author had assigned it would have it renewed, considering that what he had originally paid the author for his book covered the right to reprint it for ever. In 1777 and 1778 the government issued a number of decrees which modified this position; in particular, one provision allowed an author the right—which publishers had always denied him—to retain the *privilège* for a work, to have it printed and to sell it himself or through a bookseller of his choice. In addition, the new decrees made possible firmer measures against French publishers who produced pirated editions. In future prosecutions were to be much more numerous. Thus in 1781 a Toulouse publisher who was responsible for a pirated version of Marmontel's *Contes moraux* was fined 6,000 *l.*, one-third of which sum was to be paid to the author.

Yet under the Ancien Régime the position of the writer still remained unsatisfactory. Pirated editions of books, even those produced inside France, did not vanish overnight. After the publication of his *Études de la Nature* in 1784, Bernardin de Saint-Pierre had a most irritating experience when he was called upon to be present at a school speech day:

> J'ai été invité un jour à une distribution de prix présidée par un ministre qui en faisait les frais. . . . L'on m'avait réservé l'honneur d'embrasser conjointement avec lui tous les vainqueurs. Quelle fut ma surprise, lorsque j'en vis plusieurs, sortant de mes bras, emporter au bruit des applaudissements de toute l'assemblée, pour prix de morale et de vertu, mes *Études de la Nature* contrefaites! (Souriau, *Bernardin de Saint-Pierre*, p. 217)

It was in fact left to the Revolution to produce the first modern copyright law in France, which really safeguarded the interests of the author in his work. In July 1793 the *Convention* decreed:

> Les auteurs d'écrits en tout genre, les compositeurs de musique, les peintres et dessinateurs qui feront graver des tableaux ou dessins, jouiront durant leur vie entière du droit exclusif de vendre, faire vendre, distribuer leurs ouvrages dans le territoire de la République, et d'en céder la propriété en tout ou partie.

Another proof of the determination of French writers in the closing years of the Ancien Régime to stand up for their rights, is seen in the famous controversy between playwrights and actors, particularly those of the Comédie Française, which is chiefly known today because Beaumarchais was the leading figure in the movement to secure better terms for writers. When the *Barbier de Seville* had had its first run, Beaumarchais, who was rich enough not to bother about what he earned from his play, but who knew that many of his fellow-playwrights were in revolt against their exploitation by the Comédie Française, refused the accounts offered him by the actors on the grounds that they were not accurate. He showed up some of the tricks of the actors in the discussions which followed. In reckoning the ninth of the receipts which was due to him during the first run of his play, the actors only allowed the daily sum of 300 *l.* for the *petites loges*, i.e. seats hired by the year by patrons of the theatre, whereas the average sum which they brought in worked out at 800 *l.* The Comédie Française, like other Paris theatres of the time, was compelled to contribute a quarter of its gross receipts to the upkeep of hospitals; in practice it had compounded for a lump sum which worked out *per diem* at about one-third of the amount which it deducted from the gross receipts when presenting accounts to authors. In calculating the expenses of the theatre which were to be deducted from the gross receipts, the actors added in all sorts of items in which the author could scarcely be expected to share. Worst of all, in addition to paying him the smallest amount it dared for the first run of a new play, the actors took advantage of the regulations which laid it down that if on two occasions the gross receipts fell below a certain figure, the play ceased to be the property of the author. They had all sorts of tricks to ensure that the receipts from a play should cease to reach the necessary figure and that it should thus become their property.

The tyranny of the actors over the playwrights who produced new plays for them was by no means entirely an economic one. Unless a writer managed to keep on the right side of the actors and actresses of the company, he could have a thin time. De Belloy, the author of a highly successful patriotic tragedy, *Le Siège de Calais*, was not, unfortunately for him, on good terms with the actor Lekain. When his tragedy, *Gaston et Bayard*, was at last put on in 1772, a contemporary wrote:

Il y a au moins six ans que cette tragédie est reçue, et que les odieuses tractations de Le Kain ont empêché de la jouer. M. de

Belloy, mourant de faim, a été forcé de la faire imprimer l'année passée, ce qui a fait tort nécessairement à la représentation. . . . Si elle n'eût pas été mise au théâtre cette année, M. de Belloy se voyait réduit à un tel excès de misère qu'il songeait à reprendre le métier de comédien qu'il a eu le malheur de faire dans sa jeunesse.

After De Belloy's death the same writer added a note: 'Il a vécu plein d'honneur et d'honneurs, et il a été réduit exactement à la mendicité, qu'il cachait. Le Kain et ses confrères, en refusant de jouer ses pièces, l'ont fait mourir de misère; à la lettre, il est mort de chagrin.' He adds that Lesage's famous account of the behaviour of actors and actresses towards authors is still true: 'C'est la même chose aujourd'hui, tant cette peinture est vraie et de main de maître.' (Collé, *Journal*, III, 314-15)

An interesting commentary on this last remark is furnished by the account of a young author's tribulations in 1763 in getting a comedy of his performed at the Comédie Française. The play, when presented to the theatre, gradually reached the hands of one of the actors whom the author went to see about it:

Je vole chez lui, je ne le trouve point . . .; une grosse cuisinière est assise sous la porte cochère dans son fauteuil à bras, elle épluche nonchalamment des épinards; elle me dit, en ricanant, 'N'êtes-vous pas un poète?—Hélas, oui.—Ne venez-vous pas chercher une pièce?—Hélas, oui.—Attendez.' Là-dessus elle fouille dans le tas d'herbes, en tire mon manuscrit, et me le remet.

Tout le monde se figure sans doute la mine d'un auteur secouant, le long d'une rue, les épinards dont les feuillets de son manuscrit sont décorés.

J'admirais ces ornements, bien plus modestes que les vignettes, les culs-de-lampe, dont nos plus petits almanachs sont enrichis, quand je donnai du nez dans la poitrine d'un homme aussi distingué par ses talents que par la pureté de ses mœurs; c'était M. de Belloy. Il ne se doutait pas alors qu'un comédien dût le faire mourir de chagrin.

De Belloy, who had not yet fallen out with the actors, got his play accepted for him; but his misfortunes did not end there:

Mais, par malheur, un acteur essentiel gagnait alors de l'argent

en province.[1] On le pria fort indiscrètement de la part de
Messieurs les Gentilshommes de la Chambre de vouloir bien se
rendre à Paris. Il eut de l'humeur, promit aux comédiens qu'il
quittait de les rejoindre bientôt, arriva sans savoir un mot de
son rôle, le joua le lendemain d'après le souffleur, et savoura le
plaisir de voir tomber une pièce qui l'avait empêché de gagner
de l'argent en province. (Cailhava, *Théâtre*, I, 18-21)

Whether or not one accepts the literal truth of such stories (and
there are many others one could quote), there is no doubt that
there was extremely bad blood between playwrights and the
actors of the Comédie Française in the 1760s and 1770s.

When therefore in 1777 Beaumarchais invited his fellow
playwrights to join in founding a society, known rather pomp-
ously as the Bureau de Législation Dramatique, to protect
their interests both in Paris and in the provinces, he received
a good deal of support. What the playwrights claimed from the
Comédie Française which had, as we have seen, a virtual
monopoly in Paris, was, first, a fairer way of paying for new
plays, and secondly some arrangement which would allow the
author to retain a play as his own property, for himself and his
heirs, so long as the actors saw fit to perform it. There was also
a considerable amount of support for a plan to break the
monopoly of the Comédie Française by setting up a second
subsidized theatre in the capital. Naturally there was not complete unanimity among playwrights, and in the course of his
disinterested efforts on behalf of the profession Beaumarchais
had to put up with a great deal of bickering. Some writers
pretended to be above these sordid money questions. One
wrote to him: 'Heureusement par les circonstances je me trouve
au-dessus du besoin; je ne travaille point pour de l'argent'
(Bachaumont, *Mémoires secrets*, XXVI, 90).

Negotiations with the Comédie Française dragged on until
in 1780 the government issued a decree which was intended to
settle the matter once and for all. In practice, while it put an
end to the worst abuses of the existing system of payments to

[1] Paris actors were in the habit of augmenting their income by undertaking
provincial tours, with or without the permission of the *Premiers gentilshommes de la
chambre* who were in charge of the two privileged theatres.

authors, it tended to take back with one hand what it gave with the other. It is unfortunately impossible to state exactly what difference these reforms made to the payments received by playwrights, as the registers of the Comédie Française which give down to 1760, performance by performance, the exact amount received by the author of a new play, suddenly cease to do so, and all we have for the period between 1760 and the Revolution is a few fragments of the accounts of the theatre. From some scraps of information at our disposal it would seem probable that the total amount paid each year to authors of new plays was on the average higher after 1780 than it had been before. We certainly know that Beaumarchais, thanks to the phenomenal run enjoyed by the *Mariage de Figaro* from the date it was first put on in 1784, did very well out of the Comédie Française. While the normal run of highly successful plays in eighteenth century Paris reached at the outside some thirty performances and brought their author some 4,000 *l.* (*Mérope* had brought Voltaire as much as 6,000 *l.*), in June 1787 Beaumarchais collected 59,510 *l.* 14s. 10d. for the first hundred performances of his play; and, what is more, he continued after that date to draw money from his play as it had still not become the property of the actors.

Yet such a success was wholly exceptional, and playwrights still remained dissatisfied with their relations with the Comédie Française. There also remained the scandal of the refusal of provincial theatres to pay any royalties whatsoever to writers for the plays which they performed. Mercier, whose works were extremely popular in the provinces, described the situation thus in 1778:

> Voyez les pièces de théâtre représentées dans toutes nos provinces. Les citoyens s'y portent en foule et les applaudissent à plusieurs reprises. Jamais une obole n'en reviendra à l'auteur, fût-il dans l'indigence la plus extrême. On peut faire cent mille francs avec sa pièce sans qu'il en soit seulement informé. Tout le monde se partage l'argent, et il n'est jamais venu dans l'idée à personne que l'auteur pût en réclamer la moindre portion. (*De la littérature*, p. 60)

In 1784 Beaumarchais and his fellow playwrights attempted

vainly to make the provincial companies pay for the performance of their plays. Once again it was the Revolution which
produced a serious attempt to clear up the whole situation. In
1791, after the playwrights had presented a petition, the
Constituent Assembly passed a law which abolished the
monopoly of the Comédie Française and which established the
property of authors in their plays. The essential section ran:

> Les ouvrages des auteurs vivants ne pourront être représentés sur
> aucun théâtre public, dans toute l'étendue de la France, sans le
> consentement formel et par écrit des auteurs, sous peine de
> confiscation du produit total des représentations au profit des
> auteurs.

Satisfactory arrangements were soon made with Paris theatres,
but the provincial companies proved a harder nut to crack. In
a petition to the Legislative Assembly Beaumarchais gave an
amusing account of the furious resistance to the new law put up
by the directors of theatres in the provinces. For instance, when
he complained to the director of the Lyons theatre that he was
performing *Le Mariage de Figaro* without permission, he received
the blunt reply: 'Nous jouons votre *Mariage*, parce qu'il nous
fournit d'excellentes recettes; et nous le jouerons malgré vous,
malgré tous les décrets du monde; je ne conseille même à
personne de venir nous en empêcher; il y passerait mal son
temps' (*Œuvres complètes*, p. 636). It took some time to establish
the principle, now accepted in all civilized countries, that a
playwright is entitled to a share in the proceeds of his works
whenever and wherever they are performed; that was to be the
achievement, so far as French playwrights were concerned, of
the Société des Auteurs et Compositeurs Dramatiques, which
gradually developed out of the Bureau de Législation Dram-
tique called into life by Beaumarchais in 1777. But the results
of the action of Beaumarchais and his fellow playwrights were
slow in coming, and take us well beyond 1789.

While there seems unquestionably to have been a marked
improvement in the economic position of men of letters—
perhaps more especially outside the theatre—in the second half
of the century, so that it had by now become possible for a

writer to achieve independence and to live by his pen, it would be a mistake to imagine that patronage ceased to play an important role. Unless they possessed private means or held a job and only wrote in their spare time, the great majority of writers continued, right down to 1789, to look to some kind of literary patronage to supplement their income or at least to tide them over difficult times. A rich man could occasionally still be found to help a struggling author. It is true that the dedication filled with nauseating flattery in return for hard cash (Corneille's dedication of *Cinna* to a wealthy tax-farmer was the model of this type) had now gone out, as Condorcet indicated in his *Éloge de D'Alembert* in 1783. Men of letters, he declared,

> ont renoncé à ces épîtres dédicatoires qui avilissaient l'auteur, même quand l'ouvrage pouvait inspirer l'estime ou le respect; ils ne se permettent plus ces flatteries, toujours d'autant plus exagérées qu'ils méprisaient davantage au fond du cœur l'homme puissant dont ils mendiaient la protection; et, par une révolution heureuse, la bassesse est devenue un ridicule que très peu d'hommes de lettres ont eu le courage de braver. (*Œuvres complètes*, III, 69)

But there are a host of well-authenticated examples of patronage extended by men in positions of wealth or power to writers in the second half of the eighteenth century.

Helvétius, the philosopher and former *fermier général*, in addition to helping Marivaux, gave a substantial pension to the playwright, Saurin, and, when the latter married, gave him the capital. Other tax-farmers such as La Popelinière and d'Épinay were also generous patrons of men of letters, while a wealthy banker like Necker, before he entered the government, had made substantial gifts to impecunious writers. In 1779 a nobleman, the Comte de Valbelle, left a sum bringing in an annual income of 1,200 *l.* for 'l'homme de lettres, qui, au jugement de l'Académie, aura le plus grand besoin de ce secours et en sera jugé le plus digne'. Shortly before he was dismissed from office, the Duc de Choiseul gave La Harpe 3,000 *l.* for a play of which he had heard a reading and which, for religious reasons (it contained an attack on the practice of dispatching unwilling girls into convents), could not be performed on the Paris stage.

Perhaps the most generous private patron of men of letters in this period was Mme Geoffrin, who showed a maternal solicitude for the writers, established as well as young, who frequented her famous *salon*. She gave, for instance, annuities to a variety of writers, among them D'Alembert, and when she died in 1777 she made provision for these to continue after her death; in addition she gave all manner of presents to men of letters during her lifetime. Diderot, for instance, is said to have received from her a new set of furniture.

The princes of the blood naturally played an important part as literary patrons. The Orléans family in particular, which stood nearest to the throne, provided all sorts of men of letters with modest pensions and sinecures. The minor playwright, Collé, obtained in 1760 the post of *lecteur* to the Duc d'Orléans with a salary of 1,800 *l*. Collé was also one of the eight *secrétaires ordinaires* of the duke; the income from this post was a modest one (only 400 *l*.), but it conferred some prestige and various privileges on the holder. Again, in 1776, when a young writer produced a successful tragedy, the duke gave him a pension of 1,200 *l*., 'et comme ce jeune auteur demandait si cette grâce l'engageait à remplir quelques fonctions auprès de Son Altesse, elle lui répondit avec une bonté très flatteuse: "Cela ne vous engage à rien qu'à travailler de plus en plus pour votre gloire" ' (La Harpe, *Correspondance littéraire*, II, 57). In 1787, on the eve of the Revolution, his successor, Philippe-Égalité, established pensions of 800 *l*. for twelve writers and scientists; four of these went to members of the Académie Française and among the other writers favoured in this way was Bernardin de Saint-Pierre.

Yet, important as the patronage of private individuals continued to be, it was to the Crown that the writer of the time looked for encouragement and for the prestige which a royal pension conferred. The number of gifts, pensions, posts and sinecures which the government had at the disposal of men of letters in the second half of the eighteenth century was indeed considerable. 'Il y a peu de contrées en Europe', wrote Diderot in 1767, 'où les lettres soient plus honorées, plus récompensées qu'en France. Le nombre des places destinées aux gens de lettres y est très grand.' It is true that, naturally enough since he certainly never earned the favour of the government of the day, he qualifies this statement: 'Heureux si c'était toujours le mérite qui y conduisait! Mais si je ne craignais d'être satirique, je dirais qu'il y en a où l'on exige plus scrupuleusement un habit de velours qu'un bon livre' (*Œuvres complètes*, XVIII, 48). Mediocre or even bad writers have often gained encouragement under any system of royal patronage; in the reign of Louis XIV Chapelain was better rewarded than Corneille. Necker too, in his *De l'administration des finances*, published only five years before the Revolution, declares that 'les récompenses qu'on accorde en France aux savants et aux gens de lettres sont plus considérables qu'on ne pense communément' (II, 364). Among the items of government expenditure he lists 300,000 *l.* for the expenses of the various academies, including those of Science and Medicine, and for payments to writers. This is certainly a small sum beside the 28 millions which was the total for other pensions. Yet one gets the impression from contemporary memoirs that the amount of royal patronage, in one form or another, was very considerable both during the personal reign of Louis XV and the reign of his successor; there is no reason not to repeat the heretical view that during this period of French history the Crown did far more for men of letters than in the reign of Louis XIV.

Encouragements to men of letters took many forms. There were gifts to the authors of successful new works. The author of a new play would normally obtain a substantial sum when it was given its first performance at court—some 2,000-3,000 *l.* Very often he received a pension, generally of some 1,000 or 1,500 *l.* Such pensions, although mostly not very large, conferred prestige as well as making a useful addition to income, even though, it must be said, the perpetual difficulties of the Treasury meant that they were seldom regularly paid. All sorts of writers of the period—poets, playwrights, novelists—received at one time or another such pensions, sometimes through the influence of Mme de Pompadour or even Mme Du Barry, or

in the next reign that of Marie Antoinette. In the 1780s, for example, we find pensions being conferred on a variety of writers, including Bernardin de Saint-Pierre. In addition to gifts and pensions the government had available all manner of posts, very often pure sinecures, for men of letters. There was, for instance, the post of *historiographe du roi*; when it was vacated by Voltaire on his departure for Potsdam, it passed to Duclos and, on his death in 1772, to Marmontel; the salary was not high (2,000 *l.*), but its holder was also entitled to a free lodging and to admission to all court fêtes. In addition, there were all sorts of other posts of *historiographes* which involved equally little work; there were such posts as *historiographe de la marine, historiographe de l'ordre du Saint-Esprit*, and so on, to all of which a modest salary was attached. The Académie Française had its secretary (a post held by Duclos, D'Alembert and Marmontel between 1750 and the Revolution) who had a modest salary and an equally modest flat in the Louvre. Sedaine, the author of *Le Philosophe sans le savoir*, was appointed secretary of the Académie Royale d'Architecture on similar terms, but with 'un beau logement au Louvre'. There were in addition posts of *lecteurs* or secretaries to various members of the royal family, which were again agreeable sinecures. Most of those posts and pensions were relatively modest, but there were a small number of real plums. Thus in 1768 Abbé Barthélemy, who twenty years later was to produce *Le Jeune Anacharsis*, one of the most important works in the neo-Classical revival of the closing decades of the century, was pushed by his patron, Choiseul, into the post of 'secrétaire général des Suisses' which carried with it an income of some 20,000 to 30,000 *l.*

Another important source of income for writers in the second half of the century was the pensions provided by literary journals. These pensions were at the disposal of the government, but were paid not only by journals under its direct control, such as the *Gazette de France*, the *Journal des Savants*, and especially the *Mercure*, but also by independent periodicals, including even the *Année littéraire*, the editor of which, Fréron, roused Voltaire and the *Philosophes* to fury. The *Mercure*, for instance, provided men of letters with pensions which amounted altogether to

something like 25,000 to 30,000 *l.* a year. The situation was, as Mercier pointed out, a rather odd one:

> Le gouvernement pensionne plusieurs écrivains; mais il ne débourse pas pour cela de l'argent. Il assujettit les journaux à une taxe, et paye les gens de lettres avec les travaux des gens de lettres. Tel auteur a une pension sur une feuille satirique où il est déchiré à belles dents. Ainsi il *boit et mange son jugement et sa condamnation*; ce qui est assez plaisant. (*Tableau de Paris*, VIII, 57)

Patronage then was by no means dead even in 1789, despite the fact that writers could sometimes earn substantial sums with their pen. A clear idea of the various sources of income which could permit a writer who began his career in the middle of the century to attain to a very comfortable living is furnished by the memoirs of Marmontel. Born in 1723, he arrived in Paris from his modest home in the provinces and in 1748 scored a considerable success, as we have seen, with his first tragedy, *Denys le Tyran*. He took to heart the advice which Mme de Tencin gave him: 'Malheur, me disait-elle, à qui attend tout de sa plume! rien de plus casuel. L'homme qui fait des souliers est sûr de son salaire: l'homme qui fait un livre ou une tragédie n'est jamais sûr de rien' (I, 272). He gradually turned away from tragedy after he had made a name for himself in the theatre, and produced among other writings his *Contes moraux* which during his lifetime had an enormous success all over Europe. He was careful to keep in with the powers that be, and used the influence of Mme de Pompadour to secure, first a sinecure in a government office, then a pension on the *Mercure* and finally, in 1758, its editorship. Although he soon lost this post, he retained a useful pension (3,000 *l.*). By the time he finally married, in 1777, he had saved 130,000 *l.*, and by the 1780s he and his wife were leading a very comfortable existence:

> Sans parler du casuel assez considérable que me procuraient mes ouvrages, la place de secrétaire de l'Académie Française, jointe à celle d'historiographe des bâtiments . . . me valaient un millier d'écus. Mon assiduité à l'Académie y doublait mon droit de présence.[1] J'avais hérité, à la mort de Thomas, de la moitié de la

---

[1] At every sitting of the Academy 40 *jetons*, each worth 30 sous, were distributed among the members present.

pension de deux mille livres qu'il avait eue, et qui fut partagée entre Gaillard et moi, comme l'avait été celle de l'abbé Batteux. Mes logements de secrétaire au Louvre et d'historiographe de France à Versailles, que j'avais loués volontairement, me valaient ensemble dix-huit cents livres. Je jouissais de mille écus sur le *Mercure* . . . Je me voyais donc en état de vivre agréablement à Paris et à la campagne. (III, 73-4)

Along with other members of the Académie Française, Marmontel benefited in 1785 from Calonne's openhandedness; the value of the *jetons* was raised from 30 sous to 3 *l.*, and in addition the secretary's pension was raised from 1,200 *l.* to 3,000 *l.* So Marmontel could write in his memoirs: 'Ainsi mon revenu d'académicien put se monter à quatre mille cinq ou six cents livres' (III, 78). He was a man of mediocre talents, but one who was endowed with the necessary skill to make himself a popular writer earning substantial sums of money; and being at the same time a successful place and pension hunter, he built up for himself an extremely comfortable position. He certainly was hostile from the start to the Revolution, since he was enjoying to the full what Talleyrand once called 'la douceur de vivre' of the closing years of the Ancien Régime; indeed, his memoirs contain a scathing and most penetrating denunciation of the aristocratic revolt which precipitated the cataclysm of 1789.

Although by 1789 French writers do not appear to have kept pace with their English colleagues in the march to independence, and although they still depended in most cases to some degree on the literary patronage which was to be derived from contacts with the wealthy middle classes, the aristocracy and the court, there is no question that their economic position had greatly improved since the beginning of the century. Perhaps even more striking advances were made in their social status.

In the profoundly aristocratic society of seventeenth century France, although the man of letters might be tolerated so long as he 'knew his place' and behaved with the respect due from an inferior, he was despised and scorned. If he was insolent (or thought to be insolent), the outraged nobleman to whom he gave offence left his punishment to a gang of toughs whom he hired to beat him up. That was the fate of various writers in the seventeenth century, and a punishment with which Boileau, for instance, was more than once threatened. Such an attitude towards the writer persisted among the aristocracy for several decades of the eighteenth century. The most illustrious victim of such treatment was Voltaire himself. The incident, which took place in 1726, is best related by a contemporary pen:

> Voltaire a eu des coups de bâton. Voici le fait. Le chevalier de Rohan le trouve à l'Opéra et lui dit; Mons. de Voltaire, Mons. Arouet, comment vous appelez-vous? L'autre lui dit je ne sais quoi, sur le nom de Chabot.[1] Cela en resta là. Deux jours après, à la Comédie au chauffoir,[2] le chevalier recommence; le poète lui dit qu'il avait fait sa réponse à l'Opéra. Le chevalier leva sa canne, ne le frappa pas et dit qu'on ne devait lui répondre qu'à coups de bâton. Mlle Le Couvreur[3] tombe évanouie, on la secourt, la querelle cesse. Le chevalier fait dire à Voltaire, à deux ou trois jours de là, que le duc de Sully l'attendait à dîner. Voltaire y va, ne croyant point que le message vînt du chevalier. Il dîne bien, un laquais vient lui dire qu'on le demande; il descend, va à la porte et trouve trois messieurs garnis de cannes qui lui régalèrent les épaules et les bras gaillardement. On dit que le chevalier voyait ce frottement d'une boutique vis-à-vis. Mon poète crie comme un diable, met l'épée à la main, remonte chez le duc de Sully, qui trouva le fait violent et incivil, va à l'Opéra conter sa chance à Mme de Prie qui y était,[4] et de là on court à Versailles, où on attend la décision de cette affaire, qui ne ressemble pas mal à un assassinat. (Marais, *Journal et Mémoires*, III, 392)

It will be noticed that the lawyer who wrote this letter does not waste much sympathy on the victim of such a brutal assault. Nor did anybody else at the time, as we see from his next letter in which he again refers to Voltaire and his 'coups de bâton':

> On s'est souvenu du mot du duc d'Orléans à qui il demandait *justice* sur pareils coups, et le prince lui répondit: 'On vous l'a faite'. L'évêque de Blois a dit: 'Nous serions bien malheureux si

---

[1] The *chevalier*'s full name was Rohan-Chabot.
[2] The *foyer* of the Comédie Française.
[3] Adrienne Lecouvreur, the famous actress.
[4] The mistress of the prime minister, the Duc de Bourbon.

les poètes n'avaient point d'épaules'. On dit que le chevalier de Rohan était dans un fiacre *lors de l'exécution*, qu'il criait aux frappeurs: 'Ne lui donnez point sur la tête', et que le peuple d'alentour disait: 'Ah, le bon seigneur!' Le pauvre battu se montre le plus qu'il peut, à la cour, à la ville, mais personne ne le plaint, et ceux qu'il croyait ses amis lui ont tourné le dos. (III, 393)

This was, however, the last well-known example of such behaviour. It has an interesting counterpart at the other end of the century, in an incident of 1786, which shows how times had changed. The playwright, Sedaine, gave offence to the official who was in charge of theatrical entertainments at court, a man who rejoiced in the name of Papillon de La Ferté. When Sedaine complained about the scenery and costumes which had been provided for a play of his which was being performed before the court at Fontainebleau, La Ferté came rushing along and shouted: ' "Où est Sedaine?" Ce poète qui l'entend, lui crie: "La Ferté, Monsieur Sedaine est ici; que lui voulez-vous?" ' The official had the further humiliation of being rebuked for his manners by Marie Antoinette herself, when he complained to her about the playwright's insolence. 'Monsieur La Ferté', she told him, 'quand le roi et moi parlons à un homme de lettres, nous l'appelons toujours *Monsieur*. Quant au fond de votre différend, il n'est pas fait pour nous intéresser' (Bachaumont, *Mémoires secrets*, XXXIII, 199, 290).

Seventeenth century writers, in face of the contempt shown them by the aristocratic circles of the time, blushed for their profession and did their best to rise out of it into the circles of the aristocracy and the court, abandoning literature for some well-paid and honorific sinecure. The classic example of this is, of course, the haste with which Racine and Boileau gave up writing plays and poetry to become *historiographes du roi* and secure the admission to court circles which this appointment carried with it.

This feeling of the social inferiority of the writer died slowly in the eighteenth century. There was, we have seen, something challenging in the title which Voltaire, his shoulders still smarting from the blows of the hired thugs of the Chevalier de Rohan, gave to one of his *Lettres philosophiques* in 1734: 'De la *Considération* qu'on doit aux gens de lettres.' 'Ce qui encourage le plus les arts en Angleterre', he wrote with clear propaganda purpose, 'c'est la considération où ils sont. Le portrait du premier ministre se trouve sur la cheminée de son cabinet; mais j'ai vu celui de M. Pope dans vingt maisons.'

In the first half of the century, unless writers possessed private means, they were compelled to live a very meagre existence. Their parents were often poor or of only modest position, and generally disapproved of their embarking upon what seemed such an unpromising career, one which brought neither security nor moderate affluence. Like Diderot, many writers led a hand-to-mouth, bohemian existence in their youth and attained a modest affluence only in the latter part of their career. Though fêted in the *salons* of their day, they could not compete with the other guests either in wealth or general polish. Moreover, their wives—generally like themselves of modest social origins—could obviously not accompany them on their expeditions into polite society. Many writers of the time—at least the obscure hacks—never attained to anything as respectable as a settled home and family. They lived to the end a sordid, poverty-stricken existence, like the caricatural, but none the less realistically drawn figures depicted by Diderot in *Le Neveu de Rameau*, men reduced to the role of fawning flatterers in the households of the rich.

However, from about the middle of the century onwards the position of men of letters in the polite society of Paris ('le monde') underwent a change. Hitherto, though writers had frequented the *salons* of the capital from the time of the Hôtel de Rambouillet onwards, they were admitted, not for their own sake, but as men of letters, that is to say, they were more or less on exhibition. By the middle of the century, however, the development of social life in Paris led to an increasing levelling of ranks, at least among the people who qualified for admission to 'le monde'. People were now admitted, regardless of rank, provided they had the right manners and tone. There is an interesting comment on this mingling of social classes in the polite society of Paris in the *Considérations sur les mœurs* which

Duclos published in 1751: 'Les mœurs font à Paris ce que l'esprit du gouvernement fait à Londres; elles confondent et égalent dans la société les rangs qui sont distingués et surbordonnés dans l'état' (p. 15).

As a result of this levelling of ranks in polite society, men of letters came to be admitted to 'le monde', no longer as men of letters, but for their own sake, as individuals, and on an equal footing with people of higher rank or greater wealth. As Duclos put it:

> Le goût des lettres, des sciences et des arts a gagné insensiblement, et il est venu au point que ceux qui ne l'ont pas, l'affectent. On a donc recherché ceux qui les cultivent, et ils ont été attirés dans le monde à proportion de l'agrément qu'on a trouvé dans leur commerce.
>
> On a gagné de part et d'autre à cette liaison. Les gens du monde ont cultivé leur esprit, formé leur goût, et acquis de nouveaux plaisirs. Les gens de lettres n'en ont pas retiré moins d'avantages. Ils ont trouvé de la considération; ils ont perfectionné leur goût, poli leur esprit, adouci leurs mœurs, et acquis sur plusieurs articles des lumières qu'ils n'auraient pas puisées dans des livres. (pp. 135-6)

Inevitably the popularity of men of letters in the high society of Paris also had its disadvantages. Many writers wasted their time in the futilities of the social round, and often had neither the time nor the inclination for anything as arduous as writing books. In the chapter 'Sur les gens à la mode', Duclos himself wrote: 'L'homme de lettres qui, par des ouvrages travaillés, aurait pu instruire son siècle, et faire passer son nom à la postérité, néglige ses talents, et les perd faute de les cultiver: il aurait été compté parmi les hommes illustres; il reste un homme d'esprit de société' (p. 101). Other writers of the time frankly deplored the trend: in his *Tableau de Paris*, later in the century, the satirically minded Mercier maintained that there were no more than thirty writers in the whole of France at that date, that is, men who wrote and published regularly:

> On sait que dès qu'un auteur est académicien, il pense toucher au terme de la gloire littéraire; il ne fait plus rien que de courir

les sociétés. Il est plus souvent à table qu'à son bureau; et quand il a passé des années entières sans payer aucun tribut au public, il appelle cela le *respecter*. A qui convient donc le fauteuil académique? A tout homme qui ne veut plus écrire. (VIII, 63n.)

One must never take Mercier literally, but there is obviously a certain amount of truth in what he has to say about the writers of his day, and not only about academicians.

Undoubtedly in the closing decades of the Ancien Régime the man of letters, even if he were not a man of genius, enjoyed immense prestige in the upper-class circles of Paris. Writing after the Revolution, the Comte de Ségur contrasts the inequalities in society as a whole with the spirit of equality which reigned in the *salons* of the capital:

> Les titres littéraires avaient même, en beaucoup d'occasions, la préférence sur les titres de noblesse, et ce n'était pas seulement aux hommes de génie qu'on rendait des hommages qui faisaient disparaître toute trace d'infériorité; car on voyait fréquemment, dans le monde, des hommes de lettres du second et du troisième ordre être accueillis et traités avec des égards que n'obtenaient pas les nobles de province. *(Mémoires, I, 53)*

English travellers noted the same phenomenon in the days before the Revolution. In his travel notes for 1787 Arthur Young numbers among the advantages of life in Paris that 'the society for a man of letters, or who has any scientific pursuit, cannot be exceeded. The intercourse between such men and the great, which, if it be not upon an equal footing, ought never to exist at all, is respectable. Persons of the highest rank pay an attention to science and literature, and emulate the character they confer' (I, 85). Ségur's observations are even more strikingly confirmed by what the Scottish traveller, John Moore, has to say about the position of men of letters in Paris society towards the end of the reign of Louis XV:

> Many of those whose works you admire are received at the houses of the first nobility on the most liberal footing.
> You can scarcely believe the influence which this body of men have in the gay and dissipated city of Paris. Their opinions not only determine the merit of works of taste and science, but they

have considerable weight on the manners and sentiments of people of rank, of the public in general, and consequently are not without effect on the measures of government.

The same thing takes place in some degree in most countries of Europe; but, if I am not mistaken, more at Paris than anywhere else; because men of letters are here at once united to each other by the various academies, and diffused among private societies by the manners and general taste of the nation.

As the sentiments and conversation of men of letters influence, to a certain degree, the opinions and conduct of the fashionable world, the manners of these last have a more obvious effect upon the air, the behaviour and the conversation of the former, which in general is polite and easy; equally purified from the awkward timidity contracted in retirement, and the disgusting arrogance inspired by university honours or church dignities. At Paris the pedants of Molière are to be seen on the stage only. (*A View of Society and Manners in France, Switzerland and Germany*, I, 26-7)

One reason for the new position which French writers had won for themselves in the social life of Paris by the second half of the eighteenth century was that they now became a power in the land. They controlled that mysterious new force which, long before 1789, imposed severe limitations on the actions even of an absolute monarchy: public opinion. In one of the most interesting passages in his *Tableau de Paris* Mercier attempts to show that the Englishman who sees the French groaning under the yoke of despotism has not seen the whole picture. The passage is all the more interesting as it comes from a severe critic of the Ancien Régime:

L'Anglais aura dit: Le roi de France jouit d'une autorité presque indéfinie; il a le fer dans une main, l'or dans l'autre; il fait ployer les corps intermédiaires avec une feuille de papier; il est sûr que la noblesse sera à ses ordres quand il le voudra; la magistrature lui apporte des remontrances et se retire; le peuple n'a aucune voix, aucune force; il a livré ses biens et sa personne à son maître, qui de plus possède depuis cent ans sa fortune pécuniaire et qui d'un mot peut libérer ses immenses dettes. Il a un plus grand pouvoir encore: il défend à la pensée de paraître; il flétrit ou ridiculise les idées qui ne lui plaisent pas; et s'il n'y parvient pas pour toujours, il y parvient pour un certain temps. Il n'y a pas jusqu'à la place d'académicien qui ne soit de son choix; et Louis XIV pouvait dire à Corneille: 'Vous ne serez pas de l'Académie'.

In practice, Mercier goes on to point out, there were all sorts of limitations on the power of the monarchy and its ministers in the customs and usages of the country, reinforced by public opinion and a set of vigilant writers:

> Ainsi parmi nous la liberté publique, vivante malgré de terribles atteintes, s'appuie avec plus de succès encore sur les coutumes et sur les mœurs que sur les lois écrites. L'empire des mœurs, plus absolu que les lois, parce qu'il est perpétuel, commande la modération à ceux qui seraient tentés de ne pas la connaître; car les lois ne sont respectées ou suivies qu'autant que le législateur a eu l'art de les enter sur les mœurs et les idées nationales. Enfin, la plume des écrivains, vigilante et protectrice des privilèges que la raison a créés, les maintient et défend aux souverains d'oser les attaquer. (VIII, 143, 146)

From being the humble hangers-on of kings and great noblemen, the mere entertainers of polite society, writers had come by the second half of the eighteenth century to exercise immense power.

This fundamental point was well brought òut by Duclos in his *Considérations* as early as 1751 when he wrote: 'Cependant de tous les empires, celui des gens d'esprit, sans être visible, est le plus étendu. Le puissant commande, les gens d'esprit gouvernent, parce qu'à la longue ils forment l'opinion publique, qui tôt ou tard subjugue ou renverse toute espèce de fanatisme' (pp. 138-9). The most striking illustration of the new importance achieved by men of letters—now no longer merely the somewhat despised entertainers of a few thousand members of the upper classes of Paris, but the masters of public opinion in France itself and, beyond her frontiers, in a considerable area of Europe—is to be found in the triumphant return of Voltaire to Paris in 1778. The man who fifty years before had been beaten up by the hired thugs of the Chevalier de Rohan and then sent to the Bastille for daring to seek revenge, was fêted and treated with adulation at the Academy, the Comédie Française and in the streets of Paris. The novelty of this treatment of a man of letters was commented upon by a contemporary observer, Meister, when he wrote:

> M. de Voltaire lui-même, toutes choses d'ailleurs égales, n'eût
> point joui du même triomphe sous le règne de Louis XIV, qui
> aimait les lettres parce qu'il aimait la louange, qui favorisait le
> génie et les arts, mais qui prétendait toujours leur donner la loi,
> et qui avait imprimé dans l'esprit de ses peuples une telle dévotion
> pour le trône et pour sa propre personne que l'on aurait craint
> de commettre un acte d'idolâtrie en prodiguant à un simple
> particulier des hommages dont lui-même eût été jaloux.

The apotheosis of Voltaire, he went on, was

> la juste récompense, non seulement des merveilles qu'a produites
> son génie, mais aussi de l'heureuse révolution qu'il a su faire et
> dans les mœurs et dans l'esprit de son siècle, en combattant les
> préjugés de tous les ordres et de tous les rangs, en donnant aux
> lettres plus de considération et de dignité, et à l'opinion même
> un empire plus libre et plus indépendant de toute autre puissance
> que celle du génie et de la raison. (Grimm, *Correspondance littéraire*,
> XII, 73)

To this position of influence and power which men of letters acquired in the closing decades of the Ancien Régime, the contribution of the *Philosophes* is obvious. Not for them the notion—summed up in the famous remark of Malherbe a hundred and fifty years earlier that 'un bon poète n'est pas plus utile à l'État qu'un bon joueur de quilles'—that the writer has no social function and that his aim is simply to give pleasure to his readers. For them the writer—over and above his other aims —has the task of enlightening his fellow-men and at the same time of enlightening governments too. The influence of men of letters on the public opinion which they had helped to call into being is well summed up by Mercier—not, incidentally, a member of what one might call the party of the *Philosophes*— when he wrote in the 1780s:

> De quel abîme d'erreurs et de misérables préjugés n'ont-ils pas
> fait sortir les administrateurs des nations? Qu'enseignent-ils, si ce
> n'est l'amour de l'humanité, les droits de l'homme et du citoyen?
> Quelle question importante à la société n'ont-ils pas examinée,

débattue, fixée? Si le despotisme s'est civilisé, si les souverains ont commencé à redouter la voix des nations, à respecter ce tribunal suprême, c'est à la plume des écrivains que l'on doit ce frein nouveau, inconnu. Quelle iniquité ministérielle ou royale pourrait se flatter aujourd'hui de passer impunément? Et la gloire des rois n'attend-elle pas la sanction du philosophe? (*Tableau de Paris*, IV, 160)

Thus by the second half of the eighteenth century, thanks to the economic progress of the country, to the spread of education and to the growth of the reading public, men of letters in France had overcome their old modesty and the contempt in which they were held by an aristocratic society. They now claimed for themselves a social function of the highest importance and this claim was admitted by the general public.

So far, in discussing the status of the man of letters in eighteenth century France, we have stressed the expansion of the reading public which took place in these years and its influence on the position of the writer. That expansion can be seen very roughly, but none the less clearly, in the larger editions of successful works and the more frequent reprints and pirated editions which they went through. Works of literature were disseminated more widely than ever before—both in the different classes of society as illiteracy declined, and over the country as a whole, in remote provincial châteaux and in the towns, large and small, which were dotted over the country.

Yet there is another side to the medal which we must also examine—the relatively restricted circles to which literature continued to appeal and the very restricted world for which it continued to be written. To take the second point first. The great bulk of French literature continued to be produced in Paris and was written, in the first instance, at least, for a relatively narrow section of the population of the capital. All sorts of works—plays, poems, novels and other books—were read aloud and discussed in the *salons* of Paris before they were placed before a wider public. A considerable number of writers came, of course, from the provinces, like Diderot, or from even further afield, like Rousseau, but they produced their works in Paris and in contact with the narrow society of the capital. The concentration of the literary life of France in Paris is well brought out by Mercier when he wrote of the men of letters of his day:

> Si l'on compte qu'il n'y a point eu d'homme célèbre né en province, qui ne soit venu à Paris pour se former, qui n'y ait vécu par choix et qui n'y soit mort, ne pouvant quitter cette grande ville, malgré l'amour de la patrie; cette race d'hommes éclairés, tous concentrés sur le même point, tandis que les autres villes du royaume offrent des landes d'une incroyable stérilité, devient un profond objet de méditations sur les causes réelles et subsistantes qui précipitent tous les gens de lettres dans la capitale, et les y retiennent comme par enchantement. (*Tableau de Paris*, IV, 16)

And in Paris, as we have seen, the writers of the period mingled with representatives of the upper classes of society—with the nobility, the wealthy tax-farmers and high officials and their womenfolk—in the different *salons* which, from one end of the century to the other, flourished so abundantly that to recall the names of more than a few famous hostesses such as the Marquise de Lambert and Mme de Tencin in the first half of the century, and of Mme Geoffrin and Mme Necker in the second would be to produce merely a catalogue.

It was inevitable that the works of men of letters should reflect in all sorts of ways the tastes and outlook of this relatively narrow and select section of the community in whose company they spent a great part of their time. No doubt the works which they produced eventually reached in printed form all sections of the community who could read and penetrated to every corner of the country; yet they were conceived in a limited circle and bore unmistakably the imprint of their origin. A clearer notion of the audience in the capital for which men of letters wrote can be formed by a study of the drama and the theatres of the time, for the excellent reason that while readers might be scattered over all regions and classes of the country, the audiences of the theatres of the capital left behind in all manner of documents of the time a fairly clear notion of their size and social composition.

Despite the revival of the provincial theatres in the course of the century Paris continued to dominate the theatrical life of

France, as was natural with the capital of a highly centralized country, drawing to itself the wealthiest and most aristocratic sections of society and the best actors and actresses. Throughout the period Paris possessed, in addition to the Opéra, two privileged theatres—the Comédie Française, by far the more important of the two, and the Théâtre Italien, which was merged with Opéra-Comique in 1762 and gradually lost all its Italian characteristics. From the beginning of the century the privileged theatres had to face competition from the Théâtres de la Foire which gradually evolved a genre of their own, the *opéra-comique*, which, as we have seen, led to a fusion of the Opéra-Comique and the Théâtre Italien. By about 1760 other theatres had emerged, and by 1789 the fashionable promenade, the Boulevard du Temple, boasted as many as six. Yet despite the vogue of such theatres their contribution to literature, like that of the Théâtres de la Foire earlier in the century, was negligible. In fact, the two privileged theatres were alone of any importance from the literary point of view, and of these the Comédie Française with its monopoly of all plays of any importance which had survived from the previous century and its near-monopoly of all new plays with serious literary pretensions dominated the theatrical life of the capital.

We happen to be fairly well informed about the size of the audience which the actors of this period could expect to attract to their theatre. Given the size of the capital—a permanent population of well over 500,000 swollen by all manner of visitors from the provinces and abroad—and given the enthusiasm of the age for everything to do with the theatre, the number of spectators which the Comédie Française attracted in the period between 1715 and 1750 was astonishingly small. It fell indeed far below the average for the first thirty-five years of the theatre's existence, from 1680 to 1715. Then, after the middle of the century, came a steep rise in attendances which appears to have continued to the Revolution.

Yet throughout the period the number of spectators who might be expected to support a new play during its first run remained, by modern standards, extremely small. Thirty or so performances, attended by something like 25,000 to 30,000 spectators, remained the utmost that a playwright could hope for; after that his play had to be taken off for lack of support and might not be revived for months, or even years. Voltaire's greatest box-office success was his tragedy, *Mérope*, performed in 1743; it was given 29 times and attracted to the Comédie Française close on 30,000 spectators. There was, of course, one phenomenally successful play in our period, *Le Mariage de Figaro*, which had a first run of 73 performances and attracted close on 100,000 spectators to the theatre; but it is clear that it must have appealed to thousands of people who did not normally frequent the Comédie Française. Beaumarchais's earlier comedy, *Le Barbier de Séville*, had a degree of success which was much more in line with that normally achieved in the course of the century; 24,000 spectators paid to see it during its first run of 27 performances.

Even such figures as those for the *Barbier* represent a degree of success far greater than that reached by many important plays of the time which remained for decades in the repertory of the Comédie Française. 'Il a paru depuis quinze ans sur la scène française', commented a writer in the 1760s, 'plus d'un ouvrage digne d'y reparaître dans tous les temps. Vingt représentations, au plus, ont épuisé le concours du public' (La Dixmerie, *Lettres sur l'état présent de nos spectacles*, p. 9). A play which attracted 15,000 to 20,000 spectators continued down to 1789 to count as quite a considerable success. There is room for only one conclusion: that the public willing and able to support a new play was still small, not indeed perceptibly larger than it had been at the end of the seventeenth century.

As for the composition of these audiences, we have already seen how, in the last decades of the Ancien Régime, a few representatives of the lower orders began to find their way to the privileged theatres. It is, however, very improbable that their small numbers exercised any real influence on the sort of plays performed at the Comédie Française. The occupants of the cheapest part of the theatre continued to be overwhelmingly bourgeois. The middle classes, as in the previous century, continued to be powerfully represented in the Paris theatres, but we must not leave out of account the place occupied in them by the representatives of the upper classes of a society in which blue blood still retained an importance difficult to grasp today. French society in our period continued to be dominated by the royal family, the princes of the blood and the countless lords and ladies who inhabited Paris and Versailles.

Little more than a dozen years before the Revolution we find Voltaire upbraiding Shakespeare for daring to introduce into a tragedy such a monstrous phrase as 'Not a mouse stirring'. In his *Lettre à MM. de l'Académie Française* in which he de, nounced Shakespeare and his translator, he exclaims: 'Oui- monsieur, un soldat peut répondre ainsi dans un corps de garde; mais non pas sur le théâtre, devant les premières per- sonnes d'une nation, qui s'expriment noblement, et devant qui il faut s'exprimer de même' (*Œuvres complètes*, XXX, 363). The importance of the upper-class spectators in the theatres of his day is also brought out in his vivid description of a first night:

> C'est un grand jour pour le beau monde oisif de Paris qu'une première représentation: les cabales battent le tambour; on se dispute les loges; les valets de chambre vont à midi remplir le théâtre.[1] La pièce est jugée avant qu'on l'ait vue. Femmes contre femmes, petits-maîtres contre petits-maîtres, sociétés contre sociétés; les cafés sont comblés de gens qui disputent; la foule est dans la rue en attendant qu'elle soit au parterre. (*Correspondence*, XX, 235)

The ladies in the *premières loges* (the first row of boxes) and the most aristocratic or wealthy male spectators on the stage were an important part of the audience, socially as well as financially. When seats on the stage were finally abolished at the Comédie Française in 1759, a contemporary wrote of the change:

> L'illusion théâtrale est actuellement entière; on ne voit plus César prêt à dépoudrer un fat assis au premier rang du théâtre, et Mithridate expirer au milieu de tous gens de notre connaissance; l'ombre de Ninus heurter et coudoyer un fermier général, et Camille tomber morte dans la coulisse sur Marivaux et sur Saint-Foix[2] qui s'avancent ou se reculent pour se prêter à l'assassinat de cette Romaine par la main d'Horace, qui fait

---

[1] In order to reserve seats on the stage for their masters.
[2] These two playwrights enjoyed the privilege of free admission to the theatre.

rejaillir son sang sur ces deux auteurs comiques. (Collé, *Journal*, II, 172)

From about the same period of the century dated a very popular innovation—the institution of private boxes (*petites loges*) which could be rented by the year. Women in particular —and it goes without saying that these women belonged to the wealthiest and most aristocratic sections of Paris society—loved them, for reasons described sarcastically by Mercier:

> Il faut donc, quand on est femme, avoir dans une *petite loge* son épagneul, son coussin, sa chaufferette, mais surtout un petit fat à lorgnette, qui vous instruit de tout ce qui entre et de tout ce qui sort, et qui vous nomme les acteurs. Cependant la dame a dans son éventail une petite ouverture, où est enchâssé un verre, de sorte qu'elle voit sans être vue. (*Tableau de Paris*, II, 188)

The important place occupied by the aristocratic and wealthy sections of society in the Paris theatre audience is underlined by the novelist, Mme Riccoboni, in the preface to her *Nouveau Théâtre Anglais*, published in 1769. The crudity of so much English drama, she maintains, is to be explained by a fundamental difference in the theatre audiences of London and Paris:

> A Paris les grands et les riches suivent assidûment les spectacles. A Londres les personnes distinguées vont rarement à la comédie; l'emploi de leur temps et l'heure de leurs repas ne leur permettent guère d'être libres quand elle commence. C'est donc à la bourgeoisie, même au peuple, que l'on est obligé de plaire. (I, viii-ix)

When these lines got her into trouble with her old friend, David Garrick, she expanded her remarks and had this to say about Paris theatre audiences:

> Ici les premiers du royaume font leur séjour habituel du théâtre; les dames ont de petites loges à l'année, la comédie est le rendez-vous de la bonne compagnie. Elle ne divertit guère, mais elle occupe beaucoup. On disserte, on prône, on cabale; mille fainéants titrés n'ont d'autre ressource contre l'ennui que les chauffoirs des trois spectacles.[1] (Garrick, *Private Correspondence*, II, 561)

[1] The *foyers* of the Comédie Française, Opéra and Théâtre Italien.

Such a passage leaves us in no doubt as to the importance of the aristocratic section of the audience in the Paris theatres only twenty years before the Revolution.

Audiences thus remained down to 1789 small by modern standards, and at the same time among the spectators who frequented the theatres the members of the aristocratic and wealthy sections of the community continued to play an important part. The situation in the theatre gives one some inkling of the influence which, partly through the *salons* of the time, the upper classes of the capital throughout the eighteenth century continued to exercise both on the different forms of literature and also on language, the instrument of the writer.

# CHAPTER VIII

# LITERATURE AND IDEAS

FOR seventeenth century writers the court had been the centre of good taste. Thus for La Bruyère the court was 'le centre du bon goût et de la politesse'; for a writer on language like Vaugelas good usage was 'la façon de parler de la plus saine partie de la cour, conformément à la façon d'écrire de la plus saine partie des auteurs du temps'. This respectful and admiring attitude towards the court lingers on into the eighteenth century. In 1729, for instance, in his continuation of Pellisson's *Histoire de l'Académie Française*, d'Olivet could write:

> Car qui doute que la cour, bien loin de nuire à un bon esprit, ne soit au contraire l'école la plus propre à le former? Et une compagnie, dont l'unique but est d'affermir le bel usage de la langue, de travailler sans cesse à la perfection du goût, n'a-t-elle pas de grands secours à espérer d'un seigneur qui vit dans le centre du goût et de la délicatesse? (II, 144)

Another writer of this period of the century, Abbé Leblanc, argues that while men of letters are better judges of the written language, great noblemen are superior as judges of the spoken language: 'Les uns ont approfondi davantage les règles de la grammaire et l'étymologie des mots; les autres sont des témoins plus sûrs de l'usage du monde. C'est le concours des uns et des autres qui peut seul perfectionner une langue.' His next words —'La cour est le centre du goût et de la politesse'—are merely a repetition of the seventeenth century commonplace expressed by La Bruyère (*Lettres d'un Français*, III, 4).

As the century wore on, the influence of the court proper, established at Versailles, waned. It is true that to the end the Crown retained its importance as the dispenser of literary patronage, but because of its isolation from Paris influence on matters of language and literature passed more and more to the polite society of the capital. In her memoirs Mme Campan sums up her first impressions of life at Versailles in the closing years of the reign of Louis XV: 'De lieu de réunion où l'on vît se déployer l'esprit et la grâce des Français, il n'en fallait point chercher. Le foyer de l'esprit et des lumières était à Paris' (p. 48). In his usual blustering way Mercier sums up this loss of influence of the court in matters of taste when he writes in his *Tableau de Paris*:

> Le mot de *cour* n'en impose plus parmi nous comme au temps de Louis XIV. On ne reçoit plus de la cour les opinions régnantes; elle ne décide plus des réputations, en quelque genre que ce soit; on ne dit plus avec une emphase ridicule: 'La cour a prononcé ainsi'. On casse les jugements de la cour; on dit nettement, elle n'y entend rien, elle n'a point d'idées là-dessus, elle ne saurait en avoir, elle n'est pas dans le point de vue. . . .
>
> Du temps de Louis XIV la cour était plus formée que la ville; aujourd'hui la ville est plus formée que la cour. . . . La cour a donc perdu cet ascendant qu'elle avait sur les beaux-arts, sur les lettres, et sur tout ce qui est aujourd'hui de leur ressort. On citait dans le siècle dernier le suffrage d'un homme de la cour, d'un prince; et personne n'osait contredire. . . . C'est de la ville que part l'approbation ou l'improbation adoptée par le reste du royaume. (IV, 153-4)

Slightly earlier John Moore had noted the same phenomenon, particularly as concerns drama: 'Obedient to the court in every other particular, the French disregard the decisions pronounced at Versailles in matters of taste. It very often happens that a dramatic piece, which has been acted before the royal family and the court with the highest applause, is afterwards damned with every circumstance of ignominy at Paris. In all works of genius the Parisians lead the judgment of the courtiers and dictate to their monarch' (*A View of Society and Manners*, I, 86).

In matters of language, too, the court ceased to be the arbiter of usage. It is at least pushed into the background by the theorists of the time, who tend to stress the importance of the cultured classes of Paris in this sphere. Some writers go even further and, like Marmontel in the 1780s, speak slightingly of 'la cour, dont le langage roule sur un tout petit nombre de mots, la plupart vagues et confus, d'un sens équivoque ou à demi voilé, comme il convient à la politesse, à la dissimulation, à l'extrême réserve, à la plaisanterie légère, à la malice raffinée, ou à la flatterie adroite' (*Œuvres*, VII, 96).

The seventeenth century purists who, taking the usage of polite society and the best writers as the criterion in all matters of language, had purged the literary language of all words and expressions which did not conform to the standards of taste of this small section of the community established in Paris, had their successors in our period. They bequeathed to the eighteenth century the belief that the French language had now reached a stage of perfection from which any departure could only mean a decline, and the veneration of the eighteenth century for the great writers of the previous age gave its purists a curiously conservative attitude to language. Their aim was to avert the terrible danger of a decline in the language created by the previous age—a decline which they always saw threatening on the horizon—by fixing the French language in the state in which they had inherited it.

The *style noble*—a style noble and elevated, purged of all realistic and everyday words and expressions—extended its sway still further in the eighteenth century, invading new fields such as the novel or comedy, and becoming more and more rigorous in its application. Words and expressions which were realistic, bourgeois, plebeian or technical were banished from any work with literary pretensions. Naturally, as in the previous century, there remained a hierarchy of styles which varied according to the literary genre concerned, be it tragedy or comedy, history or the novel. 'Les styles sont classés dans notre langue comme les sujets dans notre monarchie', wrote Rivarol in his *De l'Universalité de la langue française*. 'Deux expressions qui conviennent à la même chose, ne conviennent pas au même ordre de choses; et c'est à travers cette hiérarchie des styles que le bon goût sait marcher' (p. 282). In other words, a writer had to know how to choose the terms and expressions appropriate to the particular genre in which he was writing.

According to such rules *génisse*, for instance, must in poetry replace *vache*, which was considered suitable only for prose;

expressions like 'une bonne nouvelle' and 'il vous voudra du mal' in the tragedies of Corneille are condemned by Voltaire as suitable only for comedy. In 1737, in a letter to his royal pupil, the future Frederick the Great, he gave examples of the different words which must be used in the higher forms of poetry to replace the common words of everyday life: 'Par exemple on ne dira pas en prose *coursier* pour *chevaux, diadème* pour *couronne, empire de France* pour *royaume de France, char* pour *carrosse, forfaits* pour *crimes, exploits* pour *actions, l'empyrée* pour *le ciel, les airs* pour *l'air, fastes* pour *registres, naguères* pour *depuis peu,* etc.' (*Correspondence,* VI; 278).

All sorts of devices were employed by eighteenth century writers in order to observe the conventions of the *style noble*. One method, strongly recommended by Buffon, was to use whenever possible general terms to replace words which were not sufficiently 'nobles' for high style, to use, for instance, *animaux* for *chevaux* or *édifice* for *maison*. A favourite device was, of course, periphrasis: parents became 'les auteurs de leurs jours' and children 'les gages de l'amour', the sun 'l'astre du jour' and the sky 'la voûte azurée'. The subtlest trick of all was to take words which in themselves were unsuitable for high style and so to place them that they became acceptable to the reader or spectator. Racine had shown the way in *Athalie* with his *chiens* ennobled by the epithet *dévorants* which transformed the word. Other devices were used by the eighteenth century as well as the ennobling epithet; one was to use the *mot propre*, but to accompany it by a periphrasis, for instance in André Chénier's line: '*Ce nageur mugissant, ce taureau, c'est un Dieu.*' But the ennobling epithet remained the favourite device ('Du reste *infortuné* de cet *auguste* sang' or 'ce nœud *sacré*'), along with the ennobling metaphor ('Ce triste et dernier *fruit* d'un malheureux amour' or 'La colonne *vomit* des feux continuels').

The ravages of the *style noble* in eighteenth century literature are, of course, notorious. They are naturally less visible in the tragedies of the age with their conventional setting and their exalted personages far removed from the crude realities of everday life, than in, say, the kind of poetry which attempts to describe ordinary things in an exalted style. Abbé Delille, for

instance, writing of the pleasures of drinking tea and coffee, speaks thus:

> La *fève de Moka*, la *feuille de Canton*,
> Vont verser leur *nectar* dans l'*émail du Japon*,
> Dans l'*airain échauffé*, déjà l'*onde* frissonne;
> Bientôt le *thé doré* jaunit l'*eau* qui bouillonne,
> Ou des *grains du Levant* je goûte le parfum.[1]
>
> (*Les Trois Règnes de la Nature*, Canto I)

Often periphrasis produces riddles which baffle the modern reader, and the general impression left by nearly all French poetry of the eighteenth century is of stilted language and worn-out clichés.

From the point of view of the development of the French language the eighteenth century then can be summed up by the one word, 'purism'—a purism carried to ever greater heights, one in which Voltaire criticizes the style of a seventeenth century writer like Corneille, only to be severely censured in his turn for his linguistic and stylistic lapses by the hyper-purist, La Harpe. Yet there is another side to the development of the French language in our period. The very theory of the *style noble*, as elaborated in the eighteenth century, with its paradoxical notion that, under certain conditions, any words could be introduced even into the highest forms of literature, left the way open for a wholesale invasion. Moreover, the aims of the purists—to keep the language fixed in the state of perfection to which the seventeenth century had brought it—meant a war to the death against all neologisms. Yet such a struggle was doomed to defeat; the development and enrichment of life in the eighteenth century, both in the narrow sphere of polite society and in the wider world outside it, were bound to lead to a comparable development and enrichment of the language. It simply could not stand still. Thus we find the

---

[1] Periphrases—'fève de Moka'='café', 'feuille de Canton'='thé', 'émail du Japon'='porcelaine' (Japanese porcelain as well as Chinese has influenced European china), 'airain'='bouilloire', 'grains du Levant'='café'. 'Onde' is a more elevated word than 'eau', which is used in the following line—perhaps ennobled by its place in the sentence and its relative clause. 'Thé' is used in line 4, but accompanied by the ennobling adjective 'doré'.

contradiction that even the very purists were driven to confess the weakness and absurdity of their position.

We find, for instance, the arch-purist, Voltaire, writing to Frederick in 1749 to lament that the French language, 'cette gueuse pincée et dédaigneuse qui se complaît dans son indigence', should have become so impoverished. 'Si on laisse faire l'Académie', he goes on, 'elle appauvrira notre langue, et je propose à votre majesté de l'enrichir. Il n'y a que le génie qui soit assez riche pour faire de telles entreprises. Le purisme est toujours pauvre' (*Correspondence*, XVII, 151-2). His own views in this field were relatively timid, as one might expect, and mainly limited to giving new meanings to existing words and reviving old ones. But he had some influence on the decision of the Academy to introduce into the fourth edition of its dictionary, published in 1762, the technical terms which it had hitherto scorned. In the fifth edition of the dictionary, the publication of which was held up by events until 1798, it gave hospitality not only to large numbers of archaic words, but also to a numerous selection of neologisms. The author of a dictionary which appeared in 1787 gives some idea of the rush of new words entering the language when he speaks of 'deux mille mots nouveaux introduits depuis vingt ans'.

In the second half of the century was being elaborated the technical vocabulary of the French language—in the arts and in politics, in economics and in philosophy, for instance—and it was inevitable that it should break down all barriers and invade literature. This process is already clearly visible in the first half of the century in the writings of men like Fontenelle and Voltaire when they come to popularize the scientific discoveries of their day. The enrichment of the language by the technical terms of the arts and sciences is well brought out by Diderot in the article *Encyclopédie* which appeared in 1755:

Les connaissances les moins communes sous le siècle passé le deviennent de jour en jour. Il n'y a point de femme à qui l'on ait donné quelque éducation, qui n'emploie avec discernement toutes les expressions consacrées à la peinture, à la sculpture, à l'architecture et aux belles-lettres. Combien y a-t-il d'enfants qui ont du dessin, qui savent de la géométrie, qui sont musiciens, à qui la langue domestique n'est pas plus familière que celle de ces **arts,** et qui disent, *un accord, une belle forme, un contour agréable, une parallèle, une hypothénuse, une quinte, un triton, un arpégement, un microscope, un télescope, un foyer,* comme ils diraient *une lunette d'opéra, une épée, une canne, un carrosse, un plumet!* Les esprits sont encore emportés d'un autre mouvement général vers l'histoire naturelle, l'anatomie, la chimie et la physique expérimentale. Les expressions propres à ces sciences sont déjà très communes et le deviendront nécessairement davantage. Qu'arrivera-t-il de là? c'est que la langue, même populaire, changera de face; qu'elle s'étendra à mesure que nos oreilles s'accoutumeront aux mots, par les applications heureuses qu'on en fera.

The great prose-writers of the second half of the century— Rousseau, Diderot or Bernardin de Saint-Pierre, for instance, not to mention Voltaire himself—availed themselves in their works of this rich technical vocabulary. Even plebeian language, so despised in the polite society of Paris, found its way into such writings of Diderot as *Jacques le Fataliste* and the *Neveu de Rameau* and into the *Confessions* of Rousseau, and the influence of foreign languages, Italian and especially English with the development of what was derisively called *anglomanie*, also tended to enrich the literary language.

In poetry the influence of this tendency is seen most clearly in the passion for poems about agriculture of the closing decades of the Ancien Régime. In the preface to his translation of the *Georgics*, published in 1770, Abbé Delille, the most illustrious of these didactic poets, made a plea for this type of poetry and affirmed its advantages over tragedy and comedy:

> Notre langue, resserrée jusqu'ici dans ces deux genres, est restée timide et indigente, et n'acquerra jamais ni richesse ni force, si, toujours emprisonnée sur la scène, elle n'ose se promener librement sur tous les sujets susceptibles de la grande et belle poésie. On ne peut donc savoir trop de gré à ceux qui, au lieu de grossir cette foule de drames platement imités, ou monstrueusement originaux, nous ont donné des poèmes sur les travaux des arts ou sur les beautés de la nature: c'est pour notre langue un monde nouveau, dont elle peut rapporter des richesses sans nombre.

In his translation he does not hesitate to use the technical terms of agriculture, a process which he continues in his own poem, *Les Jardins*, published in 1782, which contains the famous lines:

> Ne rougissez donc point, quoique l'orgueil en gronde,
> D'ouvrir vos parcs aux bœufs, à la vache féconde
> Qui ne dégrade plus ni vos parcs, ni mes vers.

However, for all its popularity such didactic poetry, with its use of the technical vocabulary of agriculture, was far from being the only form of verse written in France in the second half of the century. Despite the increasing liberation of prose from the shackles of the *style noble*, its cramping influence continued in tragedy and in other forms of poetry. There was still room, several decades after 1789, for the Romantic revolution which knocked off the shackles imposed on poetry by the seventeenth century purists and fastened even tighter by their successors in our period.

Literature in our period continued to be dominated by the *salons* of Paris, in which men of letters mingled with the more aristocratic and wealthy sections of the community. The influence of *le monde* on the style of so much of French literature was not limited to language, on which, as we have seen, its outlook and prejudices, reinforced by those of the purists, continued to have so considerable an effect. One reason for the success which so many eighteenth century French books enjoyed in the Europe of their day lay in the fact that they avoided all pedantic methods of exposition and sought to appeal, even when dealing with serious and complicated subjects, to the men and women of polite society in Paris, and beyond them to a public of *honnêtes gens*. One thinks here, for instance, of the light form which Voltaire gave to the most serious problems in his multitude of polemical writings, from the *contes* to the *Dictionnaire philosophique*. Montesquieu's *Esprit des Lois*, though a serious historical and sociological treatise on law, is none the less adapted to the tastes of this public; side by side with the solemn rounded periods of M. le Président we find flashes of wit and irony and a suitable admixture of spicy remarks to tickle the reader's palate, while this long work is made easier to read by its short sentences, short paragraphs and the short chapters into which all its books are divided.

It is the drama of the age that bears perhaps most clearly the mark of the tastes, interests and prejudices of the upper classes of the capital for whom the theatre was such an important occupation. Despite the presence of so many middle-class and even a sprinkling of plebeian spectators in a theatre like the Comédie Française, the aristocratic and wealthy members of the high society of Paris continued to impose their outlook on the drama of the age. The dramatists of our period inherited from the seventeenth century the tradition that the principal characters of a tragedy must be of high birth, preferably of royal blood. Though this principle was challenged in the second half of the century, only a small number of tragedies—including one highly successful patriotic drama, De Belloy's *Siège de Calais*, given at the Comédie Française in 1765 and portraying the famous episode of the Burghers of Calais—brought on the stage before 1789 characters of less exalted birth.

In the shocked comments on Shakespeare made by many French critics of the eighteenth century one of the chief charges levelled against him is that he lacked any notion of the dignity of tragedy. Instead of confining himself to portraying people of exalted birth, he brought on to the stage a motley *canaille* of artisans, soldiers and grave-diggers. Shakespeare also offended against other canons of the aristocratic taste of eighteenth century France. He had no respect for the sacred rule of the proprieties (*bienséances*) in either the themes or the language of his plays. The low manners and speech of the vulgar characters whom he introduced into his tragedies even infected those of their betters and completely destroyed the solemn, dignified tone of tragedy. Instead of rigorously excluding all comic elements and all realistic and trivial scenes from his tragedies, Shakespeare wallowed in them and thus completely destroyed the atmosphere of tragedy.

To those who have been brought up on the simple equation 'French Classical Tragedy'='The Three Unities', that these should have been the main criticisms brought against Shakespeare in eighteenth century France may seem incredible, but it is none the less true. If we look at the famous eighteenth chapter of the *Lettres philosophiques*, written when Voltaire's enthusiasm for Shakespeare was at its height, we find praise and blame neatly balanced in such phrases as 'un génie plein de force et de fécondité, de naturel et de sublime, sans la moindre étincelle de bon goût et sans la moindre connaissance des règles'. But among the rules which Shakespeare is accused of ignoring there is no direct mention of the unities; what is criticized in his tragedies is the violation of such technical rules as that of *vraisemblance* and more especially of the *bienséances* and the separation of tragedy and comedy. What horrifies Voltaire in the works of such a genius is brought out clearly by his comments on *Othello* and *Hamlet*:

> Vous savez que, dans la tragédie du *More de Venise*, pièce très touchante, un mari étrangle sa femme sur le théâtre, et quand la pauvre femme est étranglée, elle s'écrie qu'elle meurt très injustement. Vous n'ignorez pas que, dans *Hamlet*, des fossoyeurs creusent une fosse en buvant, en chantant des vaudevilles, et en faisant sur les têtes de mort qu'ils rencontrent des plaisanteries convenables à gens de leur métier.

He goes on to speak with equal disgust of *Julius Caesar* with 'les plaisanteries des cordonniers et des savetiers romains introduits sur la scène avec Brutus et Cassius'. Judged by the aristocratic standards of taste of Voltaire and his contemporaries, Shakespeare's plays were bound to seem to all but a handful of critics the very antithesis of tragedy; despite their flashes of genius, they appeared to be the outpourings of an ignorant barbarian whose only thought was to pander to the low instincts of the mob.

With only minor and generally timid modifications the *bienséances* continued to reign in French tragedy down to the Revolution. The *style noble* which likewise reflects the influence of polite society on French tragedy during the Ancien Régime was to retain its hold there until the Romantic revolution of the 1820s. Playwrights like Voltaire deplored the excessive place given to love in French tragedy, a failing which he repeatedly attributes in his correspondence to the ladies. A typical comment is to be found in one of his letters of the 1750s: 'Vos premières loges sont composées de personnes qui connaissent mieux l'amour que l'histoire romaine. Elles veulent s'attendrir, elles veulent pleurer, et avec le mot d'amour on a cause gagnée avec elles' (*Correspondence*, XXXII, 159). One may have one's doubts as to whether an interest in this particular passion is confined to women, but certainly Voltaire lays the blame at the door of the aristocratic ladies of his time.

The influence of the polite society of Paris on the development of French comedy in our period is perhaps even more striking. In his plays Molière took in all classes of society— nobles, bourgeois and peasants—but there was a marked tendency among playwrights of the eighteenth century to confine their attention more and more exclusively to the portrayal of characters drawn from the upper classes of society. The 'aristocratic reaction' which is so important in the social and political history of eighteenth century France has a curious reflection in comedy, where *Marquis*, *Comtesses* and *Chevaliers*, with an occasional *Conseiller* or *Président* or perhaps a *Fermier général*, tend to monopolize the stage. Among the numerous protests against this state of affairs which were made from the middle of the century onwards the most striking was that of Rousseau who makes the hero of *La Nouvelle Héloïse* declare, during his visit to Paris, that comedy confines itself nowadays to reproducing 'les conversations d'une centaine de maisons de Paris':

> Hors de cela, on n'y apprend rien des mœurs des Français. Il y a dans cette grande ville cinq ou six cent mille âmes dont il n'est jamais question sur la scène. Molière osa peindre des bourgeois et des artisans aussi bien que des marquis. . . . Mais les auteurs d'aujourd'hui qui. sont des gens d'un autre air, se croiraient déshonorés s'ils savaient ce qui se passe au comptoir d'un marchand ou dans la boutique d'un ouvrier; il ne leur faut que des interlocuteurs illustres, et ils cherchent dans le rang de leurs personnages l'élévation qu'ils ne peuvent tirer de leur génie.

What is more, his hero is made to argue, that is what the theatre-going public of Paris wants:

> Les spectateurs eux-mêmes sont devenus si délicats qu'ils craindraient de se compromettre à la comédie comme en visite, et ne daigneraient pas aller voir en représentation des gens de moindre

condition qu'eux. Ils sont comme les seuls habitants de la terre; tout le reste n'est rien à leurs yeux. Avoir un carrosse, un suisse, un maître d'hôtel, c'est être comme tout le monde. Pour être comme tout le monde, il faut être comme très peu de gens. Ceux qui vont à pied ne sont pas du monde; ce sont des bourgeois, des hommes du peuple, des gens de l'autre monde, et l'on dirait qu'un carrosse n'est pas tant nécessaire pour se conduire que pour exister. (II, 340-2)

The diatribe concludes with the words: 'On n'y sait plus montrer les hommes qu'en habit doré. Vouz diriez que la France n'est peuplée que de comtes et de chevaliers.'

In this same outburst Rousseau also complains that tragedy deals with subjects too remote from the experience of ordinary people. This was a theme which was to be taken up by other writers in the second half of the century, by Beaumarchais, for instance, who before he found his true vocation in comedy, wrote two *drames*, *Eugénie* and *Les Deux Amis*. In his *Essai sur le genre dramatique sérieux*, published in 1767 with the first of these *drames*, he roundly declares that the preference for kings and princes in tragedy is a matter of pure van ty, and that the use of such characters merely reduces the interest which the ordinary spectator takes in tragic heroes. 'Que me font à moi, sujet paisible d'un état monarchique du dix-huitième siècle, les révolutions d'Athènes et de Rome?' he asks. 'Quel véritable intérêt puis-je prendre à la mort d'un tyran du Péloponnèse? au sacrifice d'une jeune princesse en Aulide? Il n'y a dans tout cela rien à voir pour moi, aucune moralité qui me convienne' (*Théâtre complet*, p. 39).

The new genre of the *drame*, of which Diderot had made himself the theorist ten years earlier, aimed at portraying characters closer to the average spectator in time and in social status than those of tragedy. The *drame* was intended by Diderot to occupy a place between the two existing genres of comedy and tragedy, and to approach now more closely to the former, now, in the form of domestic tragedy (*la tragédie bourgeoise*), to the latter. He claimed for domestic tragedy that it would portray characters drawn from a world close to that of the average spectator, and not from a more or less remote past:

43  *Moreau le Jeune*, Hommages rendus à Voltaire sur le Théâtre Français le 30 mars 1778

44   Assemblée dans le désert en 1773 (near Nîmes)

Elle est plus voisine de nous. C'est le tableau des malheurs qui nous environnent. Quoi! vous ne concevez l'effet que produiraient sur vous une scène réelle, des habits vrais, des discours proportionnés aux actions, des actions simples, des dangers, dont il est impossible que vous n'ayez tremblé? (*Œuvres complètes*, VII, 146)

In a letter Beaumarchais said of his second *drame* which dealt with the commercial life of Lyons, and contains enthusiastic praise of the role of the merchant in society:

J'aurais été bien trompé dans mes vues si le commerçant que j'ai cherché à montrer dans le plus beau jour en cet ouvrage n'était pas satisfait du rôle digne et honnête que je fais jouer à un homme de son état. . . . Je souhaite qu'elle plaise aux négociants, cette pièce qui a été faite pour eux et en général pour honorer les gens du tiers état. (*Théâtre complet: Lettres relatives à son théâtre*, pp. 543-4)

Mercier, who was bold enough to argue that the theatre ought to abandon its traditional role of entertaining only the upper classes of society and should endeavour to appeal to the masses, naturally went further than Diderot or Beaumarchais in demanding that characters of the most humble birth should be portrayed on the stage. He attacks the prevailing aristocratic prejudice in the most bitter terms:

Mais voir les conditions humaines les plus basses, les plus rampantes! ajoutera-t-on encore, les mettre sur la scène! Et pourquoi pas? Homme dédaigneux, approche; que je te juge à ton tour. Qui es-tu? qui te donne le droit d'être hautain? Je vois ton habit, tes laquais, tes chevaux, ton équipage; mais toi, que fais-tu? . . . Tu souris, je t'entends; tu es homme de cour, tu consumes tes jours dans une inaction frivole, dans des intrigues puériles, dans des fatigues ambitieuses et risibles. Tu ruines tes créanciers pour paraître un homme comme il faut. . . .
    Verge avilie du despotisme, un tisserand, son bonnet sur la tête, me paraît plus estimable et plus utile que toi. Si je te mets sur la scène, ce sera pour la honte. Mais ces ouvriers, ces artisans peuvent y paraître avec noblesse; ce sont des hommes, que je reconnais tels à leurs mœurs, à leurs travaux. Et toi, né pour l'opprobre du genre humain, plût à Dieu que tu fusses mort à l'instant de ta naissance! (*Du Théâtre*, pp. 137-8)

Yet if we look at the *drames* of Diderot, Beaumarchais, or even Mercier, we find a considerable gap between theory and practice. Diderot's *Père de famille* and *Fils naturel* portray the same world as that of the comedies of the time; their characters are drawn from the wealthy and even aristocratic sections of society. In the play which Beaumarchais wrote to 'honorer les gens du tiers état', he may transport us to the despised provinces and show his main characters at grips with commercial and financial problems, but the persons he portrays belong to the nobility or the very fringe of it. Mercier, it is true, does sometimes depict quite plebeian characters—a peasant, a poor weaver, for instance—but the effect is destroyed by his fondness for the popular device of the recognition which suddenly transforms his characters of low or bourgeois birth into persons of rank or substance.

For all their timidity, such attempts to portray bourgeois and plebeian characters on the stage had in general a hostile reception from the critics. Nor was the new dramatic genre popular with the actors of the Comédie Française, and several authors of *drames*, especially Mercier, had difficulty in having their plays performed anywhere in Paris. It seems rather as if it was in the large commercial centres of the provinces such as Lyons, Marseilles or Bordeaux, that the new genre of the *Drame* enjoyed its greatest popularity. In his preface to the *Barbier de Séville*, published five years after the appearance of his second and last *drame*, *Les Deux Amis*, Beaumarchais offers ironical submission to the traditional interpretation of the functions of tragedy and comedy: 'Présenter des hommes d'une condition moyenne accablés et dans le malheur, fi donc! On ne doit jamais les montrer que bafoués. Les citoyens ridicules et les rois malheureux, voilà tout le théâtre existant et possible, et je me le tiens pour dit; c'est fait, je ne veux plus quereller avec personne.' The resistance which was encountered by the demand for a drama which would deal with the lives and problems of ordinary people, and the very timidity of its practitioners throw interesting light on the hold of aristocratic traditions in the literary world of Paris before 1789.

In the course of the century a similar demand was made in

the case of the novel. As early as 1734, when he published the second part of his unfinished novel, *La Vie de Marianne*, Marivaux spoke sarcastically of the tendency of readers to prefer characters of the highest rank:

> Il y a des gens dont la vanité se mêle de tout ce qu'ils font, même de leurs lectures. Donnez-leur l'histoire du cœur humain dans les grandes conditions, ce devient là pour eux un objet important; mais ne leur parlez pas des états médiocres, ils ne veulent voir agir que des seigneurs, des princes, des rois, ou du moins des personnes qui aient fait une grande figure. Il n'y a que cela qui existe pour la noblesse de leur goût. Laissez là le reste des hommes: qu'ils vivent, mais qu'il n'en soit pas question. Ils vous diraient volontiers que la nature aurait bien pu se passer de les faire naître, et que les bourgeois la déshonorent. (p. 57)

The same point is made in 1749 by a journalist reviewing Sarah Fielding's *Adventures of David Simple*. He begins his article thus:

> Nous sommes plus fastueux, nous autres Français, dans les titres que nous donnons aux livres de cette espèce. On ne voit guère en France de romans roturiers; ils sont presque tous de la première condition; il en est peu qui ne soient décorés du nom d'une terre érigée en duché, en marquisat ou en comté. *Mémoires du Duc de* \*\*\*, *Aventures du Marquis de* \*\*\*, *Confessions du Comte de* \*\*\*, c'est ainsi qu'ils s'annoncent dans le monde. . . .
> Si cependant il arrive que le héros ou l'héroïne d'un roman soit un paysan on une paysanne, on ne fait connaître la bassesse de leur condition que pour relever davantage l'éclat de leur fortune: *Le Paysan parvenu, La Paysanne parvenue* nous annoncent quelque chose de brillant; et l'on s'attend au moins à les voir l'un et l'autre posséder en titre de marquisat les terres que leurs pères avaient labourées. (De La Porte, *Observations sur la littérature moderne*, I, 108-9)

This last remark is interesting. Although Marivaux argued strongly in favour of a novel dealing with the affairs of ordinary people, he none the less chooses as heroes of his novels characters who, despite their humble beginnings, have by the time they relate their adventures ended up among the upper classes of society. Jacob, the hero of *Le Paysan parvenu*, is a genuine peasant's son, but he writes his memoirs as a wealthy tax-farmer; while the heroine of *La Vie de Marianne*, although at the beginning of the novel she is depicted as an apprentice to a sempstress, ends up among the aristocracy, and, although the mystery of her birth is never explained, it is hinted at the very beginning of the novel that her parents were of noble rank.

Moreover, despite the demand, voiced in various quarters, for a novel dealing with the affairs of ordinary people, critics of the time showed themselves as hostile to this tendency as they were to the *Drame*. A novelist like Lesage was criticized for not concerning himself with characters drawn from the upper ranks of society. One writer complained of his first original novel: '*Le Diable boiteux* aurait été un ouvrage charmant si l'auteur eût peint les aventures du grand monde', while another spoke slightingly of *Gil Blas* because it showed a lack of knowledge of the upper classes of society—'une connaissance plus familière et plus intime d'une certaine classe de la société que Gil Blas n'avait pas assez observée ou qu'il ne voyait que de loin'.

English novelists, especially Fielding and Smollett, were frequently criticized for concerning themselves with the lower orders, while French novels dealing with the affairs of ordinary people met with a cool reception. Thus in 1753 we find the critic, Grimm, pouring scorn on a novel which dealt with the love affairs of a young provincial who had been sent by his father to study law under a Paris *procureur*, and which consequently offers a picture of the daily life of a *procureur* and his family. The critic has nothing but disdain for such characters who are outside the narrow sphere of the polite society of the capital:

Voilà donc un roman domestique que personne cependant ne saurait lire; c'est qu'indépendamment du défaut de talent dans l'auteur, les personnages du roman sont tous des gens qui n'ont point d'existence dans la société, et dont les aventures, par conséquent, ne sauraient nous attacher. Le quartier de la Halle et de la place Maubert a sans doute des mœurs, et très marquées même; mais ce ne sont pas les mœurs de la nation, elles ne méritent donc pas d'être peintes. (*Correspondance littéraire*, II, 269)

The same critic could have nothing but contempt for the famous passage in *La Vie de Marianne* in which Marivaux depicts a quarrel between two plebeian characters, a sempstress and a cabby, over the amount of a coach-fare: 'Rien n'est mieux rendu d'après nature, et d'un goût plus détestable que le tableau que je cite.'

In the same year Grimm offers a vivid picture of the narrow circle of the court and Parisian high society to which much of the literature of the age was addressed, when he writes of autumn as being generally the season

> la plus stérile de l'année en nouveautés littéraires, parce que la cour étant d'un côté à Fontainebleau[1] et presque tout le reste des habitants de Paris dispersés dans les campagnes, les auteurs et leurs hérauts les libraires sont en usage de consacrer ce temps au repos, pour avoir, dans le temps où le carnaval fait rentrer tout le monde dans le sein de Paris, les uns des succès plus brillants, les autres des ventes plus considérables. (*Correspondance littéraire*, II, 293)

The phrase 'presque tout le reste des habitants de Paris', which could obviously apply only to the 'best people', is delightful, and forms an interesting parallel to his reference above to ordinary folk as 'des gens qui n'ont point d'existence dans la société'.

Another interesting sidelight on what many critics and readers expected in the way of social tone in the novel is provided by the way in which English novels of the time were adapted to suit French taste and their characters elevated several degrees in the social scale. Thus when the novelist Mme Riccoboni came to adapt Fielding's *Amelia* to French taste, she transformed the penniless young officer with whom the heroine elopes into the scion of an aristocratic family, while the faithful Sergeant Atkinson, his one-time orderly, is elevated to the rank of lieutenant.

Naturally the novelists of the eighteenth century enjoyed a freedom denied to the dramatist. The novel, a somewhat despised literary genre in the past, had never been seriously

---

[1] By longstanding tradition the court always spent the autumn at Fontainebleau.

hampered by elaborate rules, and the novelist did not have to present his work before the select and still aristocratically-minded audiences of the Comédie Française. Among the tremendous number of novels produced in the course of the century there were works to suit all tastes. The novelists did not cater only for the aristocratic public of what Grimm calls elsewhere 'le quartier du Palais Royal et le faubourg Saint-Germain'; he wrote often for a very wide public, scattered over the provinces of France as well as concentrated in the capital. Novels were read not only by duchesses and the wives of tax-farmers, but by what Grimm calls 'les jeunes filles de boutique de la rue des Lombards et de la rue des Bourdonnais' (VII, 479). Yet anyone familiar with the novels of eighteenth century France has no difficulty in recognizing in them the influence of the polite society of Paris, not only in their choice of characters, but in their themes, tone and general style.

The eighteenth century is not distinguished for great poetry. Indeed, it has been claimed that the greatest poet of the age was Jean-Jacques Rousseau, who wrote in prose. Not that poetry was despised; a host of writers, amateur as well as professional, turned out enormous quantities of verse. Poetry still enjoyed an immense prestige; Voltaire's fame among his contemporaries rested in part on the belief that with his *Henriade* he had at last endowed France with a great epic poem, and that in his tragedies he had proved himself a great poet. Out of all the mass of verse produced in our period little remains of interest to the modern reader except the *Poème sur le désastre de Lisbonne*, and the writings of Andre Chénier in the years just before and after 1789.

It is easy, as we have seen, to trace the influence of the polite society of the capital on the language of eighteenth century poetry. Again, among the vast output of verse in our period, a prominent place is taken by the society verse which had developed in the *salons* of the seventeenth century and which continued, with variations in fashions and forms, to flourish right down to the Revolution. For a long time after *énigmes* (riddles in verse) had fallen into disrepute with the polite society of the capital, they continued to find favour in the provinces, and to please its provincial clientèle the *Mercure* went on publishing them until 1789. It is recorded that when the poet and playwright, Gresset, retired towards the end of his life to his native Amiens, he rapidly tired of the vogue which they enjoyed in the society in which he moved. He therefore composed a parody, well calculated to pour ridicule on this type of verse. It began of course with the normal opening of an *énigme*, but ended very differently:

> Je suis un ornement qu'on porte sur la tête.
> Je m'appelle chapeau: devine, grosse bête.

Everyone, it is related, laughed at this obvious parody, except for one very serious gentleman who sat thinking it all out until suddenly he jumped up with his 'solution': 'Je l'ai trouvé, je l'ai trouvé: c'est une perruque' (La Harpe, *Correspondance littéraire*, II, 126).

Another literary fashion which flourished to the end of the Ancien Régime was the parlour-game of *bouts-rimés*, in which verses had to be composed to set rhymes. In 1784, when the Marquis de Montesquiou-Fezensac was elected to the Academy, a contemporary declared that his only literary work consisted of *bouts-rimés*. The Marquis owed his election to the fact that he was *Premier écuyer* of Louis XVI's brother, the Comte de Provence, and a contemporary epigram ran:

> Montesquiou-Fezensac est de l'Académie.
> Quel ouvrage a-t-il fait? . . . Sa généalogie.

It is related by a contemporary that two years earlier Louis XVI, on hearing of the Marquis's skill in *bouts-rimés*, set him one to do.

The society verse of the eighteenth century rose somewhat higher than such obvious parlour-games as *énigmes* and *bouts-rimés*. Though the mediaeval forms like the *rondeau* and the *ballade*, which had been revived in the *salons* of the previous century by poets like Voiture, did not long survive, poets continued to turn out *stances*, *chansons*, *madrigaux* and *épîtres*. One of the great masters of society verse in our period was Voltaire. To his contemporaries he was not only the author of

*La Henriade* and of philosophical poetry, as well as the successor
of Racine in tragedy; he was also the author of a series of light
pieces, full of grace and wit, such as his *Madrigal à Mme de \*\*\**
*sur un passage de Pope*:

> Pope, l'Anglais, ce sage si vanté,
> Dans sa morale au Parnasse embellie,
> Dit que les biens, les seuls biens de la vie,
> Sont le repos, l'aisance et la santé.[1]
> Il s'est trompé! Quoi! dans l'heureux partage
> Des dons du ciel faits à l'humain séjour,
> Ce triste Anglais n'a pas compté l'Amour?
> Qu'il est à plaindre! Il n'est heureux, ni sage.

In the epigram too Voltaire had few equals. This is how he
dispatched two of his enemies:

> *Sur le portrait de Voltaire mis entre ceux de La Beaumelle*
> *et de Fréron*
>
> Le Jay vient de mettre Voltaire
> Entre La Beaumelle et Fréron:
> Ce serait vraiment un Calvaire,
> S'il s'y trouvait un bon larron.

Fréron is the subject of another crushing epigram:

> L'autre jour, au fond d'un vallon,
> Un serpent piqua Jean Fréron.
> Que pensez-vous qu'il arriva?
> Ce fut le serpent qui creva.

In his slightly older contemporary, Piron, Voltaire found,
however, a rival, as, for instance, in the following epigram:

> *Contre Voltaire*
>
> Son enseigne est *à l'Encylopédie.*
> Que vous plaît-il? de l'anglais, du toscan?
> Vers, prose, algèbre, opéra, comédie?
> Poème épique, histoire, ode ou roman?

---

[1] *Essay on Man*, Epistle IV:
> Reason's whole pleasure, all the joys of sense,
> Lie in three words, health, peace and competence.

Parlez! C'est fait. Vous lui donnez un an?
Vous l'insultez! . . . En dix ou douze veilles,
Sujets manqués par l'aîné des Corneilles,
Sujets remplis par le fier Crébillon,
Il refond tout . . . Peste! voici merveilles!
Et la besogne est-elle bonne? . . . Oh! non!

Piron's chief butt, however, was the French Academy, which he tirelessly pursued with his wit: his most famous attack on it is probably his own epitaph, which he finally reduced to two lines, 'pour le soulagement des mémoires':

Ci-gît Piron, qui ne fut rien,
Pas même académicien.

Other brilliant epigrams came, later in the century, from the pen of the poet, Écouchard-Lebrun. Among the best known are:

*Sur une dame poète*

Chloé, belle et poète, a deux petits travers:
Elle fait son visage, et ne fait pas ses vers.

and:

*Dialogue entre un pauvre poète et l'auteur*

On vient de me voler!—Que je plains ton malheur!
Tous mes vers manuscrits!—Que je plains le voleur!

Such poems bring to life today the literary world of eighteenth century Paris.

Among the many varieties of verse which flourished in the eighteenth century, one of the most popular, at least in the closing decades of the period, was descriptive poetry. As late as 1755 a critic maintained that the prejudices of polite society would prevent the writing of poems dealing with country life:

Combien d'objets qu'on ne peut peindre en vers! Combien de termes mêmes auxquels nous avons attaché une idée de bassesse, et que nous ne pouvons suppléer que par des circonlocutions! Les travaux de la campagne, les instruments de l'agriculture sont décrits par Virgile et plaisent en latin; en français les mêmes détails seraient peu supportables, et c'est moins la différence de goût que la différence des mœurs. Ces détails champêtres étaient

très familiers aux Romains les plus délicats, mais comment mettre sous les yeux de notre monde poli des objets dont on n'entend parler qu'à ses fermiers? (Raynal, *Nouvelles littéraires*, II, 216)

In fact, as we have seen, not only did writers of the closing decades of the Ancien Régime produce poetry on the theme of country life—*Les Saisons, Les Mois, Les Jardins*, and so forth— but they also removed some of the shackles which the narrow taste of polite society had imposed on the language of poetry. Moreover, for a variety of reasons polite society from about 1760 did come to take an interest in country life and in agriculture. The influence of Rousseau mingled with the teachings of the Physiocrats and of the agricultural improvers to direct even the essentially urban outlook of the upper classes of Paris towards the land. A poet like Saint-Lambert could therefore sing in his *Saisons*, published twenty years before the Revolution, of the agricultural improvements of 'Turnip Townshend'.

> Il est, il est un art de choisir les engrais,
> Qu'au vertueux Towsend (*sic*) a révélé Cérès . . .
> Dans les champs d'Albion, sur un sable infertile,
> C'est toi qui, le premier, fis répandre l'argile,
> Fécondas l'un par l'autre, et du mélange heureux
> Vis naître les moissons sur un fonds sablonneux.
> Au sol qu'une huile épaisse humecte et rend solide,
> C'est toi qui, le premier, mêlas le sable aride;
> Par ses angles tranchants, le limon divisé
> Laissa sortir le blé du champ fertilisé.
> C'est toi qui, le premier, instruisis ta patrie
> A revêtir les monts des dons de la prairie;
> A contraindre les champs depuis peu moissonnés
> D'offrir une herbe tendre aux troupeaux étonnés.
> L'agriculteur anglais, que l'État encourage,
> Bientôt de tes leçons apprit à faire usage.   (*L'Automne*)

*Les Saisons* met with considerable success. Certainly a poet could now interest both the polite society of Paris and a wider circle of readers beyond in the problems of agriculture. Yet even a *Philosophe* like Saint-Lambert considered that peasants—particularly the poorer peasants—should be introduced very

sparingly into such poetry, as we see from the following remarks in the preface to the poem:

Il n'y faut pas placer de malheureux paysans; ils n'intéressent que par leurs malheurs; ils n'ont pas plus de sentiments que d'idées, leurs mœurs ne sont pas pures; la necessité les force à tromper; ils ont cette fourberie, cette finesse outrée, que la nature donne aux animaux faibles et qu'elle a pourvus de faibles armes. Parlez d'eux; mais ne les mettez que rarement en action; et surtout parlez pour eux.

Il y a dans les campagnes de riches laboureurs, des paysans aisés; ceux-là ont des mœurs. Ce sont, dit Cicéron, des philosophes auxquels il ne manque que la théorie; la peinture de leur état et de leurs sentiments doit plaire à l'homme de goût, c'est-à-dire à l'honnête homme éclairé et sensible.

Above all, Saint-Lambert suggests, the poet should depict the provincial noblemen who have so far been neglected:

Il y a un ordre d'hommes dont les poètes champêtres n'ont jamais parlé; ce sont les nobles, dont les uns vivent dans les châteaux et régissent une terre, et dont les autres habitent de petites maisons commodes et cultivent quelques champs. (*Œuvres*, I, 36-7)

Though we have moved far from the satirical portrait of the provincial nobleman which one finds in such seventeenth century works as Molière's *George Dandin* or La Bruyère's *Caractères*, we are still in the France of the Ancien Régime in which all but the aristocracy of wealthier peasants were deemed unworthy of a place in literature.

The Revolution finally destroyed the hold which, for two centuries, the polite society of Paris had exercised on literature through the *salons*. Paris has not, of course, lacked famous *salons* in the nineteenth and twentieth centuries, but their influence on literature has been slight: 1789 and the destruction of the society of the Ancien Régime finally put an end to the influence of polite society, in which the taste of women was prominent, on the development of both language and literature. The break with the past, so far as language is concerned, is symbolized by the preface to the fifth edition of the *Dictionnaire de l'Académie*

*Française* which, although prepared before the suppression of
the Academy in 1793, was not published until five years later.
'La vraie langue d'un peuple éclairé', declares the preface,
'n'existe réellement que dans la bouche et dans les écrits de
ce petit nombre de personnes qui pensent et parlent avec
justesse, qui attachent constamment les mêmes idées aux
mêmes mots.' The usage of polite society which, a century and
a half earlier, Vaugelas had set up as the criterion in matters
of language, is dismissed with contempt:

> On en a conclu qu'il ne fallait pas consulter *le beau langage* du
> *beau monde* comme une autorité qui décide ou tranche tout; parce
> que le *beau monde* pense et parle souvent très mal; parce qu'il
> laisse périr les étymologies et les analogies; parce qu'il ferme les
> yeux aux sillons de lumière que tracent les mots dans leur passage
> du sens propre au sens figuré; parce qu'enfin la différence est
> extrême entre le *beau langage* formé des fantaisies du beau monde,
> qui sont très bizarres, et le *bon langage,* composé des vrais rapports
> des mots et des idées, qui ne sont jamais arbitraires. (p. iv)

Long before the end of the Ancien Régime a new spirit had
been observable in French literature, one which the literary
historian labels as *Préromantisme*; the political and social upheaval of 1789 was to be matched, a generation later, by the
Romantic revolution which swept away most of the literary
and linguistic conventions on which French literature had lived
for two centuries.

.     .     .     .     .     .     .     .     .

The literature of seventeenth century France, particularly
that of the personal reign of Louis XIV which followed upon
the disorders of the first part of the period, had been essentially
conformist. If political discontent and unorthodox religious
views, though driven underground, were not entirely suppressed
even at the very height of the reign, and although in its closing
period they stand forth clearly for the modern historian to see
in the writings of Fénelon and Saint-Simon or Bayle and
Fontenelle, the great creative artists of the reign—Molière and
La Fontaine, Racine and Boileau—had poured forth paeans of
praise to the achievements of Louis XIV, while Bossuet had

celebrated in his *Politique tirée de l'Écriture sainte* the alliance between the Throne and the Altar in the doctrine of the divine right of kings.

All this was to change gradually between 1715 and 1789. The great writers of the age, in their different ways and with very different emphasis, reacted strongly against the political and religious orthodoxy of their time. Whereas the great writers of the previous age had been ranged round the King in attitudes of admiration, those of our period became estranged from the Crown and the government of their day. They pursued, despite all opposition from the secular power, their own views on religion, philosophy and finally politics in flagrant defiance of established authority.

It is well known that in eighteenth century France the attack on the Altar preceded that on the Throne. Beginning with the pinpricks of Montesquieu's *Lettres persanes*, Voltaire's *Lettres philosophiques* and a host of writings by lesser or even unknown authors, many of which could not be printed, but gave rise to a considerable trade in illicit manuscripts, the campaign grew in violence after 1760, when the Patriarche de Ferney launched his campaign against *l'infâme*, only to be outdone by the most intransigent of the *Philosophes* of Paris, Baron d'Holbach, whose *Système de la Nature*, published in 1770, preached a materialism which repelled Goethe and shocked Voltaire. There was in fact no unanimity on the religious question among all these writers. Although all rejected the established religion of Catholicism, there was no agreement as to what, if anything, was to be put in its place. There were all shades of belief and unbelief among these writers: there were deists of such very different outlook as, say, Voltaire and Rousseau; there were sceptical agnostics like d'Alembert or Condorcet; and there were men like Diderot and d'Holbach who rejected religion in any form. Yet all were united, not only in their hostility to Catholicism and behind it to any form of Christianity, but in their preaching of religious toleration. Following in the footsteps of such masters as Bayle and Locke, they denounced every form of religious intolerance.

In considering their crusade against religious fanaticism, we must bear in mind not only that the horrors of the wars of

religion of the sixteenth and seventeenth centuries were closer
to them than to us, but also that the France in which they lived
and thought and wrote was filled with an atmosphere of repression and intolerance, in which the secular power lent its
support—its prisons and its gibbets—to the maintenance of the
one true religion. The Catholic Church sought to impose on
all Frenchmen not only its rites, dogmas and moral teachings,
but also its interpretation of philosophy and history; traditionally it fought against all attempts to interpret the world in the
light of reason and science. In his *Suite de Apologie de l'Abbé de
Prades*—published anonymously in 1752—Diderot defended
Buffon against the charge that in his *Histoire naturelle* he had
contradicted the account of the origins of the earth given in
Genesis, and embarked on an impassioned defence of the rights
of science and free inquiry:

> Quoi donc! parce que Josué aura dit au soleil de s'arrêter, il
> faudra nier, sous peine d'anathème, que la terre se meut? Si, à la
> première découverte qui se fera, soit en astronomie, soit en
> physique, soit en histoire naturelle, nous devons renouveler, dans
> la personne de l'inventeur, l'injure faite autrefois à la philosophie
> dans la personne de Galilée, alors, brisons les microscopes,
> foulons aux pieds les télescopes et soyons les apôtres de la barbarie!
> (*Œuvres complètes*, I, 457-8)

What made perhaps the deepest impression on Voltaire during
his stay in England in the 1720s, coming as he did from
Catholic France where such things were almost unimaginable,
was the freedom of conscience enjoyed by Englishmen ('Un
Anglais, comme homme libre, va au ciel par le chemin qui lui
plaît') and the freedom which its philosophers and scientists
enjoyed to follow out their theories wherever they led them,
without risk of interference by the secular or religious authorities. In his *Lettres philosophiques* he contrasts the career of
Descartes, who found it necessary to leave France 'pour
philosopher en liberté' with that of Newton, who, 'né dans un
pays libre', lived his whole life 'toujours tranquille, heureux et
honoré dans sa patrie' (Letter XIV).

In France, on the other hand, the monarchy put the whole
weight of its authority behind the maintenance of the position

of the Catholic Church and its monopoly of control over men's religious beliefs from the cradle to the grave. If we are to appreciate the reasons behind the long campaign waged by the *Philosophes* for religious toleration—now with all the resources of wit and irony, now with passionate and pathetic eloquence— we must bear in mind the position to which the Protestant minority in France had been reduced since the Revocation of the Edict of Nantes in 1685.

Unquestionably, partly as a result of the campaign for tolera- tion conducted by the *Philosophes*, the lot of the Huguenots improved immensely in the course of our period. A royal decree of 1787, although it still denied them freedom of worship and excluded them from all official posts, gave freedom of con- science to 'ceux qui ne professent point la religion catholique', made arrangements for the registration of their births, deaths and marriages and secured their property. Yet even this modest alleviation of their lot came only two years before the Revolu- tion, and their position earlier, particularly before about 1760, had been very different. A royal declaration of 1724 confirmed and even strengthened the measures taken by Louis XIV against the Huguenots. It was aimed particularly against the illegal assemblies which they held in remote places in the country ('le désert'): a man found guilty of taking part in such worship was liable to be sent to the galleys for life, and a woman to life imprisonment, while the penalty for an officiating pastor was death. Only a Catholic form of marriage was recognized and children of former Protestants had to have their children baptized by their *curé* within twenty-four hours of their birth. Those 'nouveaux convertis' (to use the official phrase—the existence of Protestants as such was not recognized) who refused the sacraments when they were ill, were to be treated as apostates if they recovered, and punished by perpetual banish- ment and confiscation of their property. The declaration also continued to exclude Protestants from all official posts. The result of its promulgation and the persecutions which followed was another wave of emigration.

Partly because, in times of war, it feared the possibility of Protestant risings in regions like the Cévennes, the government did not always go as far as the Church would have liked in its persecution of the Huguenot minority. There alternated periods of severity and periods of relative calm. Yet those who were caught attending the conventicles continued to be imprisoned, and those pastors who came back to France, after receiving their training at the École des Pasteurs du désert at Lausanne, were shown no mercy when captured; as late as 1762 a Protestant pastor was hanged at Toulouse and three Protestant noblemen who had tried to rescue him were decapitated. It was in the same year and in the same town that the Protestant, Jean Calas, was broken on the wheel for the alleged crime of murdering his son to prevent him from abjuring Protestantism. Three years later, after a brilliant propaganda campaign by Voltaire, the memory of Calas was rehabilitated and compensation paid to his widow and children.

Yet though the *Philosophes* fought vigorously in favour of religious toleration for the Huguenot minority in France, their campaign against intolerance and fanaticism had much wider aims. What they sought was freedom for the individual to make his own choice of religion, even though it were deism or no religion at all. Throughout the century the Catholic Church continued to hold firm to the principle of religious uniformity, dismissing contemptuously as mere *tolerantisme* any doctrine which left religion to the free decision of the individual. Again and again in the course of the century it made its position perfectly plain. All must accept Catholicism and, if they failed to do so, the secular power must step in and use force. When for instance, in 1767, Marmontel published his *Bélisaire*, a harmless and dull plea for toleration to the modern reader who turns its pages, the success of the book was vastly increased by the condemnations which the Church authorities heaped upon it. In censuring the book the Sorbonne, the faculty of theology of the University of Paris, made perfectly clear its conception of the duties of the secular power:

En qualité de souverain, le prince a reçu de Dieu le glaive matériel pour réprimer tout mal préjudiciable à la société, c'est-à-dire, tout ce qui tend à corrompre les mœurs de ses sujets, à déranger l'ordre public, à enfreindre les lois et les ordonnances

45   La malheureuse famille Calas (la mère, les deux filles, avec Jeanne Viguière,
leur bonne servante, le fils et son ami, le jeune Lavaysse)

46  Lettre de cachet

47  The order for the arrest of Diderot (1749)

de son royaume. En conséquence, il a le pouvoir de réprimer toute publication, en quelque manière qu'elle se fasse, des fausses maximes de l'athéisme, du déisme, du matérialisme, etc., lesquelles coupent tous les nœuds de la société, détruisent le frein de la conscience, font disparaître la différence du bien et du mal, ouvrent la porte à toute sorte de crimes. Son pouvoir s'étend encore à réprimer toute autre doctrine capable d'ébranler les fondements de la religion catholique, de donner atteinte à la pureté de sa foi et à la sainteté de sa morale. (*Censure de la Faculté de Théologie de Paris*, pp. 188-9)

Though the governments of Louis XV and Louis XVI never quite lived up to the ideas which the clergy had of their duty to suppress any form of heresy, their repressive role was none the less considerable, especially as it was reinforced by the frequent interventions of the law courts, particularly the Parlements, which considered it one of their functions to suppress any form of free thought.

The government exercised a vigilant control over all books which were published either in France or abroad. No book could be published without the approval of the government, As the law of 1744 put it: 'Aucuns libraires ou autres ne pourront faire imprimer ou réimprimer, dans toute l'étendue du royaume, aucuns livres, sans en avoir préalablement obtenu la permission par lettres scellées du grand sceau.' Such permission was obtained only after the manuscript had been examined and approved by a censor appointed by the Chancellor (a similar censorship had been organized at the beginning of the century for plays). Even if a work had been approved by a censor, the author still ran the danger of seeing his book suppressed if, on publication, it aroused the hostility of the Sorbonne or the Parlement; if he offended the judges, proceedings might even be taken against him.

In practice, books provided with a *privilège* and the censor's *approbation* were not the only ones to appear in France. As Malesherbes, who as *Directeur de la Librairie* had control over the whole publishing and literary world in the critical period of the century from 1750 to 1763, put it: 'Un homme qui n'aurait jamais lu que les livres qui, dans leur origine, ont paru avec l'attache expresse du gouvernement, comme la loi le prescrit, serait en arrière de ses contemporains presque d'un siècle' (*Mémoire sur la liberté de la presse*, p. 300). Other books could be published in France, but without official approval, with what were known as 'permissions tacites'; indeed, the authorities would sometimes go even further and, provided it was done secretly, would allow the publication of books to which the clergy or the Parlement might take exception.

It would be quite wrong to imagine that the repression of 'dangerous thoughts' was carried out as efficiently in the France of the Ancien Régime as in a twentieth century totalitarian state. There were dozens of publishers scattered over Europe who would be only too ready to print a manuscript which could not be published, officially or unofficially, in France; and in Paris and the provinces too a good deal of illicit printing went on. The more strictly banned a book was, the higher its price when it was smuggled into the country or into Paris. The sale of illicit books by *colporteurs* was quite well organized, and any book could always be obtained, even though at a price; but there were risks attached to the business:

2 *Octobre 1768*. On a exécuté ces jours-ci un arrêt du Parlement qui condamne Jean-Baptiste Jossevand, garçon épicier, Jean Lécuyer, brocanteur, et Marie Suisse, femme dudit Lécuyer, au carcan pendant trois jours consécutifs; condamne en outre ledit Jossevand à la marque et aux galères pendant neuf ans, ledit Lécuyer aussi à la marque et aux galères pendant cinq ans, et ladite Marie Suisse à être renfermée pendant cinq ans dans la maison de force de l'Hôpital Général, pour avoir vendu des livres contraires aux bonnes mœurs et à la religion. Ces livres sont: le *Christianisme dévoilé*, l'*Homme aux quarante écus*, *Éricie ou la vestale*,[1] lesquels ont été lacérés et brûlés par l'exécuteur de la haute justice, lors de l'exécution des coupables.

On s'est récrié contre la sévérité d'un pareil arrêt, qu'on attribue à M. de Saint-Fargeau, président de la chambre des vacations, homme dur et inflexible, et dont le jansénisme rigoureux n'admet aucune tolérance. (Bachaumont, *Mémoires secrets*, IV, 113)

[1] Respectively a violent anti-religious work of d'Holbach, a *conte* of Voltaire, and a tragedy attacking the monastic system which could not be performed in Paris until 1789.

Voltaire's *Dictionnaire philosophique*, first published in Geneva in 1764 and reproduced in innumerable editions, had no difficulty in penetrating into France; but two years later its appearance was to have tragic consequences, and he himself was very seriously threatened even in his hide-out at Ferney. In February 1766 a court at Abbeville passed the following sentence on a young nobleman of eighteen, the Chevalier de La Barre:

En ce qui touche Jean-François Lefebvre, chevalier de La Barre, le déclarons dûment atteint et convaincu d'avoir appris à chanter et chanté des chansons impies, exécrables et blasphématoires contre Dieu; d'avoir profané le signe de la croix en faisant des bénédictions accompagnées de paroles infâmes que la pudeur ne permet pas de désigner; d'avoir sciemment refusé les marques de respect au Saint-Sacrament porté en la procession du prieuré de Saint-Pierre; d'avoir rendu ces marques d'adoration aux livres infâmes et abominables qu'il avait dans sa chambre; d'avoir profané le mystère de la Consécration du vin, l'ayant tourné en dérision, en prononçant à voix basse dessus un verre de vin qu'il avait à la main les termes impurs mentionés au procès-verbal, et bu ensuite le vin; d'avoir enfin proposé au nommé Pétignal qui servait la messe avec lui, de bénir les burettes en prononçant les paroles impures mentionnées au procès.

Pour réparation de quoi, le condamnons à faire amende honorable, en chemise, nu-tête et la corde au col, tenant en ses mains une torche de cire ardente du poids de deux livres au devant de la principale porte d'entrée de l'Église royale et collégiale de Saint-Wulfran, où il sera mené et conduit dans un tombereau par l'exécuteur de la haute justice qui attachera devant lui et derrière le dos un placard où sera écrit en gros caractères *impie*; et là, étant à genoux confessera ses crimes à haute et intelligible voix; ce fait aura la langue coupée et sera ensuite mené dans ledit tombereau en la place publique du grand marché de cette ville pour y avoir la tête tranchée sur un échafaud; son corps et sa tête seront ensuite jetés dans un bûcher pour y être détruits, brûlés, réduits en cendres, et icelles jetées au vent. Ordonnons qu'avant l'exécution ledit Lefebvre de La Barre sera appliqué à la question ordinaire et extraordinaire pour avoir par sa bouche la vérité d'aucuns faits du procès et révélation de ses complices. . . .

Ordonnons que le *Dictionnaire philosophique portatif* faisant partie desdits livres qui ont été déposés en notre greffe, sera jeté par l'exécuteur de la haute justice dans le même bûcher où sera jeté le corps dudit Lefebvre de La Barre. (Cruppi, *Linguet*, pp. 107-9)

The Chevalier appealed to the Paris Parlement, which confirmed the sentence (including the section concerning the *Dictionnaire philosophique*), and the King having refused to commute the punishment into life imprisonment, it was duly carried out on 1 July, to the stupefaction of the *Philosophes* and especially Voltaire.

It is true that no writer in eighteenth century France experienced the tragic fate of the Chevalier de La Barre; nor were any found in the Bastille when the famous state prison was stormed in 1789. Yet they lived and worked in an atmosphere of repression, of humiliating acts of hypocrisy and of secret denunciations. When Baron d'Holbach, the most radical of all the *Philosophes* in his attacks on religion in any shape or form, sought in 1756 to succeed his father-in-law in the sinecure of *secrétaire du roi*, he was compelled to furnish a certificate from his *curé*. The latter certified that 'il connaît led. Sr de Holbach pour homme de bonne vie et mœurs faisant profession de la Religion catholique, apostolique et romaine dont il remplit les devoirs avec édification et qu'il a une parfaite connaissance que ledit Sr de Holbach a satisfait à son devoir pascal de l'année dernière.' And this was the author of *Le Christianisme dévoilé* and the *Système de la Nature*.

Zealous Catholics thought it their duty to denounce to the authorities as the worst type of miscreant men like Voltaire and Diderot for holding views on religion which are today commonplace. When Voltaire was sent to the Bastille in 1726 to prevent him from taking vengeance on the Chevalier de Rohan, the *lieutenant de police* of Paris received the following anonymous letter:

Vous venez de mettre à la Bastille un homme que je souhaitais y voir il y a plus de 15 années. Il y en a 10 à 12 qu'étant allé voir à Saint-Sulpice M. l'abbé d'Albert, je me plaignis à lui du métier que faisait l'homme en question, prêchant le déisme tout à découvert aux toilettes de nos jeunes seigneurs; je voudrais être homme d'autorité pour un jour, lui dis-je, afin d'enfermer ce poète entre quatre murailles pour toute sa vie; il ne m'a pourtant jamais fait ni bien ni mal, n'en ayant jamais été connu; mais tout homme qui se déclare ennemi de Jésus-Christ, notre divin maître et bon sauveur, est un impie que nous devons poursuivre à cor et à cri. . . . (*Correspondence*, II, 14-15)

In 1747, the year after Diderot had published his *Pensées philosophiques*, the *curé* of his parish sent in the following denunciation to the *lieutenant de police*:

Le sieur Diderot est un jeune homme qui a passé sa première jeunesse dans le libertinage. . . . Les propos que Diderot tient quelquefois dans la maison montrent assez qu'il est déiste pour le moins. Il débite contre Jésus-Christ et contre la Sainte Vierge des blasphèmes que je n'ose mettre par écrit. On lui demanda un jour comment il s'y prendrait avec de tels sentiments s'il se trouvait en danger de mort. Il répondit qu'il ferait ce qu'il avait déjà fait en pareil cas à l'âge de seize ans, qu'il appellerait un prêtre et recevrait les sacrements. On se récria contre cette impiété; il ne fit qu'en rire et ajouta que pour une pure cérémonie il ne voulait pas déshonorer sa femme et ses enfants dans l'idée d'un public ignorant. . . . Dans un de ses entretiens il s'est avoué l'auteur d'un des deux ouvrages qui fut condamné par le Parlement et brûlé il y a environ deux ans. On m'a assuré qu'il travaillait depuis plus d'un an à un autre ouvrage encore plus dangereux contre la religion. Je tiens tous ces faits d'une même personne qui demeure en la même maison et qui est entrée assez avant dans sa familiarité pour savoir ce qu'il pense et ce qu'il fait. Il lui importe comme à moi de ne point paraître dans cette affaire. . . . (Bonnefon, *Diderot prisonnier à Vincennes*, p. 203)

With such denunciations hanging over their heads and with the prospect of their written works, even if published surreptitiously and without passing through the censorship, being closely scrutinized for any 'dangerous thoughts' which they might contain, the *Philosophes* were undoubtedly driven, at any rate until about 1760, to express their ideas with a caution which we must take into account today in trying to discover what they really thought. It would, for instance, be a naïve reader who took literally Diderot's profession of faith in the *Pensées philosophiques*: 'Je suis né dans l'Église catholique, apostolique et

romaine; et je me soumets de toute ma force à ses décisions'
(LVIII).

No doubt we must not imagine the *Philosophes* of our period
languishing for years in dark dungeons or ending their days
upon the scaffold; nor, however, must we fall into the opposite
excess of accepting the view that, just as to have the Parlement
order one's books to be burnt was a decided stimulus to their
sales, so being sent to the Bastille by *lettre de cachet* meant a free
and relatively luxurious spell in prison which brought profit
both to one's fame and one's purse. No doubt this was sometimes the case. In 1759 Marmontel was sent to the Bastille, and
spent a comfortable eleven days there; but his only crime was
to have recited a satirical poem about a certain duke who had
obtained a *lettre de cachet* against him as its alleged author. In
the following year Morellet was sent to the Bastille for having
published a pamphlet against the satirical comedy of Palissot,
*Les Philosophes*. In his memoirs he tells us that in prison he had
consoling thoughts which made resignation to his fate easy:

> . . . J'étais merveilleusement soutenu par une pensée qui rendait
> ma petite vertu plus facile.
>
> Je voyais quelque gloire littéraire éclairer les murs de ma prison:
> persécuté, plus j'allais être connu. Les gens de lettres que j'avais
> vengés et la philosophie dont j'étais le martyr, commenceraient
> ma réputation. Les gens du monde qui aiment la satire, m'allaient
> accueillir mieux que jamais. La carrière s'ouvrait devant moi, et
> je pourrais y courir avec plus d'avantage. Ces six mois de Bastille
> seraient une excellente recommandation et feraient infaillible-
> ment ma fortune. (I, 95)

In fact he spent only six weeks in the Bastille, and had all along
the knowledge that his crime (giving offence to certain highly
placed noblemen and ladies) was regarded as a minor one.

Diderot had not the same consolation when in 1749 a *lettre
de cachet* sent him to Vincennes. Among the works on the author-
ship of which he was interrogated by the *lieutenant de police* in
person were the *Pensées philosophiques*, burnt by the hangman
three years earlier, and the *Lettre sur les Aveugles* which had
appeared the previous month—both books which might well
have kept him in prison for years. As it was, he was released

after just over three months' imprisonment, but before leaving Vincennes, he had to sign an undertaking 'de ne plus rien publier qui, en quoi que ce soit, fût contraire à la religion et à la morale'. No doubt this incident had a profound influence on Diderot's future career and partly explains why so many of his works were published posthumously. It is obvious that he could not publish during his lifetime with any safety such a master-piece as *Le Rêve de d'Alembert*.

Voltaire had two spells in the Bastille, one as a result of his quarrel with the Chevalier de Rohan, and another which lasted nearly a year for a satirical poem on the Regent. The publication of his *Lettres philosophiques* caused a scandal; if he had been in Paris instead of Burgundy when the storm broke in 1734, he might well have joined his publisher in the Bastille. To avoid the *lettre de cachet* issued against him he had to retire for a short time over the frontier into Lorraine. In the meantime the Paris Parlement had his book burnt by the hangman as 'contraire à la religion, aux bonnes mœurs et au respect dû aux puissances'. Eleven months passed before he was allowed to return to Paris. From the time he left the capital for Potsdam in 1750 down to his triumphant return twenty-eight years later, he was an enforced exile from his native city; and when he died there in 1778, full of glory, he was denied a decent burial.

Then there is the example of Rousseau. In 1762 he published two books, the *Contrat social* and *Émile*. Despite the tremendous influence which the former work was to have during the Revolution, its publication caused him no trouble whatsoever with the French authorities. The appearance of *Émile*—with the author's name on the title-page and with its long and some-what unorthodox disquisition on religion in the *Profession de foi du vicaire savoyard*—raised a storm. This time it was not the government itself which took action, it was the Paris Parlement; it condemned the book and issued a warrant for the arrest of the author. Rousseau was compelled to flee from France and to seek refuge in Switzerland. It is true that eight years later he was allowed to return to Paris and to spend the rest of his life down to his death in 1778 living in the capital; but there is also no doubt that the prosecution launched by the Parlement in

1762 for the publication of a book which is not only one of the great works of eighteenth century France, but at the same time profoundly religious, reduced Rousseau to a wandering existence and stimulated the persecution-mania which for the last part of his life deprived him of happiness and peace of mind.

No doubt we must not exaggerate the persecutions from which men of letters suffered in the eighteenth century; but neither must we underestimate their effect either on the outlook of writers or on the way in which they expressed their ideas. After about 1760 a Voltaire, sitting safely in Ferney, or a d'Holbach, established in the centre of Paris and taking the risk that the authorities might suddenly discover that he was responsible for the publication of a mass of unorthodox writings which issued from the presses of Amsterdam, could and did say pretty well everything they wanted to say, however unpalatable their religious and philsophical ideas might be to the authorities. But most writers, especially those who were more or less dependent on their pen for a living, tended to be more cautious. 'La crainte des fagots', d'Alembert once wrote, 'est très rafraîchissante.' Some notion of the atmosphere of repression in which they lived and worked is given by Mercier in his *Tableau de Paris*:

> Il est onze heures du soir ou cinq heures du matin; on frappe à votre porte, votre domestique ouvre, votre chambre se remplit d'une escouade de satellites, l'ordre est précis, la résistance est superflue; on écarte de vous tout ce qui pourrait vous servir d'armes, et l'exempt, qui n'en vantera pas moins sa bravoure, prend jusqu'à votre écritoire pour un pistolet.
>
> Le lendemain un voisin, qui a entendu du bruit dans la maison, demande ce que ce pouvait être: *Rien, c'est un homme que la police a fait enlever.—Qu'avait-il fait?—On n'en sait rien; il a peut-être assassiné ou vendu une brochure suspecte.—Mais, monsieur, il y a quelque différence entre ces deux délits.—Cela se peut; mais il est enlevé.*

'Il n'est pas nécessaire', Mercier goes on, 'de faire un gros volume contre les lettres de cachet. Quand on a dit, *C'est un acte arbitraire*, on en peut tirer sans peine toutes les conséquences

possibles.' Not that, it should be noted, Mercier was against all
*lettres de cachet*; but there seems much point in the last sentence
of his chapter:

> Nous avons pris aux Anglais leur Wauxhall, leur Ranelagh, leur
> Wisk,[1] leur punch, leurs chapeaux, leurs courses de chevaux,
> leurs jockeys, leurs gageures; quand leur prendrons-nous quelque
> chose de plus important à saisir, comme, par exemple, la loi
> *habeas corpus*? (*Tableau de Paris*, V, 159-62)

The eighteenth century saw a growing estrangement between
the Crown, determined to preserve not only its own power, but
also that of the established Church, and those writers who
sought freedom to express their notions on religion and philosophy. The Crown had many favours to bestow on men of
letters, but these were rarely given to the *Philosophes*, however
great their fame in France and indeed in Europe. It is true that
in the 1740s Voltaire enjoyed for a while, thanks in part to
Mme de Pompadour, such favour at court as had Racine
himself fifty years earlier; he too held the posts of *historiographe
du roi* and *gentilhomme de la chambre*. But neither Louis XV nor
Voltaire found the arrangement a happy one. Towards the
end of his life Voltaire wrote: 'Ceux qui vous ont dit, monsieur
l'abbé, qu'en 1744 et 1745 je fus courtisan, ont avancé une
triste vérité. Je le fus; je m'en corrigeai en 1746, et je m'en
repentis en 1747. De tout le temps que j'ai perdu en ma vie,
c'est sans doute celui-ci que je regrette le plus. Ce ne fut pas le
temps de ma gloire, si j'en eus jamais' (*Œuvres complètes*, XLIX,
537). In 1750 he abandoned Versailles for Potsdam, where
fresh disillusionment awaited him. Louis XV, for his part, was
equally disillusioned with Voltaire:

> . . . Il le craignait, et ne l'estimait pas. Il ne put s'empêcher de
> dire: 'Au reste, je l'ai aussi bien traité que Louis XIV a traité
> Racine et Boileau; je lui ai donné, comme Louis XIV à Racine,
> une charge de gentilhomme ordinaire et des pensions: ce n'est pas
> ma faute s'il a fait des sottises, et s'il a la prétention d'être cham-
> bellan, d'avoir une croix et de souper avec un roi. Ce n'est pas la
> mode en France.' (Mme du Hausset, *Mémoires*, pp. 98-9)

[1] The eighteenth century French form of the English word 'whist' (or 'whisk').

'Il le craignait' could scarcely have been applied fifty years earlier to Louis XIV's attitude to Racine! But Louis XV hated the *Philosophes* for their unorthodox religious views. Mme du Hausset relates how he made fun of the smallness of the pension which, a few years later, Frederick offered to d'Alembert, but when Mme de Pompadour suggested that he offer d'Alembert twice the sum and forbid him to take the pension from Potsdam, he refused 'parce qu'il regardait d'Alembert comme un impie' (p. 112).

There were no favours to be expected from the court for such dangerous fellows. The *Philosophes* thus accepted with delight the patronage of foreign rulers like Frederick or Catherine the Great, partly as a balm to their injured pride at being neglected in their own country, and partly as a shield against persecution. It is difficult to imagine that in private the *Philosophes* should have had many illusions about their illustrious patrons; it is significant that, after Voltaire's unhappy sojourn at Potsdam, none of the prominent French writers acceded to pressing invitations to establish themselves permanently at the court of their patrons. D'Alembert might visit Frederick at Potsdam, yet he politely but firmly declined all invitations to settle there; it took Diderot a good ten years to make up his mind to undertake the long journey to visit his benefactress, Catherine the Great, and he had no intention of remaining permanently in Russia. For their part Frederick and Catherine enjoyed having such excellent publicity agents as the *Philosophes*, without taking their advanced ideas too seriously.

No doubt it was pleasant for the *Philosophes*, exposed to the ill-will of the government at home which, for instance, authorized the public performance of Palissot's satirical comedy, *Les Philosophes*, in which, under transparent disguises, Diderot and Helvétius were depicted as gallows-birds, to point to the favours which they enjoyed from other governments. Similarly, in the knowledge that they were appreciated elsewhere, there was some compensation for the attacks of a Fréron whose *Année littéraire* was authorized by the government while there never existed a *Journal Philosophique* in which they could have presented their own ideas to the reading public. As Grimm put it in 1765:

Tous ces auteurs si célèbres, si admirés dans toute l'Europe, sont haïs et détestés ici, et surtout généralement réputés dangereux. On entretient un homme[1] exprès: cet homme a le privilège exclusif de leur dire des sottises deux fois par mois, et ce privilège lui vaut douze à quinze mille livres par an. . . . Je ne conçois pas cette satisfaction de la nation à entendre du mal de ceux dont les talents l'ont honorée et illustrée chez ses voisins. . . . Comment se peut-il qu'un homme à talents soit digne des bienfaits des princes étrangers, à la gloire desquels il ne peut contribuer, et indigne de la protection de son souverain, dont il illustre le règne par ses travaux? (*Correspondance littéraire*, VI, 309)

Or take the letter which Diderot wrote to the *lieutenant de police* in 1770 when he was consulted by him about the manuscript of a play, *Les Satiriques* (actually by his old enemy, Palissot, though he was not aware of the fact), which attacked the men of letters of Paris. His letter concludes:

Il ne m'appartient pas, monsieur, de vous donner des conseilst mais, si vous pouvez faire en sorte qu'il ne soit pas dit qu'on ais deux fois, avec votre permission, insulté en public ceux de vo, concitoyens qu'on honore dans toutes les parties de l'Europe; dont les ouvrages sont dévorés de près et au loin, que les étrangers révèrent, appellent et récompensent, qu'on citera, et qui concourront à la gloire du nom français quand vous ne serez plus, ni eux non plus; que les voyageurs se font un devoir de visiter à présent qu'ils sont, et qu'ils se font honneur d'avoir connus lorsqu'ils sont de retour dans leur patrie, je crois, monsieur, que vous ferez sagement. (*Œuvres complétes*, XX, 12)

Here spoke injured pride; but foreign patrons also had their uses when persecution threatened a writer. When Marmontel's *Bélisaire* fell foul of the Sorbonne in 1767, he tells us in his memoirs, 'les lettres des souverains de l'Europe et celles des hommes les plus éclairés et les plus sages m'arrivaient de tous les côtés, pleines d'éloges pour mon livre, qu'ils disaient être le bréviaire des rois'. Catherine the Great translated the book and dedicated her translation to an Archbishop; Maria Theresa ordered the work to be printed in her dominions—'elle', Marmontel adds, 'qui était si sévère à l'égard des écrits qui attaquaient la religion'. Marmontel made full use of such

---

[1] Fréron.

support to disarm the authorities: 'Je ne négligeai pas, comme vous pensez bien, de donner connaissance à la cour et au parlement de ce succès universel; et ni l'une ni l'autre n'eurent envie de partager le ridicule de la Sorbonne.' (*Mémoires*, II, 284)

The difference in outlook between men of letters of the age of Louis XIV and those of the eighteenth century was well summed up by Mercier when he wrote, towards the end of the Ancien Régime:

... Jamais la prostitution du bel esprit n'a été poussée si loin qu'aux pieds de Louis XIV.

Les hommes sont de grands enfants. Quelques statues, quelques tableaux, quelques morceaux de poésie font donner à un siècle, qui d'ailleurs a été malheureux, le nom pompeux de siècle des beaux-arts, de siècle de gloire.

La révocation de l'Édit de Nantes en 1685 a passé sans réclamation quelconque de la part des gens de lettres. Nous disons donc hardiment que ce siècle, malgé sa renommée, n'était pas véritablement éclairé. Il n'en serait pas de même aujourd'hui. La littérature surveille le gouvernement et lui sauverait un pareil écart.

Qu'importe que l'on ait eu alors des épîtres poétiques de Boileau, grossier flatteur, et des tragédies de Racine, simple et fin courtisan, qui s'occupait de la grâce versatile? Ce sont là des niaiseries en comparaison des matières politiques sur lesquelles on peut répandre d'ailleurs tout l'intérêt et l'agrément que peuvent avoir ces deux écrivains. (*Tableau de Paris*, VIII, 104-5)

What then was the attitude of the men of letters of the age to political and social questions? It would be idle to attempt to sum up in some simple formula the highly complex theories on society and government which were thrown up in the general ferment of ideas which accompanied the disintegration of the Ancien Régime. There were, needless to say, enormous variations in outlook, ranging from vigorous exponents of conservative ideas (a *revolution* was, after all, necessary to create a new society in 1789) to a group of writers whose theories at least foreshadow modern socialism as well as the communist ideas which Babeuf and his group were to attempt to realize during the later period of the Revolution. Even among the group of writers whom we for the sake of convenience label as *Philosophes*, there were many differences in emphasis.

One point, however, is reasonably clear. The revolt against orthodox ideas in religion and philosophy preceded that against the existing government and society. It was in 1771, in the midst of the agitation caused by Maupeou's *coup d'état* against the Parlements, that Diderot wrote the famous lines:

> Chaque siècle a son esprit qui le caractérise. L'esprit du nôtre semble être celui de la liberté. La première attaque contre la superstition a été violente, sans mesure. Une fois que les hommes ont osé d'une manière quelconque donner l'assaut à la barrière de la religion, cette barrière la plus formidable qui existe comme la plus respectée, il est impossible de s'arrêter. Dès qu'ils ont tourné des regards menaçants contre la majesté du ciel, ils ne manquent pas le moment d'après de les diriger contre la souveraineté de la terre. Le câble qui tient et comprime l'humanité est formé de deux cordes; l'une ne peut céder sans que l'autre vienne à rompre. (*Œuvres complètes*, XX, 28)

Yet this was written only eighteen years before the Revolution and there seems little doubt that it reflects the effervescence caused by Maupeou's onslaught on the Parlements, for Diderot himself adds in the same letter: 'Pour ma part, je proteste que dans un autre temps je n'eusse jamais conçu les idées que je suis capable aujourd'hui de nourrir'.

After 1789 all sorts of counter-revolutionary writers built up a fantastic legend according to which the *Philosophes* deliberately prepared the way for the Revolution and were the forerunners of Robespierre and Saint-Just. All the responsibility for the upheaval of 1789 was laid on the shoulders of men like Voltaire and Rousseau. As a satirical song of the Restoration period put it:

> On est laid à Nanterre,
> C'est la faute à Voltaire,
> Et bête à Palaiseau,
> C'est la faute à Rousseau.
>
> Je ne suis pas notaire,
> C'est la faute à Voltaire,
> Je suis petit oiseau,
> C'est la faute à Rousseau. . . .

Yet there is a great amount of truth in the remarks made by Sénac de Meilhan, a former *Intendant*, about the limited influence of the *Philosophes* in the realm of social and political ideas:

> Les écrits de Voltaire ont certainement nui à la religion et ébranlé la croyance dans un assez grand nombre, mais ils n'ont aucun rapport avec les affaires du gouvernement, et sont plus favorables que contraires à la monarchie. Les ouvrages de Montesquieu sont des apologies de la monarchie, de la noblesse et des parlements. Le *Contrat social* de J.-J. Rousseau renferme des idées conformes au systeme de liberté illimitée qui a été adopté; mais ce livre profond et abstrait etait peu lu et entendu de bien peu de gens. L'abbé de Mably est peut-être de tous les écrivains celui qui a rassemblé le plus grand nombre d'arguments contraires aux maximes depuis longtemps suivies; mais ses ouvrages, si pesamment écrits, avaient peu de vogue . . . C'est quand la Révolution a été entamée qu'on a cherché dans Mably, dans Rousseau, des armes pour soutenir le système vers lequel entraînait l'effervescence de quelques esprits hardis. Mais ce ne sont point les auteurs que j'ai cités qui ont enflammé les têtes. (*Le Gouvernement, les mœurs et les conditions en France*, pp. 172-3)

One can scarcely imagine M. de Voltaire as a *sans-culotte* or even as a Girondin. The political ideas of a man like Rousseau seem to have made singularly little impact on public opinion before 1789 and not to have been treated as more than an exercise in highly abstract reasoning. Montesquieu certainly had more influence than Sénac de Meilhan credits him with, but in the rich confusion of his *Esprit des Lois* it was rather his stress on the privileges of the nobility and on the role of the aristocracy and the Parlements as *pouvoirs intermédiaires* which was influential; but while it served as the Bible of the privileged orders in their struggle to curb the authority of the Crown and to regain a share of political power, it was the aristocratic revolt of 1787 and 1788 which it precipitated, not the fall of the Bastille and the events which followed.

It has been argued that the Revolution would have taken place and followed exactly the same course, if there had been no *Philosophes*; but that is to throw the baby out with the bathwater. According to Condorcet, the only prominent *Philosophe* to play any considerable part in the events of the Revolution, the great writers of the movement were equally opposed to political and religious tyranny; only they changed their line of attack according to the aim they had in mind in writing a particular work:

ménageant le despotisme quand ils combattaient les absurdités religieuses, et le culte quand ils s'élevaient contre la tyrannie; attaquant ces deux fléaux dans leur principe, quand même ils paraissaient n'en vouloir qu'à des abus révoltants ou ridicules, et frappant ces arbres funestes dans leurs racines, quand ils semblaient se borner à élaguer quelques branches égarées; tantôt apprenant aux amis de la liberté que la superstition, qui couvre le despotisme d'un bouclier impénétrable, est la première victime qu'ils doivent immoler, la première chaîne qu'ils doivent briser; tantôt, au contraire, la dénonçant aux despotes comme la véritable ennemie de leur pouvoir, et les effrayant du tableau de ses hypocrites complots et de ses fureurs sanguinaires; mais ne se lassant jamais de réclamer l'indépendance de la raison, la liberté d'écrire comme le droit, comme le salut du genre humain; s'élevant, avec une infatigable énergie, contre tous les crimes du fanatisme et de la tyrannie; poursuivant dans la religion, dans l'administration, dans les mœurs, dans les lois, tout ce qui portait le caractère de l'oppression, de la dureté, de la barbarie; . . . prenant enfin, pour cri de guerre, *raison, tolérance, humanité.*
(*Esquisse d'un tableau historique*, pp. 160-1)

No doubt this passage was coloured by the events of 1789 and the following years; no doubt too in interpreting it, one would have to allow for the differences between individual authors among the *Philosophes* and the differences between what they thought in, say, 1740 and 1770. Yet of one thing there is no question: the writers of eighteenth century France played a very different role from that of their predecessors in the age of Louis XIV. And that was primarily because whereas Corneille and Molière, Racine and La Fontaine witnessed the period of French history which saw the final establishment of absolutism, Voltaire and Montesquieu, Rousseau and Diderot lived in the age which saw its gradual disintegration until in 1789 it was swept away along with the whole aristocratic fabric of the Ancien Régime.

# CHAPTER IX

# THE BIRTH OF MODERN FRANCE

THE twenty-six years between the meeting of the *États généraux* in 1789 and the final downfall of Napoleon at Waterloo wrought profound changes in France, as indeed in Europe. The France of the Ancien Régime with its absolute monarchy and its still semi-feudal society was transformed in these years into modern France, not, it is true, the France which we know in the middle of the twentieth century, but at least into a country with laws, institutions and manners immeasurably closer to us than those which prevailed in 1789. In those years much of the future history of France, down even to our own day, was moulded. In the pages which follow we shall be concerned less with the mighty drama of the Revolution and the Napoleonic era, absorbing as it still remains, than with the long-term results of the events of these years, with the transition from the Ancien Régime to modern times.

The meeting of the *États généraux* in 1789 quickly led to the formation of a National Assembly, which was followed, on 14 July, by the fall of the Bastille and the end of absolute monarchy. Between 1789 and 1791 the National Assembly (now renamed *Assemblée Constituante*) gave France a constitution, the first of many constitutions, and a new set of laws and institutions; feudalism was abolished, the power of the old privileged orders and the Parlements broken. The flight of Louis XVI and the royal family to Varennes in June 1791 and their enforced return to Paris was virtually the end of the monarchy, though it lingered on for another year.

The Revolution did not stop at the point to which the Constituent Assembly had taken it, though many of the radical leaders of 1789 would have preferred it to do so. The Legislative Assembly (1791-2) marks a more radical phase, which was partly brought about by the threat of invasion by the counter-revolutionary powers, Prussia and Austria. This period in the

Revolution was followed by a yet more extreme phase, during which control of the government was seized by the Jacobins, who were put into power by the insurrection of 10 August 1792.

After this date the Legislative Assembly gave place to the *Convention* which remained in session until 1795. It abolished the monarchy and proclaimed a republic; Louis XVI was executed in January 1793. For ten months, from September 1793 to July 1794, down to the famous date of the 9 Thermidor, the desperate struggle against counter-revolution, both at home and abroad, led to the Reign of Terror. The dominating figure in this regime was Robespierre, whose name is associated with the most radical stage of the Revolution.

His fall and execution (9-10 Thermidor) were followed by a period of reaction. The *Convention* finally evolved a new constitution and gave way to the *Directoire*, a government of five *Directeurs*, in 1795. The next four years were a period of uncertainty and lack of clear policy, as the government inclined now to the right, now to the left, in its struggle against both Jacobins and Royalists.

This regime was brought to an end by Napoleon in 1799 with the *coup d'état* of 18 Brumaire, which inaugurated a new form of government, the Consulate. Napoleon gradually made himself First Consul, then Consul for life and finally, in 1804, Emperor. The Empire which he had founded was to last exactly ten years, until his enforced retirement to Elba in 1814; its revival in 1815—the Hundred Days—was cut short by the Battle of Waterloo.

For nearly a quarter of a century, from 1792 to 1815, France was engaged in practically incessant wars. Her armies fought from Spain to Egypt and to the streets of Moscow. At its height under Napoleon French domination over Europe stretched from Spain to Poland, from North Germany to Italy, and incidentally brought in its train the abolition of feudalism over most of the Continent. The military glory of the Napoleonic era did not die with the collapse of Napoleon's Empire; it cast its shadow over the next half-century of French history. His nephew, Louis Napoleon, 'Napoléon le petit' as Hugo called him, and the Second Empire which he founded in 1852 did not vanish from the French scene until the surrender at Sedan in 1870.

At first sight the successive forms of government under which Napoleon ruled over France seem to represent a complete break with the Revolution and everything it had stood for. After seizing power in 1799, he proceeded to satisfy his own personal ambitions; he gradually made himself Consul for life, then Emperor, and, so he hoped, the founder of a new dynasty. He even created a new nobility and tried to revive the court. In his political institutions he sought to return to something close to the monarchy of the Ancien Régime, to the very negation of the principle of the sovereignty of the people proclaimed in 1789 in the *Déclaration des Droits de l'Homme*. The parliamentary institutions of his reign were a mere façade, as they were almost entirely devoid of effective power; when it was summoned, the legislature was completely servile. There was in fact no control by the nation or its representatives over taxation and expenditure or any of the acts of the government. Napoleon was clearly an absolute ruler. There was no liberty for the individual; France was a police-state in which people were arrested and imprisoned without trial. There was no freedom of the press. Only four newspapers were allowed in Paris, and their editors were appointed by the Emperor; only eighty papers were tolerated in the whole of the rest of France, and they were under the strict control of the government. The number of printers was limited, and for writers there was a rigid censorship, as both Chateaubriand and Mme de Staël, the two greatest writers of the period, found to their cost.

It is true that Napoleon undid the political conquests of the Revolution; but this was the most transitory part of his achievements and one which contributed to his speedy downfall. There is another side to his rule—a more important one, since it was to prove much more durable: his consolidation of the achievements of the Revolution. His regime did not in fact represent a complete break with the events and achievements of the ten years since 1789; he came to end the Revolution, but not to destroy all its positive results.

That the Revolution, for all its rapid changes and its complete instability, did achieve positive results is a fact that tends to be forgotten in those pictures of the period which present it as a mere orgy of almost diabolical destruction. And yet it was the Revolution which, in the intellectual and artistic sphere, endowed France with some of its most famous institutions; indeed it was the *Convention*, the most radical of all its assemblies, which, before and after the fall of Robespierre, played the leading part in this field. To the Revolution France owes not only the first outlines of a system of primary, secondary and university education, but such famous institutions as the Archives Nationales and the Conservatoire de Musique, the École Polytechnique, the Muséum d'Histoire Naturelle and the Conservatoire des Arts et Métiers. Yet in the social sphere too the Revolution had positive achievements to set alongside its destruction of the power of the two privileged orders; Napoleon's regime was to rest largely on the support of the two classes which had carried through and profited from the Revolution: the middle classes and the peasants. Indeed it was largely because he satisfied their aspirations that he rose to power.

The Revolution abolished in the name of equality the old social hierarchy of the Ancien Régime; no longer were there three different orders of citizens of different social status. Hence forth all men were equal in the eyes of the law. No longer were there two 'superior' orders in the state whose members enjoyed exemption or partial exemption from most direct taxes; henceforth all Frenchmen were to contribute to the upkeep of the state according to their wealth, not according to their social status. The Revolution also abolished the buying and selling of official posts (*la vénalité des charges*), which had been so important a feature of the social history of France during the Ancien Régime; henceforth talent and not wealth was to secure admission to the civil service and the judiciary. It goes without saying that the aristocratic monopoly of all high posts in the army, the civil service, the judiciary and the Church—one of the main grievances of the middle classes before 1789—was completely abolished.

In the economic sphere the Revolution promoted changes in harmony with the interests of the middle classes. The guilds, long attacked as reactionary monopolies, were abolished; the rigid state control over industry, which had long been denounced in the name of the principle of *laissez-faire*, was swept away. The obstacles to trade presented by the existence of internal customs barriers were removed, and the chaos of weights and measures of the Ancien Régime was replaced by the decimal metric system. A new set of laws, finally embodied in the *Code Napoléon*, gave the new society which had emerged from the Revolution a legal system which was uniform from one end of the country to the other. Its essentially bourgeois attitude to questions of property and the family has often been stressed. Property, declared article 17 of the *Déclaration des Droits de l'Homme*, was 'un droit inviolable et sacré'; article 544 of the *Code Napoléon* stresses the absolute right of the individual to make what use he wishes of his property: 'La propriété est le droit de jouir et disposer des choses de la manière la plus absolue, pourvu qu'on n'en fasse pas un usage prohibé par les lois ou par les règlements.'

All the new laws of the period which regulate relations between masters and men were tilted in favour of the property-owning classes. The section of the *Code Napoléon* which deals with the hiring of servants and workmen contains the characteristic clause:

> Le maître est cru sur son affirmation,
> Pour la quotité des gages;
> Pour le paiement du salaire de l'année échue;
> Et pour les à-comptes donnés pour l'année courante.
>
> (article 1781)

Combinations of workmen to secure higher wages and better conditions were strongly discouraged; the English Combination Acts of 1799 and 1800 had their counterpart in the legislation of the Revolutionary and Napoleonic period. In 1791 the *loi Le Chapelier* forbade under heavy penalties all combinations of workmen. It is true that, like a law of 1803, it also forbade combinations of employers; yet the real aim of these laws is clearly brought out by the much heavier penalties imposed on workmen than on their masters for infractions of the law.

The peasants too saw some at least of their aspirations realized by the Revolution. They still formed the overwhelming majority of the nation, and they had their own ideas as to what should be done on the land—ideas which they gradually translated into reality by bringing pressure to bear on the different revolutionary assemblies. Naturally there were enormous differences in the aspirations of the members of the peasantry, since conditions varied so much from region to region, and moreover there were all shades of wealth and poverty from the large peasant landowner or farmer down to the landless labourer, a very considerable class in many parts of France before 1789. It is certain that the Revolution did very little for the great mass of landless or nearly landless peasants. Yet the abolition of tithes and feudal dues did benefit many of them, as did reforms in the taxation system which led to a fairer assessment of direct taxes. At first the Constituent Assembly merely decreed that peasants were to buy out the holders of feudal dues, but in 1793, in the most radical phase of the Revolution, they were finally abolished without compensation. This measure was undoubtedly of great benefit to the peasant who owned land—and such peasants were numerous before the Revolution—since before 1789 his right of property was incomplete, as he had to make to his lord payments in kind and money and perform perhaps also certain services. By abolishing the remnants of feudalism the Revolution transformed his copyhold into freehold, that is, made the peasant absolute proprietor of his land.

Moreover, the peasants were given an opportunity to acquire more land, through the sales of Church property, the estates of *émigrés*, and the royal domain. It is true that the methods by which this land was sold did not allow the mass of landless or nearly landless peasants to acquire much of it. Some of the land owned by the *émigré* nobles was regained by them, either because it was still unsold at the Restoration or because it was bought back for them by their agents. Again, the amount of land made available for sale varied quite capriciously from region to region; in some parts of France, for instance, the Church owned practically no land, and consequently little or none came on the market. Again, it is fairly well established that the principal purchasers of the *biens nationaux*, as they were called, were the middle classes and the more prosperous sections of the peasantry. Yet even so some land probably went to the medium and smaller peasants.

Moreover, if we compare what was happening in France in these years with events in England, we see how the French Revolution strengthened the hold of the peasantry on the land at the very moment when on this side of the Channel the opposite process was in full swing. Here the enclosure movement, combined with the agricultural revolution, increased the productivity of our agriculture, but drove the smaller peasants off the land, reducing them to the status of agricultural labourers or sending them into the towns to seek work in the new factories. In France the enclosure movement, despite the nominal approval given to it by the revolutionary assemblies, went on only very slowly, as did too the revolution in agricultural techniques. The Revolution of 1789, so far as the land was concerned, acted, paradoxical as it may sound, as a stabilizing factor, in the sense that it tended to preserve, and to preserve down to our own day, the *status quo* on the land. It is wrong to imagine, as is sometimes done, that the land of France today is mainly in the hands of a vast number of small peasant-proprietors; a high proportion of the land is in fact in the hands of a relatively small number of owners. That was in fact the position before 1789, a situation which the Revolution, so to speak, froze; by preventing the mass of small peasant land-owners from being driven off the land, it maintained the mixture of small- and large-scale property which existed before 1789, although not the overpopulation of the countryside which existed before the Revolution, as in the last century and a half large numbers of the poorer sections of the peasantry have been drawn to the towns, leaving some of the less fertile parts of the country very sparsely populated.

Naturally the French peasants, especially those who had been able to acquire more land, were, like the new bourgeois land-owners, passionately attached to the Revolution. They lived in constant fear of an attempt to put the clock back, to revive feudal dues and tithes, and to seize back the *biens nationaux*, the land taken from the clergy and the *émigrés*. They supported Napoleon and his regime precisely because he confirmed the land policy of the Revolution.

The positive side of the work of Napoleon consisted in endowing France with institutions which consolidated the changes brought about by the Revolution and which in many cases have survived, with modifications, right through the nineteenth century down to our own day. Just as the Revolution had replaced the utter chaos of weights and measures which existed in France before 1789, by the simple, clear and uniform decimal metric system, so the revolutionary assemblies sought to provide one code of civil law for the whole of France, to take the place of the chaos of laws before 1789. Under the Ancien Régime the southern half of the kingdom had been under Roman Law, while the rest had been under customary law (*droit coutumïer*) which varied not only from province to province, but even from district to district. The aim of the *Code Napoléon* was to weld into a coherent whole, modifying them where necessary, the large collection of laws produced by the different revolutionary assemblies.

The *Code Napoléon*, more accurately known as the *Code Civil* since Napoleon played only a minor part in its preparation, was promulgated in 1804. It interprets in a fairly conservative sense the principles of the Revolution. While proclaiming such principles as equality before the law, freedom of conscience and freedom for trade and industry, it confirmed the abolition of feudal dues by making all land freehold. Thus the peasants were assured of the full ownership of the land which they had held as copyhold before 1789. The manner in which the new code regulated the transmission of land by will was also of considerable importance. Before 1789 in most parts of France, while the land in the possession of *roturiers* was divided up in equal shares between their children after their death, the estates of the aristocracy had been held together by the *droit d'aînesse*, which gave the lion's share to the eldest son, and by entail (*substitution*). In its equalitarian and anti-aristocratic attitude to property the *Convention* had abolished entail and had laid it down that all property should be divided in equal shares between the children of the testator. The *Code Napoléon* went back on this: although it forbade entail save in very exceptional circumstances, it qualified the principle of equal shares among the children of a testator by allowing him to dispose as he wished of a half to a quarter of his estate (half if there was only one child, a third if there were two, and a quarter if there were three or more). He could thus, if he liked, give more favourable treatment to his eldest son than to his other children, and help to keep an estate in the family for generations. On the other hand the right conferred upon heirs to insist upon a breaking up of the main part of the estate in equal shares had important consequences: over the last hundred and fifty years it has tended to a continuous subdivision of the land, one of the most striking features of the French countryside.

The *Code Civil* also maintained the Revolutionary principles affecting the family, though it interpreted them in a decidedly conservative sense. In 1791 the registration of births, deaths and marriages was taken out of the hands of the Church and entrusted to the municipal authorites. The confirmation of this law by Napoleon has its effects down to our day on the celebration of marriages in France; while the Roman Catholic Church continues to look upon marriage as a sacrament, the State regards it merely as a civil contract, and it continues to insist that the civil ceremony, which takes place before the mayor with a reading of the relevant articles of the *Code Civil*, must precede any marriage in church. The *Code Napoléon* also confirmed the institution of divorce, another question on which, then as now, the French Church did not see eye to eye with the State; it is true that the *Code* made divorce far more difficult than it had been during the Revolution, and as in everything dealing with the family put women in a very unfavourable position compared with men.

Napoleon also brought to an end the conflict between Church and State which had arisen during the Revolution over the Civil Constitution imposed upon the French clergy. In 1801 he reached agreement with the Pope over a new Concordat which recognized Catholicism as 'la religion de la grande majorité des Français'. This formula implied a rejection of the claims of Catholicism to be recognized as the state religion. The Pope had to make other concessions: he had to recognize the French Republic (this was before the founding of the Empire) and the sale of Church property during the Revolution. In return the government undertook to provide the clergy with 'un traitement convenable'. As under the Concordat of 1516, archbishops and bishops were to be chosen by the State, but invested by the Pope as spiritual head of the Church; *curés* were now to be appointed by the bishops, but from among persons acceptable to the government. A similar arrangement was made for French Protestants, both Calvinists and Lutherans, whose pastors were also to be paid by the State. Napoleon's religious settlement was to endure for over a century until the final separation of Church and State in 1905.

The educational system of France still owes much to the changes brought about by the Revolution and Napoleon. While it is true that the educational projects of the various Revolutionary assemblies remained for the most part on paper, those of the *Convention*, especially before the fall of Robespierre, were particularly far-sighted, and some interesting educational experiments were also carried out during the *Directoire*. Napoleon's influence on French education was often far from beneficent, and in some spheres, particularly primary education, his outlook was much less enlightened than that of the men of the Revolution. It is probable that primary education, especially that of girls, was in a worse position in France in 1815 than it had been in 1789; Napoleon did not wish the education of the masses to go beyond the three Rs, and a good part of the primary education provided during his reign was the work of religious orders.

It was secondary and higher education, catering for the sons (though not the daughters) of the middle classes, that interested the Emperor. A law of 1806 instituted the *Université*, a body upon which he conferred a monopoly of teaching; in practice it concerned itself with secondary education in the *lycées*, state schools founded by Napoleon, and with higher education in the re-established universities All secondary and university education was, on paper at least, given in state establishments staffed by teachers paid by the state. In practice, even during the Napoleonic period, secondary schools outside the State system had nearly as many pupils as the state *lycées* and the *collèges* run by the towns, and, with the breaking of the state monopoly of education in 1850, the so-called *écoles libres*, run by the Catholic Church, came to play an important part in French education, particularly the secondary schools which today contain nearly half as many pupils as those run by the State. Yet the state system of education, from the primary school to the university, under the control of the Ministry of Education, continues to dominate the French educational scene, partly owing to its monopoly not only of conferring university degrees, but also of the *baccalauréat*, the equivalent of the General Certificate of Education. Down to our own day, all members of the state educational system, including university teachers, remain civil servants (*fonctionnaires*).

In addition to the *Code Civil* which exercised a profound influence on the legal system of a large number of countries scattered over the world, our period also saw the creation of the complicated system of law-courts, ranging from that of the *juge de paix*, established in each *canton*, to the *cour de cassation*, the supreme court of appeal, and including the special administrative tribunals which culminate in the *Conseil d'État*. To Napoleon France also owes the Banque de France, estaclished in 1800. But perhaps the most important legacy from the Revolutionary and Napoleonic era was the system of local government and its relations with the central government.

It was in 1790 that the Constituent Assembly replaced the chaotic administrative regions of the Ancien Régime by a new division of the country into departments; each department was later divided into *arrondissements*, beneath them into *cantons*, and at the base came the smallest unit of local government, the *commune*. When Napoleon seized power, he reimposed on France the rigid system of centralization which goes a long way back into the history of the Ancien Régime when the agents of the central government in the provinces, the *Intendants*, assisted by their *subdélégués*, exercised strict control over local government. Using the new framework of department, *arrondissement* and *commune*, he installed a *Préfet* in each department, a *sous-préfet* in each *arrondissement* outside the departmental capital, and a mayor in every *commune*. The system has naturally been much modified since Napoleon's day, especially in the direction of giving greater power to the elected bodies—the *conseil général* of the departments and the *conseil municipal* of the *communes*. Yet the framework remains very much the same as that created by Napoleon a century and a half ago. Although the mayor is now elected by the *conseil municipal*, he is only bound by decisions of that body in matters of purely communal concern, since he remains what he was made by Napoleon: a state official charged with carrying out certain acts on behalf of the government. Again, although the *conseils généraux* have been given wider powers, the *Préfet*, along with the *sous-préfets* and other officials under his control, continues to represent the central government in the department and to exercise a very considerable authority.

From these examples it is clear that the Revolution was not a mere orgy of destruction and that Napoleon's empire was not simply a colourful episode in French history. In the place of the society destroyed by the Revolution a new society was created. In the course of some twenty-five years the evolution was completed which transformed the absolutist, semi-feudal France of the Ancien Régime into a modern state with new institutions and new laws. In contrast to England with its slow, evolutionary historical development, France underwent in this quarter of a century a rapid and complete transformation.

The social and political privileges which the clergy and nobility had inherited from the Middle Ages were destroyed; absolute monarchy, based on the doctrine of the Divine Right of kings, was utterly and finally rejected. The peasantry was strengthened in its hold on the land, while the middle classes passed from a state of social and political inferiority to the dominant position which they were to occupy in the nineteenth and twentieth centuries. New laws and institutions, a new system of administration, of education, a new relationship between Church and State, were set up in conformity with the new society which had emerged in the revolutionary period.

These twenty-five years have left their mark on French social and political history for the last century and a half. 1789 represents in a dozen senses a decisive moment in French history. Even today the break with the past which took place then marks the dividing-line between Left and Right in French political life; and the influence of the events of these years made itself felt not only in France, but over the whole of Europe as well as in many other corners of the globe.

# SOME SUGGESTIONS FOR FURTHER READING

## I. Social and Political Background

A. Cobban, *A History of Modern France*, Vol. I. *Old Régime and Revolution, 1715-1799*. Harmondsworth (Penguin Books), 1957.

F. L. Ford, *Robe and Sword, the Regrouping of the French Aristocracy after Louis XIV*. Cambridge (Harvard University Press), 1953.

*Histoire de France*, ed. M. Reinhard, Vol. II. R. Mousnier, *La France de Louis XV*; M. Reinhard, *La Crise Révolutionnaire*. Paris (Larousse), 1954.

P. Goubert, *L'Ancien Régime*, Vol. I, Paris (Armand Colin), 1969.

C. Kunstler, *La Vie quotidienne sous Louis XV*. Paris (Hachette), 1953.
*La Vie quotidienne sous Louis XVI*. Paris (Hachette), 1950.

G. Lefebvre, *Quatre Vingt Neuf*. Paris (Maison du Livre Français), 1939.

R. Mandrou, *La France aux XVII^e et XVIII^e siècles*, Paris (Presses Universitaires), 1967.

H. Methivier, *L'Ancien Régime*, Paris (Collection "Que sais-je?"), 1961. *Le Siècle de Louis XV*, Paris (Collection "Que sais-je?"), 1966.

E. Préclin and V. L. Tapié, *Le XVIII^e Siècle*. Paris (Presses Universitaires), 1952. 2 vols.

P. Sagnac, *La Formation de la Société Française Moderne*, Vol. II. *La Révolution des Idées et des Mœurs et le Déclin de l'Ancien Régime (1715-1788)*. Paris (Presses Universitaires), 1946.

H. Sée. *La France économique et sociale au XVIII^e siècle*. Paris (Armand Colin), 1925.

## II. Literary Background

J. Bertaut, *La Vie littéraire au XVIII^e siècle*. Paris (Tallandier), 1954.

A. Brulé, *La Vie au XVIII^e siècle. Les Gens de Lettres*. Paris (Seheur), 1929.

A. François, *La Langue postclassique* in F. Brunot, *Histoire de la langue française des origines à nos jours*, Vol. VI, Part II. Paris (Armand Colin), 1932.

M. GLOTZ and M. MAIRE, *Salons du XVIIIᵉ Siècle*. Paris (Nouvelles Éditions Latines), 1949.

G. LANSON (ed.), *Choix de Lettres du XVIIIᵉ Siècle*. Paris (Hachette), n.d.

J. LOUGH, *Paris Theatre Audiences in the Seventeenth and Eighteenth Centuries*. London (Oxford University Press), 1957.

K. MARTIN, *French Liberal Thought in the Eighteenth Century. A Study of Political Ideas from Bayle to Condorcet*, 2nd edition. London (Turnstile Press), 1954.

D. MORNET, *La Pensée Française au XVIIIᵉ siècle*. Paris (Armand Colin), 1932.

   *Les Origines intellectuelles de la Révolution Française, 1715-1787*. Paris (Armand Colin), 1933.

M. PELLISSON, *Les Hommes de lettres au XVIIIᵉ siècle*. Paris (Armand Colin), 1911.

L. RÉAU, *L'Europe Française au Siècle des Lumières*. Paris (Albin Michel), 1938.

The period of the Revolution and Napoleon would require a special reading list to itself. Along with A. Cobban's *History of Modern France* (listed above), the following works provide an introduction to the period:

A. GOODWIN, *The French Revolution*. London (Hutchinson), 1953.

L. HALPHEN and P. SAGNAC (editors): *Peuples et Civilisations: Histoire générale*. Vol. XIII. G. Lefebvre, *La Révolution Française*. Paris (Presses Universitaires), 1951. Vol. XIV. G. Lefebvre, *Napoléon*. Paris, 1953, 4th edition.

J. GODECHOT, *Les Institutions de la France sous la Révolution et l'Empire*. Paris (Presses Universitaires), 1951.

There is no complete modern edition of Arthur Young's *Travels in France* except in the French translation of H. Sée (Paris, 1931, 3 vols.). The most useful modern English edition is that by C. Maxwell (Cambridge University Press), 2nd edition, 1950.

# INDEX OF AUTHORS QUOTED

*The editions listed are not necessarily the earliest, but are those referred to in the text*

D'Argenson, *Journal et mémoires*, ed. E. J. B. Rathery, Paris, 1859-67, 9 vols., 31-6, 113, 119, 126, 161, 162, 175, 176-8.

Arnould, *De la balance du Commerce et des relations commerciales de la France dans toutes les parties du monde*, Paris, 1791, 3 vols., 72.

Bachaumont, *Mémoires secrets pour servir à l'histoire de la République des Lettres en France de 1762 jusqu'à nos jours*, London, 1777-89, 36 vols., 234-5, 253, 263, 306.

Barbier, *Chronique de la Régence et du règne de Louis XV (1718-63)*, Paris, 1866, 8 vols., 33, 85-6, 91-2, 105, 115-16, 118-19, 140-1, 152-3, 155, 156, 157, 169-70, 172, 173, 174, 176, 178-9, 182.

Barnave, *Œuvres*, ed. Bérenger de la Drôme, Paris, 1843, 4 vols., 128-9, 132.

Beaumarchais, *Œuvres complètes*, ed. E. Fournier, Paris, 1876, 255.
*Théâtre complet*, ed. R. d'Hermies, Paris, 1952, 95, 288, 290.
*Théâtre complet: Lettres relatives à son théâtre*, ed. M. Allem, Paris, 1934, 289.

Besnard, *Souvenirs d'un nonagénaire*, ed. Célestin Port, Paris, 1880, 2 vols., 42, 60, 77-8, 99-100, 108-9.

P. Bonnefon, 'Diderot prisonnier à Vincennes' (*Revue d'histoire littéraire de la France*, Vol. VI, pp. 200-24), 309.

Bouillé, *Mémoires*, ed. F. Barrière, Paris, 1859, 96, 111.

Boulainvilliers, *État de la France*, London, 1737, 8 vols., 128.

Burke, *Reflections on the Revolution in France*, London, 1790, 201.

Buvat, *Journal de la Régence*, ed. E. Campardon, Paris, 1865, 2 vols., 145.

Cailhava, *Théâtre*, Paris, 1781-2, 2 vols., 252-3.

Calonne, *Discours prononcé dans l'Assemblée des Notables le 22 février 1787*, Versailles, 1787, 217-18.
*Mémoire sur l'imposition territoriale* in *Collection des mémoires présentés à l'Assemblée des Notables*, Versailles, 1787, 218.

Mme Campan, *Mémoires sur la vie de Marie-Antoinette*, ed. F. Barrière, Paris, 1876, 160, 278.

*Censure de la Faculté de Théologie de Paris contre le livre qui a pour titre 'Bélisaire'*, Paris, 1767, 304-5.

Chateaubriand, *Mémoires d'Outre-tombe*, ed. E. Biré, Paris, n.d., 6 vols., 111-12.

L. Claretie, *Lesage romancier, d'après de nouveaux documents*, Paris, 1890, 241.

*Code Napoléon*, Paris, 1808, 324.

Collé, *Journal et mémoires*, ed. H. Bonhomme, Paris, 1868, 3 vols., 251-2, 274-5.

Condorcet, *Esquisse d'un tableau historique des progrès de l'esprit humain*, ed. O. H. Prior, Paris, 1933, 319.
*Œuvres*, ed. A. C. O'Connor and F. Arago, Paris, 1847-9, 12 vols., 204, 256.

*Correspondance secrète du Comte de Mercy-Argenteau avec l'Empereur Joseph II et le Prince de Kaunitz*, ed. A. d'Arneth and J. Flammermont, Paris, 1889, 2 vols., 199, 219-20.

*Correspondance secrète inédite sur Louis XVI, Marie-Antoinette, la cour et la ville de 1777 à 1792*, ed. M. F. A. de Lescure, Paris, 1866, 2 vols., 197, 213-14, 219, 228.

Croÿ, Duc de, *Journal inédit*, ed. Vicomte de Grouchy and P. Cottin, Paris, 1906-7, 4 vols., 116, 161.

J. Cruppi, *Un avocat journaliste au XVIIIe siècle: Linguet*, Paris, 1895, 307-8.

*La Déclaration des Droits de l'Homme et du Citoyen et la Constitution de 1791*, ed. M. Bouchary, Paris, 1946, 125, 324.

Delille, *Les Géorgiques*, Paris, 1770, 283.
*Les Jardins*, Paris, 1782, 284.
*Les Trois Règnes de la Nature*, Paris, 1808, 281.

*Dictionnaire de l'Académie Française*, Paris, 1762, 2 vols. (4th edition), 16n., 22n., 53n., 57n., 61n., 79n., 235n.
Paris, 1798, 2 vols. (5th edition), 60n., 66n., 107, 300.

Diderot, *Œuvres complètes*, ed. J. Assézat and M. Tourneux, Paris, 1875-7, 20 vols., 157, 192, 244, 257-8, 289, 302, 309-10, 315, 317.

John Law, *Œuvres complètes*, ed. P. Harsin, Paris, 1934, 3 vols., 144.

Le Blanc, Abbé, *Lettres d'un Français*, The Hague, 1745, 3 vols., 277.

A. Le Moy, *Le Parlement de Bretagne et le pouvoir royal au XVIIIe siècle*, Paris, 1909, 227.

E. G. Léonard, *Mon Village sous Louis XV d'après les mémoires d'un paysan*, Paris, 1941, 61-2.

Lesage, *Histoire de Gil Blas de Santillane*, Paris, 1715-35, 4 vols., 238-9.

Lévis, Duc de, *Souvenirs et portraits*, ed. F. Barrière, Paris, 1879, 198-9.

Louis XVI, *Journal*, ed. L. Nicolardot, Paris, 1873, 197.

J. de Maistre, *Œuvres complètes*, Lyons, 1884-1931, 14 vols., 3.

Malesherbes, *Mémoires sur la librairie et sur la liberté de la presse*, Paris, 1809, 305-6.

Mallet du Pan, *Mémoires et correspondance*, ed A. Sayous, Paris, 1851, 2 vols., 229.

Mathieu Marais, *Journal et mémoires*, ed. M. F. A. de Lescure, Paris, 1863-8, 4 vols., 31, 137-8, 262-3.

Marie-Antoinette, *Correspondance secrète entre Marie-Thérèse et le Comte de Mercy-Argenteau avec les lettres de Marie-Thérèse et de Marie-Antoinette*, ed. A. d'Arneth and A. Geffroy, Paris, 1875, 3 vols., 196, 198, 200, 209.

Marivaux, *La Vie de Marianne*, ed. F. Deloffre, Paris, 1957, 291.

Marmontel, *Mémoires*, ed. M. Tourneux, Paris, 1891, 3 vols., 5-6, 225, 226-7, 238, 245, 260-1, 315-16.
*Œuvres*, Paris, 1819-20, 7 vols., 278-9.

*Mémoire touchant l'origine et l'autorité du Parlement de France, appelé 'Judicium Francorum'*, n.p., n.d., 154-5.

L. S. Mercier, *De la Littérature et des littérateurs*, Yverdon, 1778, 254.
*Du Théâtre, ou Nouvel essai sur l'art dramatique*, Amsterdam, 1773, 289.
*Tableau de Paris*, Amsterdam, 1783-9, 12 vols., 27-8, 67-8, 88, 89, 103, 105, 114, 118, 122-3, 245, 260, 265-6, 267-8, 269-70, 271, 275, 278, 312-13, 316.

Mirabeau, *Mémoires*, ed. Lucas-Montigny, Paris, 1834, 8 vols., 115.

H. Monod-Cassidy, *Un Voyageur-philosophe au XVIIIᵉ siècle, l'abbé Jean-Bernard Le Blanc*, Harvard U.P., 1941, 237.

Montesquieu, *Lettres Persanes*, ed. A. Adam, Geneva-Lille, 1954, 146, 147.

J. Moore, *A View of Society and Manners in France, Switzerland and Germany*, London, 1779, 2 vols., 4-5, 266-7, 278.

Morellet, *Mémoires*, Paris, 1821, 2 vols., 310.

Necker, *Compte rendu au roi*, Paris, 1781, 55, 113, 213.
*De l'Administration des finances de la France*, n.p., 1784, 3 vols., 50-1, 70, 83-4, 85, 117, 258.

Baronne d'Oberkirch, *Mémoires*, ed. L. de Montbrison, Paris, 1853, 2 vols., 115.

Pellisson and D'Olivet, *Histoire de l'Académie Française*, ed. C. Livet, Paris, 1858, 2 vols., 277.

Piron, *Œuvres complètes*, Paris, 1776, 7 vols., 296-7.

Public Record Office, State Papers 78/297, 207.

Raynal, *Nouvelles littéraires* in Grimm, *Correspondance littéraire* (q.v.), 297-8.

*Recueil des réclamations, remonstrances, etc. au sujet de l'édit de décembre 1770*, London, 1773, 2 vols., 189.

*Remonstrances du Parlement de Bretagne au XVIIIᵉ siècle*, ed. A. Le Moy, Paris, 1909, 183.

*Remonstrances du Parlement de Paris au XVIIIᵉ siècle*, ed. J. Flammermont, Paris, 1898, 3 vols., 135, 137, 139, 168, 174, 175, 176, 178, 184-8, 203-4, 207, 208, 210-11, 220-1, 222-4.

Rétif de la Bretonne, *La Vie de mon père*, ed. H. d'Alméras, Paris, n.d., 14, 60-1.

Mme Riccoboni (transl.), *Le Nouveau Théâtre anglais*, Paris, 1769, 2 vols., 275.

Richeprey, *Journal des voyages en Haute-Guyenne*, ed. H. Guilhamon, Rodez, 1952 (only Vol. I published), 21-2, 107.

Edward Rigby, *Letters from France, etc. in 1789*, ed. Lady Eastlake, London, 1880, 15.

Rivarol, *De l'Universalité de la langue française*, ed. T. Suran, Paris, 1930, 279.

Mme Roland, *Mémoires*, ed. C. Perroud, Paris, 1905, 2 vols., 104.

J. J. Rousseau, *Confessions*, ed. L. Martin-Chauffier, Paris, 1933, 57-8.
    *Correspondance générale*, ed. T. Dufour, Paris, 1924-34, 20 vols., 232-3, 235, 236.
    *La Nouvelle Héloïse*, ed. D. Mornet, Paris, 1925, 4 vols., 287-8.

Saint-Lambert, *Œuvres*, Paris, 1823, 2 vols., 17, 54, 298-9.

Saint-Simon, *Mémoires*, ed. A. de Boislisle, Paris, 1879-1930, 43 vols., 86, 123, 127, 135-6, 138.

Sedaine, *Le Philosophe sans le savoir*, Paris, 1766, 94.

Ségur, Comte de, *Mémoires, souvenirs et anecdotes*, ed. F. Barrière, Paris, 1879, 2 vols, 130, 266.

Sénac de Meilhan, *Le Gouvernement, les Mœurs et les Conditions en France avant la Révolution*, ed. M. F. A. de Lescure, Paris, 1862, 51-2, 92-3, 318.

Sieyès, *Qu'est-ce que le Tiers État?* ed. E. Champion, Paris, 1888, 97, 229-30.

M. Souriau, *Bernardin de Saint-Pierre d'après ses manuscrits*, Paris, 1905, 250.

Mme de Staël, *Considérations sur les principaux événements de la Révolution française*, London, 1818, 3 vols., 129, 131, 132, 219, 221.

Talleyrand, *Mémoires*, ed. Duc de Broglie, Paris, 1891-2, 5 vols., 103-4, 110, 124.

Turgot, *Œuvres*, ed. G. Schelle, Paris, 1913-23, 5 vols., 24-6, 29-30, 37-40, 52-3, 121-2, 205.

Véri, Abbé de, *Journal*, ed. J. de Witte, Paris, 1929, 2 vols., 42, 194, 196, 209, 212.

Véron de Forbonnais, *Recherches et considérations sur les finances de France*, Basle, 1758, 2 vols., 71.

# INDEX